ADVANCE PRAISE FOR *INTUITIVE HEALING*

'Dr Judith Orloff eloquently describes how to integrate the care of the body with other dimensions of health and healing, one that embraces emotional and spiritual transformation as well as the physical. The path of love and intuitive healing she presents, and the powerful tools she provides, may change your life.'

Dean Ornish, M.D.

Author of *Love and Survival*

'By directing our attention to the missing factor in healing – our own mind – Dr Judith Orloff guides us on the path to the wisdom we forgot. At long last, medicine is awakening to the powers of consciousness and Orloff is one of the reasons why.'

Larry Dossey, M.D.

Author of *Reinventing Medicine*

'*Dr Judith Orloff's Guide to Intuitive Healing* is a tour guide of essential wisdom and innermost healing. It is a timeless work of depth, courage, and heart. It will bring a positive light to many lives.'

Richard Carlson, Ph.D.

Author of *Don't Sweat the Small Stuff*

'An excellent resource for those ready to explore their role in health, wellness and living.'

Bernie Siegel, M.D.

Author of *Love, Medicine and Miracles*

'I am delighted to endorse yet another wonderful contribution Dr Judith Orloff has made in the field of human consciousness. Dr Orloff's work is not only needed by the social mind in order to understand the future of health care, but it is also a masterpiece of educational data.'

Caroline Myss, Ph.D.

Author of *Anatomy of the Spirit*

'Judith Orloff represents an approach to our daily concerns that has yet to be fully appreciated. Intuition is not an exceptional talent you practice one day of the year. It can be a way of life. Dr Orloff offers clear, accessible advice on how to make this fundamental and life-opening shift from the anxiously controlled life to one that is open to opportunity and creativity. She is a reliable guide with a good bedside manner.'

Thomas Moore
Author of *The Care of the Soul*

'Wise, accessible, compassionate, funny and authentic, this book can help you listen to the voice of intuition, live a more satisfying and joyful life, and connect with the body's natural healing powers.'

Joan Borysenko, Ph.D.
Author of *Minding the Body, Mending the Mind*

'This book gives an opportunity to go even deeper into our understanding of what intuitive healing means. The main thing missing in modern medicine is intuition. Dr Orloff shows us how to connect with our source and to make use of our intuition. I highly recommend this book!'

Louise Hay
Author of *You Can Heal Your Life*

'This is a work of great depth as well as practical insight into realizing the potential we all have for healing ourselves and others. The spectrum of techniques Dr Orloff offers, the skills she teaches us to use in awakening and applying intuition help us turn a page in our human development. It is rare that one finds a book that is at once both pragmatic and evolutionary.'

Jean Houston Ph.D.
Author of *A Mythic Life*

'Judith Orloff brings intuition into the healing arts. Her book is a great contribution for our deeper understanding and transformation.'

Marianne Williamson
Author of *A Return to Love*

ABOUT THE AUTHOR

Judith Orloff M.D. is a practising psychiatrist and an assistant clinical professor of psychiatry at UCLA. She has been featured on *CNN*, *PBS*, *ABC News* and in *USA Today* and is an international lecturer and workshop leader on the inter-relationship between medicine, intuition and spirituality. She lives outside Los Angeles.

Also by Judith Orloff
SECOND SIGHT

Intuitive Healing

Five Steps to Physical, Emotional and Sexual Wellness

Judith Orloff

FOREWORD BY
DEAN ORNISH

RIDER

LONDON · SYDNEY · AUCKLAND · JOHANNESBURG

In loving memory of my mother and my father

First published in 2000 by Times Books,
a division of Random House, Inc.
This edition published in 2000 by Rider,
an imprint of Ebury Press, Random House,
20 Vauxhall Bridge Road, London SW1V 2SA
www.randomhouse.co.uk

Random House Australia (Pty) Limited
20 Alfred Street, Milsons Point, Sydney,
New South Wales 2061, Australia

Random House New Zealand Limited
18 Poland Road, Glenfield,
Auckland 10, New Zealand

Random House South Africa (Pty) Limited
Endulini, 5A Jubilee Road,
Parktown 2193, South Africa

The Random House Group Limited Reg. No. 954009

Papers used by Rider are natural, recyclable products made from
wood grown in sustainable forests.

Printed and bound by Mackays of Chatham plc, Kent

A CIP catalogue record for this book
is available from the British Library

ISBN 0-7126-0605-X

I have faith in all those things that are not yet said.
I want to set free my most holy feelings.
What no one has dared to want
will be for me impossible to refuse.

—Rainer Maria Rilke

AUTHOR'S NOTE

I'VE WRITTEN THIS BOOK in the hope that it will help you work more effectively with your doctor and other health professionals. This book isn't intended to be a substitute for medical care; no book can be that. However, I hope you'll share it with the health professionals with whom you work; I believe that all healers can benefit from a more intuitive outlook in their delivery of care, just as I believe that all patients can benefit from a more open and trusting relationship with a caring doctor.

Please note that, to protect their privacy, I've disguised the names and identifying characteristics of my patients described in these pages. My friends have kindly granted me permission to use their stories and real names. I am grateful to the many patients and friends—mentors all—who have shared their experiences with me for this book.

ACKNOWLEDGMENTS

My gratitude to many people who have supported my writing:

Richard Pine, literary agent, whose integrity, expertise, and devotion never cease to inspire.

Betsy Rapoport, editor of my dreams, seer and champion of this project.

Kitty Farmer, who has masterfully organized my workshops and lectures and with loving commitment disseminated my work.

Paula Cizmar and Thomas Farber, whose dedicated insight helped me shape and achieve this book.

Terry Schoonhoven, visionary muralist, who, with ability and kindness, provided the text's illustrations.

Rabbi Don Singer, Sensei, guide, friend, spiritual sounding board.

Berenice Glass, who hears the whole truth and does not judge.

For their skill and enthusiasm I want to thank the extraordinary people at Times Books: Tina Constable, Chip Gibson, Carie Freimuth, Mary Beth Roche, T. J. Snyder, Suzanne Wickham-Beaird, Regina Su Mangum, Steve Ross, Sabrina Hicks, Tracy Howell, Linda Pennell, and Mindy Schultz.

Also, my appreciation to friends and family for their suggestions and encouragement: Mila Aranda, Barnet Bain, Barbara Baird, Kathy Bishop, Barbara Biziou, Dannion Brinkley, Laurie Sue Brockway, Ann Buck, Janus Cercone, Vicki Chang, Jane Daly, Barbara Dossey, Dr. Larry

Dossey, Gay Norton Edelman, Arielle Ford, Linda Garbett, Michael Go-erden, Peter and Tara Guber, Angelika Hansen, Brian Hilliard, Brother James, Jonathan Kirsch, Michael Manheim, Dr. Richard Metzner, Catherine Miller, Stephen Mitchell, Mary Manin-Morrissey, Dean Orloff, Dr. Theodore Orloff, Dr. Dean Ornish, Dr. Phyllis Ostrum-Paul, Candida Royale, Lisa Schneiderman, Madeleine Schwab, Stephan and Hayden Schwartz, Marc Seltzer, Benjamin Shield, Stephen Simon, Chris Snyder, Leong Tan, Russell Targ, Suzanne Taylor, Roy Tuchman.

Finally, every physician is also a student: I am indebted to my patients and workshop participants, who continue to teach me so much.

FOREWORD

Dean Ornish, M.D.

IN THE LAST DECADE, more and more people have been seeking a new kind of medicine. Many are finding that the limited world of high-tech, invasive procedures, managed care, and six-minute doctor visits is often unsatisfying for both doctors and patients. A study released by the Kellogg Foundation today found that one in three Americans thinks the medical system is critically ill.

According to recent surveys, the majority of physicians would not recommend medicine as a career for their sons or daughters. Also, there is a growing frustration with attempts to control medical costs by limiting access to care rather than addressing the underlying causes of suffering and illness.

In *Dr. Judith Orloff's Guide to Intuitive Healing*, Dr. Orloff eloquently describes her vision of how to integrate the care of the body with other dimensions of health and healing, one that embraces emotional and spiritual transformation as well as the physical. She helps to bridge different worlds. An accomplished, traditionally trained physician, she also blends intuition and spirituality into her practice. When I first met Judith, I was impressed by her passion to help others find their inner voice and their own personal truths. Her manner is gentle, but her commitment to this goal is fierce.

In my work, I have found that pain and suffering in all its forms, including illness, can be a powerful doorway for transforming our lives for the better. While we don't look for suffering, sometimes it is unavoidable. Conventional medical training teaches us to kill pain, numb pain, bypass pain, or distract ourselves from pain. In this book, Judith describes how we can use the experience of pain and suffering to help clarify our values, to sort out what matters most to us and what doesn't. Sometimes the most meaningful changes in life are the most difficult to measure, but they can be experienced.

Love is a powerful doorway to reach the deepest parts of ourselves, to hear the still, small intuitive voice within that most spiritual and religious traditions describe. In my experience, that voice speaks very clearly but very quietly with information that can be profoundly useful, even healing.

This book can help you access your own inner voice more directly. In an era in which we sometimes question the validity of our own experiences and in which polls may substitute for leadership, being able to access your intuition has powerful applications in practical and transformative ways.

Your intuition may make it easier for you to change your diet, to exercise, to quit smoking, to manage stress more effectively. Health information and satisfying the intellect is important but not usually sufficient for most people to make and maintain beneficial changes in diet and lifestyle; if it were, no one would smoke. It's not because of a lack of information—everyone who smokes knows it's not good for them. We need to work at a deeper level.

Love enables us to contact our deepest intuitions. The idea that love heals is not a new one, but an increasing number of scientific studies now document that people who feel lonely, depressed, and isolated are many times more likely to get sick and to die prematurely. On the other hand, many studies show that anything that promotes feelings of love, intimacy, and community also promote health and longevity. For example, several studies have shown that people with cancer who participate in support groups often improve not only the quality of life, they also lengthen survival.

To me, the ultimate goal of healing is not to live forever but to learn to live more fully and joyfully, with an open, compassionate heart. The path of love and intuitive healing that Judith describes in this book and the powerful tools she provides may change your life.

—Dean Ornish, M.D.,
founder and president, Preventive Medicine Research Institute; clinical professor of medicine, School of Medicine, University of California, San Francisco; author, Love and Survival *and* Dr. Dean Ornish's Program for Reversing Heart Disease; *October 7, 1999*

CONTENTS

Author's Note   vi
Acknowledgments   vii
Foreword by Dean Ornish, M.D.   ix
Introduction   xiii

PART ONE: *The Body*

1. What Is Intuitive Healing? A First Look at the Five Steps   3
2. Visions of Health and Prevention   18
3. Sacred Healing Partnerships   44
4. If Illness Comes: How You Can Use Intuition
   to Heal Yourself   69
5. Death As Healer and Teacher   101

PART TWO: *Emotions and Relationships*

6. The Emotional Path of the Warrior   129
7. Centering and Protection   155
8. Finding Light in Darkness   176

9. Honoring Relationships — 203

10. A Final Good-bye — 232

PART THREE: *Sexual Wellness*

11. Passionate Sex, Deep Spirit — 243

12. Awakening Sexual Power — 262

13. A Return to Beginnings — 282

14. Sexual Energy's Healing Gift — 304

Afterword — 324

Selected Reading — 327

Resources — 331

Index — 335

INTRODUCTION

WE ARE THE KEEPERS OF OUR OWN HEALING. We are the keepers of an intuitive intelligence so powerful it can tell us how to heal. The time has come for each of us to claim it again. Never forget: It is your right to heal. It is your right to look inside yourself for the answers.

We are the vanguard of a health care revolution as profound as civil rights or feminism. I see a worldwide uprising fueled by courageous people like yourself, demanding that their spiritual and intuitive voices be honored in the healing process. Your passion makes a difference. It will change things. It already has. Attitudes are shifting. I meet medical practitioners and patients everywhere who rail against the icy sterility of technological interventions alone—no matter how miraculous—when simple kindness, love, and an awe for our inner vision is sacrificed.

We physicians have forgotten so much. We desperately need to restore our sense of the visionary, fight to keep the spirit of medicine alive. The future of medicine lies in the integration of intuition and technological advances, the wedding of heart and mind. Too many in health care have sadly lost sight of this, so much so that the designated healers of our culture can't even remember they can see. They walk around with a blindness that is deadly, a blindness that dictates in traditional psychiatry, for example, that "claims of sixth sense and clairvoyance" be written off as psychotic delusion or fraud. This is what I was taught in medical school at the University of Southern California and during my four years of psychiatric residency at UCLA. It is still the standard for medical practice today. Visionless, too many caregivers fail to grasp that the healing of ourselves, our patients, our beloved planet is contingent on the awakening of our compassion, intuitive foresight, and humility before the mystery of Spirit.

I'm defining intuition as a potent form of inner wisdom not mediated by the rational mind. Accessible to us all, it's a still, small voice inside—an unflinching truth-teller committed to our well-being. You may experience intuition as a gut feeling, a hunch, a physical sensation, a snapshotlike flash, or a dream. Always a friend, it keeps a vigilant eye on our bodies, letting us know if something is out of sync.

We all possess within us an intuitive healing code that contains the blueprints for our health and happiness, and for the survival of everything that is good here on earth. This code is written in a language of silence, metaphor, imagery, energy, and knowings that may seem alien until we are taught to decipher it. I want to share what I know of this code with you, although I'm always learning more. As you begin to understand its nuances, its secrets, the code will come to seem like the most familiar language of all, one you uttered before you ever had a memory of anything material, one that doesn't require a spoken voice to comprehend.

My expertise is as a psychiatrist and practicing intuitive. I'm writing this book to introduce you to the practical techniques I employ in my life and teach to patients every day about using the power of intuition to heal. As you read this book you'll learn to truly listen to your body's needs. You'll recognize warning signals and act on them to help prevent illness. I'll give you skills to access vital information from meditation, dreams, and remote viewing (a way of intuitively tuning in) to make sense of your life when it's most confusing. The insights you gain from these techniques will lend reason, compassion, and meaning to events such as illness, loss, or despair that the rational mind alone has a limited capacity to appreciate. You'll be shown a method of utilizing your body's subtle energies to heal pain, panic, depression, and other symptoms.

Reach back in your experience. See if you can't remember a special time when you listened, really listened, to what seemed invisible yet felt so true. Maybe it was an inner call to enter a career, a sudden inexplicable attraction to the person you were destined to marry, or simply a strong impulse to contact a good friend you hadn't seen for years. That indisputable sense of rightness is an echo of the code I'm speaking of. You deserve such certainty about all decisions. Even if you feel out of touch with it now, let me help you find it again. This is the kind of intuition around which I've built my psychiatric career and personal life. Without it, I don't feel complete. Without it, my patients get only a fraction of who I am as a healer, and they suffer as a result. Without it, I miss the joy, clarity, and vision to catalyze positive changes in my patients' lives and my own. I won't allow anything to keep me from that anymore.

In my first book, *Second Sight,* I shared the struggles I went through reconciling my intuitive skills with the world of science. I told of the loneliness and fear I felt as an only child in Los Angeles who could sense the unspoken and know things about people without them saying a word. My abilities frightened my physician-parents. I wasn't allowed to talk about my premonitions at home. In desperation I used to gaze up at the stars and pray that a spaceship would land in my front yard, to take me away to my real home. The alienation I felt in those days isn't necessary for any of us now.

Today intuition is my greatest passion. I am grateful to the many angels in my life, teachers who've patiently walked me through my fears. In my psychiatric practice I now depend on intuition for every aspect of patient care. I use it with my orthodox medical training to guide my options for treating patients. The messages I receive from images, dreams, and knowings direct me, along with my intellect. I teach patients to trust their inner voices as an authentic source of truth. I am blessed to travel around the country giving workshops on intuitive healing to auditoriums full of extraordinary people—health care professionals and general audiences alike—who long to embrace their ability to see. Our numbers are rapidly expanding. We can now seek one another out for support. The great gift I received from publishing *Second Sight* is freedom to acknowledge my intuitive voice and speak out about it, despite my fear of what my medical peers would think.

Response from readers, colleagues, patients, and workshop participants has been more generous than I ever dreamed. I've received thousands of letters and calls from every kind of person you can imagine—physicians, rabbis, nuns, prison inmates, schizophrenic patients, housewives, showgirls, FBI agents, high school honors students, even a group of ninety-something teachers in Oklahoma, who've been guided by their intuitive insights to inspire young children to learn—all dedicated to finding their inner voices. These are my heroes. These are people who've seen the good that comes from allowing the invisible code I speak of to manifest in loving service.

This is not a fringe phenomenon. It has gone mainstream. So many of us are tired of staying numb and asleep; we long for the kind of exhilaration only intuitive and spiritual awakening can bring. Come wake up with me. Begin to lift the veils before your eyes. Heaven is not some faraway place, separated from life. Intuition will enable you to see the beauty, passion, and exquisite light that have always been there.

In my first book I addressed the general theory and practice of intuition; in this book my focus is on teaching you specific intuitive tools to access healing wisdom from within.

I use the phrase "intuitive healing" in this book to emphasize the intuitive ingenuity we all have to tap into, to maintain and optimize our life force. My main theme is simple: Our intuition can open us up to our spirituality and show us how to be more healthy and whole. If you're in good health, you'll want to know about intuition because it can help you stay well and recognize messages that prevent illness. If you or your loved ones need healing, you'll also want intuition to show the way.

I'd like you to think of healing in the broadest terms. It may involve a complete resolution of symptoms, a "cure," or it may not. On a profound intuitive level it also pertains to the self-knowledge and soul growth achievable during illness or as death approaches. Our perception of these passages is key. In good health or ill, if we aim for self-compassion, inner listening, and a deepening link with the divine, we're engaging in an act of love, which is inevitably transformative.

To map out the healing process, a fundamentally nonverbal realm, I'm presenting a framework of five intuitive steps. You can depend on these steps, as I do, to clarify all aspects of your life. Count on them to guide you. They can augment decisions you make about traditional medical care or offer creative alternatives. The five steps are

1. Notice your beliefs

2. Be in your body

3. Sense your body's subtle energy

4. Ask for inner guidance

5. Listen to your dreams

No matter what you're dealing with, these steps are cogent tools. I urge you not to leave your healing to chance. By being accountable for your intuitive needs, you can better nurture yourself. Throughout this book I'll illustrate in detail how you can draw on these steps to take an instinctively informed, proactive role in your health.

Intuitive Healing is divided into three parts. In "The Body," I highlight the vital role intuition and your subtle energy system have in maintaining your physical health, in self-diagnosis, pain control, and accelerating healing. This part also explores why death is not to be feared and how we can intuitively tap into it as a creative resource in life. I'll also present a primer on choosing health care practitioners who blend spiritual, intuitive, and technical skills.

The second part, "Emotions and Relationships," stresses how your path as a spiritual warrior is to dig to the core of your emotional life and mend wounds with compassion. It illustrates how intuition leads to breakthroughs in anxiety, depression, and emotional blocks, even if traditional psychotherapy hasn't. It describes the importance of energetic centering and protection. You'll learn about the intuitive use of antidepressants and other medications. You'll see how intuition can strengthen good relationships, salvage bad ones, and help you select well-matched partners.

The third part, "Sexual Wellness," presents sexual energy as a powerful connector, an oasis for nurturing our troubled spirituality. Sex is more than physical love; it is an intuitive way of being in the world, an energetic opening to life, nature, and spirit. It can make you feel vibrant, bring vitality to the rest of life. You'll discover how to awaken your sexuality, whether you are in a relationship or not, and how to direct erotic power to heal symptoms from depression to back pain.

Years of medical practice have taught me that our physical, emotional, and sexual well-being are bridges to one another, collaborators in an elegant interplay. Not to acknowledge their connections precludes complete healing. We are all multifaceted, though we may have drifted far from our power. I'm asking you to be brave, to reconcile your many sides with more heart than you've experienced before. If you split off even one aspect, you inflict a violence on yourself. Refocus on the five steps, integrators that will hone your energy and keep your health at its peak.

There comes a time when we must decide if we are committed to a life based on heart. With regard to healing, this commitment means coming to compassionate terms with the light and dark forces that shape us, excluding nothing. Remember this when you greet all the angels and beasts on your path. As your heart opens, so does your intuition. Your intuition will teach you how to see and how to love. It will instill in you a renewed faith to face anything.

As I write this it is the year 5758 in the Jewish calendar, the year *enya,* which means, "You shall intuit." In this spirit I invite you to delve deep as you read this book, perhaps travel to new territory. Try to stay open. Risk with me. There is magic in what is invisible. Allow yourself to be touched. Be innocent again so nothing is kept from you. You can feel the intuitive code everywhere: in the warmth of your breath, your body, in the soft rustling of leaves in the wind, in the sea at midnight. Be very quiet. Listen carefully . . . the moon, the earth, the stars all know its secret. Now let them whisper it to you.

PART ONE

The Body

1

What Is Intuitive Healing?

A First Look at the Five Steps

> In every beginning there is a magic power . . . that
> protects us and helps us to live.
> —Hermann Hesse

*T*he twilight shimmered violet, bathing the New England hills. Just overhead I could see the planet Jupiter radiant beneath a sliver of pale summer moon. A magical sight, strengthening me. The early evening, still warm, was balanced between light and shadow—as we all are—pointing me toward what was to come.

I was on my way to lead a workshop on intuitive healing for 150 inmates at a women's correctional institution in Connecticut. I'd been invited to speak by a prison caseworker and gifted intuitive, Marcelle, who'd read my book *Second Sight*. On the phone we connected instantly. She was tough and funny, with the voice of a street kid straight out of Brooklyn. "These women have blown it," she said. "They've made terrible choices about their lives. Come teach 'em to listen to the wisdom inside. They'll love it. It'll do 'em good." I was honored. I jumped at the chance. Once more I was amazed by where life was taking me. Intuitive healing in a prison? Approved by the warden? During my medical training at UCLA, could I ever have imagined such a moment?

I'm not saying I didn't feel anxious about going there. I'd once visited a high-security men's prison—an enlightening but unnerving experience. I know it's irrational, but whenever I get around people in government uniforms, I feel guilty, like I've done something wrong. It's a reflex. Even if I'm not speeding, I squirm whenever a police car trails me. Plus, I have to admit the mere thought of getting locked up and being told what to do throws me into a stone cold panic. I guess it's a combination of a touch of claustrophobia, my dread of arbitrary rules and regulations, and my need to know that I can escape instantly from any situation if I choose to leave. I'm always the one who likes to drive my own car places . . . just in case.

My tension eased as I wound up to the entrance. Surrounding the prison were acres of lush grass lined with umbrella-shaped crab apple trees and clusters of fragrant knotty pine. I marveled at the flocks of purple-feathered turkeys and black Canada geese that lived wild, protected on federal land. Marcelle greeted me, smiling: "Welcome to Danbury." I gulped. Universes collided. There she stood, brown-skinned and exotic like a gypsy in her long, colorful floral skirt, jet black hair flowing—a hint of her Lebanese ancestry. But looming behind her was a double-wire fence made of razor blades with dagger points. I braced myself, took one long, deep breath. We headed in.

Prisons are not places of curves or color. Everywhere I looked there were angled concrete slabs, beige rectangular compounds, square vaulted doors that slammed shut at lockdown, and bleached-out benches, all screaming ninety degrees. Marcelle and I walked through the yard—about the size of two football fields—and entered the auditorium, a landscape that looked bleak but, even so, vibrated with palpable energy. For me a great gift of being an intuitive is the ability to sense what cannot be seen. Now, here, I felt invisible spotlights warming me like the sun, coming from the women's eyes. All around I watched hundreds of eyes looking up at us, questioning, searching, shining. Rough edges and softness mixed. Mysterious oval brown African eyes, wise crones' eyes, others bright blue or green. I could sense the humming of anger and fear, the restlessness beneath their skin . . . and at the same time a subtle glow permeating it all.

"Good evening, ladies," Marcelle cheerfully greeted the crowd. "I'd like to introduce you to Dr. Orloff." I walked up onto the stage, cautiously sat down. I felt tiny, scanning the huge auditorium packed with a sea of khaki-uniformed women. I knew the externals of our lives couldn't have been more different. Also, I was a perfect setup to be stereotyped. Psychiatrist and intuitive healer from California? Come on. How many people, particularly on the East Coast, could have a field day with that? If only I came from the Midwest! I wondered if I'd be heard at all. I had to remind myself that the sign-up sheet for this workshop had been filled within twenty minutes. These women had all chosen to come, to give up their free time.

I began with basics. "How many of you were warned by your intuition not to commit a crime but didn't pay attention?" Nearly everyone raised a hand.

"How many of you have ever known your health was in danger but ignored the signs your body sent?" Hands went up again.

"How many of you have sensed a relationship would be abusive but got into it anyway?"

"I knew on the first date!" a hefty blond shouted out from the back. Everyone laughed, knowingly.

Clearly, many of these women had received signals to avoid difficulties but hadn't listened. Still, I was surprised by both their honesty and their self-knowledge.

Over the next hour I was hit with a barrage of questions.

"What is intuitive healing?" a woman asked.

"Most of all it means getting in touch with your heart to hear your intuition. Then using that information to heal. The first step," I said, "is finding that still, small voice inside that tells you the truth about things. A kind of guardian angel. You have to be very quiet to hear it."

"I've tried. I can't hear it," she said. "The noise in my head is too loud. I can't stop thinking about my son. I can't stop thinking about getting out of here." *Getting out of here:* I knew I was hearing a refrain that haunted this place, a not unreasonable monomania.

I was aware of this woman's anguish. How could one not be? But my task was to convey to her that we all have our concerns—our obsessions. It was right to want to get out of prison. It was right to be thinking about her son. But to start to heal she had to find quiet. "In the beginning," I explained, "it's natural to have thoughts. Our laundry list of things to do, our hopes, dreams, fears—even the most valid of these must be temporarily set aside if we want to find our intuitive voice. The mind's babble goes on forever. The secret is to learn to meditate. Practice being quiet a few minutes each day. You can do it longer when you're ready. Each time a thought comes, train yourself to focus on your breath. This will help you find the silence."

I looked around at the faces in the room. The women seemed to be right with me. I gathered myself, pressed on. "How many of you meditate now?" I asked, expecting only a few hands. Nearly half the audience responded; I was delighted. I must have conveyed my astonishment. "We have meditation and yoga classes every day here," someone called out. Astounding—not at all my vision of prison.

During this discussion I noticed that a stern, pale woman in the front row was getting edgy. Her dark eyes, caked in black mascara, looked wired and impatient. (I later found out she was a convicted murderer.) Her hand shot straight up, demanding my attention. In truth, I was afraid not to respond. "Can we please stop talking so much?" she snarled. Oh no, I thought, now it's coming. The room fell silent. I glanced over at Marcelle, but she looked perfectly calm. Meanwhile, the woman just kept staring. She wanted something from me, but what? I wasn't getting it—that was obvious. Finally, she said, exasperated, "I'm sick of just talking. I want to know what intuitive healing *feels* like. Can't we meditate here? Can't you *please* show us?" "Yes!" other voices chimed in. I breathed a sigh of relief. Of course.

So, that August evening in Danbury Federal Prison, 152 women meditated together. With fluorescent lights glaring, a disembodied voice barking orders over the loudspeaker in the yard, we closed our eyes and breathed. "Begin by focusing on your heart," I said. "Slowly . . . start to feel the love inside you. Don't force it. Opening to love is how you listen. Then the voice of your intuition can be heard. Let love flow to any part of your body that's ill or in pain. If an image comes, note it, don't dwell on it. But later see how it can help you heal. Stay aware only of your breath. If you're in emotional pain, let the love completely surround you. Just take it all in." For nearly twenty minutes this gathering of women—convicted of murder, child abuse, embezzlement, conspiracy to overthrow the government, bank robbery—communed, laughed, wept. Some experienced a glimpse of love, for others it was much more.

Love resonates from universe to universe. It transformed a prison auditorium into a place of worship. Whenever a group of people come together with the intention to heal, it's strong medicine. Whenever we sincerely look inside our hearts for love, magic takes hold. At Danbury I saw once again that no matter how far down any of us have gone, there is always the promise of redemption. I'm grateful to those women for the openness they shared and their courage to heal. It has helped make me brave. Every one of us has suffered illness. We've all felt hurt, betrayed, disappointed. We all have to seek so hard to find love.

With love comes freedom. I know the danger of metaphor, comparisons made too easily. Still, I must tell you that the prisons we live in, external or internal, have power over us only to the degree we allow them to define who we are. Or, for those of us outside the razor-wire fence, only insofar as we deny they exist. Consider Nobel Laureate Nelson Mandela's decades of incarceration. Despite horrific conditions, never did he succumb to racial hatred or abandon his principles.

Like Mandela, the inmates I met and their moment of healing offer us mirrors to see ourselves more clearly. Beyond the issue of how cruel an environment we come from, and the real misery and costs of poverty, some of us are better than others at controlling our emotions or not acting them out destructively. These women teach us an essential intuitive truth: the potent interconnectedness of us all. That is to say, we're all more similar than not. It might hardly seem so. After our meditation, because I was an intuitive, the inmates hounded me to predict the outcomes of their court cases, their release dates, whether or not they'd be paroled. They were beset with real-life concerns not my own. Even so, I never stopped feeling the similarities. We are all of one heart, inextricably bound. For each of us, if we want to relieve illness or despair, love must be the lens through which we view ourselves and the world. The specifics vary from life to life, but the task remains the same.

Take my experience in this prison as a starting place, a very human microcosm of our hunger to heal. For us all love is the underpinning of intuitive healing, the essence of all things spiritual. What is within and without. Darkness and light. The Answer. In the tradition of my spiritual teacher, there is one path, the Tao, upon which all other paths converge. Whether you find the love I speak of in conventional religion, quiet contemplation, or the radiance of the moon, you must know in every cell of your being that it's real and unconditional. Not an abstract concept or remote goal but an accessible, trustworthy force in your daily life. If you can't feel it, let me help show you how. All it takes is innocence and an open mind. Just wait. Miracles lie ahead. The spiritual path we travel is very wide and built of the sturdiest earth and stone. It is prepared to support every aspect of who you are and more. Whether you are in excellent health or ill, happy or not, there isn't a single part of yourself that is unwelcome on this journey.

Let me tell you specifically what intuitive healing means. It is listening to your body's signals—your inner voice and heart, your spiritual connection—to find out how to become more physically, emotionally, and sexually whole. Intuition gives you a head start on preventing illness. By sensing warning signs you can act sooner to restore the integrity of your internal defense system, sometimes before symptoms appear. Human beings are all manifestations of energy. If illness comes you can learn how to intuitively balance your body's energy to accelerate regeneration and repair. The knowledge you gain from listening translates positively to all areas of your life. It gives you practical direction to approach every problem.

Intuitive healing is integrative. It means respecting the intelligence of your analytical mind but also calling on a deeper wisdom to guide you. It's a dance. Your intellect and intuition are allies; they can work together well. Just remember that the intellect, no matter how brilliant, is limited by its linear focus. It can see only so much. In contrast, intuition is multidimensional, can penetrate surfaces, offers solutions about your health and happiness that the mind alone cannot appreciate. The difficulty is that the mind's chatter is often so loud it drowns out the knowledge within. I'll help you find that knowledge again.

Intuition also inducts you into the realm of genius—where ideas, imagery, and dreams ignite, making healing an absolute reality even when science deems it impossible. As a physician I've heard how many times my patients were told by well-meaning doctors, "Your disease is chronic. You'll just have to live with it" or "The only way to feel better is to take this pill." Such advice can be dangerous, debilitating, untrue. There are always options; to find them may require you to become a kind of revolutionary. Dare to go beyond conventional medical wisdom. Trust that you *can* awaken your inner vision. When you do the answers will become clear—although at times totally unexpected.

Get ready to be surprised. A cosmic sense of humor is at play here. A mischievous trickster may seem to be running the show. You ask for solutions—you will be given them. Try not to be fooled, and don't underestimate their significance. On the surface the advice you receive may seem outrageous, impractical, the last thing in the world you want to do. You don't have a clue how you'll put it into action. Don't jump to conclusions. Logic deceives.

The most unlikely scenarios of healing may be the most inspired. I'm living proof. In my early twenties I had an explicit dream that told me I was to be a psychiatrist, to gain the credentials to help validate the psychic field. Me, an M.D.? In those days nothing could have sounded more unappealing. I was a hippie. I was living with my artist-boyfriend in a loft in Venice Beach, a clerk in the towel department at the May Company. Also, my parents were physicians, as were most of their friends. Ugh. Very boring. I gravitated to creative types on the fringe. I'd just begun to explore my intuitive side, working as a researcher at

UCLA with the parapsychologist Dr. Thelma Moss. At least I knew enough by then to believe this dream could come true. Not that I ever thought it would. Around that time my parents sent me to a career counselor. She tested me, then told me the results. I'll never forget her words: "Whatever you do," she said, "don't go into the helping professions." Suppose I'd followed this advice? I would've missed my real calling. Luckily, my dream rescued me. Its energy propelled me through fourteen years of medical training.

The intuitive messages you receive can be life-changing. Please listen. Only good can come. Even so, I know how easy it is to fixate on what you're already pursuing, what you've come to feel is right for you. I have this struggle all the time. I'm asking you simply to allow for other possibilities, as I've learned to do. Reserve judgment. See how your future unfolds. There's often a synchronicity; opportunities may present themselves. If so, go with them. Watch where they take you. Change of this kind always has a component of the unpredictable. It can be mysterious, beguiling. Be prepared to smile.

In this spirit I now want to present your road map for the journey. Here's a first look at the five intuitive steps that can transform your health and life. They provide the structure I'll refer to throughout the book. Each step represents an indicator that can help you avoid illness, replenish energy, and bring insight into any problem. In every chapter I'll take you through each step thoroughly. Utilizing this structure will enhance your intuition, or enable you to find it.

Step 1. Notice Your Beliefs

Your beliefs set the tone for healing. Positive attitudes accentuate growth, negative attitudes impair it. Honesty is required to flush out counterproductive perceptions so ingrained you may not realize how pernicious they are. If we examine our beliefs, we won't be subject to subterranean undermining influences. Our beliefs trigger biochemical responses. No organ system stands apart from our thoughts. What you believe—what you really believe—programs your neurochemicals. I'm not suggesting that you be Pollyannaish or put on a happy face to please, but that you be absolutely true to yourself. This will liberate you from unconscious impulses that impede your healing.

Step 2. Be in Your Body

Your body is a richly nuanced intuitive receiver. You must be in it completely to heal. This may require some adjustment. We're trained to function from the neck up, denying the rest of our bodies. I want you to reorient yourself, to respect the intellect but delight in your physicality as well. Being aware of the sensuousness of the body can open intuition. This may mean noticing the early signs of pain so you can act on them, trusting your gut about relationships, or awakening your sexuality. We can't afford to ignore such life-informing signals. Being attuned to your body is a treasure.

Step 3. Sense Your Body's Subtle Energy

Tapping into your body's subtle energy can heal. From an intuitive standpoint we are all composed of vibrantly colored energy fields (whose centers are called chakras) that emanate from us. These can be sensed. They contain truths about our physical, emotional, and sexual needs. Energy has different manifestations, from erotic to psychic. Invisible to most people, it can be sensed with intuition. To heal you must first learn to identify energy. Then you can direct it to specific parts of the body. Feeling energy can be very sensual. I assure you, it won't be all work!

Step 4. Ask for Inner Guidance

A range of answers lies within you. To access them I'll focus on two intuitive techniques: meditation and remote viewing. *Meditation* is a state of quiet that amplifies the intuition. It is the foundation of my spiritual practice. In practical terms meditation lowers blood pressure, relieves stress, can help reverse heart disease, even retard aging.

The method I'll show you is to focus consciously on your breath, to contact a soundless inner pulse. This is your intuitive core. Your breath will take you there. Once you're accustomed to the quiet, you can use *remote viewing,* an intuitive technique to move through both time and space. It enables you to tune in to the past, present, and future, or to visualize a person, place, or situation, even at a great distance. With this knowledge you can help diagnose illness by picturing the body's organs, predict proper treatment, appraise current therapies—all mandatory when conventional medicine seems unable to find a cure. Remote viewing also reveals emotional and sexual blocks; it can even let you check someone out before you get involved. All this is possible: College students have been taught basic remote viewing in a few sessions.

Step 5. Listen to Your Dreams

Intuition is the language of dreams. We speak it every night, during the REM state, the phase of sleep when our brain waves impart secret healing formulas. This mystic symbology—images, messages, scenarios—has rules different from those in our waking life. A dream's tone can be as restorative as its content; the nonverbal often presides. Also, in dreams revelations about illness and relationships are conveyed. Dreams do heal, but first you must retrieve them. During sleep we experience a kind of amnesia. To the intellect dreams are alien, language that does not compute. Dreams cannot be captured by the rational mind alone; intuitive memory is needed. As you learn how to remember and interpret dreams, you'll be able to draw on this form of healing.

You CAN APPLY these five intuitive steps to every health challenge in your life, as well as every emotional or sexual issue. I live them every day—in my medical practice, my relationships, dating, choices about health or new directions. As you read on you'll see how the steps pertain. They are yielding, expansive, reflecting possibilities. Try not to cling to any one too tightly; simply allow them to illuminate. You may be more compelled by one step than another. For example, since childhood I've been a prolific dreamer—every night dreams articulate my inner truth like nothing else can. Find the most natural outlet for your intuition. Have fun. Give yourself permission to explore.

The form your intuition takes may vary: images, dreams, sounds, gut feelings, a sense of knowing, a kaleidoscope of creative flow. Often while I'm working with patients snapshotlike flashes come through. In a split second I receive a world of information. It's exciting. As a physician I've come to depend on these moments of insight. Notice if such flashes happen to you. Write everything down immediately in a journal. The material can be relayed quickly, but it slips away if undocumented. Watch closely. We all have our intuitive styles. Discover yours. As you read this book, try to put each of the five intuitive steps into action. Take your time. Experiment. See what your experience is.

QUESTIONS FOR REFLECTION

- Do you consider yourself an intuitive person? If so, how? If not, what intuitive qualities would you like to develop?

- Do you believe your intuition can heal? What old ideas tell you it can't? Can you set them aside and stay open to new possibilities?

- What kind of healing do you most need? Are you ready to receive it?

- What would it mean to your life if you did?

As I continue to define intuitive healing, I want to stress that the spirit with which you approach it is critical. Looking inward is a sacred act. Deep healing is a state of being graced, not an entitlement. Humility is required. I understand that realizing you can pick up intuitive information about the past, present, and future can be seductive. I've seen too many people get hooked in by their egos, lose track of ethics and priorities. We must be grateful for knowledge that points us toward wellness, and never become overly impressed with ourselves.

The link I want to convey is this: First, come from your heart. Then and only then, request intuitive direction. Your sense of humanity and kindness must guide. This ensures perspective. For me the one truth that remains constant is how little I know. I am privileged—as you will be—to see certain things, but remember, what we see is a mere speck in the mystery.

The heart stabilizes. It offers strength you never knew you possessed. It gives clarity that seems to emanate from some force greater than yourself. The heart allows you to survive the insurmountable. We cannot always control the events of our lives, but we can determine our attitude.

I have a patient who recently lost her husband of forty years to pancreatic cancer. They had had a love affair since high school. The thought of being without her husband was unbearable to her. Shortly before he died, she left a message from his hospital room on my answering machine: "I feel like I'm climbing an icy cliff to a tent with no exit. It's bitter cold. The wind is howling. But pushing up between the shafts of ice, I see patches of beautiful, tiny red flowers."

Tears welled up in my eyes. I know all too well how life can put us face to face with our edge—then push us over into emotional territory that appears unrelenting. As for this patient, intuition expands the capacity to see, instills courage. The flowers she spoke of are the blessing intuition bestows on us. Our capacity to discern such flowers, in whatever situation, is our antidote to fear. It's not that my patient's anguish was any less excruciating. But she can teach us that in the most dire circumstances there's the possibility for magnificence and the connection to spirit, to hope.

It's important to grasp that intuitive healing begins with the individual but is not simply personal. We become catalysts for something beyond the self. As we turn to love more and more, we generate energy others can feel. I am talking about "presence," being able to radiate love without saying a word. Just standing next to a person with this quality brings enormous comfort. Our goal is to become people of presence. The love each of us generates radiates into the world, expanding ripples on the pond, not limited by time or space. Love has a voice. It has compassionate arms that reach out from you to your family, your community, the globe.

Every human being has an empathic bond to the entire ecosystem. This dynamic is an interchange: our impact on the environment, its effect on us. I'm not talking simply about the physical repercussions—for example, of destroying the rain forests and global warming—though I'm not trying to minimize such devastation. I'm also saying that on an intuitive level if our environment is wounded, *we* are wounded. There is an energetic continuum between our bodies and the natural world. We aren't separate from the earth or what happens in our cities. There is a flow through all of life that we can feel with practice. Many of us sense this to be true. Yet even our best intentions to improve planetary conditions can be misguided.

On a recent trip to Berlin, I visited the northern part of the city, where the wall used to be. It was a chilly, overcast October afternoon when we arrived at Checkpoint Charlie—the famed American military post in what was once a heavily guarded gate between East and West. My host, a German bookseller, couldn't have been more ecstatic about all the "positive" changes happening in the city since the wall had come down. I gazed over to what had been East Berlin. As I saw what he meant, I was shocked. Where there used to be monotonous Soviet-style scenery, a droning gray newsreel, now endless blocks of ultramodern high-rises were under construction as far as the eye could see. Cold and angular, they mimicked the harshest of Western aesthetics. "What progress!" my host exclaimed. My heart sank. Political oppression and a totalitarian state were gone. This was clearly good. But "progress" alone could not mend this precious land.

Berlin: a living metaphor for the difficulty of resolving the divisions within us. Something more profound was required. Why were no forests being planted? No gardens, no flowers, no honoring of the earth? No ceremonies of purification? I'm not arguing against urbanization per se. But in a place so embattled, it's just not enough. I strained to find even an echo of healing. I knew that this misunderstanding of progress doesn't have to be so. We must be more careful. Healing comes from the inside out. Any other way is illusion.

Intuition and illusion can never coexist. The opportunity that intuitive healing offers is to look at life's entirety with fresh eyes. To inspect and discard any limited notion of your creative capacity for wellness. Try not to compare yourself with anybody else—whether you're recovering from illness or simply want to find ways to improve your energy. Your path is unique. Let your intuition guide you. For instance, if your doctor presents you with a course of action that feels wrong, don't hesitate to question it. You have every right to reexamine what healing means to you, not to compromise your ideal. This is something I've been forced to confront myself.

Picture this scene: medical rounds at a major teaching hospital. A group of stiff young residents and an attending cardiologist, all in white coats, stethoscopes in hand, gather around an elderly woman's bed. She's just been admitted for a heart attack. She looks scared. Except for a few questions, the doctors barely speak to her. Each resident listens to her heart, then her lungs. They review their findings. The woman says nothing. When finished the doctors politely excuse themselves and dutifully file out the door behind the cardiologist.

Cut to five minutes later. A cleaning person comes in smiling, humming an old Otis Redding tune. "How you doin'?" he asks cheerfully. The woman perks up. They chat a little. "Hang in there," he says, and pats her on the back. "You're lookin' good." She laughs. He gives her the high sign, winks as he says good-bye. He has no advanced degrees, but clearly he does have a heart as big as the room.

Such scenarios occur in hospital rooms every day. Seeing this over and over again, I've had to ask, Who's doing the real healing? Let's return to our discussion of presence. The energy we exude makes a difference. It can heal. Others can feel it. The quality of heart the cleaning person radiated is something we all must aspire to. Technological skills and heart make for a powerful duo in healers.

To expand our understanding of healing, we must call on our intuition, have more compassion for ourselves. Let's reconsider an essential premise of Western medicine: Healing is equated only with health. On the surface this sounds logical, but from an intuitive perspective it is just a fraction of the truth. There is healing to be found in even the most trying phases of our lives, if we have the capacity to perceive it. In some cases healing may mean being disease-free, as we ordinarily assume. But I want you to try to understand, healing also may entail going through depression, living with chronic pain, or surviving cancer. The root question we all have to confront is, Must illness be a failure? I think not. The moment we try to dictate the terms of our healing, we eclipse a greater wisdom that can intercede in our lives. I don't want to give you the idea that I'm blind to the often cruel realities of our experience. Practicing medicine, I have seen nearly every kind of condition that human "flesh is heir to." I'm not saying illness and loss aren't terrifying. None of us would choose them. Still, it is undeniably true that healing can occur in the most unsuspected ways.

The real problem may be giving up some of our expectations. Let me tell you about my father. At seventy-seven he had until a year before been a physician his entire adult life. Of course, as I have, he'd seen the full spectrum of human illness over the decades of his career. Then my father became the patient. Like his own mother, he had Parkinson's disease. What this meant was that my father was slowly losing his ability to walk, to swallow, to speak, to remember. He couldn't fight infection like he used to, was at risk of contracting pneumonia, which could be fatal.

Even though I'm a doctor, seeing my father in this condition tested all my beliefs about healing. I'd been devastated, watching him deteriorate physically in such a short time. I longed to hold on to him, but he was disappearing before my eyes. When I visited he was usually propped up for support in his favorite red velour armchair. His large blue-green eyes, identical to mine, would stare up at me without bitterness, with innocence. I'd have to control myself, but I wanted to cry. He was defenseless, like a baby. I would've done anything to protect him. I was his only child. "Hi, darling," he'd always say as I walked in the room. Since I was a little girl, I'd loved it when he called me darling. "I'm glad to see you, Daddy," I'd say, kissing him on the cheek.

My father had been a kind of loner all his life. He'd never talked much about feelings—his or mine—even though more than once I'd badly needed him to. A radiologist, he spent his days alone in darkrooms developing X rays, diagnosing disease, dictating medical reports. At night he'd be glued to Lakers or Dodgers games on TV. This would drive my mother crazy. "I'm going to get rid of that TV!" she threatened over forty years of marriage, but never did. My mother, also a physician, was intensely social. Despite my father's protests she used to suit him up in a tux (he'd look so handsome) and drag him to lavish parties or political fund-raisers. Every year she'd plan exotic vacations—Israel, the Italian Riviera, the Sahara—and off they'd go. My father liked to complain about traveling, but in reality he loved every minute of it. My mother had died of cancer four years before. Dad hadn't been himself without her.

With good reason you might assume, as I did, that losing a wife and developing Parkinson's disease would be hard to construe as preconditions for my father's healing. I certainly would never have wished such a fate on him. But what I witnessed was that, in so many ways, my father had blossomed. More than once I'd shake my head to make sure I was seeing what was right in front of me. But that's how the truth is; sometimes it takes time to absorb.

For instance, at my father's request he'd begun living in an assisted care facility in Westwood, several miles from my place. He'd told me on many occasions he felt secure there. At first I cringed at the thought of him being anywhere but home. I viewed his moving into such a facility as my failure. We all know the negative stereotype of retirement "hotels." And, in fact, let's not kid ourselves—too often they're true. Still, where my father lived turned out to be a lifesaver for him. The place was filled with people—mostly women—who doted on him, made sure he ate enough, worried about his aches and pains. He actually looked forward to group therapy sessions, where for the first time he'd learned to express his feelings. Every Monday evening we'd go to dinner at a neighborhood delicatessen (he'd order a pastrami sandwich; I'd sip cabbage soup) and just talk. My father, an expert at reticence, a virtuoso of emotional silence. It may not seem like much to you, but for me this was a miracle.

One stormy December night after dinner, from out of nowhere my father declared, "I have to remember, there is so much sky around me." I was astounded. I had my father defined as what he'd always seemed to be: linear, practical, not a person who verbalized the poetic. It came to me that often when people are preparing for the end of life they receive unexpected flashes of insight or beauty. I studied my father's face: things were changing.

It was getting late, time to say good night. We were walking back toward his room when off in the distance we heard music. My father's face lit up. "Let's go," he said, waving me in the direction of the dining hall. More surprise! My father was famous for ducking social events. But what did I know? I followed him. There was a group of residents, seniors ranging from 60 to 101 years old, some snapping their fingers, others up and dancing as best they could to a Brazilian beat. What a scene! Three musicians, themselves rather elderly, were proudly attired in sequined gaucho costumes. They came in once a week to provide entertainment.

"Judith, I want to dance so much," my father said. I almost started to laugh: I just couldn't believe this was happening. "I'm scared," he continued. "What if I can't? I don't want to make a fool of myself." But before I could respond, there he was, walker and all, inching his way toward the linoleum dance floor. I was in a dream. Surely Lucille Ball and Desi Arnaz would be darting past him any moment. Seeing my father's courage, everybody began to applaud. The music of the samba filled the room—drums rolling, castanets clacking, maracas shaking. Outside a cold winter rain was pouring down, wind so strong it made the shutters rattle. There was a clap of thunder, then another. For an instant I felt the future, with all its losses and gains, even his eventual passing, rushing toward us. But here, safe inside, moved more than ever by how much there was to learn, I watched my father dance. Soaring. Soaring.

2

Visions of Health and Prevention

If you want to see what your body will look like
tomorrow, look at your thoughts today.
—Navajo saying

An electric hum ignites the room. The staccato pulse of beepers. Bodies in motion. Doctors glued to house phones answering pages. All around me the unmistakable adrenaline rush of being on call.

I don't usually get nervous when I give a talk, but seconds before I address this audience of physicians, Agnes, a second-year psychiatry resident, announces helpfully that the head of her program recently stormed out in the middle of a video on a topic similar to mine. *Now* she tells me! And, of course, there the man is, first to arrive, planted dead center.

I'm at the University of Nevada Medical School, about to make a presentation at grand rounds—a defining ritual in modern medicine: each week physicians in hospitals and academic settings gather to debate topics related to patient care. The amphitheater is jammed. There are over one hundred psychiatric residents and clinical staff members, the largest turnout they've ever had, I'm told. From the podium I gaze up at rows and rows of impeccably dressed psychiatrists. I half-expect them to lift off, floating on air. This must be Woody Allen's version of heaven . . . or hell!

I take in a slow, deep breath and reflect on the title of my talk, "How to Use Psychic Abilities to Excel in Patient Care." Suddenly beads of cold sweat erupt all over my body. I'm well aware this is sensitive territory, more than a little bit dangerous. As far as I know this is the first time such a topic has been presented for serious consideration to a medical staff anywhere. I could be mocked, doubted, dismissed out of hand. My professional reputation is at stake.

I try to read the faces of the skeptical crowd. I have to remind myself that traditional psychiatrists view anything psychic as a sign of psychosis, don't believe it exists, or associate it with the sleazy psychic phone lines bombarding late-night television viewers. To use psychiatric lingo, I'm up against a lot of resistance. Even so, my apprehension feels more firmly rooted than the occasion warrants—strangely unrelated to this here and now. It lives deeper within me. I've sensed it before: a kind of haunting resonance with a past I can't quite remember, a time when it was unsafe even to mention such things. I gather up my courage. Today my message is that the practice of medicine must change: We must honor our capacity to contact an inner knowledge that tells us how to help prevent and treat illness.

Then I begin my talk. As the minutes pass I feel both rapt attention and polite restraint. There is also the palpable tension of expectation— the questioning will soon commence.

Right after the applause a serious-looking resident puts out feelers. "I don't mean to be the guy snarling in the back of the room," he starts, "but you've already lost me. Psychic? Come on! Are you actually trying to say it's real?" he baits me. "If so, what's the big difference between psychic and intuition?"

"I see them as being on a continuum," I respond as calmly as I can. I gain nothing by being provoked by hostility; I'll stay on the high road. "Intuition to me is more than the common experience of gut feelings and hunches all good doctors pride themselves on. I'm talking about a specific psychic capacity each of us has: We can all learn to receive detailed internal guidance about how to avoid illness and stay healthy. I've just recently decided to stick to the term *intuition* to describe both, whenever people seem to have trouble hearing me. *Psychic* can have too many negative connotations." (It'd been too late to correct the wording for this talk.) Even as I say this, I feel sad I must be so wary of this word, yet I realize for some it is a turnoff.

The debate continues. "How will I know if my intuition isn't just a projection?" "How does intuition help us diagnose and prevent disease?" "Can we teach patients to notice warning signs before they get sick?" "Do messages about our health come in dreams?" So many questions: I barely have time to answer them.

For me a miracle took place that afternoon. Despite the opposition in the room, despite the rigorous training these doctors had under-gone, the revering of technology at the expense of instinct, a dialogue about the healing role of intuition had begun. I was touched to learn that the residents were in heated discussion for hours afterward. Even the head of the department thanked me for coming. Jokingly, he said, "You've been looking at me so kindly I can hardly stand it!" Everyone laughed. I laughed too. Still, I couldn't help but wonder why kindness would come as such a surprise.

My goal in speaking at this medical school was to present new treat-ment options using intuition as a tool. I never expected everyone to agree with me. And, clearly, there were people I didn't get through to at all. It was like speaking to slabs of granite! Yet many others lit up. I realize each of us must come to terms with how much we are willing to trust intuition. It is a deeply personal understanding that shapes our core beliefs about the extent of change we are capable of. Is science enough to keep us well, or is our sense of inner vision a resource we also must turn to? If I was able to offer this audience of doctors permission at least to start exploring these issues, I'd succeeded. As the poet Rumi so beautifully puts it, "Out beyond any ideas of wrongdoing or rightdo-ing, there is a field. I'll meet you there." This day was just the beginning.

NOW I WANT to take you on the next phase of this journey. I'm going to lead you into some intimate areas you may never have explored: the spaces between your thoughts, the unspoken messages you receive, the inspirations to be found from silence, from dreams, or even from lis-tening to the language of starlight. I'll be presenting many ideas about prevention and healing that may seem impossible to your rational mind. Such subtleties elude it. Instead, seek out and trust your intuitive experience of the practical approaches I offer. Put them to the test.

Consider this concept: Illness can often be detected and reversed long before physical signs appear. Echoes of illness precede its occur-rence, oscillating through the tiniest particles within you. It's like feel-ing a nearly motionless wind brush against your skin. To your ordinary awareness it may be imperceptible—yet, intuitively, you can tell it is there. I will show you how to tune in. Reach beyond the ordinary to dis-cover how to sense early on and predict minute changes in your self-awareness.

You have a healing code within that contains vital information about ways to stay healthy, in many cases to resolve illness before it takes physical form. I also appreciate that this is not possible or appropriate in every instance. I want to reemphasize that sometimes our healing may be intended to come from the illness itself; this need not represent failure on our part. The learning we derive from illness must never be minimized. It may not always entail physically "curing" the disease. But illness can be a catalyst for developing self-compassion, softening our egos, trusting our intuition, defining what's truly important to us. Though no one would ever choose to be sick, illness is a demanding teacher that initiates change in us like nothing else can. It sets the stage for the opening of our hearts. Spiritually speaking, deep healing is a matter of perspective, sometimes involving more that a symptom's "cure." Some illnesses are preventable, but in every case deciphering your own healing code is key.

To help you begin this deciphering, let's jump into the practical application of the five intuitive steps. I'll illustrate the process to follow whenever you want to receive intuitive hints about your health. For now let's address prevention. In future chapters we'll focus on illness. Here I will present each step with a special emphasis on how to sense subtle energy.

In traditional medicine these intuitive steps are easily overlooked; they are invisible, can't yet be reliably quantified. Slowly familiarize yourself with every step. Get to know each one like you would a good friend. They have life and breath and magic. This process is not static. Allow it to continue to teach you. The approach I'm describing may challenge you to take a more assertive role in your medical care than you've ever considered before.

Step 1. Notice Your Beliefs

I have a patient, Marcie, who loves to eat fresh oranges and stare out at the ocean. Nothing makes her happier than watching waves break on the shore. The cast of golden light on the water as the sun filters through. The massive winged pelicans diving for fish. The surf's phosphorescent glow as night falls.

Marcie is a newspaper reporter. Her beat is politics. She has passion for her work but sometimes overdoes it. Her calendar is packed— interviews, press conferences, breaking news. It's hard for her to take time out for herself. Sometimes the thought would cross her mind, If only I had a cold. Then I could stay home, lie in bed, and look at the ocean. Of course, she didn't listen. She'd convince herself, I feel fine. There's too much to do. Then, like clockwork, within a few days a cold would arrive.

Beliefs are powerful. Beliefs can set a tone for certain realities to occur. Our bodies are very intelligent. They need to get their rest. They need to be pampered and feel good. If a thought comes along that says to the body, In order to get the rest you need, you have to get sick, the body will comply. It's not that Marcie wanted this. She just wouldn't slow down. "Beliefs and illness are connected," I told her. Like many of us she intellectually realized this but hadn't put it to the test. She needed to experience it as real. Now, whenever catching a cold starts to sound good to Marcie, she knows to take a day off. That day in bed, eating oranges—and once in a while even succumbing to a scoop of chocolate-chip ice cream (not low-fat!)—spares her the symptoms of a full-blown cold. Permission to play hooky occasionally is a gift Marcie has learned to give to herself. It renews her. Rarely does she get a cold anymore.

Marcie had a choice about her health, as you do. Your mind and body are linked by an intricate intuitive circuitry. Notice the pattern of any recurring beliefs or emotions that occur before an illness. They may well be premonitions. Another patient of mine, a comedy writer for television, has an ulcer that periodically acts up. What tips him off at least a week before any symptoms is that he loses his sense of humor. A comedy writer's worst nightmare: Nothing seems funny anymore. Everybody and everything irritates him. He now knows to jump on this cue, to take special care of his stomach to ward off an attack.

Your body responds to your mind's beliefs, conscious or unconscious. Thoughts such as This job is eating me alive, Life's not worth living, I'm scared to death, You're giving me a heart attack, I'm so tired I feel like keeling over—all can transmit potent messages, even self-fulfilling prophecies to your brain chemicals, tissues, and cells. In *The Artist's Way*, Julia Cameron astutely points out that while many of us cringe at the thought of positive thinking—too Pollyannaish, all those aphorisms—we have no problem telling ourselves we're stupid, fat, ugly, failures.

Part of the problem may be a lack of inspiring, believable role models. We're shown either saccharine, inauthentic figures who "think positive" or heroic lives that end badly. It becomes a truism in our minds that great artists finish their days as alcoholics or suicides, or that the noblest political figures are inevitably assassinated. We have to free ourselves from such thinking, begin to associate creativity with optimism. Negativity mesmerizes by preying on our fears, distorting reality. It's important to realize this, notice when fear takes over, and begin to reprogram your thinking.

Thoroughly search yourself for negative beliefs. Visualize health, not illness. Cultivate a growing optimism that replaces fear-based thinking with hope and empowerment. One of my closest friends, Berenice, suffered third-degree burns over her entire body from a house fire. Later she survived two occurrences of malignant skin cancer. "I don't ever worry about my health," she told me. "I have absolute faith in the strength of my body to overcome adversity." Berenice, now seventy, visualizes being physically and mentally vital into her nineties. She is committed to making this a reality.

I resisted positive thinking for a long time. For years I'd recoil whenever people would say to me, "Think positive." All I wanted to do was rebel. It reminded me of those horrid moments as a child when my parents would say, "Smile for the camera" or "Put on a happy face." Of course I never would. I resented anyone telling me how to be. Please understand, that's not my intention with you. Nor am I implying that positive thinking can be solely responsible for either promoting wellness or destroying it—such notions are simplistic, misleading. What I am suggesting, though, is that your attitudes about health shape your capacity to achieve it. You must strive to be more loving with yourself to sustain the most nurturing biochemical and psychic environment in which to heal.

It is this quality of love that penetrates to an unspoken life within you, a divine microbiology. On a subliminal level cells speak. As you grow more open, listen with your intuition as Hesse did to what he called "the teachings my blood whispers to me." That blood goes back generations. You are not only the genetics you carry; you hold your entire ancestral history. The beliefs your mothers and grandmothers had about their health, the illnesses they experienced and how they dealt with them, still affect you today.

The other day, going through a safe-deposit box containing documents belonging to my parents, I came upon a piece of paper dated June 23, 1976. My mother's name was typed in capital letters on the top. It was a pathology report. It said she had malignant lymphoma. I froze, remembering the suffering this disease had caused her, re-living her death four years before. The loss of her, that unrelenting siren moaned right through me all over again. Was it so important to her, this lymphoma, that she preserved its original documentation for me to find years after her death? What was she trying to tell me? Yet there the notice was in the same stack of papers as my birth certificate, my report cards from grammar school (she must have kept every one), my first lock of baby hair. Lymphoma was one such milestone for my mother. And I couldn't help but wonder, Would it also be mine?

Our parents' beliefs about illness cast light on our beliefs about ourselves. My mother, herself a doctor and very brave, nonetheless defined herself by her ultimately terminal lymphoma, giving it even more power than it had. I realized it was vital to disengage from such thinking. The illnesses of our lineage do not have to become our own. It is critical not to feel obliged to inherit something that doesn't belong to us. Or to misread the bond with our loved ones as including their illnesses. Genetics may dictate the transmission of a disease, but we can do much to break our intuitive link to such a process. Most important, notice your fears. It's natural to empathize with what your loved ones are going through. Still, be careful not to overidentify with their illnesses or the difficulties they have coping with them. Fear acts as a negative magnet. Do your best to let it go. Releasing fear offers a reprieve. This alone could very well liberate you from reliving even your relatives' genetic patterns.

We can't always regulate what happens to us in life, but the quality of our passage is up to us. Become accustomed to looking at your beliefs as intuitive guideposts, both as precursors to illness and as ways of deflecting it. Prevention is more within your grasp than you may think.

Step 2. Be in Your Body

For years it never felt safe for me to be in my body. It seemed alien, a container that was much too small. I felt trapped. I wanted out. Overwhelmed by too many feelings, I hovered numb just a few inches above my skin, disconnected. It seemed as if I rarely breathed. I hid from my sensuality. Yet so much of being in the body is a sensual experience: inhaling the fragrance of night-blooming jasmine, hearing the soft hoot of a owl, feeling the head-to-toe electricity of being attracted to another person.

We take a lot for granted. We forget to honor the sensuality of being human. Slow down. Notice how good it feels to breathe, eat, walk, meet a friend's eyes straight on. It took exploring my intuitive side, gaining comfort with opening up, to recognize that the body is an elegant intuitive receptor, sensitively registering the most delicate input. For you to become fully aware of your intuition, it's not enough to occupy only your mind. Inhabit your body. You can't afford to have one foot out the door.

Our society puts a premium on the ability to tough out adversity. We celebrate people who ignore their bodies' danger signals in order to achieve—a macho or macha delusion that can lead to big health trouble. At a hospital staff meeting at UCLA one November, I ran into a medical colleague with a thriving practice. Usually tanned and fit, he looked ghastly. He confided, "My shoulder's killing me." "How long?" I asked. He paused, sheepish. "Since last May. I've been too swamped to have an orthopedist look at it." So typical of a doctor! As if ignoring pain would make it disappear. Almost six months? More than anyone he should've known better. He had good intentions, like many of us, but failed to act.

It's vital to retrain yourself to override mechanisms you've developed to push through discomfort. To prevent illness I'm going to show you how to pay special attention to physical distress signals. Honor your body's messages; don't discount them. Simple, prompt action is sometimes all it takes. If you're tired, rest. If you're hungry, eat a delicious meal. If you're stressed, get a relaxing massage. The price of not listening? You come down with the flu; your back goes out. You still don't listen? The thermostat gets turned up until you do.

Heeding early warnings protects your health. Your body is programmed for survival. Familiarize yourself with how it speaks to you. It wants you to be well. It will tell you if you are not. Hippocrates wrote over two thousand years ago, "There is a measure of conscious thought throughout the body." This is practical wisdom you can live by. To get a head start on warding off symptoms, get used to detecting the quieter messages your body sends. Some of them you may recognize right away.

QUESTIONS FOR REFLECTION

- Do you ever walk around feeling "off center"? Oddly numb? Out of focus? Detached? As if you're somehow missing a beat? How long do you tolerate this sense that your body just isn't right?

- Do you sometimes feel "toxic," as if you're coming down with the flu though there are no other signs of it?

- Have you experienced unexplainable symptoms that may have gone on for years? A knot or emptiness in the pit of your stomach? A lump in your throat? An aching heart?

- Do you ever have a distressing sense of rawness or feeling exposed? Does everything seem to get to you and you feel you have no defense?

If you answer yes to any of these questions, it's worthwhile to begin by taking a general inventory of your health and stress level. What areas can be improved upon? Examine everything: amount of exercise, alone time, your relationships. Make sure you're allotting enough space to recharge your batteries. Although the above changes may seen relatively minor, on an intuitive level they indicate early difficulty. To start, do your best to pinpoint and remedy problem areas. Later, in the subtle energy section of this chapter, we'll go into solutions in greater depth.

To discern your body's warnings, both quiet and blatant, requires increasing sensitivity to nuances of physicality, the knack of sensing smaller changes before they become full-blown. Mindfulness is key. Denial is the antithesis of intuition. You must do what you can to get past it. What is its fundamental root? Could it be we're not just denying the messages our bodies send but denying we have bodies at all?

The level of deep self-care I'm proposing must stem from an intuitive appreciation of the preciousness of your physical form—a radical shift of consciousness, not simply a change of behavior. I understand this is asking a lot. After all, the majority of us never even have the chance to glimpse our own anatomy, a glaring oversight in our basic education. You could easily live an entire lifetime without knowing what lies beneath your skin. How strange that no one thinks to question this! The beauty of our internal workings, the awe that comes from witnessing them, is everyone's essential right. We all possess a gorgeous three-dimensional universe within us that we ignore at our peril. We've grown so accustomed to accepting surfaces as fact, viewing only a fraction of who we are, especially where our bodies are concerned. We must delve beneath these surfaces to wake ourselves up.

My own wake-up call came in anatomy lab when I was a first-year medical student. It was totally unexpected. I was as squeamish as most of us would be about cutting into a body, particularly a dead one drenched in formaldehyde. Even before dissection, what a foul smell! And why me anyway? The premonition I'd had years before told me I was to become a psychiatrist. That was the plan. No mention of cadavers. Oy! I had no desire to dissect a brain, kidney, liver. Though I'd never acknowledged it, I'd grown up with a kind of revulsion for the body—a culturally conditioned response shared by most of us. Especially the sight of blood: The last thing I considered it to be was sacred. Not until I was forced, week after week, to touch tissues, organs, and bones, commit their structure to memory, did the magnificence of the body become apparent to me.

Later as a resident "scrubbing in" on major surgeries, I had the awe-inspiring experience of watching a heart linked to a labyrinth of blood vessels beating in a patient's chest, of feeling the textures of a uterus, ovaries, and lungs—an honor each of us deserves if we desire it, simply as an initiation into what it means to be human. Imprinted in my memory is the energy of each organ, its smooth, moist texture, its overall warmth and glistening color. Now, when I intuitively tune in to patients, these diverse frequencies are easier to sense.

There is an ancient ritual among the Iglulic Eskimos in which a shaman uses supernatural abilities to "divest his body of his flesh and blood" so that nothing but his bones remains. He must then recount all the parts of his anatomy, speak aloud each bone by name. And so the shaman gains power and self-knowledge by honoring the very structure of which he is composed. Becoming conscious of your structure will help complete your self-image, bring awareness to your body and its patterns to help prevent disease.

I recommend to you what I strongly suggest to everyone in my workshops: Go out and buy a copy of and *Start Exploring Gray's Anatomy: A Fact-Filled Coloring Book*. Or, if you have a special interest in the workings of the mind, check out the children's book *Brain Surgery for Beginners: A Scalpel-Free Guide to Your Insides* (see Selected Reading). It is filled with detailed, easy-to-understand color drawings, which will provide you with a well-rounded, delightful overview of the brain. Review each book from cover to cover. See yourself in every illustration. Take out your crayons. Choose your own color scheme. Have fun. You can also try the surgery channel on cable TV, but many people find it too clinical, un-appealing. Better, visit your local bookstore and check out the many CD-ROMs for children on the human body such as *3-D Body Adventure and A.D.A.M., The Inside Story.* Watch one closely. Then, for an even more direct experience, go to a medical supply store and get a stetho-scope. As I encourage all my workshop participants, play doctor with a friend. Take each other's pulse. Practice listening to your friend's heart, lungs, abdomen. *Ca-thunk, ca-thunk.* Woooshes. Gurgles. Kids love these sounds, have a giggle fest experimenting. Just as they do, really get into it. Compare notes. Take a careful look at how you are made.

In the process learn that every human being is composed as you are, sharing the basic structure yet unique. To start, get a general idea of the different systems of the body: digestive, respiratory, circulatory, urinary, neurologic, among others. What role does each play in keeping you healthy? Then go through the major organs. Where is your pancreas lo-cated? Your bladder? Your heart? What function does each organ serve? How does it support life? Most important, this knowledge will demystify the body, liberate it from the realm of the unknowable, the unspeak-able, or taboo. The goal is not to overphysicalize your structure but to become acquainted with it.

The more intimately you know your physical makeup, the more suc-cessful and intuitively driven any health-related intervention you undertake will be. For instance, if you're in excruciating pain from pass-ing a kidney stone, being able to visualize your kidney gives you a con-crete focal point where you may tune in. Like a laser you can zoom into the problem area and help heal it utilizing a technique of mobilizing subtle energy I will teach you. Do the same thing if you're having surgery or undergoing any medical or dental procedure. Before, dur-ing (if you're awake), and afterward, visualize the location of the diffi-culty. As your intuition develops you'll learn to direct energy to it; I'll explain how later. Your intuitive participation makes healing easier, faster, with fewer complications. Knowing your anatomy allows you to apply intuition to localize and sense subtle energy shifts preceding ill-ness (increasing the odds of preventing it or making an early diagnosis) and gives you a map of where to aim healing energy if illness comes.

Your presence in your body awakens it. "Can this be me?" you might ask. Your anatomy may seem so mind-blowing, it's hard to relate to, like a foreign country. But slow down. Take it all in gradually. Notice any resistance you have to what you are seeing. It's natural. Gently come to understand how it keeps you from connecting to your physicality, your primal core. Stay with it. In good time your resistance will melt. Increasingly, being in your body will be a joy. Your sensitivity to detect and act on messages the body transmits will grow.

Your body deserves to be worshiped. As a result, of course, you will learn to love yourself more. The innocence with which you approach your body, curious yet humble, will expand your awareness of the human experience. Committing to a life truly *in* your body can't help but rearrange your priorities. It has mine. Without forcing it, listening to your inner workings will become second nature to you, a seamless way of being in the world.

Step 3. Sense Your Body's Subtle Energy

Think microscopic. Think tinier than microscopic. Imagine your body: the intricacies of its flesh and blood. But also picture another dimension, made of energy that penetrates and extends many feet beyond your skin. What is this energy? It is an intuitive language of the body. It is the essence of who we are, a subtle vibration underlying everything physical, both living and inanimate (including objects such as rocks, furniture, and jewelry). Some of us may see it more easily; other may feel it. If we reduce ourselves to the smallest components, energy is what we find. To Hindu mystics, it's *shakti*. Chinese medical practitioners call it *chi*. It's the radiant "aura" seers through the ages have reported. Even Western medicine is starting to catch on. An exciting new subspecialty has emerged: energy medicine. Drawing on ancient Hindu and Buddhist systems, it recognizes our bodies and spirits as manifestations of energy composed of seven midline centers called *chakras*. Any imbalances in these centers cause disease.

Here's an overview of the chakras to make them easy to visualize. Now you'll have a reference point to use throughout the book as you learn more about this system. Of course, the depth and mystery of the chakras is known only through experience; this simplification is just a start.

A MINIGUIDE TO THE CHAKRA SYSTEM

Chakra	Location	Function	Color
First	Genitals, anus	Sexuality	Red
Second	2 inches below belly button, midline	Sexuality, nurturing, balance	Orange
Third	Solar plexus	Emotions, power drive, need to control	Yellow
Fourth (heart chakra)	2 inches above diaphragm, midline	Compassion, love	Green
Fifth	Throat	Communication, speaking your truth	Cobalt blue
Sixth (third eye)	Forehead, between eyebrows	Intuition, intellect	Purple
Seventh (crown chakra)	Top of head	Spirituality	White

I'd like you to get used to picturing your body in terms of chakras. Go through the table and see where the chakras correspond to parts of your body. Visually orient yourself. Then spend at least a few minutes exploring how each chakra feels. Sitting quietly, take as long as you like focusing on each one. Pay attention to any heat, cold, tingling, pressure, emotions, or whether sensations fade or build. Routinely practice this. Daily awareness of chakras activates them. Even if it takes you a while, keep at it. As we progress through the chapters, your ability to sense the chakras will grow.

It's important to know about chakras to maintain optimal health and prevent illness. Energy can be perceived in a generalized way, but reading chakras allows you to break it down into distinct, body-specific components. By being in closer touch with your body, you can detect if it's functioning well or requires special care. Intuitive information about your deepest physical, emotional, and spiritual needs is transmitted through the chakras. Interpreting these signals is life-sustaining.

Energy medicine has different assumptions than Western health care that I'd like you to consider. One is that you are matter and also the light that surrounds it. You are color, constantly changing, reflecting your moods and health. Sometimes gold or the deepest crimson, or the loveliest blue and green and white light shooting like flares from your skin. All this outside the spectrum we ordinarily see. Within these colors are invisible tendrils possessing an exquisite ability to absorb and feel another person's energy, even from many feet away. These intuitive receptors are so exacting they sense infinitesimal changes in your health and how others affect it.

Let's look at energy in terms of your everyday life. Have you ever met someone at a party and liked her immediately? It wasn't so much what she said or did, but how wonderful she felt to be around. Or remember that time you were working on a project with a man who seemed perfectly nice but you always came away drained? You were responding to another person's energy. In a very real way the energy people give off can have an influence on keeping you well. You can't interact with someone without having this reciprocal exchange. Know this. Whenever possible surround yourself with others who feel good to be with, who nurture you, not those who sap you dry. Your body is constantly processing energy, fine-tuning itself to people, places, situations.

Take the concept of personal space. Ask yourself, Is there a certain distance (one foot? two feet? ten feet?) you prefer keeping from others when you talk to them? Do you get uneasy when your personal space is violated? We've all met people who are so oblivious, they're practically on top of you when you talk. Do you find yourself edging away? Then do they irritatingly edge closer? There is an unseeable energetic border around you that sets a comfort level. Intuitively you sense this. In response you unconsciously learn to negotiate energy at a very young age. The result? You adopt body language—crossing your arms, talking with your hands, raising your voice—that keeps this border intact. In doing so you communicate to others a distance they must keep that feels best to you.

How can knowing about energy keep you healthy? To get a better idea we need to zero in on the dynamics of how illness works. Let's slow down the entire process. Begin to see illness as a progression—it never just appears out of the blue. Look at it this way: Energy-wise, by the time a heart attack, stroke, or migraine (so-called acute illnesses) "hits," you've already traveled far down an illness's course. Subtle shifts precede cellular change. The secret is to catch imbalances in your body long before you have pain or a full-blown disease.

To do this attend to the quieter signals your body sends—energy warnings that may occur before any obvious physical cause. Emptiness, numbness, exhaustion, a knot in your stomach, a lump in your throat, mysterious aches and pains—these generalized symptoms are notoriously elusive, often defy ordinary explanation. Nonetheless, to feel well you need to know what's causing them.

Most likely, if you experienced these sensations and then consulted your doctor, you were given a physical exam and a battery of tests, which turned out all negative if your symptoms were energy-based. "You're fine," your doctor told you, sending you on your way. Now you were probably even more confused, doubting yourself. Be aware that energy expresses itself in forms medical science can't yet explain. The problem is that, when it comes to energy, most of us don't know the right questions to ask or where to turn for help. So we do nothing. We are forced into becoming tolerant of physical states that are not good for us—a setup for later negative repercussions on our health.

To detect imbalances in yourself, you need to realize that energy in its simplest form is something we initially perceive as vibration. It's so subliminal we often miss it. I want to share with you the way I tune in to energy so you can get used to it. I practice this technique every day. Let me show you how.

BODY SCANNING

Close your eyes. Take a few deep breaths. Relax. Find a comfortable position. Gently focus your attention on only your body. How does it feel? Notice any physical discomfort, or areas that are at ease. Get a baseline. Then try to pick up your subtle energy. Ask yourself: Do I have any waves of tingling or buzzing anywhere? Rushes of heat, cold, or goose bumps totally unrelated to the outside temperature? If so, can I pinpoint the specific organ involved? Can I sense in it a particular feeling of well-being or vibrance? Or does it feel flat, depleted, ill?

You may perceive energy as a hum, a color, a quivering. These may show up in surprising locations—your sinuses, ears, liver, spine. Some parts of your body may feel alive, especially sensitive, others dull, aching, or numb. Let your imagination go wild. Notice how these sensations vary. You may feel things in places you never even knew existed. This is good. You'll get to know your body well, a positive start to prevention.

Practice. Practice. Practice. Discerning such fine energy takes time. Meanwhile, your mind will help you out. It constantly translates vibration into forms you can more easily recognize. For example, into imagery and emotions. Patients have shared with me striking descriptions: the accountant who felt as if a steel rod was shooting down his back; the young girl with a black cloud over her heart. You may have had similar powerful images. Or how about this? Have you ever experienced the strange feeling that parts of your body are congested, blocked, or shut down with no physical evidence to support it? That sadness is bottled up in your liver, or there's anger in your joints? These are ways subtle energy speaks to you, offers leads about your health. As an intuitive I've trained myself to tune in at this level. I teach my patients to do so too.

Take a peptic ulcer. Let me present a typical progression, tracking from early energy warnings to appearance of symptoms:

> waves of goose bumps ➤➤ feeling physically off ➤➤ a knot in the stomach ➤➤ localized anger ➤➤ image of clenched fist ➤➤ a feeling of blockage ➤➤ increased stomach acid ➤➤ stomach pain ➤➤ ulcer forms

I have a patient, George, who used to suffer gallstone attacks a few times a year. They'd be so severe he'd sometimes land in the hospital on morphine. His internist recommended surgery, a logical suggestion. But George didn't want to go that route; he preferred trying naturopathic medicine first. So he did, taking a high-potency pain remedy with no luck. Then, through our work together, George observed something that ordinarily would've flown right by him: For most of the day before an attack his abdominal area would feel "clogged" and unusually hot—actually giving off heat. His internist couldn't explain it, but George was becoming more aware of energy. "Use this knowledge," I advised. "The next time the heat comes, why not immediately take the medicine?" Bingo. From that day on George had fewer attacks and milder pain if there was a flare-up. Why? He was treating the predisposing energy disturbance—excessive heat and congestion—before it had a chance to evolve into pain. This skillful intervention broke the pain cycle before the actual symptom occurred.

Phase one of prevention is to backtrack to the energy origins of your illness. Phase two is to discover what actions to take to correct the imbalance. It may mean changing your lifestyle or diet, meditating more, getting into therapy to face difficult emotions, undergoing "energy work" (Chapter 4 will take you through specific hands-on energy techniques), resting, stopping smoking, taking the right medications early on. Maybe you know exactly what to do on your own. If not, seek out a knowledgeable practitioner to help pinpoint your solution.

A writer-friend of mine always feels as if each nerve ending in his body is exposed right before his back goes out. Every sound, smell, even a person accidentally bumping into him on the street, seems like an assault. From an astute physical therapist he's learned to recognize these signals that announce to him, You must unglue yourself from the computer and return to yoga. If he listens—jumping to correct the energy imbalance—in no time he regains his center and is spared weeks of excruciating back pain.

Sometimes, though, it's not that simple. Let me tell you about Diane. For over two years she lived with the nagging feeling that "something wasn't right" in her body. It wasn't that she was sick. When she'd consult her doctor, he'd always be reassuring and give her a clean bill of health. Nevertheless, she felt "off," as though she couldn't shake a mild flu. Diane was a public school administrator who dreamed of selling real estate. She loved beautiful houses and wanted a schedule of her own making. Still, whenever she really thought about changing jobs, she stopped herself. The perks she'd accumulated over fifteen years in the school system—medical insurance, retirement plans, an excellent salary—were just too good.

So for very logical reasons she remained at a job that was not her passion. In our sessions we talked about the potential risks. "It's not an ideal choice," Diane admitted, but she was determined to live with it. Of course, this was her call. I had to respect it. Several years passed. Her life went on. One day she noticed a lump over her throat: it proved to be a fast-growing form of thyroid cancer, the same disease her mother had suffered decades before. Diane had surgery, then went through grueling chemotherapy, which left her nauseated and made her hair fall out. Toward the end of these treatments, she said to me, perfectly at peace, "I'm going to do it. I'm going to leave my job."

Now Diane sells real estate in Malibu. She's been in remission from cancer for over seven years. These days she looks forward to going to work; her body feels good. Every spring, on the anniversary of her diagnosis, she takes a walk at dawn by the ocean and says thank you to God for the life she's been given. Diane's new career isn't perfect— sometimes her finances are unnervingly unsteady—but she makes out just fine. "There's a purpose to everything," she says. Though it hasn't always been easy, she's learned the lessons of her body well.

I tell you about Diane both to share with you a happy ending and to assert how vital it is to take your body's discontent seriously. I don't mean to oversimplify the causes of Diane's illness. I appreciate that a variety of factors other than her job, including genetics, came into play, as is true of all disease. Nor am I implying that if you don't listen to your body you'll inevitably get cancer. We've all heard of extreme examples: the chain-smoking grandma with every ache and pain in the book who's about to turn one hundred, cancer-free; friends who're oblivious to their bodies' signals yet seem to be okay. It happens. But is it preferable to live this way? You must decide. Who gets sick, who doesn't can't be reduced to a pat formula. There's no guarantee that if you do everything right you'll stay healthy. However, I am saying that many times you may be forewarned about oncoming pain or illness and fail to realize it. If you choose to act on the energy changes your body communicates, it will pay off. I understand the kind of close listening this requires, how inconvenient making lifestyle changes on the basis of such subtleties can be. In the whirlwind of our busy lives, it's all too tempting just to write them off. But at what price?

What I am offering you is a new way of taking care of yourself—a chance to assume a proactive role in preventing a great deal of illness. This doesn't mean you have to be an obsessive. Be observant of energy, not overly focused on it. Your sensitivity will blossom. Look at it as the upside to the lesson of the princess and the pea. You remember: That stormy night the princess arrived at the palace, soaked and bedraggled, the prince doubted she was the real thing. Her sensitivity to a tiny pea he placed beneath a stack of mattresses proved she was royal, worthy to rule a kingdom. I promise you this: If you are mindful of your body's subtle energy and become accountable for it, your health will improve. I've seen how true this has been for my patients, my friends, and myself. The choice is yours.

Step 4. Ask for Inner Guidance

I believe from the moment we are born to the day we die, we have guidance and protection all around us. Call it your guardian angels, your ancestors, a higher power, or simply love, we are not as alone as we think. The difficulty is that most of us are born not remembering we can "see"; we perceive there is nothing there.

Whenever I'm confused about an issue in my life and need direction, I ask for intuitive guidance. I may not know how to help a patient or how to protect the health of a loved one or myself. I've analyzed the pros and cons, evaluated relevant statistics; I've listened to the advice of people I respect. Still the answer isn't there. No option I've considered feels right. Now what? Have I reached a dead end? Yes—but only intellectually. When we arrive at this point, it's time to seek a different kind of truth, one that comes from looking inward.

Sometimes your guidance will just appear, no request necessary. You'll be walking down the street and *bam!* It hits you. Or you may be in the shower, which if you're like me is a psychic phone booth. The hot water drenching my body, the relaxation it brings, is like magic. Suddenly answers come. Even if you haven't formally enlisted help, in certain times of need an internal alarm goes off on its own. A patient of mine in his twenties, an avid marathon runner, was dragging around exhausted for days. No one knew why. He swore he wasn't depressed. He ate well. His blood tests and physical exam were normal. One afternoon walking out of a neighborhood restaurant, he spotted a homeopathic pharmacy down a small flight of stairs next door. He'd been by it a million times, never noticed. Now this strangely compelling feeling—irresistible really—seemed to pull him inside. It didn't matter that he knew nothing about homeopathy. It was in this pharmacy he was given a formula for his cure.

Tuning in to guidance about your body can keep you feeling your best. Whether it arrives unsolicited or you invite it in, your intuition will notify you. It's always thrilling to me, this inner link with such a creative intelligence. Be sensitive to your physical responses—a chill up your spine, the tiny hairs of your neck standing on end, a flushing of your face, a quickening of breath. Your body's telling you you're on track. Sometimes you'll experience an immediate "Aha!" as though a bright light had flipped on. Other solutions—in the form of images, sensations, premonitions—zing with energy. For me they often come through in snapshotlike flashes. See what happens to you. Whenever you're inexplicably drawn, as my patient was, to a specific place of healing—a pharmacy, a workshop, a t'ai chi class, a clinic—pay close attention! Or notice if you feel impelled to work with a particular medical practitioner. Don't let these opportunities pass.

How do you request guidance? The most powerful tool I know is meditation—a lifeline to the part of you that intuits what's right if you'd just pause to hear. Meditation bypasses the mind. If you want the strong inner connection I'm suggesting, you must begin to quiet yourself. It's a very different posture from thinking, the exact opposite of "working" to figure a problem out. Pure receptivity. No effort required. Let's say you have painful recurring migraines. At the beginning of your meditation, you might ask, How can I keep my headaches from coming back? Place your request. Close your eyes. Get very still. Then wait. Focus only on your breath. If thoughts come—and they will—return to your breath each time. The pressure is off. No expectations. Remain open. Allow yourself to be surprised. If a solution pops up while you're sitting there quietly—great. If not, meditate again later. With experience you'll find the answer.

I know of a woman who underwent a radical mastectomy of her right breast for cancer. Two years later, after the birth of a daughter, she discovered a large mass in her left breast. Her family panicked. She was on the verge, but before she went over the edge, she sought guidance in meditation to check out if her cancer had returned. Not trying to think up solutions, she simply posed a question, then waited. Within minutes a distinct image came through: Milk ducts in the area of the mass were blocked from breast feeding. *This* was the source of her problem. Every cell of her body agreed. A chill of recognition shot through her. From the clarity of her vision, she knew she was fine. Not long after her diagnosis was confirmed by ultrasound.

We are wired for intuitive guidance. But how does it work? The synapses of perception: mere electrochemical transmissions from cell to cell, or is something more involved? Who we are, how we are made, has mystery. I am moved by the intricacies of our physical form. Don't you see? *We are the miracle.* I have to believe that this truth more than qualifies each of us to acknowledge the wisdom of our bodies, to sense the infinite love from which all guidance comes.

Step 5. Listen to Your Dreams

Last year on Christmas Day I had a decision to make—a big one. My seventy-seven-year-old father with Parkinson's disease was in the hospital with pneumonia, nearly delirious from a fever of 104. He looked like death warmed over. I was devastated. He barely recognized me. Was his time up? I wondered. So did his doctor.

Along with antibiotics there was only one thing left to do, his doctor concluded: "We have to put a permanent G-tube in your father's stomach." I froze. This meant that he would never eat real food again. No more pastrami sandwiches on rye, his favorite. He'd have to live with a six-inch plastic gastrointestinal tube inserted through his skin, sewn into his stomach. Ensure, that horrible canned supplement, fed through the tube, would be his only sustenance. Not a pretty picture. But if it would save his life? I understood the thinking behind this choice. The theory was that Parkinson's disease had caused my father's swallowing muscles to stop working properly. As a result food intended for his stomach ended up in his lungs. Thus, he was susceptible to recurrent pneumonia.

Still, something didn't feel right. So I did what I always do when I'm too involved to intuitively see clearly: I sent out an SOS for a dream. That night it came:

> *My father and I are having dinner at a table with a simple white cloth. He looks happy, physically fit. I watch him eat; he savors every bite. He says nothing. Suddenly he looks up at me. His eyes turn a radiant emerald green. They are loving and bright. I fall into them. Then all at once I know: It's okay to put off the decision about the tube.*

I woke up certain of this.

Once my father's infection resolved, I took him home. A few weeks later he met Janice, a lovely eighty-nine-year-old widow ("an older woman," as she put it!). They fell in love. She gave him a new lease on life. They'd go out for Chinese food, would hold hands in the movies, stroll side by side with their walkers in the park. Without a doubt this was worth every minute of his doctor's obvious frustration with me, that look he gave me implying that I was trying to kill my father. I didn't tell the doctor about my dream. I feared it would only have made matters worse. Not long after that my father winked at me and said, "I'm under your wing." I understood. By following my dream I'd spared him the hardship of rushing into a premature decision. I'd bought him precious time.

There is a healing instinct within you that can manifest in dreams. You'd be surprised at the straightforward health advice they give, either spontaneously or on request. Tips on food, preventive therapies, treatment options constantly come through—but we miss them. Once remembered the essence of many of our dreams is lost because we, or our

therapists, misinterpret them. A patient told me about a recurring broc-
coli dream. "You can't be serious," he said, chuckling. "It's actually trying to tell me what to eat? A vegetable?" Yes—it was. We often dismiss
such practical suggestions as meaningless. But sometimes a cigar is just
a cigar.

Keep it simple. Try something new. If you dream of eating a luscious
mango, run out, devour one. Or when, in a dream, you're soaking in
natural hot springs, make a date to go. I have a friend who dreams of a
health spa in Mexico every few years when she's overly stressed. She
takes it as a signal to make a reservation. How do you know if the advice
you receive is right? What if you feast on an entire, incredibly scrumptious, gigantic chocolate mousse cake in a dream? Does that mean you
should run out to buy one, then eat the whole thing? Of course not.
Who needs the calories or the bellyache? Count on common sense to
direct you. Though some intuitive flashes may seem impractical or unexpected, the authentic ones will never suggest anything to jeopardize
you or anyone else's physical welfare. So, for instance, if you have heart
disease and a dream tells you, "It's okay to smoke cigarettes," don't do
it. Question all messages that risk your health. Along with this guide-
line, begin to familiarize yourself with traditional dream interpretation.
I suggest Carl Jung's classic text *Man and His Symbols,* or take a look at
Creative Dreaming by Dr. Patricia Garfield (see Selected Reading). These
are good ways to jump in until we go deeper into analyzing dreams in
Chapter 4.

In addition, there's an intuitive level to understanding dreams of
which I'd like you to be aware. Reliable intuitive information stands out
in very specific ways. Watch for these clues:

- Statements that simply convey information
- Neutral segments that evoke or convey no emotion
- A detached feeling, like you're a witness watching a scene
- A voice or person counseling you—as if you're taking dictation from
  an outside source
- Conversations with people you never met before who give instruc-
  tions about your health

I've found that my most dead-on intuitions either come across as
compassionate or have no emotion at all. I once correctly dreamed that

a patient was going to have a stroke. Of course I was alarmed. But the information itself at the moment I received it was uncharged. Develop a careful eye as you practice separating the content of your dreams from your reactions to it. Soon you'll be able to tell what is reliable health guidance and what is not. You'll know just what to do with that chocolate mousse cake.

Be aware that your dreams go by different rules than your waking life. Get ready for a mind shift. Physical laws no longer apply. Gravity changes. In dreams you can fly! Remember as a child (or adult) when you took off wingless, soared over mountains and valleys below. Health-wise, this is a reminder of the vitality and freedom that is in you. Silence is pregnant. A dream's tone can be as restorative as its content; a revelation about staying well can come through someone's eyes rather than words, as it did with my father.

You are in partnership with your dreams. Initiate an ongoing dialogue with them. It's like consulting the wisest old-time family doctor you can imagine who knows you inside out. You can ask your dreams anything—even what seems most impossible. How can I keep my blood pressure down? What about my hip pain or allergies? Are there ways to stop catching so many colds? No question is trivial if it is meaningful to you. Expect answers. Some will be direct. Others may require interpretation, which I'll teach you as we go on.

Dreams can keep you well. Dreams provide answers. But first you must retrieve them. How many nights have you awakened with the most amazing dream you were certain you'd recall? The next morning it was gone. Our memories deceive. During sleep we experience a kind of amnesia. Dreams are not of the rational mind. Your intuitive memory is what is needed. Here is a method I recommend to remember your dreams. It's helpful to practice it each day. Soon it will become second nature to you.

FOUR STRATEGIES TO REMEMBER YOUR DREAMS

1. Keep a journal and pen by your bed.

2. Write a question on a piece of paper before you go to sleep. Formalize your request. Place it on a table beside your bed or under your pillow (like you did as a child when you made a wish to the tooth fairy).

3. In the morning do not wake up too fast. Stay under the covers for at least a few minutes remembering your dream. Luxuriate in a peaceful feeling between sleep and waking, what scientists call the hypnagogic state. Those initial moments provide a doorway.

4. Open your eyes. Write down your dream immediately; otherwise it will evaporate. You may recall a face, object, color, or scenario, feel an emotion. It doesn't matter if it makes perfect sense—or if you retrieve a single image or many. Record everything you remember.

When you're finished refocus on the health question you asked the previous night. See how your dream applies. One, two, or more impressions about the who/what/where of your solution may have surfaced. My own answer to preventing recurring sinus infections came in a dream: the flash of an acupuncture office. An elevator. An old Chinese man. A rush of vitality. These were my signposts. Take note of yours. Get in the habit of recording your dreams regularly. Be assured I've never met anyone who can't be taught how to remember. Keep at it. If your answer doesn't come the first night, try again. More details will emerge, rounding out the picture. Then look to your daily life for evidence of what your dream tells you. The woman's face you glimpsed for that split second could just be that of the healer you've been searching for.

I'll let you in on a secret. One of my favorite ways of conjuring up dreams is to turn on music at twilight as the moon rises and dance. You can try it too. Instantly I'm out of my head, into my body (a basic formula for intuitive awakening—memorize it!). In my living room, gazing out at an expanse of purple ocean and pastel sky, with no one to please, I gyrate wildly to Nirvana's heavy metal blasting, boogie to Miles Davis, or glide like a raven on the wind's currents to haunting Gregorian chants. Tension dissipates. Energy surges up my spine. I leap, spin, twirl faster than light. I flash yellow on the horizon—then become invisible. No more mind. Memory returns. Dreams fly through me. I become them. I am open. I can see.

I CAN SEE. I am guided every day by the five intuitive steps I've just presented. They have become my eyes. They can be yours too. The intuitions about your health I speak of and live by are ordinarily without boundary and are unseen. As you go through these steps they highlight truths about your body, providing a framework in which to recognize them. Ordering allows for a simple, focused understanding. I have a great respect for structure as long as it facilitates our freedom. Go through the steps with this in mind. In future chapters you will see how they apply to your emotions and sexuality as well. With each health question you ask, be prepared to expand or contract in response—whatever fluid motion is called for. Surrender all preconceptions about your healing. This realm I'm attempting to outline ultimately escapes definition. The mastermind of all things intuitive, the brains behind the scene, is of an infinite source.

To begin to grasp this, for a moment imagine yourself as a tabula rasa—literally a clean slate, open to fresh possibility. With this "beginner's mind" I'd like you to consider, maybe for the first time, what spirituality means to you. I'm not necessarily referring to any specific religion or upbringing, although you can draw on them if you like. I'm alluding to an abiding sense of communion with a compassionate, wise essence within you and without. Before all else it is there: a force that knows no limits of love. Each day I turn to it with my heart for the intuitions I am blessed with. It is the most important relationship I have. Seek this relationship out for yourself before a health crisis hits. Make it real. Then, in times of good health or not, you'll have more clarity to draw on. In my years as a physician I've seen that, for the faithless, healing can be difficult—they don't believe in anything, even themselves. Whether you define spirituality as a universal intelligence, God, the life force, or simply love, it is through our connection with this sublime presence that our intuitive awareness and capacity for wellness expands.

About the mystery, Albert Einstein said it well: "Human beings, vegetables or cosmic dust—we all dance to the mysterious tune, intoned in the distance by an invisible piper." More and more of us are able to hear. In modern medicine the question of spirituality looms increasingly large. Over twenty medical schools, including Johns Hopkins, Brown, the University of Chicago, and Loyola, offer a spirituality course, Faith and Medicine, as part of the regular curriculum. The goal is to introduce students early in their training to the interrelationships among spirituality, prevention, and healing. This is revolutionary! The S word was never even mentioned when I was in medical school.

Enduring true belief can be hard earned. My patient Lynn has taught me we each must find it in our own time. She wanted to believe but didn't. A college history professor, wickedly irreverent and smart, she winced at anything New Age ("woo-woo" she called it) and refused to set foot in a metaphysical bookstore. Even so, every few years, in crisis, Lynn would ask me, "How can I get in touch with my spirituality?" From experience I knew talking about it would get us nowhere. Push-pull. Start-stop. Her ambivalence was just too strong. "I need proof," she declared just last month. "Okay," I said. "Then go home and ask the universe for a sign." She looked exasperated. "I need practical advice. Don't be ridiculous." I'd heard this before. I stood firm. "Oh . . . all right. I guess it can't hurt to try." She was indulging me.

A week later Lynn called my office, bursting. "Judith, you're going to love this." She told me her story: One winter afternoon, after feeding Zsa Zsa and Ava, her two chickens, she decides to take her horse for a ride. Heading down a familiar dirt path near her home in the canyon, she comes to a grove of fragrant eucalyptus. She stops and waits. Quietly she says to herself, "Please show me a sign." A gentle breeze comes up. She feels peaceful . . . and within minutes there is a loud *whoosh*. Suddenly out of the trees thousands of monarch butterflies take flight all around her. Orange-and-black-striped wings fluttering from ground to sky. The area, she knows, is a monarch sanctuary during the colder months, but this is beyond belief. At exactly that instant, puttering down the street comes a beat-up VW Bug driven by a young Rastafarian man with shoulder-length dreadlocks. He pulls up next to her, rolls down his window. Marijuana smoke wafts into the air. "Look at this!" she exclaims, marveling at the swarm of butterflies. Grinning wide, his brown eyes shining, he says to Lynn, "You see. God blesses you." Then he disappears down the road.

Imagine the genius it would have taken to orchestrate that scene! It was tailored perfectly for Lynn. How could it be? What really happened? Whether the message Lynn received fully sank in or not, she'll never forget that day. It's funny about spirituality. We can see evidence of the most miraculous sights right before our eyes, and still we have to think about it, to mull it over, evaluate. Such is the nature of our minds. What if, just once, you let yourself go, accept the gift unconditionally? I dare you. What do you have to lose? And to gain? Breathe fire into what is dormant in you: your intuitions about a healthy body, your sense of spiritual power from which all your intuitions come. Make these connections count. They will last a lifetime. Open yourself to knowledge of how to heal. Let the mystery touch you. It is everything, everything.

3

Sacred Healing Partnerships

I swear by Apollo the physician and all the gods and
goddesses to benefit my patients. With purity and
holiness I will pass my life and practice my art.
—Hippocratic Oath

When I was a little girl, my mother, a family practice physician, used to take me along on house calls in her white Cadillac convertible. Not exactly the old horse and buggy out on the prairie. Fast-forward to the early sixties in Beverly Hills. Me—terribly shy with my ponytail, pedal pushers, and penny loafers—and my mother, a dynamo dressed head to toe in Chanel. We'd drive down palm-lined Rodeo Drive to the estates of Bel Air. Her elderly patient Mrs. Hormel (remember Spam, forerunner of all canned meats? That was her family) was too sick to leave the house. So Mother came to her, as she did with other patients. That worn-out old black leather bag of hers, bulging with tools—stethoscope, blood pressure cuff, reflex hammer, tuning fork, bandages, gauze—had an irresistible mystique. When no one was watching, I'd play with them all, imagine their power. I'd picture how my mother would close her eyes very tight, wrinkle her forehead, and concentrate as she examined Mrs. Hormel's heart and lungs. In absolute silence, just listening so long. How could I ever forget such caring? Or the birthday parties I spent with Mrs. Hormel and her family (she and I were both born on June 25). This was my initiation into sacred healing partnerships, the sphere of people they touch, how deep they go. On cold winter nights, after a full day of patients, I still curl up under the warmth of the thick red afghan Mrs. Hormel knitted for me. My mother was my role model. She taught me much about being a good doctor.

An only child, I grew up in a household where the bonds of medicine and family were inextricably mixed. My father, a radiologist, and mother used to discuss their patients at the dinner table. I'd hear about open-heart surgeries, triplets, diarrhea, death; no detail was taboo. Not exactly my idea of a relaxing meal, but this is how it was. So I took it in, partly fascinated, partly repelled, more than a little relieved for the breather I'd get whenever conversations veered off into shopping or golf.

Later, as a teenager, I was a rebel: being a doctor like my parents was the last thing I wanted. Whatever my feelings, though, medicine proved to be my destiny. To begin with, I came from a long lineage of physicians, a total of twenty-five on both sides of the family. Cancer researchers, gynecologists, internists, orthopedic surgeons, specialists in infectious disease. Further, I inherited a legacy of intuitive healing, although for most of my life it was kept hush-hush. Only when my mother was dying did I learn that my grandmother, my mother, my aunt, my cousin, and her daughter all had the intuitive gifts with which I've been blessed. (Of those five women, three were physicians!)

A doctor to be without realizing it, I was receiving extraordinary preparation as a child. I knew most of my mother's patients, and they knew me. This had its advantages. The high point was the day my mother took me to the hospital to bring Mick Jagger homemade chicken soup! Unforgettable. My mother's patients were my extended family. After my mother's death many of them found her impossible to replace. Her brand of medicine, they told me, was becoming extinct.

In the last decade the geography of medical practice has drastically changed. Managed care dominates choices of practitioners, hospitals, and treatment. It is divided between restrictive health maintenance organizations (HMOs) and preferred provider organizations (PPOs), which offer a wider range of possible doctors to see. In addition, medicine has become more complex; dazzlingly expensive machines have replaced the trusty old black bag. Most of our country's 740,000 physicians are specialists. The days of the archetypal family doc are sadly gone.

At a recent talk on intuition in medicine I gave to forty psychiatric interns and residents in Los Angeles, I asked, "How many of you are going into private practice?" No one raised a hand. I was appalled. "What's stopping you?" I inquired. They had financial considerations— yes. Would they succeed? Would patients come? Is the market oversaturated? Then, the real doozy: In private practice, as designated HMO providers, did they want to hassle with the endless red tape it takes to get paid? Or the inordinate HMO control? Very practical considerations. I sympathized. However, I also came away knowing the problem went deeper. A critical factor was missing. Why a doctor—or any healer—decides upon a certain career direction I believe has mystical significance. It's not only a matter of logic, it's a calling of the heart. These psychiatrists in training were clearly intelligent, devoted, and hardworking, but what was chillingly obvious was that they hadn't been taught to listen for the call.

I want to guide you through the process of selecting a health care practitioner to match your needs. I'll point out qualities to look for and those to avoid. I'll begin by presenting you with commonsense guidelines, then build on these utilizing the five intuitive steps. Who you let touch your body, prescribe medications, and counsel you about vital health strategies is one of the most important decisions you'll ever make.

I stress from the start that all therapeutic relationships are partnerships; healing always goes two ways. I've never worked with a patient who hasn't contributed to my own healing as well. I'm grateful for what each person has shared with me over the years. At the same time I must acknowledge that in this partnership, despite our equal footing as human beings, there are inherent inequalities. I have gone through fourteen years of medical training; I have specific knowledge and clinical experience to call on that my patients just don't have. That's why they come to me. Even so, I don't support the archaic, disempowering, patriarchal view still prevalent in medicine that implies, I'm the doctor. *I'm* taking care of *you*. Don't question me. Rather I'm suggesting a relationship based on mutual respect in which you and your doctor work together. You deserve to have a voice in your medical care. If necessary, you must fight for it.

The burden for having a good relationship can't be on just your doctor's shoulders. I'm constantly shocked at how many bright, capable people absolutely fail to tell their doctors the truth. A patient of mine once got pregnant and decided to have an abortion. She went to a public clinic for the procedure. Intentionally, she never told her own gynecologist a thing about it. I emphasized how vital it was for him to have a complete and accurate health record, yet still she refused. My patient was ashamed. Of course I empathized. But I also knew such withholdings between patient and doctor are dangerous. Responsibility for clear communication goes both ways.

Once that's understood, what can you reasonably look for in a practitioner? I took an informal survey among colleagues and friends. Nearly everyone agreed: "I must have faith in him or her. I must feel connected. He or she must be technically skilled." Herein lies the dilemma. Suppose you find a surgeon who's a whiz in the operating room but has an arrogant, offensive manner? Does that mean he shouldn't perform surgery on you? Or, alternatively, what if you meet the nicest doctor in the world but her treatments don't seem to be helping? The solution? Whenever possible, find balance. For those situations that are less than ideal, aim for an intelligent compromise.

Let me lead you through the dos and don'ts of selection. Many of us have stuck far too long with a health care practitioner when we didn't follow our intuition on whether he or she was a good fit for our needs. I'm asking you to take a more assertive stance: smart and probing but always respectful. The object is not to mow someone down but to uncover information to see if you're compatible. At the same time, don't be afraid to ask questions. I suggest you interview your doctors before you allow them to care for you. Get a feel for their approach. Seek out someone who blends intuitive and technical skills, implementing as many of the following guidelines as possible.

QUALITIES TO LOOK FOR IN A HEALTH CARE PRACTITIONER

Notice if he or she:

• **Takes time to listen to you**
Does he or she pay attention and let you fully explain why you are there? Is there good eye contact, or is your doctor staring down at a file, clipboard, or computer screen?

• **Is technically qualified**
Does your practitioner have solid credentials? For example, an M.D., Ph.D., or R.N.? Is he or she licensed? Is your alternative healer certified, with a good track record with patients? Do you know anyone who can vouch for his or her high level of care?

• **Isn't offended if you ask for a second opinion**
Is your doctor open and nondefensive about getting another point of view if one's needed? Will he or she recommend a trustworthy colleague?

• **Presents you with options and is knowledgeable about (or at least open to) alternative health techniques**
Are you told the pros and cons of a few possible treatments? If you ask, for example, about acupuncture, will your doctor react with an open mind? If you say, "Here's an article about my condition, would you be willing to read it and discuss it with me?" how does your doctor respond?

• **Honors your intuitions and preferences about your body**
If you say, "I don't feel good about this plan of action," does your doctor factor that into the decision making? Or will he or she chide you. "Be serious, that's not very scientific." Does your doctor encourage you to know your body's needs?

QUALITIES TO AVOID IN A HEALTH CARE PRACTITIONER

Notice if he or she:

• **Rushes you through an office visit**
Are you interrupted by your doctor taking phone calls? Do you overhear him or her making dinner reservations or golf dates? Does your HMO doc really make those fifteen minutes count? Or is he or she abrupt? Distracted? Do you get cut off repeatedly or before you're finished explaining why you're there?

• **Approaches you with a demeaning "holier than thou" attitude**
Are you told, "I'm the doctor. I know what's best for you?" Does he or she insist on using complex medical terminology even though you've said it confuses you? Does your doctor refuse to explain things in simple terms?

• **Isn't professionally accredited or technically skilled**
Is your doctor unlicensed? Has his or her license ever been revoked? Do you know of any complaints of wrongdoing from other patients?

• **Makes you feel guilty or foolish for asking questions**
Does your doctor dismiss or minimize your concerns, remarking, "You're overly sensitive" or, even worse, "You created your illness"? Is he or she patronizing, saying, "It's over your head. I can't explain your condition in a way you'd understand"?

• **Doesn't return phone calls within twenty-four hours**
When calling, are you told, "The doctor's busy and will have to reach you later"? Does the doctor then not get back to you promptly? Is he or she hard to locate during an emergency? Do you have the sense that your doctor's always tied up with something more important than you?

With these criteria in mind, how do you find the best referral? For both alternative and traditional doctors, in or out of HMOs (of course, HMO rosters are more restricted), the most reliable source is either a health care practitioner you trust or a good friend. They know the type of person you prefer, styles you'd click with, your criteria for professionalism. In addition, you can consult a major hospital in your area for listings of staff physicians. Your state medical board will tell you where physicians were trained or of any disciplinary actions. For alternative practitioners contact the American Holistic Medical Association, the American Holistic Nurses Association, or medical centers that have alternative medicine programs (see Resources). Although some mind-body specialties—chiropractic, osteopathy, acupuncture—require state licensing, others—such as homeopathy and naturopathy—do not. In general when seeking referrals avoid the yellow pages, physicians' advertisements, unlicensed practitioners, or those who charge outlandish fees.

When interviewing doctors, alternative or traditional, ascertain their credentials. It's fine to ask: Where were you trained? Are you board-certified (physicians take a test to determine competence in their specialty)? What hospital do you work out of? Or, if the doctor isn't hospital-based, How long have you been in private practice? If these credentials are sound, you're off to a good start. Other pluses: affiliation with a medical school or university; membership in professional organizations such as the American Medical Association. Any reputable doctor will discuss these issues with you.

Deep healing depends upon the chemistry and respect you share with your caregivers. If the qualities you need in a doctor are missing, it is your duty and right to find someone else. If you belong to an HMO, you still can choose among primary care doctors assigned to your plan. Take time to pick the right person. Or, if you're unhappy with your HMO doctor, request a change. Your effort in finding a compatible match will pay off. The best scenario: You'll find a doctor you're in sync with. Or, if you must see someone with whom you lack rapport, there's still hope. I'll show you ways to turn the situation around.

Now let's see how the five steps can be invaluable in your selection process. I'll emphasize remote viewing, a form of guidance I've come to rely on in determining whom to consult. I offer it to you as a productive new tool. To gain an intuitive edge on choosing a healer, go through each step and see how it applies.

Step 1. Notice Your Beliefs

Your immune system has eyes and ears. It takes in everything. The beliefs caregivers convey about your health can directly affect your body. If a doctor is open-minded and exudes hope, you're given a loud and clear communication. Search for practitioners who don't let statistics dictate their beliefs. Avoid those who define healing solely in terms of numbers. For instance, if your doctor declares, "Your cancer has only a 30 percent cure rate," he is setting up a defeating self-fulfilling prophecy—disregarding your spirit's tenacious urge to survive. Too often doctors overemphasize statistics supporting nonsurvival rather than our wondrous capacity to heal. Healing is full of mystery, unique to each of us, not reducible to the sterility of limited odds. Of course, statistics are indicators for choosing a treatment. If chemotherapy is 90 percent effective in eradicating a tumor and surgery only 25 percent; this will inform your decision. But once the decision's made, if your doctor believes it's possible for you to get well—despite statistics—you can be sparked by the strength of that conviction, especially in moments of despair.

We physicians hold the faith for our patients. It is a beacon of light in the darkness. Look for it in your healer's eyes, the tone of her voice, her words, her touch. On your first meeting, especially if you are ill, your doctor's faith must be palpable. Years of experience have convinced me that your and your doctor's combined faith about your ability to heal shapes recovery more than any other factor.

My friend Helen, a savvy health magazine editor, found a physician she's crazy about. "What most impressed you?" I inquired. Helen smiled. "You might think this is a little thing," she said. "In the questionnaire I filled out before we met he asked, 'How would you prefer to be addressed?' I felt he valued my opinions from the start. It meant so much." This hit home, my being a Judith who constantly has to ward off people's tendency to call me Judi. "Then what?" I went on. "How did you feel when you talked to him?" Helen didn't hesitate. "He looked me straight in the eyes," she said. "Not all around the room, like so many doctors—right at me. His office was packed, but he made me feel I was the only person in his universe." This was their first meeting. The man did nothing but take Helen's medical history. Still, she left his office feeling better. I was struck by her experience. The potency of sacred partnerships is that you come away feeling valued, as Helen did—seen through the lens of who you really are, not as someone wants you to be. The doctor Helen found knew well how to set the stage for healing.

There are physiological repercussions to the attitude with which you are approached. Your healing is not just about calling your doctor with symptoms. As with Helen, it involves building blocks. From the instant you set eyes on someone, your healing unfolds. In sacred partnerships intuitive currents are created, enriching with time. Check out your practitioner's beliefs. See if they enliven and inspire you. Survey the scene: If you really want the whole scoop on your doctor, eavesdrop in the waiting room. Stretch to hear what other patients say about him or her—or ask them directly for their opinions. There's nothing more reliable than a good referral. Also, notice how your doctor treats the staff. It's a foolproof measure of how the doctor will treat you.

Beware of negative messages. Insensitive healers are notorious for toxic pronouncements. How many of you have heard, "You'll always have chronic pain," "We can't cure this; our goal is maintenance," "You can't heal yourself," or "The only way to get better is to take this pill." Don't buy into these notions. Be wary of "always" and "never." Stay away from practitioners who don't offer alternatives, or who say, "It will only get worse," "There's no hope," or "You just have to live with it." Such statements aren't just irresponsible, making you feel bad; they can do real harm. In *Be Careful What You Pray For,* Dr. Larry Dossey calls them a form of medical hexing. Statements like "You're a walking time bomb," "You're living on borrowed time," or "You could have a heart attack at any moment," Dossey says, can act as "lethal curses." If internalized, they can program a patient to die, even cause sudden death.

If your doctor hexes you, see right though it. At this point you should respond, "Your negative attitude makes me feel we've reached a dead end. Do you have a more constructive way to discuss this?" An acceptable reply would be, "I wasn't aware of how what I was saying sounded. Thanks for bringing it to my attention." An unacceptable reply is, "I just told you the truth. I'm not going to sugarcoat it." In essence, such a doctor has doomed you. But hexes have power only if you give it to them. Don't feed into the fear. It may be time to consider looking for someone new.

I know how difficult it is to assert your needs when you're not feeling well, particularly if you're up against an authority figure. You're vulnerable. You deserve to be taken care of, nurtured, able to let your guard down completely. This is true for us all. Still, the reality of health care demands you stay alert: You must question, with respect, not hostility, any plan or message about your health that doesn't feel right.

One summer, while vacationing on a horse ranch in the wilds of Idaho's Sawtooth Mountains, I was kicked in a closed corral by an angry mule. At the moment of impact this pointy-eared critter looked like the Devil to me. Worse, the whole thing was an embarrassing metaphor about my *own* stubbornness, at best. The injury was serious. I got woozy every time I dared to glance down at my ankle. All I could see was a grisly mix of muscle and bone. Back in L.A., when my orthopedic surgeon saw it, he grimaced. "Looks pretty bad," he said. "You'll probably have chronic pain in that ankle the rest of your life." Quite an indictment—the kind that whirls endlessly round in your head. He was the expert; I was seeking his advice. Had I believed my doctor's statement, it could've turned into a life sentence.

Luckily, my intuition saved me. Something inside said my ankle would be fine. I trusted this. Now, except for a little creaking before the rain comes, my ankle is all right. My doctor is tops in his field. His comment was not malicious, nor was it medically misinformed. At its most benign level, however, it lacked tact. More troubling, his prognosis went exclusively by the book; he didn't think to factor in his intuition.

For this reason you must factor in your intuition with your doctor. Make it the filter through which all medical information passes. Weigh and measure fact and instinct. Know you have a choice. It's up to you to determine your beliefs about healing as well as the attitude you take with your doctor. Your approach, especially with difficult practitioners, makes a huge difference. In these situations I've watched too many intelligent, well-intentioned people, driven by their frustration, only aggravate matters.

Kim is a psychoanalyst and feminist, unafraid of taking a strong stand. Not long ago her father had a massive stroke. While hospitalized he was placed in a physical rehabilitation program. After three weeks he had only gotten worse. His doctor told Kim, "There's nothing more the hospital can do." He strongly advised that her father be discharged to a nursing home. Once there, Kim's father continued to deteriorate. Naturally she was upset, and she frantically placed numerous calls to the doctor. He became harder and harder to reach. Kim was beside herself. The dynamic escalated: The more unresponsive the doctor, the more demanding she was once she got through. "Why isn't my father getting better? Can't you do more?" she prodded.

Finally, she scheduled an appointment. The doctor, in a starched, buttoned-up white coat, sat her down in his office. He closed the door. In an icy monotone he delivered his speech: "Let me tell you how it's going to end," he said. "Your father is going to remain in a nursing home the rest of his life. He's going to go downhill steadily. He's going to get an infection, probably pneumonia, which will be terminal. It may take six weeks or six months. But this is what's going to happen." Wham: it hit her. The cold, hard "facts." Kim was speechless. She felt as if she'd been flattened by a ten-ton truck. Whether the doctor's aim was blunt fact telling or, possibly, retaliation against Kim's aggressive stance, the result was destructive.

Kim had a right to feel frustrated before this last encounter. She had a right to feel dismissed. Many of us would've justifiably behaved as she did, goading the doctor into a blowup. Too busy reacting, locked in a counterproductive struggle with the doctor, she let her intuition go out the window. The result? Kim's best intentions backfired. The same might be true for you. To break this pattern, check in with your intuition for wiser ways to proceed.

Hard truth time: When you confront difficult practitioners, appreciate just how tough they can be. There's no point in kidding yourself. They didn't finish medical residencies without surviving years of hundred-hour workweeks that pushed them to the limit. Some doctors, not surprisingly, emerge with enormous chips on their shoulders. Let's not mince words: Doctors aren't always sweethearts! But even in the face of an angry, capricious physician, you are not without power. Your responses can be both tactical and spiritual.

Tactics: Be Zen. Keep your center. Think aikido: The more aggressive your opponent, the more yielding you become. Use his force to your advantage. Don't meet resistance with a clenched fist. This has nothing to do with "giving in," surrender, capitulation, being dominated. Disarm your opponent by surprise. First, show appreciation. Say simple things like, "Thank you for the medication. It really helped" or "It meant a lot that you saw me so quickly." Stress the positives. Most likely, being so difficult, such doctors don't hear appreciation very often. They're used to power struggles, not praise. Often, despite their credentials and sometimes extraordinary, hard-earned expertise, they're wounded people. When dealing with them, begin with clarity— seeing them as they are and, simultaneously, reminding yourself of your goal. These are tactics to deflect negative energy. As for expressing frustration or anger, now's not the time to "share" with your doctor. But neither must you repress your feelings. Acknowledge them to yourself, or share them with a friend.

I'm not saying this is easy, but it's a start. Even better, however, is to focus on who *you* are in this situation, the conscious path you want to follow—that is, the path of love. The goal here is to connect with the better part of your doctor (they all have one, believe it or not), to offer a centered self who elicits a centered response. Enlist your practitioners as allies. No ambushes. No sneak attacks. No massive retaliation. Look them straight in the eye and say, "Your opinion is important to me. I value your skills" or "I appreciate what you've done for me." Body language and tone are critical. Muster as much humor as you can. Words won't have impact if you're gritting your teeth, glaring, or keeping your arms folded in defense. This is an exercise in compassion: the good in you finding the good in them.

Now, tone set, gradually educate them about your needs. Always frame questions constructively, inclusively, saying, "What can *we* do about the situation?" rather than "Why haven't *you* done more?" Begin a thought with, "I feel it would really help if . . . what do you think?" instead of accusing with, "You're neglecting my father!" Choose the high road. Set off a love bomb. All the while remain firm about your needs. Whether you see a dramatic turnabout or a partial improvement, I predict you'll be pleased.

If you must undergo open-heart surgery, you're going to select a surgeon who's a master technician. She may lack a warm bedside manner—but you'd be a fool not to go with her. There's a grace to knowing how to function within limitation. Your surgeon may not become your best friend, but you can improve the communication with her. If, for instance, your surgeon is using technical language you can't understand, pin her down. "I'd really appreciate it if you could walk me through my case more slowly" will be more effective than "Didn't they teach you how to talk to patients in medical school?" Be diplomatic. Choose your battles. Suppose your doctor's closed off to the spiritual aspects of healing but provides superb physical care. It might be wiser to keep your beliefs private. Make the most of a situation that isn't ideal. Accept what is positive; discard the rest. Be sure your expectations are realistic.

All this said, I believe the nature of the doctor-patient relationship is shifting in a positive direction. This is even reflected in the priorities and attitudes of HMOs. A recent survey reported in the *Los Angeles*

Times showed that of three hundred HMO executives interviewed, 90 percent believed personal prayer, meditation, or spiritual practice can aid medical treatment and expedite the healing process. Most, however, thought it would be some time before such interventions were covered by health care providers. The majority of plans currently disregard the link between spirituality and well-being. Typical of the HMO credo, the executives reserved the right to support such coverage in the future if it proved to save money and increase patient satisfaction. There's more to come here. Stay tuned.

A counterpoint to the restrictive HMO mentality, a renaissance I feel privileged to be part of, is sweeping modern medicine. Physicians, therapists, nurses, and healers in traditional and nontraditional settings hunger to incorporate intuition and spirituality into patient care. More and more of us are speaking out. We're becoming less of a secret society.

Just look at the revolution in alternative health that has exploded in the past decade. Homeopathy, herbology, Chinese medicine—our country has been taken by storm. Prayer has been proven to enhance the recovery of cardiac patients in a landmark study conducted at San Francisco General Hospital. Therapeutic touch is a form of energy healing employed worldwide. Many major medical schools, including Harvard, Stanford, UCLA, and Beth Israel in New York, have programs devoted exclusively to alternative care.

Holistic medicine has gone mainstream. A recent Harvard study published by the *Journal of the American Medical Association* states: "Patients are increasingly seeking to identify a physician who is solidly grounded in conventional orthodox medicine and is also knowledgeable about the values and limitations of alternative treatments." In response to this trend, the Office of Alternative Medicine at the National Institutes of Health (NIH), established by Congress in 1992, is looking at everything from diet and nutrition to energetic therapies and mind-body control. In Bob Dylan's words, "The times they are a-changin'."

My own passion is to bring spirituality and intuition into traditional medicine. Then we'll be able to choose from the best of both worlds. As an intuitive and a physician, I'm working to build a bridge with the current health care system. What I'd like to see is first-year medical students learning to take an intuitive history as part of the routine physical exam. It provides information as vital as your kidney function or blood pressure. Your style of processing energy in the world and your intuitive relationship to your body make a dramatic difference to your health. If your doctor respects this, you will come out ahead.

QUESTIONS FOR REFLECTION

- Do you see a potential for partnership with your health care practitioner? How can your intuition enhance communication between you?

- Are you honest with your practitioner about the kinds of health care that are right for you? Do you prefer traditional or alternative medicine? Or both?

- Do you feel free to describe frankly your body's needs in simple, direct language? Are you withholding any information or feelings? If so, what?

Step 2. Be in Your Body

I was once referred to a doctor who loved to smoke cigars. Not in my presence—but in his private office I saw mounds of squashed brown butts in ashtrays all over his desk. The odor of cigars seemed to exude from the very fabric of the furniture, even from the rug. Worse, when he bent over to listen to my heart, his lab coat and hair reeked of it. My body recoiled. It was intolerable, but I never had the nerve to mention this to him. I figured it was a lost cause. He probably wouldn't stop smoking in his office anyway. I just never went back.

Notice your body's response to your doctor. The chemistry between you must be right. Consult your senses. Ask yourself: How do you feel physically around him? Are you at peace? Tense? Nauseous? Do your shoulders tighten? Do you feel safe? Your body registers a confidence level, an index of compatibility. As is true of any intimate relationship, once basic comfort and trust are established (your body delicately reflects this), you've formed a strong foundation. Then, when health challenges arise your doctor can be a soothing influence. You'll face whatever comes up as a team.

Make sure your doctor's style matches yours. Here it's a matter of preference, not right or wrong. Even if you've never considered this before, you're entitled to explore some honest questions: Are you more at

ease with a reserved doctor in a white coat who addresses you from behind an official-looking desk? Your body may relax with that coolness
and distance. Or maybe you go for a motherly physician in a flowing
dress who's more homespun? You feel warmth and caring when she
gives you a hug. However, if you'd rather not be hugged by your doctor,
this may not be the woman for you.

Pay attention to the quality of your doctor's touch. It communicates
a lot. Is she gentle? Rough? Before listening to your lungs, does she
warm up the stethoscope, or is it ice cold? Does she gag you with a
tongue depressor while checking your sore throat? Is she sensitive to
your pain threshold? Unfortunately, a doctor's touch may also seem seductive or intrusive—kissing you on the lips or cheek; patting you on
the butt. Mention these incidents immediately so they're not repeated.
In a tone that lets him or her know you mean business but isn't inflam-
matory, say, "I don't feel comfortable with that. Please stop it." If your
doctor continues to behave inappropriately, you'll certainly want to find
someone else, perhaps even file a report.

When it comes to your body, it's essential to give your doctors firm
yet respectful feedback. Make them aware of how you feel. It's more
productive to say while your doctor is examining your abdomen,
"Could you please apply a little less pressure?" than to say, "What's
wrong with you? Are you trying to hurt me?" Even when the doctor
must use some force, as in checking the prostate, you must still feel free
to say, "Stop. That hurts." A good doctor will back off, try to be more
gentle. I understand you may have to temper your reactions to improve
communication, but the less accusatory you are, the better. Putting
your doctor on the defensive won't change his or her behavior.

How do you know if you should write a doctor off? Use your body
as a barometer. Ideally, select someone with whom you feel physically,
emotionally, and spiritually secure. Short of this, there's a large gray
zone. Maybe your connection is lukewarm but he has great suggestions
about your care. Or she could be a tad unresponsive though well-
meaning; more bookworm than people person; somewhat brusque but
kind; or perhaps overly enthusiastic, in need of toning down. These im-
perfect relationships may be worth nurturing. But whenever your body
is repelled by a doctor—for example, you get nausea or a headache, or
feel drained—or if you're verbally demeaned and for *whatever* reasons
don't feel safe, this doctor is not for you.

All healers must show respect for your body in actions and words.

When your doctor greets you with "It's wonderful to see you today," it's a very different message from "Hmm. Looks like you need to lose some weight," followed by an annoying wink. Your doctor's job is to compassionately point out health areas that may require your attention, not to criticize. To heal, you need a protective environment. One patient told me that whenever she'd go to her gynecologist, his twenty-something nurse would instruct her to undress. Then the nurse would just walk off, never giving her a sheet to cover up in. So there my patient would be sitting, naked, when the doctor walked in. Unacceptable—yet until our talk she was reluctant to speak up—to either doctor or nurse. Don't forget, you have rights. Make your needs known.

A few years ago I consulted a therapist who had a photograph of his girlfriend on a shelf in full view. She was posing on the beach, her gigantic breasts straining the top of an itsy-bitsy bikini. It was hard for me to admit, but it made me feel awkward. I questioned myself. What kind of liberated woman was I to have such a negative reaction to her body? Was I a prude? Still, for better or worse, her obvious attributes made me critical of my own. Why would this therapist have to display such a picture? What did it say about how he viewed women? Was he sexist? I never returned to find out. For me—and the majority of women I asked—this photo was too provocative, inappropriate for a therapist's office. Yet, from all indications this man's practice was full. People react differently. Don't hesitate to voice your opinions. You must determine if your doctor's attitudes make you feel proud of your body or not.

Some doctors are in awe of the workings of the body. They are excited to share this awe with you. Let it rub off. In the course of treatment they may give you opportunities to see into your inner space. I encourage you to take them. Learn from your doctor when she educates you using pictures, models, X rays, or the visual results of certain tests. Notice if your body resists; try to figure out why. Remember, your capacity to heal is amplified by looking through the windows of your body, embracing how you are made. Even if your stomach is tied up in knots in this situation, now isn't the time to retreat. Gentle nudging by your doctor can get you over the hurdle.

My patient Budd, a first-time father, nearly fainted by his wife's side when her obstetrician performed an ultrasound of her pregnant belly, a truly benign event in which a sensor is placed with adhesive on the skin below the belly button and conveys an image to a video monitor. A big, burly man, Budd turned white as a sheet as he heard the *lub-dub* of his baby's heartbeat and saw the outline of his baby's anatomy, from genitals to lungs. Then, ala-ka-zam! His squeamishness turned to delight; he marveled at the new life of his daughter before him. Budd wouldn't have missed this moment for the world.

A sacred partnership predicated on love for the body can transform your shame, fear, or hesitation into a true appreciation of the miracle. It will promote your health. Let your doctor be the catalyst: Look to him or her as model and guide. During the selection process, call on your physical intuition for assistance. Healing flows from the rapport you have with those treating you. Trust your body to lead the way.

Step 3. Sense Your Body's Subtle Energy

Your practitioner may be extremely competent, simply on the basis of her knowledge and kindness. Some, however, possess an additional quality that sets them apart: They can transmit healing energy through their presence and touch. Reflect on your experience—have you ever been treated by someone who makes you feel better just by walking in the room? Or when she examines you, tension in your body melts away? Or the edge is taken off your pain? Some healers are born with this gift; others develop it. They bring special meaning to Hippocrates' words: "All things sacred are to be imparted only to sacred persons." Whenever possible choose such a person to care for you.

I learned much about energy from a healer named Hadi. I consulted him for recurring sinus problems. From Teheran, Osted "Hadi" Parvarandeh spoke broken English. But on our first visit that didn't stop him. Chattering away in a maddening mix of English and Farsi, he kept pointing to a hodgepodge of gaudy photographs lining his office walls, showing off his patient's "auras." Ugh. We got off to a bad start. This guy was going to help me? He proceeded to lay his hands on my forehead. For five minutes he sat by my side and "sent energy," his stomach growling the whole time. I was annoyed; his obvious hunger was distracting. I left his office ready to write him off as a quack.

"Where do you want to go for dinner?" my friend asked afterward in the car. Totally uncharacteristically, I was overcome by a craving for Middle Eastern food. It wasn't until I was devouring my falafel that I caught on to what had occurred. While Hadi was sending energy to me, he'd also transmitted his hunger and taste in food. He was the one who wanted the falafel—not me! My friend and I burst out laughing. The point here is that despite my open-and-shut negative assessment of this man, he had skill. I realized then that clearly he could send energy I was receptive to. On that basis—setting aside his personality—I decided to go back. Through his touch my sinus problems were cured. Over time I came to see it was cultural differences that had caused me to misjudge and undervalue him. The language barrier between us made me misinterpret his pride in his work as arrogance. It didn't ultimately matter that we hardly ever exchanged a word of English. Energy transcends language. Returning to Hadi's clinic on many occasions, I got used to his ways. I came to love him. He was able to heal me.

How do you find someone like Hadi? For starters, there are over thirty thousand nurses in the United States who practice therapeutic touch, a form of energy healing. (For referrals, contact the Nurse Healers Professional Associates listed in Resources.) In ideal circumstances you'll find doctors, even dentists, who work with energy as well. Some practitioners are "medical intuitives" who can make a physical diagnosis in person or at a distance, evaluating you with intuition alone. An increasing number of M.D.'s, themselves unskilled in this area, have such a person on their staff. Of course, as in all professions, there are varying levels of expertise. What can you expect? Ask yourself, Was the intuitive diagnosis accurate? Or, with energy work, do you show progress during the first few weeks? Not all practitioners can, like Hadi, cure specific symptoms—those gifted few are harder to find. But any experienced healer can balance your energy, give it a jump start, get you better faster. Again, it's generally wiser to stick to those with credentials. Energy work can go hand in hand with traditional treatment or it may be adequate by itself.

Practitioners who appreciate the dynamics of energy will offer more sensitive care. The practice of medicine has subtleties physicians aren't taught in school. I have a friend whose internist talks about his patients with cancer whenever he draws her blood. Though I'm sure he doesn't intend to, he sets a negative tone. He's simply oblivious to energy. Especially when the skin is punctured or surgery is performed, the words of our caregivers, the atmosphere that surrounds us, must be loving. We're at our most vulnerable. What they say and do affects us on many levels. When you're cranked back in that dental chair, mouth wide open, poised for a root canal, a little healing energy coming from your dentist's hands will mean a lot. My mother, during physical exams, sent energy to her patients through her touch. She taught me that healing occurs each step of the way. It's the journey, not just the destination. Every moment, every interaction counts.

Step 4. Ask for Inner Guidance

Now it's time to turn inward. Here's how. I want to let you in on a practical technique I swear by called remote viewing. It's a way of sizing up prospective healers before you even meet them. By intuitively focusing on their names and noticing any images, impressions, or insights that strike you, you'll get a good take on your compatibility. Along with the previous steps remote viewing will ensure you'll make a better-informed choice. Use it and you'll have a potent magnifying glass illuminating a universe of information unattainable by logic alone. Far out, you say? Before you decide, listen to this.

For over twenty years the CIA, DIA (Defense Intelligence Agency), and NASA spent $20 million on top-secret military research that Stanford Research Institute scientists were forbidden to discuss until 1995. These findings were first made public on Ted Koppel's *Nightline*. Why such cloak-and-dagger intrigue? Because they used remote viewing to help gather intelligence. The government's aim was to direct this type of intuition to locate foreign arsenals, determine the status of overseas nuclear testing, and be forewarned of Soviet military strategy during the Cold War. For us peaceful warriors remote viewing can benefit healing, from picking practitioners to diagnosing illness and promoting our health. We'll be doing all this throughout the book. Even if you haven't tried the technique before, you can learn it now. In controlled laboratory settings college students with no previous experience have been taught the basics in just a few sessions.

Whenever I'm deciding on new doctors to treat me, my patients, or loved ones, I do a remote viewing to check them out. I look at it this way: It saves time and money, and gives my intuition a say in whom to form a sacred partnership with. There's an instinct to matchmaking that must come into play. With remote viewing, though, we don't have to be face to face with someone to make a good match. Remember, intuition isn't limited by space or time. Einstein himself said: "The distinction between past, present, and future is only a stubbornly persistent illusion." Thus, I routinely screen potential practitioners—

and also patients—to get an overall sense of who they are before laying eyes on them. In my personal life and medical practice, remote viewing gives me a head start on determining the best course to take.

Let me lead you through an easy exercise to start. It can be done either before you've met someone or after. Your goal, in this case, is to find the right healer. The proper mind-set? Have faith you can do it. Set doubts aside. Feel the wonder while you explore. Here are some logistics. Allow for about ten minutes. Shut off the phone. Close the door. Be certain you'll have no interruptions. To tune in, the first name of the practitioner (the one he or she goes by) is all you need. It doesn't matter if many people have the same name. There may be a million Bobs in the world, but don't worry. Set your intention. Focus on your Bob. Names are sacred. The specific intuitive vibration unique to that individual will come through. Notice the nuances of how you respond. Take care not to interpret what you are sensing. Analysis kills spontaneous flow. Remain neutral. Be an empty rice bowl waiting to be filled. Simply note what you pick up. Review it later. This process is like daydreaming. Impressions come that just seem right, even if they don't rationally track.

TUNING IN TO NAMES:
A REMOTE VIEWING EXERCISE

1. Settle into a relaxed position, sitting upright on a cushion or chair. Take a few deep breaths. Slowly inhale and exhale, quieting your thoughts. Spend a few minutes in meditation. Calm yourself. Allow all tension to melt away.

2. When you're ready, say aloud the first name of the healer you're considering. Hold the name lightly in your mind. Try to think of nothing else. While focusing on the name, open yourself to all sensations. Register them. It's important not to react to what you perceive. Scan your entire body. Are you at ease? Energized? Anxious? Suddenly tired? Relieved? Repelled? Is there a sense of trust, or are you protecting yourself? Don't hold back. Do you notice images, colors, or impressions? Vibrant colors may indicate a strong life force, muted tones, an energy deficiency. Are you comfortable with what you see? Does it disturb you? Perhaps an entire scenario is playing out. Allow it to unfold. No effort is required. If you then choose, you may go on to ask specific questions. Should I work with this person? Will she help me? Notice how you feel. Simply log your responses, don't judge them.

3. When you're finished, jot the details down in a journal. Later, compare how they correlate with your in-person experience of the practitioner. Factor your remote viewing intuitions in with data the other steps have provided. Weigh your priorities. Consider the overall picture.

The process I am describing—allowing your impressions to take form, then fitting them into the gestalt—is the basic formula for remote viewing a practitioner's name. As far as privacy goes, I've found that if someone doesn't want to be read, I either sense nothing or else feel I'm hitting a brick wall. When that happens, out of respect I don't attempt to force it. Use these criteria as guidelines. If you sense an opening is there, feel free to proceed. Some of your impressions may be concrete, others metaphorical. Jump on those that zing with energy. Be wary of ones that fall flat. See how they compare. Perhaps you'll receive instant "knowings"—a full portrait of a person zooms through in a split second. Indicators like these will reinforce when you're on target or off. Soon such distinctions will become second nature to you—as will the cosmic humor that infuses the intuitive realm.

So you think people look like their dogs? Watch this. I once tuned in to a highly regarded internist I was thinking of seeing to get an intuitive take on him. In a flash I got an image of a feisty, wild-eyed Chihuahua, relentlessly yipping at me, charging and clamping its tiny teeth onto the hem of my jeans. What could I be in store for? I filed my impression until this doctor and I met. At first glance he looked nice enough. Then he opened his mouth. It was all over. He yapped at me so fast and furiously, he reminded me of a Chatty Cathy doll gone haywire. It wasn't a stretch to understand why I'd read him as a half-crazed Chihuahua. He could very well have been the most brilliant doctor in the world—but I couldn't take it. His style was not for me.

By contrast, one of my workshop participants told me he did a remote viewing on his therapist before they met. He received no imagery at all. However, when he focused on her, he felt complete and utter peace. An auspicious beginning for a relationship that continues to transform his life in positive ways.

Allow time to gain confidence in your remote viewing ability. The good news is that no intuitive step I discuss stands alone. Work them all together. If you're shaky about your reading of a practitioner's name, see how it matches up with information you've received from the other steps. Form an integrated profile. As with any skill, with practice your expertise will grow.

Especially in the early stages, it's crucial to neutralize your inner censor. When I first tried remote viewing, at age eighteen, I really wanted to impress the people at UCLA with whom I was working. They were more advanced at this than I was; I felt I needed to look good. All I did, though, was sabotage myself, suppressing intuitions I judged to be weird. Only slowly did I come to realize that, as in a dream, what seemed most strange or unsettling was often most accurate, the path to revelation. Thus, it was through censoring that I learned not to censor. This wasn't easy. Fortunately, I received lots of support and permission from my colleagues. I offer the same to you.

Intuition awakens connections. Remote viewing is a structure that holds intuition intact. It will help you evaluate people and relationships more clearly. Allow it to assist you in your choice of a practitioner. I promise it will.

Step 5. Listen to Your Dreams

When I think of dreams I see a sunlit library lined with rows of books stretching as far as the eye can see. Gold-leaf-edged volumes with all of our biographies, including our health histories, meticulously inscribed by a steady pen. As we live they are being written, yet some information has always been there: ancient wisdom accessible to contemporary minds. It can guide. If you want to find a healer who'll make a real difference to you, consult your dreams. Before going to sleep pose your question; the next morning record the response. Establish an ongoing relationship with your dreams. Interact. You can ask anything.

USING DREAMS TO CHOOSE A HEALER

Look to your dreams to

- Get a sense of a practitioner before you meet
- Round out the picture of someone you're working with
- Decide among a few possible candidates

- Receive clarification on specific points
- Get a read on someone when your waking intuition is clouded
- Affirm your choice

I'd like you to get into the habit of turning to your dreams as you would a therapist or good friend. Picture them as a hard drive on a computer. Once you learn to access it, the information is yours. Your quest for a doctor is an ideal circumstance to test this out. By addressing a question about a practitioner to your dream, then setting your intention to recover the answer, you're programming your subconscious to respond. You're activating memory. The solution will come. Your question may be Is this doctor right for me? Your answer? One possibility: The dream is a blur but you wake up with a gut feeling that securely reinforces your choice. Alternatively, someone in a dream might tap you on the shoulder and say directly, "Stick with him. He's the one." Typically solutions fall somewhere in between. If you need a quick response not steeped in metaphor, make that clear. Specify your terms. Dreams are alive. They hear you. Begin to rely on that.

In very special circumstances you may find that you dream of a healer long before you've met. On another plane your relationship is already established. Years ago, before I was introduced to my spiritual teacher and before his move from Malaysia to the United States, I dreamed of him. Not his face but his essence. The instant I saw this man in person, I knew. That essence, of love and mischief mixed, was unmistakable. Ours was clearly a reunion. It wasn't that he reminded me of anyone else. Many times in dreams I had been with *him*.

When this happens to you, stop. Take notice. Be on intuitive alert. An opportunity is at hand; your dream will point the way. If in it you feel the person is a positive influence, the dream can be a harbinger of good fortune for your health. If your dreams paint the person as negative, take it as a sign to stay away. Or maybe your medical treatment has already started. Then one day it strikes you: Oh my God, I've seen his face before! Suddenly you realize where. In dreams you've interacted. A word of caution—in dreams your healers can take many forms. Don't be disappointed if yours doesn't appear all-knowing, in flowing white silk robes on windswept dunes in the Anza-Borego Desert. She may be just a pesky crone in rags who's hot on your tail. No matter, stick to what your intuition tells you about this person. Act on it. You'll know what to do.

In sacred healing partnerships dreams of your healer may mirror your highest self—the you that is courageous, that has the resources required to get better. If in a dream your doctor is compassionate and wise, know that this is a portrayal not only of him but of you too. When you work with a gifted practitioner (M.D. or not) who's also a healthy role model—a double jackpot—your healing necessitates that you imprint his qualities, just as a baby chick instinctually does with its mother. In such a trusted relationship he is your teacher. You are the student. So, in your search for a healer, note what your dreams tell you. Keep a close eye on the qualities I've described.

OUR CULTURE IS YEARNING for a return to high-quality, personalized health care. The Academy Award–winning film *As Good As It Gets* powerfully voices this collective cry. In it a struggling waitress with a severely asthmatic son is trapped in the bureaucratic clutches of an HMO. Just getting approval to see a lung specialist is a Herculean feat. Jack Nicholson, her well-to-do would-be suitor, comes to the rescue. How does he woo her? Riches? Love songs? Not in our health care climate. Nicholson wins the waitress's heart by sending a compassionate, competent pediatrician to make house calls on her ailing son. Nicholson becomes her champion. She's free at last from the impersonal HMO. Chalk up one more victory for man versus the machine. But what of other solutions? Can reform occur within the system? Bottom line, in or out of HMOs, as our practitioners grow more enlightened, when spirituality and intuition become standard medical practice, the nature of how patients are treated must evolve.

There is a need for a new kind of hero in medicine. Not the omnipotent saver of souls whose mission is to cure our every ill, an archetype whose dark side is to feel like a failure if he doesn't succeed. Illness, pain, and death defeat him. What kind of hero is that? We're long overdue to let this myth go. We must reenvision our hero as human, a person of bravery, intuition, and heart—skilled yet at times limited (as we all are) by shortcomings. Most important, this is someone who can sit with our pain, not run from it. And, in a health crisis, someone who can stand in the center of the fire with us instead of shrinking back.

More physicians I meet are longing to embody this change. They're tired of bowing to technology at the expense of their humanity, reject being the sort of doctor Samuel Taylor Coleridge called "shallow animals" who "imagine that in the whole system of things there is nothing but Gut and Body." In many ways Western medicine has become a prisoner of its own success, hostage to the rigors of science that have fueled its advance.

I've received too many letters from doctors in training who are miserable. They long to nurture their intuition and spirituality, integrate it with basic medicine, yet many programs are still unequipped to meet their needs. Desperate, these students ask me: "Should I drop out? Go into a different career? Take Prozac?" My answer is always, "We need you. Complete your education." I advise them on how to find like-minded peers and establish a support system outside their training program. This can get them through. Credentials offer grounding. They lend weight to a practitioner's credibility. I feel proud to say I've successfully convinced many interns and residents around the country to stick their schooling out.

In an era when the umbrella of alternative health includes both turbaned crystal healers and board-certified M.D.'s, credentials can weed out frauds. I look forward to the day when alternative medicine has a working peer review system. Already Dr. Andrew Weil has started the Program for Integrative Medicine, certifying physicians at the University of Arizona in Tucson. Dr. Larry Dossey's *Journal of Alternative Therapies,* geared toward medical professionals though enlightening for everyone, provides another such forum, as does the growing National Federation of Spiritual Healers in Great Britain. Meanwhile, until we have a more broad-based peer review system, scrutinize carefully those you go to as healers.

Be an informed consumer. What constitutes a quack? Be suspicious of grand claims of cures (often steeped in pseudoscientific jargon) not anchored in science. Don't get bamboozled by anyone who insists that his is the only way or that you must divorce yourself from other medical approaches. Some quacks imply their method is higher, better, wiser than any other, that they have a direct line to God. Or worse, that they are beaming down wisdom to only a select few. Look out for subtle racism or gender preference signifying the "chosen ones." These are truly dangerous beliefs. Beware of people who charge exorbitant fees or who try to hook you emotionally or financially, seeking to control not empower you. Go toward those who are humble. Follow your intuition; use good common sense.

My patient Jan, a Harvard-trained urologist in her forties, is an elegant example of how technology, intuition, and spirituality can merge. As you may know, the subspecialty of urology (and also most of surgery) is a notorious boys' club. The male and female genitourinary tract has traditionally been a domain treated strictly by male physicians. Jan, a gorgeous, brilliant blond, defies tradition. She practices surgery in a masculine world not by becoming masculinized—a knee-jerk accommodation made by too many women doctors—but by keeping her femininity and intuition intact. Talk about a gutsy role model!

Reflect on the ambience of a typical operating room: surgeons and nurses in baggy greens and paper slippers, scrubbed hands sealed in skintight latex gloves, masked faces showing only eyes. The patient, out cold on the stainless steel table, is hooked up to an IV. A plastic tube may be inserted through his mouth, down an airway to help him breathe. Monitors record blood pressure, pulse, respirations. Scalpels. Clamps. Sutures. Everything is mechanical, sterile, cool. An environment, I'm sure you'll agree, that could benefit from a little human warmth.

I'm not talking about the free-for-all of sexist jokes, tales of hopped-up Ferraris, or holes in one at the club I heard about from hotshot doctors during my surgical rotation in medical school. I'm referring to what Jan does. To her the operating theater is a holy space. Before the procedure begins she silently says a prayer for her hands to be guided, for the surgery to be a success. Her aim is to exude a loving, positive presence, knowing how attitude and subtle energy can support the healing process. From the first incision to the closing stitch, Jan augments her technical expertise by sending energy from her hands into a patient's body. Throughout the operation she has respect for the patient while he is unconscious, and she profoundly acknowledges how intuitively receptive each of us is in this anesthetized state.

There you've got it: two approaches, two sensibilities, comparable skill. In the end you're entitled to find a practitioner who makes you feel at home, has a philosophy compatible with yours. Always remember, in every aspect of health care, you have options. It's up to you. What kind of healer will you choose?

4

If Illness Comes: How You Can Use Intuition to Heal Yourself

Disease is as old as life, but the science of medicine is
still young.
—Jean Starobinski, medical historian

*I*n the beginning, illness was very different than it is today.

Visualize Africa. Five million years ago. Grasslands lush and green.
The rolling fecund earth. Sweet, fresh water. Our father and mother
progenitors wandered from place to place, searching for food. Carbon
dating fills us in on our forebears' day-to-day health charts: They suffered injuries and arthritis; their life spans were shortened by a harsh
environment—yet most infectious disease was nonexistent. Our ancestors' small roving bands didn't stay put long enough to pollute water
sources or create refuse that attracted disease-spreading insects.

These early people were practically free from many of the health
problems that plague "civilized" culture. As humans swarmed the
globe, they were colonized by parasites, viruses, bacteria. The fittest of
our predecessors developed immunity to compensate, surviving Dar-
win's age-old evolutionary struggle. The inception of our patterns was
set in our primal blood.

What can our species's past tell us about illness? What archetypes
have arisen over the aeons? The "sick role" has taken on many personas. The leper: stigmatized because the disease was so disfiguring; the
epileptic: deemed divine; the schizophrenic: the holy fool; childhood
illnesses: rites of passage into maturity. History also teaches us that most
cultures and healing systems have acknowledged the intuitive relationship of the sick person to the cosmos—planets, stars, oceans, rivers,
ancestors, the interplay of heaven and earth. Where does healing orig-

inate, if not from our resonance with natural forces that affect our bodies?

Take the Grecian isle of Kos in the fifth century B.C.E.: a sanctuary, created by Hippocrates, the legendary father of medicine, where the sick were soothed by soft breezes and the ebb and flow of the sea. A person recovered as the integrity of nature was allowed to reassert itself. How different from Western medical tradition, which reduces illness to the micromechanics of the body, tissues, cells, intricate strands of DNA's double helix. Our physical form now orbits in its own self-confining cosmos. Healing no longer comes from moonlight, sky, or trees.

I am presenting this chapter on illness as a call for integration. I want to counter what the poet William Blake condemned as "single vision," the nineteenth century's obsession with the scientific method. I offer you a more organic approach. Hush . . . Become still. Tune in closely. Is there really a separation between the two-thirds of you that is water and the pull of the sea? Between the earth's rotation, revolving night into day, and your circadian cycles of sleep? How can sensing these intuitive interconnections foster health? This is what I will show you. Ministering to your body, and all that harmonizes with it, will be protective against illness. Your task is to realign with the positive forces within you and without. With everything.

Down this road you'll have many decisions to make. Open-heart surgery? Medication? Meditation? Should I wait to act? Look to my dreams? Even your manicurist has an opinion. How will you know what to do? Stop long enough to turn inside. Waiting for you, always, is your intuition. Whether you go the traditional medical route, dance wild-haired and naked at full moon on the stroke of midnight, do both, or pick something in between, your choice must come from an unbiased inner authority. It wants what is right for you. It will tell you when and how to proceed. It could care less about statistics if they don't intuitively apply to your particular health situation. Even if chemotherapy is recommended, it must also feel right. The emphasis of this chapter will be to teach you how to know. In the face of illness it's essential you remain centered, sort through the reams of information that may be thrown at you, discern fallacy from truth.

Illness, for many, is an initiation by fire. Take the warrior's stance: strong and sure in times of adversity. Something to strive for. Intuition is the engine that drives. There is much to learn—enormous possibility.

I want to reiterate: Our healing may take the form of getting well. It also may take the form of acute or chronic illness. Great compassion is required. No judgment. No failure. No blame. My spiritual teacher says, "If it is true gold, you need not be afraid of the furnace." When illness comes adopt this strategy: Search for the white light in everyone who treats you, the interventions you decide upon, and all that you do.

Step 1. Notice Your Beliefs

Who gets sick? How can we get well? Is illness simply a result of genetics and other physical factors, or does something else come in? Intuition? Spirituality? Your mind-set is the stage on which your health history plays out. What you believe is not of purely intellectual interest. The views you hold must be able to soothe you like a lullaby when it really counts. It's good to read books, attend lectures and workshops about healing—but in the end your convictions must get you through. Start now. Claim for yourself a sound vision of what health and illness mean.

Let me tell you a story.

There was once a little old man who lived in a pine forest. He was known far and wide as the Great Healer. His cottage was filled from floor to ceiling with books: magic spells, sorcery, medicine, science, a whole section devoted to jokes that would crack him up. Animals would come to visit. By firelight he'd teach them the healing arts. They'd all curl up and read long into the night. Man, deer, coyote, rabbit, frog, the great owl. They'd turn each page and learn the Secrets: ways to heal with energy and dreams, love of the body, power of the heart, communion with nature, simplicity, kindness to the self and one another, and of course a good, hearty belly laugh. They believed in the Secrets, lived by them.

In our society we're too often separated from such harmony with the natural world and ourselves. Healing is something we do when we get sick, not a way of life, as in my story. It's important to articulate: What beliefs do you live by? Are they sustaining? Can you depend on them in periods of crisis and despair? Determining your stance on illness is pivotal, whether you ever get sick or not. Why? Because it crystallizes your priorities—not just about health issues but about how you face everything. Faith, courage, compassion, humor, intuition, hope—

don't wait until the last minute to find them. How you cope with getting ill is how you cope with any stress. The difference may be that when your health is poor, the volume is turned up, your limits stretch.

Is crisis an opportunity, as the components of the Chinese ideogram suggest? Or is this only a rationalization for a situation that is really unredeemable? To clarify, let's learn from intuition. It tells us that everything is not as it seems. There are layers of perception, meaning upon meaning. Talk about magic and mystery! Yes, illness is challenging, as is any hero's path. What is being asked of us? All heroic challenges, physical or not, have one thing in common: a call for heart. What I'm proposing is that this call is more important than anything else we will ever do, the raison d'être of being alive. Especially if we're sick or in pain, the lessons of love don't always come easy. We must fight for self-compassion and the intuitive link with a loving force that heals. Of course, none of us would ever want to be sick or in pain. But if we are, loving-kindness, in all its ramifications, will offer us the strength we need.

QUESTIONS FOR REFLECTION

- Do your beliefs give you strength during illness? If not, are you ready to find ones that do?

- In a health crisis, what role does your intuition play? How far would you trust it?

- How do you treat yourself when you get sick or are in pain? If you're self-critical, how can you turn this into self-compassion?

- Do you believe love can heal? How about humor? Are you willing to put them to the test?

A healing life, in periods of illness or health, requires that you embrace a positive belief system. But before you do you must bite the bullet: address up front all the internalized negative voices that sabotage your getting well. Hear what they have to say. Allow the whole unseemly cast of characters we all know so well to surface: the martyr, the victim, the persecutor, the wounded child, the critical parent, the faithless one. You must recognize your opponents in order to defeat them. If I miss anything, you fill in the blanks. Does any of this sound familiar?

What did I do wrong? Why me? It's hopeless. It's unfair. I'm worthless. I'm a bad person. Poor me. I'm a victim. I'm being punished. I'm never going to feel better. I'll have chronic pain all my life. I'm destined to inherit the same disease as my mother. I'm no good. I'm powerless. I'm weak. I deserve to be sick. I can't heal myself. I caused it. I'm cursed. I'm not spiritual enough. I hate myself for getting sick. I don't have options. No God would allow me to be in such pain. God has forgotten me. God is angry at me. What's the use? I might as well give up.

Many of us spend a lifetime creating and listening to negative voices. Where do they come from? Why do they so inexorably persist? To begin with, they echo the words of parents, teachers, and other authority figures as well as normal individual insecurities. Further, body chemistry plays a role: When serotonin levels are low, depression can ensue. Also, our species' history makes us anticipate danger to survive. In addition, we use anxiety to motivate ourselves or to defend against being let down. If we expect the worst, it's harder to be disappointed. The problem is, we become driven by negativity, addicted to it. Consider the endless mayhem in the evening news. Finally, bear in mind that in intuitive terms negativity has an inherently noisier, more frenetic, and stronger charge than the more even, subtler signal of the positive. Generally, as a novice, you pick up traumatic events and emotional upheaval before anything else. Even in ordinary life our attention is compelled more by the train wreck than by the system that works nearly all the time.

As you can see negative voices have many sources, much power. To exorcise them requires reconditioning your focus, replacing fear with faith. First, expose the tirade. Hold nothing back. Go straight for the boil. Charge like a samurai; lance it. In one swift blow. Second, summon every ounce of compassion you can muster to combat these untrue, unkind beliefs. Don't buy into the fear. Third, tell these insufferable voices, "Thank you for sharing," and keep moving on.

I ruefully appreciate from my own experience how tenacious negative voices can be. They feed on our apprehensions and on the part of ourselves that is reluctant to be large. Just when you think they're gone—they're ba-ack. Nonetheless, there comes a point when you must decide if you want a life that is fear-driven or one founded on love and hope. Establishing this premise is tantamount to bringing your healing to the next level. Remember, each gain will be incremental. You'll catch the negative voices faster; you'll dismiss them more quickly. Significant improvement, but it's also true that the process is ongoing. Here's a perspective to help silence the negative voices.

FOUR STARTING POINTS OF A POSITIVE BELIEF SYSTEM

1. *The body is holy.*

Your body is a temple. It houses spirit and blood, light and the interweaving of the material you. *Everything* about your body is holy: every secretion, every orifice, every physiological function contributes to your survival and well-being. Why in our culture are parts of the body taboo? Who do you suppose was one of the most respected physicians in ancient Egypt? Iri, keeper of the royal rectum, the pharaoh's enema expert! Enemas, believed to have been of divine origin, were a widely touted Egyptian practice to purify the gastrointestinal tract. What areas of your body do you appreciate, perhaps even slave over to be attractive? Your skin? Your hair? Your eyes? Not surprising, given our culture's narrow definition of glamour. To heal, we must expand our notion of what is beautiful. Send love everywhere. See where you hold back. What about your body evokes shame, self-loathing? Your internal organs? Your secretions? Sweat? Tears? Saliva? What about excretions? Urine? Feces? Menstrual blood? Reassess what is devalued, even unmentionable. Take an honest inventory.

For vibrant health (not just making it through the day), you must slowly but surely recondition your biases. If necessary, reinvent the wheel. Rebel against our culture's myopic vision of the body. Counter conformity. Unlearn what you've been taught. You do this case by case. Menstrual blood as a source of shame? No. It's part of the cycle of preparation for creating life. Tears something to hide? No. They're a form of release, a healing. And so on. With each bodily function we have to appreciate such a miracle. Meditate on it. Contemplate it. Pray to be able to fully apprehend such truth. Beauty comes from the inside out—literally! Whenever you abhor an aspect of your anatomy, even on an unconscious level, you deprive it of energy and love, the essential fuel for healing. Create a more positive vision of your physical self. Then if illness comes you won't be trying to heal a body you may hate.

2. *It's healthy to express your emotions about illness.*

If you get sick, express yourself. Feelings of upset, anger, depression, or fear about your illness or another's can be stepping-stones to compassion. Give yourself permission to be who you are. The patients I'm most concerned about are those who go numb, suffer in silence, or are stoic to the point of shutting down. Each of us is entitled to our own coping style, but we must ask ourselves: Does it bring peace? Will it facilitate healing? Give us strength? Whatever your way is, be authentic. The goal is to shine light through darkness, never dwell in it. You have the right to voice even what may seem forbidden.

For example, I got very angry as my father's Parkinson's disease was growing worse. I agonized watching him deteriorate. I wanted to be a good daughter, to be loving, to stay on top of things, support him 110 percent—but the pressure kept building. My life was besieged with demands: nurses, hospitals, physical therapists; he couldn't walk; he couldn't sleep; his mind was confused; he required twenty-four-hour care. All this plus he became irritable, constantly snapping at me. One night I cracked. On the phone with a childhood friend who's been with me through thick and thin—and whose mother was also chronically ill—I blurted out: "I wish he'd just die!" Silence. Had the line gone dead? Finally my friend said, "Judith! That's horrible! How can you say that about your own father?" Then *click*. She hung up on me.

What had I done? Was I wrong to express such a thing? Was I a monster? Well, no. What my friend didn't understand was that I didn't *really* want my father to die. But I did need to vent. Not to my father, of course. I had to find another outlet. By surfacing the feeling, I was able to let it go, to regain compassion. My process was a progression. I inched forward. I fell short. I tried again. To feel love, all obstacles must be removed. What if I'd denied my feeling, held it in? Where would it have gone then? For even the best of friends, sharing taboo emotions may be new territory. This will be safer with some people than with others, but it's worthwhile to explore. Just know that if anger, fear, resentments about illness become frozen, they'll keep you from your heart. We are human beings, not saints. Cut yourself some slack. Feelings are not facts, they're energy. If your aim is compassion, releasing this energy productively can get you there. Believe in love that much.

3. *Spirituality will help you heal.*

Science and spirituality mix. An odd couple? Not at all. Over two hundred scientific studies have shown that spirituality is good for your health and promotes recovery from illness. Take cardiac disease. In 1995 the Dartmouth-Hitchcock Medical Center found that for heart surgery patients, a major predictor of survival was religious faith. For those without spiritual beliefs, the death rate was three times higher. As for blood pressure, another survey reveals that churchgoers have lower blood pressure than nonchurchgoers, even when smoking and other risk factors are considered. Let's also look at the elderly. A National Institute on Aging study found that geriatric patients were physically healthier and less depressed if they attended regular spiritual services. Across the board research underscores the necessity of not waiting until illness or pain comes to draw on spirituality as a resource for healing and health.

Is there a center in our brain for spiritual experience? Our prefrontal cortex, which evolutionary biologists say enables us to form complex beliefs, as in religions, is 200 percent larger than expected in a primate our size. Simply put, we're wired for spirituality. But can the transcendental experience itself be pinpointed? Scientists currently associate it with a part of the brain called the limbic system. When this area is electrically stimulated during surgery, some patients report visions of angels or devils. And brain tumors, which overexcite the limbic system, can trigger enhanced, sometimes obsessive, spiritual awareness. Which came first? God or the brain? Intuition aside, as Detective Joe Friday of *Dragnet* always said, "Just the facts, ma'am." What scientists *are* willing to conclude is that the brain and spirituality are interrelated; if you cultivate a belief in something greater than yourself—traditionally religious or not—you'll have a better chance of staying healthy longer and healing faster if you become ill.

4. *You don't have to act out life's traumas in your body.*

It is not necessary to resolve an emotional trauma by getting sick. What happens is this: A trauma—a heartbreak, death, or loss—occurs, then your body intuitively encodes it as energy. If you do your best to deal with the difficulty, you can get a jump on resolving it. If not, the conflict will fester, may translate into physical symptoms or emotional distress. Without even realizing it many of us wait for a health crisis to give us a more lucid perspective on our lives, make long overdue changes, or motivate us to work through past traumas. We use the energy of crisis to create change. I'm asking you to reappraise this strategy. By doing so you may spare your body much pain and suffering.

At a recent workshop I was giving, a woman told the group a touching story. Her mother was a Holocaust survivor who, thirty years after the war ended, was diagnosed with uterine cancer. After the malignancy was surgically removed, she said to her daughter, weeping, "Thank God. Now the Nazis are finally out of my body."

Think about it. The significance this woman attributes to her cancer poignantly conveys to us the impact our beliefs can have. Must we develop actual tumors to exorcise the demons in our lives? Please be clear, this woman never sat down and said to herself, Okay, to heal I must get cancer. Who among us would? The process is treacherous because it's subliminal. Your body takes your beliefs, conscious or unconscious, seriously. Whether you're ill or not, examine your beliefs and retain only those that serve you. Do you unknowingly use illness or pain as a means of conflict resolution for traumas of the past? If so, take a second look. What other options do you have? Psychotherapy? Energy work? Meditation? Asking your dreams for guidance? Consulting a spiritual counselor? Prayer? Talking with a good friend? Do whatever it takes. Formulate a life-affirming belief system about how to prevent illness and heal. It is the underpinning upon which a sustained recovery is based.

What other factors contribute to illness? Take the classic overachiever. Slaving away late at the office one night, he practically blacks out and is rushed to the hospital with a perforated peptic ulcer. You could easily conclude it was caused by a combination of stress and his gastric acid skyrocketing from one too many spicy enchiladas. Or, that unconsciously he'd become sick to receive the much-needed nurturing that would come from a good doctor's care. What other "secondary gains" did he accrue from being ill? Love? Attention? Time off from work? Time out from a relationship? Peace and quiet? A good rest? Whenever any of us gets sick, there are numerous physical and emotional components.

With this in mind, even so, I want to caution you against too simplistic an explanation of illness. There are other meanings too. The ecosystem of humankind and nature is intuitively bound. No life-form, human or not, stands alone. We all swim in the same waters, can feel our collective reverberations. How is it possible to talk about any individual's health without also considering the overall health of the planet? Could illness, in part, be the body's desperate attempt to reequilibrate itself with a planet fighting to survive? Depression, chronic pain, autoimmune diseases, in which the body literally attacks itself, are growing at apocalyptic rates. There's a parallel between our suffering and the relentless assault on the earth, the ravaging of rain forests, underground nuclear testing, pollution of air and oceans. Can we empathically feel our planet's cry? Do our bodies mimic the disease we are inflicting? How do we reconcile this breach?

However you conceive of illness, an element of mystery always exists. There's so much we still don't know. It's been popular the past decade to assign all kinds of meaning to symptoms, but this isn't always possible. As a physician I've learned to have awe for what is unknowable in ordinary terms. It's fine to seek a rational explanation for why you or someone you love becomes ill. But sometimes there just doesn't seem to be one. Your four-year-old develops a brain tumor. How could there ever be a good reason for that? Yet you must accept the situation and not lose faith in God, yourself, or your child. Is this too much to ask of you? Or is this single act alone, faith in the face of the greatest possible loss, more significant in the cosmic scheme of things than any one life itself, no matter how dear? An extremely hard call. Each of us must grapple with these self- and universe-defining spiritual issues.

In all types of illness, from cancer to a cold, never fail to remember the mind's capacity to heal, even what has been deemed unhealable. By lovingly learning to focus your intuition, you can strive to cure or at least improve any health situation. I first came to understand this in a roundabout way.

In 1970 I was working as a research assistant in a parapsychology lab at UCLA. Part of my job was to follow up on calls from people reporting "ghosts" in their homes. It's always amused me how many people in Los Angeles believe their houses are haunted. They'd describe electronic machinery flipping on and off uncontrollably, objects flying around the room, unidentifiable voices, footsteps, apparitions. Wild stuff! What we investigators mostly concluded was that, even if the manifestations were authentic, they were misinterpreted. In general they seemed to be extensions of the anger and frustration in a family rather than related to any specific house. When the family moved the phenomena followed them. As tempers flared episodes increased. Ghosts weren't haunting the hall; we were seeing psychokinetic energy in action, a living laboratory of how the power of the mind literally alters its surrounding environment. The real revelation for me was: If the mind can make a cupboard door flap open and shut, it can also—if properly directed—heal the body.

This brings us to an appreciation of a world where positive beliefs, emotions, and actions are prime factors in getting well, can even stimulate our immune response. A world where our defense against illness is related to a bodywide communication network we can take an active part in programming. A mix of science, instinct, and mystery, this is how intuitive healing can benefit you.

Step 2. Be in Your Body

You can't heal your body unless you're in it. Sounds reasonable, right? Then how come the instant most of us get sick we check out, the sooner the better? We feel pain or discomfort, we get scared, we withdraw. We're out of our bodies so fast, the last thing on our minds is to rally every iota of awareness and energy to the part of us that most needs attention. You might ask, How would this help? Let me explain. Intuitive truth 1: The more love and consciousness you bring to your body when it is ill, the better chance you'll have of mending it. Intuitive truth 2: If you resist discomfort, it will persist. If you soften around it, it will lessen.

Let's get specific. You have what you're going to discover is appendicitis. First signs? You're in agony, curled in the fetal position on your bed. Your body is sending out a frantic SOS. Something's really wrong. You have no choice but to listen. You head for the emergency room. You need surgery. No way out. Next thing you know, you wake up in recovery, sans appendix. You made it. Your acute pain obviously had a purpose. It got you, fast, to the hospital. Some pain is short-lived. You have it. It's treated. It's gone. Even with pain of this kind, however, there's no question that informed attention is an asset. From the onset of a health crisis, focusing your intuition can get you past all-too-human resistances. For instance, people frequently die of heart attacks, failing to heed the warning of their angina. As they say, Denial is not just a river in Egypt. Intuition combats denial. By tuning in to pain, you'll get a more incisive take on how to deal with it. But, in general, here is a strategy that never fails: Loving-kindness. Conscious softening. Releasing resistance and fear. Not forsaking the body. This is where you begin.

What if pain becomes chronic? My patient Meg, a corporate attorney used to being in charge—a control freak, really—was diagnosed with a bulging lumbar disc. Compressing the sciatic nerve, this disc caused excruciating pain in her lower back and down her leg. Pain became Meg's enemy. Drawing on techniques honed in years of legal warfare, she went on a crusade to eradicate it: antiinflammatories, ice packs, acupuncture, physical therapy, gradual exercise. She did everything her doctor told her. Still the pain was there. The more she dreaded it, the worse it got. One day she hobbled into my office, cane in one hand, cell phone in the other. An impossible juggling act, heartrending to see. On the verge of tears, she said, "I can't take it anymore. I hate this pain. I just want to get rid of it." Of course she did. Any of us would. But Meg was working against herself.

I had to teach Meg something contrary to her style of being in the world. She just wasn't going to be able to conquer her pain. She'd have to harmonize with it. For a bold spirit like Meg, this would be no easy task. Nor was this issue hers alone. So often in medicine we have it backwards. We attempt to repair the body without consulting it. Pain has its own spirit, language, intelligence, rhythm. Pain is absolutely alive. It will speak to you, not in the usual sense but on an intuitive level. First, open up communication. Odd as it may seem, ask your pain—or any illness—for help. Healing is a collaboration, an opportunity to learn from a sometimes demanding but most enlightened master. Approach your pain with deep respect. If you do, it will respond, point the way toward getting well.

All this I was communicating to Meg. Not surprisingly, she listened with visible skepticism. Perhaps you too have doubts. To further explain, let me tell you of the ancient Buddhist practice of Tonglen. Tonglen says to heal from illness you must actually become it. The paradox is that by taking illness on with compassion, you may be released from it. Aversion only worsens suffering. In *The Tibetan Book of Living and Dying*, Sogyal Rinpoche tells this story: "There were many extraordinary cases of people, who when they heard they were dying of a terminal illness, gave away everything they had, and went to the cemetery to die. There they practiced taking on the suffering of others; and what is amazing is that instead of dying, they returned home fully healed." Rinpoche also tells of lepers who cured themselves by breathing in, actually becoming one with their terrible disfigurement and pain, then transforming it with compassion. We in the West must understand that compassion is more powerful than pain and provides a potent protection against it.

As a physician, I wasn't about to ask Meg to go to Tibet or take on the misery of the world. I did want her, however, to apply aspects of Tonglen to managing her pain. The use of breathing for pain relief is hardly alien to our culture. Lamaze, a breath technique for natural childbirth, has eased many mothers through labor, brought lots of babies into the world. Building on this principle, I worked with Meg first to develop compassion for her body. Second, to embrace her pain, breathe it in, no withholding. Third, to utilize compassion to abate it. Drawing on Tonglen and my own intuitive practice, I gave Meg these guidelines. For relief of pain, or as an approach to resolving illness, you can apply them too.

MEETING THE MASTER:
A MEDITATION FOR DEALING WITH PAIN AND ILLNESS

1. Relax into the discomfort. Don't try to change it or rid yourself of it. Simply let the pain be. Gently breathe through any tightening, fear, resistance. Loosen your grip. Get to know the geography of your pain. Map it out. Become familiar with it.

2. Intuitively tune in to the discomfort. Does it have color? Texture? Emotion? Is it hot? Cold? Does it move or stay in one place? Do you notice images? Sounds? Scents? Memories? Ask the discomfort: What can I learn from you? How can I ease my pain?

3. Focus lightly on the discomfort. Feel it completely. As you inhale, breathe all your pain in. Visualize it as a cloud of dark smoke. Let it flow throughout your body, right to the core of your compassion. Now picture every last bit of the black smoke dissolving, purified by love. As you exhale, imagine this love as clear white light. Send it back to your area of discomfort. Breathe in pain. Breathe out compassion. Breathe in pain. Fill the pain with the healing breath of compassion.

Meg initially struggled with this meditation. But, despite her forceful nature, she began to see progress. Her pain gradually let up. For Meg—and most of us—the premise of this meditation is radical. It says that by actively engaging discomfort, we can transmute it, a form of mystical alchemy never to be misconstrued as succumbing to weakness or admitting defeat. *Harmonizing with pain and illness will relieve them, not make them worse.* I know this goes against much of what we've been taught. Still, the fact remains that Meg—and each of my patients who've trusted enough to explore this in therapy—have experienced significant reduction in pain or improvement in an illness, even when all else had failed.

Working with Meg, I also saw more clearly the difference between pain and suffering. At the risk of oversimplifying, pain is a physiological sensation. Or, as in Chinese medicine, a blockage of chi, our life energy. Suffering, by contrast, is our response to pain, not necessarily related only to the present. Pain, both physical and emotional, adds up. Unresolved pockets of pain fester. Any or all of them can be unconsciously reactivated with a new illness or injury. In Meg's meditation her past surfaced: an image of a childhood blanket she'd wrap up in to feel safe. Memory flashes of parents who ignored her. Never having anyone to turn to for comfort. One pain ricocheted off another, then another. Her lumbar disc was merely the focal point of a constellation of pain. Though Meg didn't realize it, this compounded her suffering. Here I could help.

The practice of Tonglen gave Meg the courage to mend past wounds and change present behaviors. It allowed compassion into many areas of her life. She never expected that part of her healing would be to allow other people to support her: letting a friend drive to the movies; asking a stranger to carry her bags when traveling. Meg's success wasn't only that her back pain subsided. Much about her started to melt: her rigidity, her tendency to beat herself up whenever she'd make a mistake, her impulse to give to others rather than take time to savor or receive. She has become more mindful of beauty. The glistening sunlit boughs of magenta bougainvillea arcing over her front porch don't go unnoticed anymore. Of course, Meg didn't achieve this overnight, but an extraordinary new pattern had begun. Self-compassion is the most enduring antidote to pain or illness I know, a kind of oxygen that can revitalize. Moving toward it is a lifelong path.

I never lose sight of how relentless chronic discomfort can be. Try to consider it a Zen koan, a spiritual riddle containing layers of meaning. Look to your body for the answer. Feel into the pain or illness. Listen to it. Learn from it. There's no guarantee your distress will miraculously lift, though it might. But what will happen is you'll enter into a relationship with a force that will provide clues on how to heal. A very different philosophy from just swallowing a pill, sitting back, and waiting for the pain to leave.

YOUR BODY ALSO GIVES you leads about recovering from pain or illness through its internal pictures. If you get sick you may have to undergo certain tests—X rays, ultrasound, CT scans, MRIs, endoscopy—some more grueling than others but all with their intuitive upside. I'd like you to begin to consider these tests a training ground where you can learn to zero in intuitively. I can't overemphasize the importance of having a distinct mental image of the part of you that needs to be healed. These tests offer you that. Their visuals are structural reference points that further ground you in your body.

Only in the last century was gazing into our body possible. In the early 1800s, Dr. René Laënnec invented the first stethoscope. Instead of using the traditional ear-to-chest method, he rolled up a tube of paper to keep a proper distance between his ear and a female patient's well-endowed breasts. This fastidious improvisation, amplifying her heartbeat, was in fact a major breakthrough into hearing the noises of our bodies. Later the first gastroscopy (a test using a scope to look into the stomach) occurred when a professional sword swallower, at the request of a physician, ingested a pipe a foot long containing a lamp and lens. By the turn of the century there were X rays, and by the 1950s there was ultrasound, sound waves too high to be heard by the human ear. The era of three-dimensional imaging took off in 1976. First CT scans utilized X rays; later magnetic resonance imagery (MRI) eliminated the need for radiation.

Such cutting-edge technology, making our bodies transparent, opens doorways of mystical perception. Of course, most of us don't look at it this way. With good reason we abhor going through tests (some are truly unpleasant). Our doctors rarely think to show us the results, let alone instruct us with them. And, be honest, do you ask to see the actual studies? Probably not. We have a conditioned squeamishness, viewing the interiors of our bodies as forbidden, repugnant, alien. I'm suggesting that you reevaluate this mind-set, discover the luminous essence the structure of our bodies imparts.

My patient Ralph just underwent a colonoscopy. He'd been dreading it, putting the appointment off for months. I thought they might have to handcuff him to get him there. Actually, his wife drove him. At the hospital a specialist inserted a flexible scope up into his colon. A video monitor magnified everything to detect disease. His doctor was a cheerful sort. During the procedure he asked Ralph, "Do you want to see your colon? Just watch the screen." Ralph cringed and broke out in a cold sweat. "I was scared to death," he admitted. "Gross. The last thing I needed to see was the inside of my own colon. Besides, what if there was something wrong?" Ralph kept his eyes locked shut the entire time.

During our next session I reviewed a copy of Ralph's study with him. His diagnosis was spastic colon, probably caused by stress. "How about going over the pictures together?" I suggested gently, fully respecting his right to say no. "Use this test as a road map. Intuition's a laser. Target your focus. Then you'll know where to direct your intention to heal." Ralph rolled his eyes. "I'm afraid to look. Why should I? I'm no doctor. I won't understand what I'm seeing. I won't like what I'm seeing anyway." Honoring Ralph's not unreasonable anxieties about the sanctity of his colon, I walked him though his resistance. Though viewing tests is usually considered the province of doctors, I explained to Ralph that it doesn't take a rocket scientist to get a general understanding of them. The films of his colon provided a clear picture of his problem. With it Ralph had a focal point with which to tune in intuitively, gather information, and send energy.

Intuitive healing is always body-interactive. Why not put your medical procedures to intuitive good? Why deny yourself such an asset? When traveling in a foreign country, wouldn't you prefer to have a guidebook? I know tests can be scary, especially if something is wrong. Even so, don't miss the magic of seeing into your body, a connector between you and the substance of which you are made. The martial arts concept of *mu-shin,* or "no mind," means no separation between mind and body. Power flows from this unity. Our physical self, our emotions, a healthy body or an organ with disease—our capacity to heal strengthens as we become one with it all.

Step 3. Sense Your Body's Subtle Energy

When my mother was dying of cancer, I used to hold her in my arms in the hospital. Plagued with insomnia, she'd toss and turn all night. Tranquilizers and painkillers didn't solve the problem. What did work was for me to cradle her head in my lap and send energy to her. She told the nurses proudly, "I don't need sleeping pills when my daughter comes to visit. She puts me in a trance with her hands." My mother would often drift off hugging a tiny carved statue I'd given her symbolizing longevity, an old, bearded Chinese man whose eyes were looking up at heaven. My mother was slowly slipping away. My heart, my energy was the gift I had to give her.

Never underestimate your energy's ability to ease suffering, accelerate healing, even cure disease. Building on the discussion in Chapter 2, we know that our bodies are composed of energy centers known as chakras. In Sanskrit, *chakra* means wheel or circle. A chakra is often portrayed in sacred art as a lotus blossom or a spinning wheel. Medical intuitives are trained to make a diagnosis by sensing imbalances in the chakras.

Now I'd like to focus on the heart chakra. If you or a loved one becomes ill, your heart is a priceless resource. I don't mean this in a metaphoric sense. I'm referring to a specific energy center in your body that directly affects your health. The heart chakra is one to four inches in diameter, located in the middle of your chest, a few inches above the diaphragm. You can sense it by placing the palm of your hand over this area. Whenever I do energy work on a patient or myself, I focus on my heart and allow its force to move through me into the other person. The heart chakra is the main generator that fuels our healing system. What does it feel like? How can you activate it? Here is what you do.

MEDITATION: OPENING THE HEART

1. Get very quiet. Relax your body. Breathe in . . . Breathe out . . . Your breath provides a focal point to come back to center. Gently place your hand over your heart chakra and hold it there. Now get ready to visualize.

2. Concentrate on a person, place, or animal that you really love. For starters, it may be simpler to picture cuddling your pet or taking in a gorgeous sunset rather than focusing on a person. Whatever moves you. There is no right or wrong. The purpose is to feel love, in a general sense to notice how its energy equivalent localizes in your midchest.

3. Pay attention to sensations in your heart chakra, no matter how subtle. Warmth. Cold. Tingling. Vibration. Pressure. Constriction. Expansion. Compassion. Joy. Let it happen. Don't hold back. Even discomfort . . . let it open. It will evolve. As you practice, a vortex of positive energy in your heart chakra will build. This is the hub of your healing. During illness or pain, tap into it.

First, get used to sensing your heart energy. Then, when it's real to you, learn to impart it. The secret? Be a vessel through which love flows. No need to strain. *You* aren't doing it. The instant you overpersonalize the process or claim credit for it, you'll become drained; the current will cease. Practice sharing energy with a friend. Place your hands over her chest. Focus on your heart chakra opening. Spend a few minutes allowing love to go freely from your heart, down your arms, out your palms into your friend. Then reverse roles. Have her direct energy back to you. This technique can be used to help anyone in need, not just friends. The quality of love I'm asking you to access is selfless, unconditional. No ego involved.

This concept took me quite a while to understand. Patients would come into my office sick or in pain. *I* wanted to make them feel better. *Me.* Not some elusive universal force. True to my medical training, I tried hard. But at what cost? At night I'd drag myself home and flop into bed, depleted. I had to learn to surrender, to become empty so I could be filled. You know you're doing something right when you come away from sending energy refreshed. Love feeds you as much as it does the person you're healing.

You never know when this technique will come in handy. Once, while I was speaking at a local book club, Jane, my hostess, broke down in tears. "I'm in terrible pain," she apologized. "I think it's a gallstone attack. Can you help me?" The room fell silent. All eyes turned to me. Now these twenty women—mostly housewives living in privileged Palos Verdes Estates—had no experience in sending energy. My book *Second Sight,* which they'd just read, was their only reference. Still, here we all were, faced with someone in pain. I asked Jane to stand next to me. I placed my hand over her gallbladder. I took a breath. I focused on my heart. I requested energy to flow through me, out my hands. I instructed the women to do the same. We all formed a circle around Jane. As if by instinct, one by one, each woman lovingly came forward sending her energy. A sea of hands on Jane, in a living room decorated for Christmas with the faces of radiant angels.

The power of the moment was such that Jane's pain eased, then stopped. This was atypical—usually her attacks persisted for hours. Relieved, she felt strong enough to call her doctor. The next day her gallbladder was taken out. Jane swears, "The ladies of my book club saved me." The energy we sent got her through the night until she could have surgery. This evening was remarkable: These women experienced for the first time what it was like to take part in healing, a down-to-earth demonstration of how effective working with subtle energy can be.

Practice makes perfect. This is a skill everyone can learn. The more you do it, the better you'll get. When you're injured or ill, direct energy to yourself where it is needed. Be specific. If you have tendinitis in your elbow, place your hand over the area—aim energy right toward it. What about cancer? In the same way visualize saturating every last millimeter of your tumor with love. Ditto for a broken arm, migraine headache, or other aches and pains. What results can you expect? In most cases, at the very least you'll feel replenished. Sending energy gives your body stamina when it has stalled. I've also seen dramatic turnabouts of symptoms: A child's asthma disappears, arthritis pain resolves, fibroid tumors shrink. I believe that many so-called spontaneous remissions from disease occur because the body's energy system becomes realigned. This is a wild card, for which traditional medicine has no logical way to account. Subtle energy has an integrity of its own, goes where it's needed at the proper time. Try to let go of expectation. Come from your heart—that's what's important; you can't dictate the outcome. Then trust your body's response—whether it's a return of vitality or a complete reversal of illness.

I strongly encourage you, especially if you're sick, to get comfortable working with your own energy. You may also want to consult a doctor of Chinese medicine, savvy in balancing your body's energy, or an energy healer. Either approach will augment conventional therapy, not conflict with it. (I always recommend you inform your conventional doctor of any alternative therapies you're trying.) Most physicians diagnose and treat illness on a gross level, predicated on what is seen or measured by tests. A lot of good can be accomplished on this basis. However, sometimes much more is needed. Particularly when you feel no positive response, I urge you to draw on all available options.

Many Western physicians lack the training to identify subtle energy disturbances that can cause symptoms. Too often people with real physical problems are written off as hysterical, hypochondriacs, or malingerers. Where does this leave you? You're being told nothing physical is wrong, yet you don't feel well. This is crazy-making. If your symptoms escape medical definition, don't give up. Fatigue. Pain. Nausea. Insomnia. Headaches. Urinary frequency. Muscle spasms. These are just a few of the culprits that often go unexplained. Maybe your doctor isn't knowledgeable about energy. I suggest you refer to the skills I presented in Chapter 3 to seek out a practitioner who is. When your energy needs are met, "unexplainable" complaints can resolve. Your wherewithal to heal will peak, bolstering your body's defenses to fight disease.

Being accountable for your subtle energy can counteract illness, safeguard your health. Take contagion. Germs are everywhere. Why do some people fall prey to them and others don't? Did you catch the flu just because that man on the subway kept sneezing on you? If so, why didn't your friend sitting next to you get it too? What constitutes immunity? Let's look at the extremes. On numerous occasions the performer Michael Jackson has been photographed wearing that infamous surgical mask in public. Must we go to such lengths to prevent infectious disease? Our society puts a premium on hygiene, as meticulously detailed by Nancy Tomes in *The Gospel of Germs:* cough shielding, the white toilet designed to be easily scoured of microbes, vacuum cleaners ridding households of disease-spreading dust. Even women's hemlines were purposely raised in the 1800s to avoid collecting bacteria.

Are infections merely about the transmission of germs? Immunity depends on white cell function, genetics, environmental pollutants, our thoughts, emotions, stress level, personality styles. Psychoneuroimmunology, a groundbreaking field linking immunity and the mind, correlates life-affirming attitudes and behaviors with wellness. Given this, consider again the Buddhist belief that compassion (your heart's expression of subtle energy) is our greatest defense against disease. How can all these factors work together? By opening your heart you can create an immunosupportive system in your body. Positive thoughts, a loving perspective on your illness and yourself, as well as the ability to direct energy consciously give us potent ammunition against disease.

Building heart builds immunity. There are numerous causes of illness. Rest assured, you have many more means of combating it than you're told in traditional settings. One of these is subtle energy. Sensing energy fine-tunes your body's functions and will point the way to healing.

Step 4. Ask for Inner Guidance

Being ill can be confusing. You're on an emotional roller coaster. Statistics, probabilities, therapeutic options, survival rate projections will be swirling around in your head. It's natural to feel overwhelmed. How do you make an informed decision about treating an illness? One that you'll feel good about twenty years from now when you look back. What should you do? First, collect the facts, but don't stop there. Take all the time you need to listen intuitively. No matter how impressive the scientific evidence, your choice must sit well with you. Slow down. Don't panic. The patients I've worked with who've felt happiest about their selections of therapy have consulted their intuition at every stage.

When you're deciding on the best way to treat an illness, ask yourself the following questions:

- What does my gut say? Is it tied in knots or relaxed? Does an option feel "right" or "off"?

- Do I sleep better or worse at night thinking about a particular approach? Does going ahead with it make me feel more at peace?

- When I quietly tune in, what images, impressions, or knowings come? Are they telling me to go ahead? Wait? Seek out another alternative? Pose specific questions to your intuition. Evaluate the response.

Succinctly formulating questions and requesting guidance for intuitive problem solving is a form of remote viewing. Put this question-answer strategy into action. You'll gain a more rounded picture of how to proceed in the here-and-now as well as in the future. Recall that remote viewing is not limited by the constraints of time or space. It is a technique whereby you can access your intuition to obtain foresight about people, places, and health-related interventions. Simply center yourself, setting aside the ups and downs of the day. Ask your question. See what intuitions come. Factor them into your decision. For instance, will a treatment succeed? Visualize yourself going through it. Do you see a positive outcome? If so, what are the details? Are you healthier? More energetic? Free from pain? If not, think twice about proceeding. Whenever possible get a clear sense of the results.

How do you know if your intuitions are accurate? Can you separate them from your hopes and fears? For example, if your doctor strongly recommends chemotherapy for your cancer, how can you be sure that your fear of its infamous side effects won't cloud your judgment? To make sure the process is pure, do this: Be an open channel. Don't micromanage your intuitions. As I've emphasized, pay special attention to those that are either completely neutral, with no emotional charge, or else conveyed with compassion. I've come to depend on these factors to gauge reliability.

I was once in session with a patient I'd known for years and cared for very much. While she was talking about job stress, I suddenly had the strong intuition she had diabetes, though nothing she related even remotely pointed to it. My first reaction, naturally, was dismay. But I knew from experience to slow down the inflow of information to determine my intuition's validity. Once I did I realized my impression, as it came through, was neutral. My instinct was to hold off mentioning it. I only suggested, on the basis of her stress symptoms, that she get a physical exam. She agreed. Her doctor ordered a routine blood panel, and an elevated glucose was found, diagnosing early diabetes. Just as I have, you can train yourself to separate your emotional reaction to what you're sensing from the original intuition. Then you'll have a more astute take on whether it's authentic.

I'm also privy to another form of intuition in my work. When it first happened it took me by surprise. In the middle of a session with Larry, a teenage boy, I suddenly saw another male face superimposed on his. I thought my eyes were playing tricks on me. I blinked—still it was there. Nobody had ever mentioned this in medical school. Had I totally lost it? Fortunately, I didn't go down that road. Instead, I decided to focus on the face, inquire directly how it could assist Larry. To my delight, I received extremely pertinent input, such as "Ask him if he's been suffering headaches." I did and he had. I was on to something. By exploring his headaches—the psychological and physical roots—Larry found his symptoms gradually ameliorating. With another patient the face of the comedienne Gilda Radner, who died of ovarian cancer, appeared. Sadly, it forewarned me that my patient would share the same diagnosis.

In my workshops I started to feel out if other therapists experienced anything similar. Bingo! Many had—but they were skittish about all the raised eyebrows they'd encounter if they dared mention it. The magic of surfacing such "taboo" intuitions is the relief it brings. Now, out in the open, a professional exchange could begin. Whether this face represents a visual premonition, a benevolent guide, or a reflection of a past life, it's a therapist's friend. When it occurs I pay attention, take advantage of this worthy intuitive asset.

Asking for guidance is very practical when it comes to your health, particularly during a medical crisis. For me it has been a lifesaver. Let me walk you through how it can work. Over a few short months I watched my father's Parkinson's disease take his life, as he had known it, away from him. My dear father, totally dependent. I, his only child, watched powerless, heartbroken. "We can't handle him any longer," the kindly nurse from his retirement home told me. "You'll have to find a facility providing more comprehensive care." Oh God. A nursing home. Part of me had sensed this coming for a long time, but I couldn't bear to think about it.

So my journey into the netherworld of nursing homes began. Envision it. Not being able to care for yourself or think straight. Needing constant supervision. Relying on the good graces of caregivers you've just met. I plunged into this very real and painful aspect of elder care in our society. I asked to be guided. I clung to my intuition for clarity. I prayed for my heart not to shut down. Sometimes this is all you can do. I was my father's only advocate. I couldn't afford to succumb to fear. There was an answer for him, a place where he'd be well cared for and happy. This, my intuition told me. It was a compassionate truth I felt down to my core. Also, I kept seeing an image of a sun, which carried no emotional charge. It was related in some way to my father's solution, but I didn't know how. Was I just making up what I badly needed to believe? My intuition, a blend of compassion and neutrality, told me otherwise.

I kept going. In the worst of nursing homes I witnessed near-Auschwitz conditions, dormitories of demented patients stacked inches from one another. I fought not to be sucked into this vortex of despair. Not my father. Not there. Even the "better places" didn't feel right. It seemed I was getting nowhere. Could my intuition have been so off? I doubted myself. Even so I struggled to recenter.

Way down on my list, outside the neighborhood I'd been considering, was a facility called Vista del Sol. When I visited there I immediately breathed a sigh of relief. The place was perfect: garden apartments connected to a nursing home that my father could transition to when the time came. It wasn't until that moment that I understood the significance of my recurring intuitive image. A chill shot through me. In Spanish, *vista del sol* means "view of the sun." In the chaos of my search, I just hadn't made the connection.

The purpose of this story is to give you a realistic appreciation of what asking for guidance will bring. Don't wait for a vision that will magically make your health concerns fall into place. It could happen, but more often your intuition will be a compass pointing the path to wellness. At first you may not have the slightest clue what a particular intuition signifies. Don't dismiss it just because it doesn't make apparent sense. The events of your life will explain its relevance. Keep your eyes open. Stay with it. Discover your answer. If doubts come (they do even for those of us who have great faith in intuition), bring yourself back to center again. Clarity will return. When it comes to your health or a loved one's, trust intuition and you won't go astray. Your challenge is, as mine was, to keep the faith in what your guidance tells you.

I look at guidance as a kind of prayer, a way of seeking an inner direction and contacting a spiritual force that can heal. We don't have to deal with illness all by ourselves. There are others out there—people we've never even met—waiting to assist us. During my father's illness I discovered prayer lines—groups of dedicated people all over the world, related to various churches and humanitarian organizations (see Resources), who will pray for you or a loved one if you are in need. Literally thousands of volunteers rotate in round-the-clock shifts to send positive thoughts and healing energy your way. The cardiologist Randolph Byrd's pioneering study of cardiac patients at San Francisco General Hospital showed the power of prayer to heal. Those who were prayed for had a higher survival rate, were less likely to require antibiotics, and had fewer complications than the group not prayed for. Impressive statistical findings. I put my father on every prayer list I could get my hands on. You can take advantage of them too. Even in health situations that don't seem to have an obvious answer, prayer is another resource on which you can draw.

Step 5. Listen to Your Dreams

Over two thousand years ago in ancient Greece, dreams were sacred. Healing shrines honoring them towered over the cobalt Mediterranean Sea. Pilgrims who were sick flocked on foot—or were carried on litters—from all parts of the world to visit the renowned Temples of Asclepius. The divine physician, Asclepius, was not human but God: son of the mighty hunter Apollo, he was the giver of dreams that cured. Special incubation chambers were set up for the sick, who'd enter "temple sleep" and request a healing dream. In preparation they were bathed in rose water, the sweet scent of incense wafting through the air. After a night in this sanctuary, priests, not physicians, would interpret their dreams. The temple walls were inscribed with dramatic testimonials of cures: "Hermodikes of Lampsakos was paralyzed in body. In his sleep he was healed." The Greek culture revered the therapeutic properties of dreams in a way we've forgotten.

In our world science's vigilant efforts to quantify illness could profit by collaborating with dreams. Relegating hard science to one camp and visionary dreams to another is a no-win proposition for everyone. The two can work together. In sleep our inhibitions fall away. Dreaming is hinged on the surrender of our thinking minds. More healing is possible without our ordinary walls intact, when creativity is at its peak. Healing equals Creativity. In terms of your body, dreams offer brilliant solutions to health issues that may never have dawned on you before: how to diagnose and treat symptoms, relieve discomfort, even forewarn of illness. If I get sick dreams are the first place I turn. It doesn't matter how worried I am about my situation; the sanity, ego-free perspective, and wisdom of dreams anchor me.

What can dreams reveal about your body that even your doctor doesn't know? Can dreams diagnose illness? Listen to what happened to the author Marc Barasch. While putting in demanding hours as the editor in chief of *New Age Journal*, he had an unusually vivid dream. It made him afraid he had cancer, though he had no specific symptoms. Still, the dream haunted him. In *The Healing Path: A Soul Approach to Illness*, he writes:

> *An iron pot filled with red-hot coals hangs under my chin. . . . I feel the heat sear my throat, and I scream, the sound becoming hoarser, a raw animal desperation, as the coals gnaw my larynx. "Please, God, bring me out of here!" . . . I feel a black no-exit despair.*

The next morning Marc awoke devastated. The clarity of the dream, its sense of utter immediacy, compelled him to seek a medical opinion. Can you imagine going to your doctor symptomless, with only dream in hand, requesting a physical? In ancient Greece, no problem. But now? Marc had trouble convincing anyone to take him seriously. People reassured him: "It's just a dream," "You're overly stressed," "It's a metaphor for your fears." All plausible, but for Marc too pat. Blessed with chutzpah and an abiding belief in intuition, he persevered. Finally, he persuaded a doctor to examine him. A tumor that turned out to be thyroid cancer was found in his neck. Surely not a desired outcome.

Even so, prompted by the dream, timely treatment was initiated, halting the spread of Marc's cancer.

If you have a dream about your body, consider its message. As with Marc, it may be offered to you. Or you can formulate a question regarding your health. As I've previously suggested, before you go to sleep, ask for a straightforward dream to explain the matter. The more specific your request, the better. Record the response in your journal. If the answer isn't clear, continue doing this for a day, or a week, until you're satisfied. Maybe you're exhausted but don't know why. Perhaps you're torn about whether to have surgery. That's okay. See what your dream has to say. In those notoriously treatment-resistant illnesses— chronic fatigue syndrome, fibromyalgia (spasms of the neck and shoulders, aka the computer disease), or other intransigent pain— dream solutions can be of real value. They're equivalent to getting a second opinion. Avoid being locked into linear, medically definable interventions. Be aware that intuitive dream-wisdom does exist—whether it comes straight from the spirit of Asclepius, a higher power, or your higher self. It has something useful to say about your healing.

There are indications of whether a healing dream is intuitively accurate. Remember to look for these tried-and-true touchstones:

- Exceptionally vibrant imagery, colors, or sounds
- An oddly impersonal tone, neutrally imparting information
- A sense of indisputable "knowing" in your body
- A crispness and clarity to segments

Your relationship with dreaming is dynamic: You ask for a dream, you receive one, you interpret it. It may take a while to get in sync with the flow, but it will soon feel natural. You'll learn to work with your own symbols to get the knack of intuitive dream interpretation. Dream books, spelling out what imagery means, will give you a starting point, but ultimately they are limited. I would suggest reviewing Carl Jung's *Man and His Symbols*. For instance, you'll learn that ocean, in Latin *mare* or mother, is associated with emotions, feminine energy, the collective unconscious; fire associated with passion; birth with creativity, new beginnings. Acquaint yourself with such traditional interpretations. Apply each to your dream, but don't stop there. Build on them by seeing what unique truths your symbols hold for you. The Talmud says an unanalyzed dream is like an unopened letter. Here is a simple technique I use when intuitively interpreting my dreams:

FOUR TIPS ON INTUITIVE DREAM INTERPRETATION

1. On awakening record your dream immediately in a journal; you'll forget it if you don't.

2. Notice those images and dream symbols to which you're especially drawn or those that move you. Highlight them in your journal.

3. As soon as possible, go into meditation. Enter a neutral, receptive state. Gently hold the symbol in your mind. No analyzing, just let it hover. Specifically ask to be shown its significance.

4. Pay particular attention to any images, scenarios, memories, or physical sensations that arise. These intuitions come from the deepest part of you. They will explain your symbol.

Let me take you through a few examples of interpretation. In his psychoanalytic practice Freud noted that dreams can be physiological premonitions of illness. Still, two dreamers may have identical images about their health with radically divergent implications. What to do? Watch carefully the elegant role your intuition plays.

A few years ago, I dreamed I was diagnosed with AIDS. At the time everything in my life—projects, relationships, vacations—seemed to be falling through. Even the plumber couldn't seem to get it together to fix my toilet. I started getting grouchy, complaining a lot, becoming generally ungrateful. Then the dream came. It was so realistic, I woke up with my heart palpitating, panic-stricken. Thank God I was only dreaming, I thought the nanosecond my eyes cracked open. I rallied to attention. From that day on I counted my lucky stars to be alive. There's nothing like the threat of losing your health to bring an instant attitude adjustment! But how did I know my dream wasn't a premonition? To determine this, I had to try to set aside my fear—not easy, but essential—so I could accurately see. Next I got very quiet and inwardly posed a hard question: "Is my dream telling me I'm going to get AIDS?" I stayed open. As I listened with my intuition, it didn't ring true. No goose bumps. No lightbulbs flipping on. No affirming imagery or waves of recognition. I trusted myself. My dream was about not illness but life:

It was an attention-getting plea that succeeded in renewing my appreciation for living.

Now shift gears. Consider the same theme, different interpretation. My patient Ben also dreamed he had AIDS. Here is part of his account:

> *I'm wasting away in a hospital bed. My son is trying to murder me. He's injecting the AIDS virus into my veins through my IV. I feel strangely detached, like a witness to the scene. I watch myself struggling to stop him, but I'm paralyzed.*

A chilling vision. What message is this dream screaming out? Ben's son, at twenty-one an addictive gambler who refused to get a job, was emotionally and financially sucking him dry. Ben had enormous difficulty setting limits. This behavior, the dream emphatically announced, was killing Ben. Was the threat of AIDS literal? Or was Ben's dream simply a graphic expression of anguish and fear? How did he find out?

I helped him focus. Then I had Ben intuitively project into the future. Did he see himself with AIDS? What was the connection with his son? These were wrenching issues for him to confront. "It's like a gong went off in my solar plexus," Ben reported about his meditation. "I felt sick in every cell of my body. If I didn't act . . . if I didn't do something different with my son . . . I had the awful sense that the dream would come true. A heaviness hit me like I was sinking into a bed of quicksand."

Ben's dream was a harsh reality check, which he was wise to take seriously. It was a battle—but to preserve his health (and not enable his son), he changed his behavior. What would've happened if he hadn't? What if he had ignored his dream? Would you have taken that risk? What does *your* intuition say?

Some dreams paint an uncompromising picture of the stakes involved. The signs Ben attended to—the detached witness state he experienced and the total body confirmation—gave credence to the dream's intuitive content. Watch out for these qualities. If they're present you may need to take your dream at face value, a radical leap that could have far-reaching implications for improving your health or another's.

There are also dreams that communicate previews of what's to come, though you might not be able to avert it. For instance, it's the night before your camping trip to the Sierras. You dream you break your leg. You're not happy about it, but you heed the warning. While hiking you're especially careful—yet an accident still happens. Why did you have the dream? How can it benefit you?

My friend Brother James is a Benedictine monk and a healer. In his original letter to me he wrote: "In the midst of my life as a religious monk, people look to me for answers. I sometimes have dreams foreseeing illness in others that I can do nothing about. This upsets me tremendously." He told of the following dream:

I see a man I know from church. At a distance I watch as a bolt from a crossbow pierces him in the heart. I just stand there. It's clear. There's no way anyone can stop it.

The next day Brother James did some frantic phoning. Sadly, he discovered that the man he dreamed of had just had a heart attack. Confusion set in. Here was Brother James's dilemma. Living in a spiritual tradition dating back to 500 C.E. in which prayer can heal, he wasn't even given a chance to implement it. What purpose did foreknowledge of his parishioner's heart attack serve?

I see it this way. Prescience, whether in dreams or awake, is light-producing. There is something sacred about bearing testimony or being a witness to events as they unfold. Everything I see, whether a patient's illness or a joyful celebration, reflects the fullness of life, the ebb and flow I'm privileged to be part of. I need to be quite clear: Being intuitively receptive doesn't guarantee having the power to change everything you see. If you dream of illness you can't prevent, it's not purposeless or a foreshadowing of doom. View it as a healing light, a good omen. It's a tribute to the depth of intuitive resources you have available to meet the challenges ahead. Monk, therapist, or housewife, in the intuitive realm you must avoid getting hooked by codependency issues, shouldering too much responsibility for what is not yours. The wise and necessary imperative is to know what you can reasonably take on.

Sometimes, however, it is appropriate and possible to intervene in health matters. To clarify, your intuition will guide. To know if, when, and how to tell someone about a dream, always ask yourself these questions:

Will this information benefit the person?

A "yes" may express itself as a comfortable gut feeling, a burst of energy, a lightbulb flipping on, a sense of moving forward. A "no" can feel like you're hitting a brick wall, a thud, a hand pushing you away, a knowing of "don't go there." With practice you'll learn what yes and no feel like to you. If you are unsure, don't act. Keep tuning in until you get a clear message.

What is the most sensitive way to communicate?

Before speaking, put yourself in the other person's position. How could you best hear this news? Be kind, and never present yourself as the sole authority (even experienced intuitives are sometimes wrong). For instance, while a friend is painting his study, you dream he falls, breaking his leg. You could relate your dream, saying, "In case it's true, it may be worthwhile to be extra careful." This alerts the person without causing panic. An approach to avoid: "Watch out. I dreamed you're going to break your leg!"—a setup for a self-fulfilling prophecy. Get used to checking in with your intuition about phrasing; sometimes saying less is more. Err on the side of understatement, not hyperbole. If you dream a cousin has cancer, you might express only, "I dreamed you had a health problem. To tell you the truth, I don't know if it's accurate. Would you be willing to indulge me and see a doctor?" The ideal strategy is to be gentle but persuasive.

Dreams offer insight and at times can heal. Often the change can be subtle: a kink in your neck is gone, cold symptoms wane, a headache vanishes. Over the years I've dreamed that my spiritual teacher performs energy work on my body. I wake up invigorated. You may not even remember the details of your dream, but the next morning you feel indisputably better. Rarer, but still possible, are dramatic examples like the one my friend Linda told me.

When Linda was a freshman psychology student, she developed a lipoma, a benign fatty tumor at the base of her spine. In one month it had grown to the size of a billiard ball, causing considerable pain. She consulted a doctor, who suggested surgical removal. But Linda wanted neither a stressful operation nor the toxic side effects of general anesthesia. At home before she went to sleep, Linda prayed, "Please show me what to do." That night she dreamed there was a huge syringe next to her bed. Seemingly on its own, the syringe pierced the side of her neck, traveled the length of her spine, and extracted a milky fluid from the lipoma. When she awoke she recalled everything and rushed straight to the mirror. The lipoma was gone.

We are capable of dreams that mend the body. We can invite them in, or they can be offered as gifts. Most of us will experience more toned-down versions of healing than Linda did, yet her experience illustrates what can take place. When we interact with our dreams, tap into their curative potential, we cross into a realm many people deem science fiction. I am here to say that it is not so. As a physician I've seen the down-to-earth therapeutic impact dreams have had on my patients' well-being and my own. My hope is that I've imparted to you the health-enhancing implications of the intuitive messages your dreams convey. Witnessing such positive change so consistently over years of clinical practice has sustained me before the science behind it is fully documented.

HEALING OUR BODIES. How far does the mystery go? Neurochemicals, troops of white cells poised to protect, the right balance of medication and meditation, intuitive guidance, dreams, our subtle energy and positive beliefs. These elements constitute the core of our healing system. The intelligence of our bodies is programmed to help keep us well. But to what extent? How can we maximize a conscious link with our physiology? Exciting evidence is surfacing that our organs themselves contain intuitive blueprints for our healing. That they literally possess "cellular memories" for all that happens to us, including our medical conflicts and resolutions. Could it be possible to communicate intuitively with our organs? If so, what would the implications be for our health?

In *A Change of Heart,* Claire Sylvia, a high school teacher, gives an intriguing account of her heart-lung transplant. According to hospital policy, the donor's anonymity was to be preserved—yet she started dreaming of him. She actually saw what he looked like, learned his name, got to know him. Never had she experienced anything like this. After her transplant she developed odd cravings for chicken nuggets, green peppers, and beer, and she took on different personality traits, memories, behaviors. Desperate to make sense of these changes, she used clues communicated to her by the donor in dreams to track down his parents. To Claire's amazement she located them. They affirmed that her unfamiliar food cravings and behaviors all belonged to their son; it was his name and appearance that kept showing up in her dreams!

The concept of cellular memory is not new. It was first recognized when describing the immune system. Decades after being inoculated with the polio vaccine, for instance, our bodies retain an active recall of that viral antigen. In the same way it follows that our organs, tissues, and blood may contain concrete memories. Claire Sylvia is the living testament. Many more transplant patients are reporting similar experiences. Relating this to the five steps I'm presenting, we'll see that illness can be understood and more readily abated by looking further than even the brain—toward an intuition that is organically seamless with our body's atomic core. There is a certain humility to this stance, a fairer distribution of instinctual knowledge. Thus, during illness contact the intuitive information your body stores and let it work for you.

There are possibilities within illness that you may not anticipate. Who of us would ever choose disease? Still, if it is upon you, begin to look at it as a form of healing not punishment. The shamanic premise that illness is a profound spiritual initiation applies here. See all health challenges with these eyes and the night sky will be lit up with a million stars. If you don't there will be only darkness. It is your decision. Illness is not failure. Approach it as a student; accept what it has to teach. Ride the dragon. Let your spirit grow strong. *Vocatus atque non vocatus deus aderit.* Invoked or not invoked, the god is present.

5

Death As Healer and Teacher

> To die is different than anyone supposes, and luckier.
> —Walt Whitman

*S*o you think death isn't funny? On a flight from Chicago to Los Angeles, I was seated in economy class in the middle of a group of twenty saffron-robed Tibetan monks. All of us, packed like sardines, headphones glued to our ears, cracking up watching a *Seinfeld* episode. The theme was fear of death. "Whaddaya mean, am I afraid of death?" George blurts out in his friends' coffee shop hangout. "Are you crazy? Of course I am. Who wouldn't be?" Spoken like a true New Yorker. The monks roared with glee. For George it was downhill from there. He launched into an angst-ridden tirade. Pacing, fidgeting, sweating: a neurotic poster boy for our collective anxiety. The monks could barely contain themselves. Truly, it was a priceless scene. Can you imagine having such a lighthearted view of death? A belief so strong in the eternality of the spirit that fear of dying might strike you as absurd?

Such cosmic humor comes not only from faith but from intuition. Facing what death is brings freedom, brings knowledge, brings peace. On a basic level facing death gives insight into our biological cycles, an appreciation for the defining rhythms of being human. This alone is magnificent. But suppose there's something more? How can we know? How can we reach further than our dis-ease? Here's where intuition comes in. Why not use it to get a closer look at what we're dealing with? Is death an end? A beginning? A doorway into another realm? Is it really as unknowable as they say? Or can our intuition peer into territory that, for our rational minds, is inconceivable?

I invite you to investigate. We're on the threshold of seeing death in a deeper way. When Columbus set sail from Spain, critics predicted he'd fall into oblivion at the earth's edge. Instead, a new world was found. How does this analogy relate to understanding death? Our journey is internal, our compass inner-directed. The irony is, if we approach the edge we're most afraid of, we might find it never existed. Fear perpetuated the illusion. Delving into death may seem like a gamble. I know that trusting your intuition this much takes courage. I also know it may entail a suspension of disbelief. But hear my conviction: To live life joyously, you must encounter death head-on.

Fear of death stops us. When left underground it insidiously haunts our lives. We make it the bogeyman. Every day as we grow older, it looms closer. We find it morbid to speak of, shield our children from its inevitability, avoid it in every possible way. But who's fooling whom? What's the good of procrastinating? Don't put off dealing with death until the final moment—if you're sick or, even worse, about to die. A saner, certainly more liberating approach is to come to terms with these issues early on. This is a quality-of-life decision, not just a position to take when you depart—as you surely will.

Medicine must adopt a more enlightened view as well. So much of health care is permeated by physicians' lurking dread of death. From birth, and throughout our medical care, that aversion is instilled. For most physicians death is a failure. The fact that death, in certain cases, may be the perfect healing is overlooked. By this I mean that the lessons of dying, of death, and beyond, are vital contributors to our spiritual growth—the striving for self-compassion, the dissolving of ego and our physical form, the faith found from such surrender, all are revelations. Here we can reconcile monumental forces: This is why stories about death make me feel whole. And as for what comes after? Could this represent a healing too? So many mysteries. There comes a time when each of us must leave this earth. We need our doctors to recognize that moment, defer to it, and usher us out of this world with as much dignity and optimism as possible.

I know how hard such yielding is for doctors. They're conditioned, trained, sworn to fight for life. It's almost antithetical to their nature to get out of the way. *Harrison's Principles of Internal Medicine,* the medical students' Bible, says it well: "No problem is more distressing than that presented by the patient with incurable disease, particularly if death is inevitable." When my mother was clearly dying, in a coma for days, I had to be the one to broach the necessity of hospice care with her doctor. The inescapable reality that she was terminal, that the kindest thing we could do was relieve her pain, and let her go, went unspoken far too long. My mother's physician, her lifelong friend, admitted, "I didn't want to face it. It was too painful even to consider losing her. I should have done more." He'd been in denial. I felt for him, but simultaneously my world was collapsing. I'd needed him to take the lead. He hadn't.

My goal in this chapter is to facilitate a reevaluation of death. I ask you again to invoke the Buddhist notion of beginner's mind, blend it with intuition, and see what you learn. I can tell you that when you die there's nothing to be afraid of; your spirit is luminous, timeless, strong. But each of you needs to find this out for yourself. It's your right to make sure. Think of how such knowledge will alter your concept of aging. Of loss. Of grief. Of life. I want to give you an uplifting look at a passage with a bad rap. Getting an intuitive appreciation of death brings solace. It also better prepares us to help loved ones or patients pass on. The artificial boundary between life and death is more permeable than we think.

Step 1. Notice Your Beliefs

You are entitled to believe whatever you want about death. You are entitled to a death of your own choosing. There is no right or wrong, only a feeling of comfort. The difficulty is that if you're being driven by fear or haven't afforded yourself permission to consider many points of view—traditionally religious or not—you sacrifice the freedom of asserting your own stand, one that is intuitively sound.

To many cultures death is not the enemy. For example, consider the Irish wake, a celebratory send-off for the deceased. The Native American belief of "dying into wholeness." The Buddhist concept of afterlife and reincarnation. And, in Mexico, on the eve of October 31, the beloved annual festival *la dia del la Muerte,* the Day of the Dead. Streets are packed with people shaking rattles, dancing, wearing sequined death masks in tribute to the change that death brings. Children devour chocolate skulls, delight in blowing up paper skeletons with firecrackers. On the outskirts of towns, cemetery grounds are overrun with families partying at grave sites in the hope of luring spirits of departed relatives back with the music and edibles they loved, even portable televisions set to their favorite programs.

What's wrong with this picture? Death, a reason to have fun? For many of us it's a mind-blowing proposition. To achieve an earned optimism about death we must reappraise our preconceptions. Apprehension may be a knee-jerk response to what we've been taught (or not taught) rather than a genuine intuition. I'm always amazed at how firmly rooted certain assumptions about death can be. Over and over again intelligent, sensitive people seem to me stymied, thwarted, blocked. Now's *your* chance to start anew. Call it a collaboration between intellect and instinct, a sincere effort to arrive at a core-felt personal truth. You don't have to justify your conclusions to anyone. But they must feel authentic to you.

FOUR MYTHS ABOUT DEATH

MYTH 1: *You Have to Be Sick to Die*

At age eighty my grandmother was losing her memory, but her body was strong. She spent her last years in a retirement home a few miles from me. The night she died I was the one they called; my parents were traveling and couldn't be contacted. I was told that Grandmom had been sitting in her favorite rocking chair, eating a vanilla ice cream cone. When she finished she mentioned to her companion how delicious it was, slumped over, and died. No fanfare. No fuss. A perfect departure.

Illness isn't necessarily a prerequisite for death. Harrison's *Principles of Internal Medicine* goes so far to say: "The diseases to which humans ultimately succumb do not alter very greatly the predetermined life span. Indeed, if it were possible to avoid them all, the average life span would not be lengthened beyond ten years." Even without disease death is inescapable; parts wear out. An old tape in need of reprogramming is that sickness and death are irrevocably united, that there is no other way to die. Buddhist tradition tells of illustrious Zen masters, still healthy, who proceeded to die. Legends say they knew exactly when their moment of death would come. No fear. No regret. Without any sign of illness, they prepared themselves, bathed, shaved their heads, gathered their students together for a few final words, closed their eyes, and were gone.

Fixated, we equate death with disease, but we may not need to get sick at all. Could it be that sometimes dying is more a function of proper timing than of age, stress factors, or genetics, that death need not involve severe physical decline? My Jewish grandmother and the venerable Zen masters (what extremes!) are two role models that attest to this. I'm not saying that illness can always be avoided when you die, or that you've failed if it can't. I'm simply encouraging you not to feed into a self-fulfilling prophecy that may be untrue or to reflexively brace yourself for the worst. Our exit from the body can go many ways, some easy, some more vexing. A nonfear-based approach to death can only help.

MYTH 2: *Death Is Contagious*

Looking for a conversation stopper? Try mentioning death at a party. Watch how quickly people look stricken, poised to stampede out of the room. What kind of mentality does this express? The D word has an aura of superstition around it, as if merely uttering it will bring it on. What about the converse? Will not speaking of it make it go away? I know many otherwise self-aware people who act just this way. When you get down to it, the norm in our society is to see death as morbid—even contagious, as though it is an infectious disease.

When my patient Holly's mother was dying, her best friend barely called. In those months she seemed to disappear. Holly felt abandoned. During their rare conversations her friend sidestepped the issue: Her life was crazed, she was on deadline, her husband's family was in town, yada yada . . . Only after Holly's mother passed away did her friend level with her. "I was a coward," she apologized. "I know this will sound weird, but I was afraid to get too close. I didn't want your experience with death to rub off on me."

Many people feel the same way. Do you? If so, don't beat yourself up. It was brave for Holly's friend to be so honest. That's a start. From there, move forward. Just know that the most contagious element of death is your fear of it. What you resist sticks to you like glue, an intuitive truth you can depend on. Evaluate your beliefs about death. Release them from the realm of superstition. Allow the sunlight to heal attitudes you may never have unearthed before.

MYTH 3: *You Are Only Your Body*

In the sixties I was a wild teenager. I experimented with drugs. I wrestled with my intuitive self, curious one minute, running from it the next. Ignoring consequences (who thought about those then?), at four-teen I tried LSD. In my bedroom I was standing in front of a mirror. I watched fascinated—transfixed, really—as my face started to age. I saw myself at twenty, thirty, sixty, eighty. It was odd; I should've been afraid, but I wasn't. There I was, a wrinkled crone, then a mere skeleton, then powder, then I vanished. But through it all, astonishingly, I felt the same. At this young age I learned a lesson I'll never forget: I was more than my body.

I'm certainly not suggesting that you take drugs, or that they are necessary to reach such a revelation. Intuition alone is sufficient. In my naïveté I bumbled into a cosmic truth, one that coincides with the be-liefs of cultures ranging from ancient Egyptian to Native American: The body is temporal. It houses our spirit while on earth. Intuition can teach us that we are in the body but not of the body. It offers greater in-sight into this relationship than the mind will bring. Knowing firsthand that you are more than your body can reassure you and transform your thinking about death.

MYTH 4: *Death Is an End*

Death may not be as dangerous as we think. In fact, it could be the safest thing we'll ever do. My Iranian healer, Hadi, had a sudden intu-ition he was going to die. Though in good health, he informed his fam-ily and calmly set about putting his affairs in order. A month later he suffered a terminal stroke. His family called to notify me. Hadi's kind-hearted message to his patients was simply, "Good-bye and good luck." I was upset, concerned his relatives would be crushed. But they ex-plained to me, "In our culture we view death differently than you do. Hadi came here. He was of service to people. And now he's moved on. He lived a full life. Of course we'll grieve, but we also understand that death isn't final." The family's attitude was not unfeeling or complacent but full of compassion and faith that the spirit exists beyond time and space.

At the least it is undeniable that loved ones live on in our memories. In this sense death can never be an end. When I was six my grandfather told me, "When I'm gone, just look up at the brightest star in the sky. It will be me watching over you." To this day, thirty years after his death, I see him there. Can people live on in energy too? Is it possible to feel them, communicate with them? Can the power of the heart be our con-nector? Here is where I'd like you to stretch a little. Use your imagination; sense what's possible. Remember that, on an intuitive level, time and space blur. Given these new parameters, reach beyond this life. Open up. See how far your intuition will go.

WHY IS THE SUBJECT of death so charged? Our fears so monstrous? How can we quell them? Even spiritual leaders are not immune. While I was having lunch with a local rabbi with a huge, devoted congregation, he reluctantly admitted how burdened he felt, constantly inundated with deaths. Conflicted about death himself, he was confused by each person's passing. He could hardly bear presiding over another funeral. My heart went out to him.

If unresolved, fear becomes gargantuan. A Japanese newspaper reported a true story of a Tokyo commuter possessed by a phobic dread of dying in a tidal wave. "I am terrified of water, and death by drowning is my greatest fear," he said in an Associated Press report. To hedge his bets against drowning, he'd devised inflatable underwear that could expand to thirty times its original size. One day he accidentally set it off in a crowded subway. "My underwear were crushing everyone in the carriage until a passenger stabbed them with a pencil."

The beast stirs. What are we so afraid of? Let's get down to it: Pain. Lack of control. Lack of choice. Unfinished business. Missed opportunities. Fear of the unknown. Hell. The Devil. Purgatory. Isolation. Oblivion. Limbo. Maybe there's nothing there. Loneliness. Being alone. Abandoned. Lost. Depressed. Miserable. Disoriented. Uh-oh, no God? Estranged from people we love. Separation from the earth. Being judged. Punished. Powerless.

There it is. Do any of these fears hit home? Feel free to add others. You must name your fears before you can liberate yourself from them. Doing this exercise, realize the big difference between your fear of the grief you'll suffer from losing someone and your apprehension of the actual transition of death. From accounts of people who've had near-death experiences, the passage itself is enjoyable. So pleasant, in fact, that most have no desire to return. Grief, by contrast, can torment—but if we don't shut down, it will ultimately lead us to open our hearts more.

Grieving, we must mourn all attachments to our loved ones' physical state. We can no longer run to the phone to call them, give them a hug, or hear their voices. Granted this is an enormous loss to confront. Even so, for closure to occur an intuitive disconnection from their bodies is required—healing comes when we can begin to see them as more than flesh and blood. This doesn't mean we won't adore them as much as ever. We simply must become accustomed to communicating in a different way: with our intuition. In dreams, meditations, and quiet moments, see if you can feel your loved ones close by. Let your grief be the impetus for honing a keener intuitive sense.

The memorials to grief are the gravestones we erect, the burial plots where we place the remains of our most precious ones. They are expressly for us survivors, places of return so we can remember. I recommend everyone visit a cemetery. Check out the headstones. Engraved on them are haikus of our essence. On my mother's stone, at her request, is her favorite motto, "Never say never. Say maybe." On other stones nearby are "Don't sweat the little things," "A beloved mother and wife," "A just man," "A survivor," "A woman of valor," "A man who loved." Pertinent messages about life. Cemeteries can be power places where we set our priorities straight, reconnect with loved ones and ourselves. They need not be morbid. Nor need they be on earth! In Tokyo there's a shortage of land. One temple is working toward the ultimate space solution—the virtual tomb. After a loved one's ashes are scattered, relatives will be able to visit his or her cybertomb on the Internet. There'll also be virtual candles and the chanting of virtual monks.

I recently found out that since 1928 over sixty thousand weddings have been performed at Forest Lawn cemetery in Los Angeles. How could this be? Are there just a lot of weird people out there? Was there a bargain rate? Or were these couples simply so at ease with—oblivious of?—the life-death cycle that they'd choose to marry in a cemetery? I called to inquire. The "wedding coordinator" was an upbeat man who told me that, yes, Forest Lawn did use the same chapel for weddings and funerals—but he assured me the events were scheduled at different times. And, yes, during the wedding ceremony you could see the cemetery outside. With as much tact as I could muster, I asked, "Why would someone *want* to be married at Forest Lawn?" A real pro, the wedding coordinator seemed used to the question. "We model our chapels after the old-time European churches. In the past, marriages, christenings, and burials were all performed in the same village church. The cemetery would be next door. It was accepted by everyone. Death wasn't separated from the rest of life as it is today."

I had to admit, his argument made sense. Still, those village churches weren't surrounded by acres of grave sites with dozens of

Acropolis-like mausoleums. Nonetheless, the notion that there need be no separation between the sacraments of life and death surely contains insight. It might even be a sane alternative to our society's ingrained death phobia.

Is it possible to shed such intense negative conditioning? To awaken, we must try. Nothing forced. Nothing too ambitious. Baby steps will do. Forget marrying at Forest Lawn! Imagine visiting an old town church in the south of France, set for centuries at the heart of the seasons of human life. Beautiful, isn't it? Life and death both present but not opposed. Allow yourself to intuit the totality of your humanness. Take in the oneness. With the marriage of heaven and earth comes unification. When death, grief, birth, life, and loving couplings evidence themselves as distinct, shining points on a sacred mandala, we can become whole.

Our acceptance of the life-death cycle and the finiteness of the human form gives opportunity for closure. A time of satisfaction that all is complete. It affords us a say about how our deaths may be. The circumstances—where you die, who you die with—are a personal matter. A reflection, liberating to anticipate. It could be that you prefer to just let death happen, not think too much about it at all. That's one way. There are also others. Let's look at the very different deaths of three American authors.

Shamelessly aiming to shatter society's taboos and phobias, Timothy Leary turned his death from liver cancer into a festive public event. In a moment-to-moment update of his dying process, even his last words, "Why not?" and "Yeah," were posted on the World Wide Web. Then, along with those of Gene Roddenberry, creator of *Star Trek*, Leary's ashes were shot into space via satellite. In contrast, Carlos Castaneda, anthropologist and sorcerer, shrouded his death in secrecy. The press didn't get wind of it for months, nor did his best friends. No funeral was held; his ashes were whisked off to an unknown location in Mexico. As for Buckminster Fuller, this genius was in robust health at eighty-seven. However, he died of a sudden heart attack while visiting his comatose wife in the hospital. He'd commented days before that she was clinging to life only because she didn't want to leave him behind. Did something in Fuller's psyche pick a moment, just let go? After months of hanging on, his wife died thirty-six hours later.

I hope these stories provoke you to delve freely into what your beliefs are. Be creative, not bound by convention. Discard the outmoded, the fear-driven; adopt a position that intuitively rings true. Most of all, let your heart dictate the stand you take, allow it to evolve over the years. A conscious relationship with your life and death deepens the reach of your healing.

QUESTIONS FOR REFLECTION

- What are your views on death? How have they changed with time? What has influenced you?

- What would allow you to come to terms with death, to not view it as an enemy? What do you most need to know from your intuition to console you?

- Do you believe in an afterlife? Why? Why not? Are you still uncertain? If so, are you ready to use your intuition to explore such a possibility?

Step 2. Be in Your Body

When does science deem the body lifeless? What legally constitutes physical death? In recent times the definition has shifted from cardiac arrest to "brain death," as exemplified by a flat EEG. According to a Massachusetts General Hospital report, death has occurred when all brain stem and spinal reflexes are gone. So is that it for us? Is that all there is?

As a medical intern at Wadsworth VA Hospital in Los Angeles, I had the privilege of working on a hospice unit, a separated ward where terminal patients, many without families, were sent to die. My main job, I found out, was to pronounce people dead. No one could have adequately prepared me for such a task. I had always imagined that when people died they would appear much the same as when alive, only more at peace. In part that was true. More striking, though, the body looked plastic, hollow, a mere shell, resembling a motionless statue in a wax museum. The eerie, impersonal vacancy of flesh alone replaced a once-luminous force. Spiritless, the body's brightness dimmed; its essence vanished. Such visible contrast accentuated the spirit's place, allowed me to better intuit it.

One way to gain evidence that you exist distinct from physical form is to view a dead body. If the time ever comes that you're a witness to someone's death at bedside, consider not looking away. Or, at a funeral with an open casket, note what you see. Observe the body carefully. Notice the skin, the eyes, the face. Compare your impressions with how the person looked in life. Is it different? Odd? Distorted? More beautiful? In what way? Do your best to remain open to your reactions. Are you fascinated? Do you feel afraid? More centered? Repelled? What is your body telling you? It's natural to be put off. But see if you can go further. Take a breath. Relax. What else can you pick up? Stay aware of any intuitive flashes, images, or knowings you may have. Place the palm of your hand a few inches over the skin. What do you feel? Try to sense if energy is radiating from the body. You may perceive it as heat, pressure, or subtle vibration on your palm. Notice everything. There's wisdom in the experience: Witnessing the absence of spirit acutely accentuates awareness of what spirit is.

I know the mere mention of a dead body sets into play numerous resistances: We're not supposed to look; we're not supposed to touch; it's creepy, disgusting, weird. Slowly but surely, begin to desensitize these misinformed views. Reorient yourself. It's a beautiful thing to learn about the body, in all its phases. See what you discover. I've found that by rooting out old conditioning we make room for new knowledge. Surprising missing pieces, reflecting the enduring brilliance of your spirit.

My friend Don, a Zen Buddhist and rabbi, told me of a touching Jewish memorial service he participated in. In preparation for the burial the deceased woman's body was lovingly washed with water and scented oil by her closest female relatives and friends, then reverently clothed in her meditation robes. Afterward the men joined them. It was not a chore for the women or distasteful. Rather this ritual was a final chance to exhibit tenderness toward a loved one's body, to purify it.

I heard this and felt instantly relieved. A part of me I'd been doubting was affirmed. When my mother was lying in an open coffin, my impulse was to embrace her one last time; to fix in my sense-memory the feel of the body that had birthed me. I placed my arms around my mother. I closed my eyes, resting my head gently on her chest. Strange, to be so close and not hear my mother's heart beat. Her skin was cold, rigid, but very smooth. I wanted to stay near her body, watch it, hold it, until I felt ready to let go. But I stopped myself. People were staring. Was I doing something wrong? No one else, including my father, showed even the slightest desire to get near her. They all looked at me, impatient, awkward. A difficult moment, a difficult day. I didn't intend to make it harder for anyone. Not wanting to offend, I joined my father in the next room.

When a loved one dies his or her body need not be off-limits. You're entitled to have contact with it if you choose. I've worked with patients who've had little need for such interaction as well as those who've wanted it very much. We each have our own intuitive rhythms of letting go. It's important to honor yours. Death means physical separation. That we must accept. But your experience of disengaging has much to do with you. This process is never easy. But by giving yourself time with a loved one's body, you can bring gentleness to closure, soften the adjustment to loss. At such sacred moments a primal interchange occurs, a body-to-body farewell. A meeting of fire, water, air, and earth, all we're made of. A time to bow to another, paying final tribute to the material form—then to move forward into life and the future.

During the dying process the body also needs to be properly watched over. Typically in a hospital setting with terminal patients, nurses and doctors grow remote, tentative; they physically pull away. A patient receives clinical care—blood pressure and heart rate are recorded, IV's refurbished, sheets efficiently changed. Functional contact, that's about it. The discomfort is palpable. Too many caregivers, including physicians, have distaste in their eyes. They may try to hide it, may be unaware it's there. Communicating fear, conscious or unconscious, isn't useful. I know that when I die I want people around me who can shine light, won't treat me like I have cooties.

We can assist our loved ones' transition out of the body; or, when it's our turn to go, they can assist us. This is a great service. Whether at home or in a hospital, it's very special to be surrounded by those who have faith in the ongoing life of the spirit. Hospice workers and dedicated round-the-clock nursing assistants are unacknowledged heroes on the front lines; they are trained to sit with the dying, to impart courage. They know to do this. Whenever possible, choose people like these (doctors as well) to be around you. Before the moment comes, try to find out what your practitioners believe about death; request to have those present who are unafraid. As you leave your body, your friends and caregivers will give you a gentle liftoff. Let the love in their eyes be the last sight you see.

When you die it's your right to decide what happens to your body. This is a matter of preference, not merely convention. Perhaps you prefer to be buried next to your beloved husband, along with generations of family. Maybe not. Perhaps you want to be cremated, ashes scattered when Jupiter rises over the Caspian Sea. It is your say, no one else's. My mother's dearest friend, Elizabeth, before her recent death at eighty-five, declared, "I want to be buried next to Maxine [my mother]. We lived in the same condominium building for years. Why can't I be with my friend?" Different, yes, but a sweet request. It took some doing—Elizabeth's relatives were buried elsewhere—but her daughter respected her wishes. When the time came she was buried right across from my mother, neighbors in life and death. I know this: At Elizabeth's funeral I was there, standing by my mother's grave.

Birth. Life. Death. The body transforms. It matters how you approach its care. There is a lightness than comes from standing back, acknowledging its cycles. By grasping the bigger picture, you can find a meaningful purpose and perspective to your life. Maybe you'll even get an intuitive peek at what happens beyond the body. Wouldn't that be something?

Step 3. Sense Your Body's Subtle Energy

Dear Judith,
I recently visited my grandmother, who's 102 years old. The doctors said she had only a few days to live. I'd never seen a human being in such a state—just skin and bones. She rarely opened her eyes. When she did, it was like she was looking into the dark. She didn't recognize me. I couldn't do much but hold her hand. Surprisingly, I felt a very strong life force. From this I knew she'd live longer than the doctors thought. I was right. In the past few months she's gotten stronger. She even sits up at a table and is eating again. This makes me very happy.

When I received this letter from my friend Ludwig in Germany, I was struck by the sensitivity he showed to his grandmother's subtle energy. Simply by touching her hand, with no words exchanged, he felt the life within her. "A warm, tingling sensation rushed from my grandmother into me. An undeniable aliveness, almost like an electrical charge or zing," Ludwig wrote. He was able to know what the doctors didn't. Ludwig's recognition of his grandmother's still vibrant core energy was a sure sign that she wasn't ready to die. Despite her abnormal medical tests and drastic physical deterioration, the energy Ludwig described is always diagnostic of life, not death. Our life force is perceptible. It's important that you get used to discerning it.

Life has a certain feel, death another. Get to know the difference. The best way is to close your eyes and hold a friend's hand. Notice everything about it. Is it warm? Cool? Tight? Relaxed? Can you feel a pulse? Then, beyond the physical, see if you can detect a passage of energy between you. You may sense it as a soft breeze, a vapor, electricity, a vibration, a transmission of emotion, even love. It might filter slowly or gush into you. No matter, register it all. Sensitize yourself to the intricate patterns of energy flow. Connect it with life.

In contrast, when someone is about to die, the intensity of his or her energy wanes. If you hold a dying person's hand, it often feels distant, faint, fading, diluted, as if something is trying hard to bubble up to the surface yet can't. Given the chance to be with someone nearing death, I hope you take it. See what you perceive. Feel for yourself how different life's energy is from death's. During medical school I spent long nights sitting with the dying, sensing the fluctuations of their energy—as death approached and when the moment arrived. It was mesmerizing, never morbid. I watched, witnessed, remembered. To me, this knowledge was indispensable. Shadow and light juxtaposed. Next to death, life more fully defines itself. You can almost see it, flickering, fine strands of silk-light braiding, unbraiding, dissolving before your eyes—substance, then substance no more. Be still and the energy will dance for you. Let death teach you about life.

When I was working in the hospice, it became evident that some patients starting dying many months before their actual deaths. With awe I tracked their energy as it gradually disengaged from the body. A delicate molting took place. Death wasn't abrupt or possible to pinpoint, as it is usually thought to be. No sudden jolt, rather what felt like a measured departure, in sync with a steady metamorphosis. The volume seemed to be slowly turned down. This taught me that how we leave this world is as unique as how we're birthed into it. Caring for dying patients, I could tell energetically when the transition began. Thus, I could be more understanding of my patients' needs.

To be loving with the dying we must know when to let go. Energy will tell us this. As my beloved fourteen-year-old Labrador retriever Pipe was dying (she waited until I graduated from my psychiatry residency at UCLA), I called my mother from the animal hospital. She rushed across town to meet me. Arriving, she saw me sitting in the kennel holding Pipe in my arms. "You must say good-bye and leave," she advised. "Pipe will fight to stay alive as long as you're with her." I knew my mother was right. My energy was holding Pipe here. As difficult as it was, my mother and I went home. My dog died soon afterward.

When a loved one is nearing death, your intuition will communicate what to do. In the moment you must surrender all expectations about how the passage will occur. Perhaps you wanted to be with your favorite uncle at the time of his death. And there you were at his side, loving him completely. Sometimes what you long for may be what's right. But if you find that your intuition demands another plan, you must improvise. Let the subtle energy you perceive determine proper action.

You may empathically sense the onset of the dying process. My father had been dying for months. His doctors hadn't said so, but I knew. The bloodline we share echoed within me that certainty. I felt his spirit receding. A part of me—an aspect of my subtle energy—was dying along with him. I sensed this as an islet of warmth dissolving, a vibration stilled, a thread still woven within but now null and void. Language describing the approach of death is often poetic. I recommend reading *Japanese Death Poems: Written by Zen Monks and Haiku Poets on the Verge of Death*, compiled by Yoel Hoffmann. A tribute to the centuries-old tradition of *jiseri*, the "death poem," this collection presents hundreds of accounts of what dying feels like. Poignant, hilarious, profound, they've been recorded during the last moments of each poet's life. These poems portray the variations of the language of subtle energy.

Discover what your language is. The energy shift that occurs when a loved one dies is an adjustment all survivors must make, though most people remain unaware of it. We have no context within which to define the experience. Loss and subsequent grief are wrenching partially because in them we sacrifice a piece of ourselves, one not requisite for survival yet one whose absence leaves us vacant, vulnerable. This energy-based phenomenon needs to be recognized while we're grieving. It will add clarity, a bittersweet awareness making closure more complete.

Another enigma to the cycling of energy is fascinating to observe. Have you noticed that sometimes shortly after a grandparent dies, a grandchild is born? Or when a wife passes on after years of marriage, the husband soon follows? I can only speculate why. Webster's defines infinity as "a part of a geometric magnitude that lies beyond any part" and as "a distance so great that the rays of light from a point source at that distance can be regarded as parallel." Infinity . . . Can you imagine? The seamlessness of life and death—the responsive filling of a vacuum that results from transformation. On and on it goes. What can we learn from it?

My cousin Dean had the ingenuity to map the process. He and his wife, Gayle, were trying to conceive a baby for months with no luck. During this period Gayle's mother was dying of colon cancer. The month following her passing, Gayle got pregnant. Not only that, but it occurred to Dean to notice that she conceived on the anniversary of his father's death, and that their child's due date was his father's birthday! Was this coincidence or something more?

What I know is this: Energy has continuity. As quantum mechanics dictates, matter and energy are neither created nor destroyed—they undergo constant transmutation. Ancients recognized the mysticism and energy of numbers as well as the effects of the stars' positions on earth's events (births, deaths, the rise and fall of governments and cultures). These ideas, distilled, are a function of energy flow; death illuminates its cycles. Your intuition is the way in. Let it be innovative in its inquiry, so you can know. You—who are part of nature, part of life— must learn of death too. Only then will the circle be complete.

Step 4. Ask for Inner Guidance

Let me tell you a surprising thing I've intuited about death. I hope it will diminish your concerns and console you. I've come to see death as a creative force we can draw on in life. It is so much more than the dissolution of the body, as the myopic Western view suggests. Most of us are oblivious to death's life-affirming properties. I've learned from intuition that death is present from the instant of birth, throughout our day-to-day existence, and when we depart.

There's a remote viewing meditation I take people through in my workshops to allow them to experience firsthand the multidimensional nature of death. My purpose is to show that death is nothing to dread, that you exist beyond the body. You may approach this exercise having had a lifelong spiritual practice that has prepared you to meet death with equanimity and faith. Or perhaps this subject has always made you anxious. Or maybe you've preferred not to think much about death at all, to take it as it comes. It's true—sometimes the act of dying itself may be the only preparation required for the transition. Simple: You learn as you go. The mind expands. The veil lifts. Much becomes clear. Then it's over. But if you are interested in intuitively learning of death in the here-and-now, let me gently guide you. This may be a leap, I realize. We're at a point where you must trust your intuition. The ordinary mind can't lead you there. Your spirit can. Take a chance and see.

EXPERIENCING DEATH:
A REMOTE VIEWING MEDITATION

1. Sit upright in a relaxed position. Take a few slow, deep breaths. Feel the warmth of your breath as air passes through your lungs, out your mouth. Be completely present. For a few minutes inhale, then exhale. Take your time. Relax and gradually soften.

2. Now, as you become more settled, focus on what you love the most. It could be a person, a place, the first sliver of autumn moon, or even your connection with spirit. Whatever you choose, let beauty and love surround you. Allow your heart to open until you feel centered and secure.

3. When you're at ease, get ready to silently invite death in. Try to let go of preconceived impressions or images of death. If they appear, let them pass. Picture death as a presence, an energy, a force. At a pace that feels safe, ask death to come nearer. Go as slowly as you like.

First visualize death as being ten feet away from you. What do you sense? What do you see? Colors? Fragrances? Sounds? Take it all in. Acclimate yourself to the experience. Then, at the proper time, gradually decrease the distance. Five feet . . . three feet . . . two feet . . . a foot. No rush. At every stage, ease into it. How do your perceptions change? What more are you learning? Notice any spontaneous visions or new ideas, but don't hold on too tight. Keep focused on your breath. Stay open. Rely on your intuition to signal when to proceed.

4. Once a comfort level is established, allow yourself to slowly merge with death. Melt into the energy. Become one with it. Dissolve into spirit as your body naturally slips away. Pure energy. All heaviness recedes. You grow lighter and lighter.

Take a moment to orient yourself. How do you feel? Calm? At peace? Confused? Exhilarated? What are you observing? Is there silence? Music? Light? Does anyone or anything look familiar? Notice it all. Cling to nothing. Breathe into the vastness. Breathe out, unbound by physical constraints. Breathe into the sweetness. Breathe out all pain

and concerns. Breathe in and grow large in spirit. Breathe out and relinquish the body you've left behind. Breathe in the utter bliss of spirit.
Breathe out the boundlessness of love. Edges yield. No separation. No
holding. Effortless. You are light as a feather. Let death carry you. Float.
Rise. Soar. The sky is never-ending. Discover how luminous and free
you are. Linger until the experience feels complete. Remember what
happens. In the future, you can come here again.

5. Gradually prepare yourself to return to your body. Clearly picture
your physical self. Allow gravity to draw you back to your body, toward
earth and the material. With gratitude, inwardly acknowledge what
you've been shown. Then solidly reconnect with feet, arms, chest, neck,
and head, fully grounding yourself in your physical form. Give yourself
all the time you need to make this adjustment.

If during this exercise you feel frightened or hesitant, it's okay to
stop. Let what you've gained sink in. At a later time, when it feels right,
you may go further. Some people prefer to practice this meditation in
increments. Check in with yourself. Honor your own pace.

I promise you, intuitively looking into death is possible and safe.
When you think of it, is sleep so dissimilar to death? Every night we
jump into bed, close our eyes, and drift off, no longer weighted down.
Then gone, out of our bodies. Every morning we return. This remote
viewing can be much the same. Many people fear that if you try to explore death, you'll die. Not true. Some evenings, after an exhausting
workday, I purposely meditate and seek death out. For years I've gone
to death to replenish myself. I also turn to it if I'm creatively blocked.
Bursts of ideas can break through, solutions I hadn't conceived. Death
is a muse that inspires, energizes. It makes sense that we benefit from
the same creative boost when we finally transition out of the body.

I utilize this meditation to enable patients, terminal or not, to diffuse fear. Often when one nears death there's an urgency to glimpse
what lies ahead, an instinctive need to know. In such cases I integrate
this exercise into psychotherapy. One of my roles as a physician, I believe, is to support patients through this transition. Even if someone is
in perfect health, a remote viewing of death can be pertinent. Not only
as a look at what's upcoming but as a doorway through time to a holy
place where we partake of the freshest of waters—then resume our lives
renewed.

In the same way, the near-death experience gives a more informed perspective about the goings-on beyond this life. These days nearly everyone—housewives, children, doctors, mystics, Larry King!—seems to be having one. Often near-death experiences are prompted by acute traumas—auto accidents, the stopping of the heart during surgery, head injury. Physical shock seems to trigger a perceptual opening, a peek into a realm we might not otherwise see. Some commonalities are reported: a feeling of absolute peace, a vision of white light, a tunnel, a meeting with loved ones who've died, even a complete life review, demanding a compassionate accounting for all that has taken place.

If your experiences of death differ, don't worry. Perceptions can be fiercely individual. One is not more enlightened, desirable, or accurate than another. Many factors come into play. Suppose you don't have the slightest desire to be met by your dearly departed relatives? Or perhaps you were a loner in life with few personal ties. Does that mean no one will greet you? To know, I suspect we must see ourselves with loving eyes. Taking this perspective, what do you see? Intuition reinforces to me over and over again love's uncompromising power. I have every confidence that we'll encounter precisely what we inwardly wish for and need, regardless of our path in life. An angel, a daughter, a father, a betrothed, a beloved pet, or a shining light we call home: no matter the messenger, the gift our intuition offers is the assurance of meeting a love greater than we'd foreseen.

Step 5. Listen to Your Dreams

Death is not off-limits in our dreams. It appears repeatedly in many forms. Dreams make death more knowable. They can educate us about the dying process and what lies after. Even if death seems scary to you while you are awake, it can feel perfectly natural, posing no threat during sleep. When we're asleep our fear often becomes a nonissue. It does not translate. From an intuitive standpoint death is an invisible border where ordinary and nonordinary reality converge. Dreams can be the bridge.

Observing my dreams and those of patients and friends over the years, I've found that themes of death fall into three categories: (1) premonitions of death, ours or another's; (2) deceased loved ones offering messages or assurance they're okay; (3) information about assisting someone who is dying. All these dreams are ways of saying that what happens to us when we pass on is part of a process, accessible through intuition, and that our consciousness survives.

THE THREE CATEGORIES OF DEATH DREAMS

1. *Premonitions of Death*

Warnings of death often come in dreams. A famous example is Abraham Lincoln. A few days before his assassination, he noted a dream in which he saw a corpse resting on a platform in the East Room of the White House. He was shocked to see it was himself—the victim of a killer's bullet, a premonition he proved destined to live out.

People worldwide have told me about dreams that accurately predicted the death of a loved one. A New Jersey construction worker reported, "I dreamed my mother came to say good-bye. Though in good health, the next day she suddenly died of a massive stroke." A granddaughter shared, "Recently my grandfather dreamed he was playing mah-jongg (a game he loved!) with a circle of relations who had already passed on. They announced that the one empty seat left at the table was reserved for him. Grandfather died soon after." A high school student said, "I dreamed I was hurried out of my sleep to serve as a chaplain for one of my best friends, who was dying. The next day in class we learned that he had suddenly passed away in an accident."

What is the purpose of such dreams? How can they serve you? Most important, they are a tribute to your sensitivity, self-knowledge, and openness to love. Love is a conduit for intuition. It facilitates close communication with those dearest to you, sometimes even with seeming strangers. I realize that foreknowledge of a death may be upsetting. Still, I urge you also to view it as evidence of a sublime rapport, an expression of truth.

Once you've received such a message, what should you do? Each time ask yourself, How can I use it to be of service? Always intuitively check out if it's appropriate to share. For example, What does your gut say? Do you feel queasy or good about intervening? Does a lightbulb flip on, indicating, Yes, go ahead? Is a force pulling you forward? Or are you hitting a brick wall, shutting down? Such signals will advise you. Sometimes, if you alert someone of danger, harm may be avoided. But if you strongly sense death is impending, it may be wisest to say little unless you're intuitively certain it would benefit someone to know. What you *can* do is nurture the person involved. Do what is possible to be supportive. That's sufficient. More isn't necessarily better. Never underestimate the good that can result from even the smallest kindness. If you find you're unable to alter an outcome, you can still witness whatever unfolds, empowered by your intuition in the most compassionate way.

This brings me to Lucille. At a yacht club luncheon—of all places!—where I was guest speaker, a woman told me an endearing story. When her devoted husband of forty years was dying, she dreamed he was leaving her for another woman named Lucille. "Who's Lucille?" she cautiously asked him, after recounting her dream. "You must be kidding! Never heard of her," he said, flabbergasted. "Leave you? Are you nuts?" Her dream made no apparent sense. A few months passed. Her husband died. Bringing flowers to his grave one day, she glanced over at the inscription on the adjoining stone. Guess who? Lucille.

Some dreams of death are conveyed with the lightness of cosmic humor. The laughter consoles. Other such dreams simply offer straightforward data, there for preparation if you're paying attention. I hope you'll take both types seriously. Watch for premonitions of death in dreams. Write them down in your journal. Make a star beside those that feel particularly on target. Note if they come true. You are capable of intuiting death before it comes. Know this.

2. *Messages*

Frequently after loved ones die they appear in our dreams to assure us that they're all right. They know how much we worry. Often they look younger, healthier, happier, no longer sick or in pain. I've had numerous visits—all tender, encouraging—from my deceased grandfather, grandmother, uncle, mother. My intuition reinforces their authenticity. I accept these dreams at face value. How can you know if such messages are real? Are they mere wish fulfillments or fantasies, as strict Freudians would say? No one can answer this with conviction but you. If you have such a dream, evaluate what your intuition tells you. Do you have chills of recognition? A crystal-clear knowing? A sense of being uplifted? Of joy? An image that rings true? Depend on your intuition to see.

People on the verge of death often dream of deceased loved ones coming to get them, announcing it's time to go. Nearing death, while in a coma, my mother cried out one night, "Mama, Papa, go back. I'm not ready to leave with you." Though unconscious, she frantically waved them away. My mother was so reluctant to let go that a few days before, barely able to stand up, she'd dragged my father to Armani, where she bought herself a new suit. My mother fought death to the end. Some people are like that. Some aren't. Regardless, the moment *will* come. A telling sign: when a messenger appears in a dream, sometimes in the form of a friend or family member.

The bond with ancestors after death is a revered Native American tradition. We all maintain an ongoing intuitive exchange with ancestors. If you want to try to experience this, before you go to sleep request that they appear in a dream. It seems in this medium it's easier for ancestors to materialize. I have a patient who considers his departed great-grandmother, a farmer's wife of Ukrainian descent, his guide. When he has a problem to solve, he asks her in dreams for direction. It is a sacred request. The concept of blood ties, surpassing time, is worth intuitive investigation. See what you find. You could link up with new allies. Treasure the messages they impart. In *The Prophet* Kahlil Gibran wrote, "Trust in your dreams, for in them is hidden the gate to eternity."

3. *Information About Assisting Someone Who Is Dying*
Dreams about death can be service-oriented. They will give you instructions, solicited or offered spontaneously, about how to do all you can for the dying. It could be as simple as, "Bring your auntie chicken soup" or "Kiss your little sister on the cheek." No requests are frivolous. I've learned to do exactly what my intuition tells me. You may not know the significance of the action, but the dying person will.

Some of you may literally be called into service with the dying through your dreams as well as your life experiences. I've worked with many hospice nurses, therapists, and physicians who present similar profiles. Typically, from a young age they have repeated dreams about death or must deal with an inordinate number of people around them dying. Relatives, friends, even distant acquaintances seem to drop like flies. This is a special situation—disturbing if not properly interpreted. Death sometimes appears most frequently to those who are best suited to work with it. If death keeps popping up in your dreams or daily life, consider the possibility.

Surrender assumptions. Your role in service to others may be unexpected. This is what my dreams have taught. Even so, at times I jump to conclusions. For example, a few months ago I woke from a dream with a phone number I couldn't place rolling around in my head. What's this? I thought and jotted it down. At the risk of looking foolish or even alarming a stranger, the next day I dialed the number. What's the worst that can happen? I thought. A machine picked up, with a pleasant woman's voice. I introduced myself, practically reciting my résumé to assure her I wasn't a nut: "I'm a psychiatrist, an intuitive, author of *Second Sight,* on the staff of UCLA. I had this dream with your phone number in it. If you feel like it, please call back." That afternoon Carla did. "I just read your book!" she exclaimed. "I'm opening up a practice as a healer. I've been praying for some support." To top it off, she'd just moved into a new apartment—I was her first call. Aha! I thought. Carla and I were destined to work together. Fate! I invited her to a workshop I was giving that weekend. Clearly, our relationship was meant to be.

As it happened, when Carla and I met it was instantly obvious we didn't click. Despite our mutual interest in healing, we had little in common. So why the dream? Could I have been so wrong? Not exactly. Carla made a strong connection at the workshop with one of the participants, a woman with ovarian cancer. Over the next few months Carla served as her soul support, helped her die. In the larger scheme of things, my lack of simpatico with Carla had no bearing at all. This scenario wasn't about me. I'd simply been the messenger.

When you are assisting the dying, dreams can tell you where to go, what to say, what not to say, what to do. They can be amazingly explicit, requested or not. It's as if some greater force out there is especially passionate about the good we're capable of in this area and is not mincing words. It is imperative to help people die in the best way possible. If your dreams direct you to do so, please take notice.

Throughout this chapter I've presented death as a mirror that can more richly reflect life. To crystallize your priorities, allow yourself to consider: What if you had only one year left to live? How would you spend your time? In *A Year to Live* Stephen Levine, a Buddhist teacher and pioneer in the field of death and dying, proposes just this. It is a provocative meditation about life as well as death. I recommend that everyone give it a try. Why? It will make you mindful of real meaning in your life, weed out all else. It will define an end point to your physical form from which you can gauge your mortality. It will open up the possibility of what comes after, not as a footnote when death approaches but as a lifelong contemplation. Just as Socrates advised on his deathbed that we should "always be occupied in the practice of dying," many spiritual traditions stress the wisdom of acknowledging the advent of death throughout life. The aim is while alive to seize every moment, to intuit that our spirits defy any time line the intellect may superimpose.

Intuition teaches the shortsightedness of the time-bound conventions of our world. It gives a glimpse into knowing that our earthly existence is simply a blip on the screen. Perhaps to our loved ones who've passed over we don't seem to be separated at all. Missing us may not even occur to them. Could our perceptions of time be merely subjective? Our minds tell us that life is divided into seconds, minutes, days, and years that unfold sequentially; intuition reveals a oneness, a non-clock reality superseding the linear. Here's death's challenge: It impels you beyond the ordinary to view all existence in extraordinary terms.

Such dropping away of boundaries manifests the magic of intuitive communication. For instance, if someone close to you is unable to verbalize, or in a coma, you can still make contact. Words need not limit you. Listening in silence or in dreams to the unspoken, feeling in your body another's subtle energy, is a function of intuition. It may take being with a dying loved one to truly know the power of this choice. Everyone may swear that such an interchange is impossible, but don't be dissuaded. See for yourself.

My friend Frank did. His mother-in-law, after multiple ministrokes, was confined to a convalescent home. She had severe dementia, convinced it was 1942, when she had lived on a horse ranch in Kentucky. Her bright blue eyes rarely opened. She'd lie in bed moaning, flailing around. Rarely uttering a word, eating nothing, day after day she was virtually nonresponsive. No one knew what to do. Two weeks before she died, Frank was inspired by an explicit intuition. For a few hours each afternoon, he was guided to tell her stories about the high points of her life. Always he'd emphasize, "What a wonderful wife, mother, and mother-in-law you've been." Sitting next to her, holding her hand, Frank would have this one-way conversation. Or was it? Each time he'd begin the stories, she'd calm down. All moaning would cease. Frank knew that the love in him was speaking to the love in her. His mother-in-law died serenely late one summer day in the middle of a story, Frank at her side.

Death can bring unanticipated healing. For Frank it was demonstrating acceptance, faith to act on intuition, and steadfast love. For his mother-in-law perhaps it was the grace to receive when her physical and mental faculties were nearly gone, to find peace in the stories of her life as they transported her into the transcendent. Who of us can judge what is most essential for a soul? As a physician I'll do my best to save life, but when death looms, I yield. The big picture: If healing embraces actualizing spirituality, not just keeping the body well, death can be the vehicle.

How will our final moments unfold? One patient told me of a colleague, a detective-mystery writer, who was dying of AIDS. His friends knew he was wild about the Beatles, had Beatles tapes going nonstop by his bed. Wouldn't you know it? When the time came for him to pass on, the track playing was "All You Need Is Love." Who could have choreographed such an exit? Soon this man was to get to the bottom of the most elusive whodunit of all.

The chilling film *DDead Man Walking* underscores how pivotal the very end of life may be. A brutal racist murderer on death row seeks out a nun as spiritual adviser, requesting she be with him when he dies. Unrepentant until hours before his execution, he finally becomes truthful about his crimes because of the strength he takes from the nun's unswerving compassion for him. In the end he seeks redemption. "It figures that I have to die to find love," he says to her, weeping. "Thank you for loving me." At the instant of lethal injection, the nun instructs him to look straight at her: "I want the last thing you see in this world to be the face of love."

The love that surrounds life and death makes both luminous. Search your intuition to shape a philosophy about the cycles of spirit. No one else can determine this for you. Believe in what you find. Especially with death, recast complexity into what is fundamental. Strive to intuit what is innocent and true. Cherish what you learn. Let it dissipate your fears. As Aldous Huxley wrote, "Lightly, my darling, lightly, even when it comes to dying. Nothing ponderous or portentous . . . Just the simple fact of dying and the fact of the clear light."

PART TWO

Emotions and Relationships

6

The Emotional Path of the Warrior

We ask ourselves: "Who am I to be brilliant, gorgeous,
talented, fabulous?" Actually, who are you not to be?
—Marianne Williamson

*T*wo devils are sitting at a booth in a diner talking shop. Winged creatures with dull yellow eyes, sallow complexions, bristly red tails. Pretty scary-looking. One devil reprimands the other: "You let humans off far too easy. There's only one approach that works: hell and damnation. I swear by it." The other devil shakes his head. "Why waste all that effort?" He snickers. "Just leave them alone. They'll do it all to themselves."

Some indictment. One that we're not obliged to cooperate with. Our challenge, as emotional warriors, is to live a different kind of life than these demons assume. That is, to see ourselves—shortcomings and all—with compassion, not beating ourselves up at every opportunity. Then we can start to heal. This entails a radical shift in self-perception, an all-inclusive inquiry into who we are. No hiding. No part left out. Here's where many of us hit a wall. We're ashamed of feeling depressed, inadequate, anxious, as if this implies we've failed or done something wrong. Nonsense. A patient once apologized, "I wish I could be calling you about something more spiritual. But I'm having panic attacks. I can barely leave the house." I felt for him, but he had it backwards. Facing panic *is* a courageous spiritual act. This was his chance for a breakthrough!

There's a misguided expectation that we're supposed to be happy all the time. Let's set this straight. None of us is immune to the ups and downs of being human. Emotions—all of them—are the precious nuts and bolts of the spiritual journey. Heal from the inside out and you can set yourself free. I often work with patients who appear to have everything. Yet many are lost, unhappy. More isn't always better. No matter how many houses you own, or how impressive a bank account, if you're full of self-loathing, even the most exquisite rose can't touch you. We view the world through the lens of how we feel about ourselves.

I'd like to address a common misconception: If you're spiritually evolved you won't have emotional conflict. Well, maybe if you reach Nirvana—but not in this world. The earth is not an enlightened planet. Surprised? It's a place where we learn: there is light as well as adversity. The Indian sage Ramana Maharishi said, "We have heaven and hell within us." Try to accept this. It's our nature. However, the real payoff of banishing your demons is that your load lightens. You loosen up. Life becomes more fun. You begin to see the cosmic humor of it all. What a relief! Learning never stops. On my deathbed I'll probably still have another issue to address. The universe is kind; it wouldn't consider depriving me—or you—of one last chance to grow.

Look at it this way: You're enrolled in Spirituality 101. The objective is to develop compassion. Enter your most contentious emotions: fear, loneliness, alienation. If you stay open, you *will* feel them. It took me years to catch on that all of experience is meant to awaken, not needlessly torment. Go with it. See what you can gain. Not easy, but essential. A great gift I received was a fierce faith that each of us has the capacity to triumph over crises and emerge stronger. This has extraordinary value. Further, for me healing is never purely personal. We must do what we can to help others. The healers—and people in general—I trust most are those on a lifelong path of self-discovery (not the ones who claim to have "arrived"). Once our beasts no longer intimidate us, we can pass courage along.

Here's a formula for healing everything from anxiety to abuse: *Darkness is transmuted into light by love.* A practical alchemy. Give yourself latitude in expressing self-love. No rules: just your personal truth in the moment. Suppose you're depressed. You may decide to enter psychotherapy, take antidepressants, not take antidepressants, go on a meditation retreat, call a time-out with your mother, or build sand castles on the beach. Follow your intuition. If you've lost touch with it—stop. Find someone to help you reconnect. This is fundamental work I do with all my patients. Part of healing is reaching out. If you can't love yourself (those times may come), you must let others love you until you can. When I've sunk the lowest, what has saved me over and over again are the eyes of my friends shining on me.

When facing emotions, try this. First, be honest with yourself about your feelings. Also, sharing them with a friend or therapist can work wonders. Sometimes any empathic listener will do. In medical school I'd often pour my heart out to my dog. Ears pointed, eyes fixed on me, she listened unconditionally to every word. Most important, find a safe outlet to surface your feelings. Airbrush nothing. Take all the time you need to sort them through. Then—and this is critical—move on. To persist in rehashing issues (sometimes for years!) without progress is counterproductive. There may still be some loose ends. That's okay. You can return to them when the right time comes. Many of us in therapy get lost in the enchanted realm of childhood traumas rather than utilize the knowledge we've gained to go forward.

People are crying out for a new model of psychotherapy. Everywhere I go they're asking for the same thing: "I've been in traditional treatment. Now I want to grow on a spiritual and intuitive level, but my doctor can't take me there. He'll think some of my experiences are crazy!" Take heart. The intuitive therapist is the next wave in health care: someone who doesn't dismiss your dreams and inner visions but blends them with psychological expertise and knowledge of the body into a comprehensive picture of who you are. In this section of the book I'll give you a concrete look at how I work with patients using the five intuitive steps—a tack quite different from traditional therapy.

As an intuitive therapist I see my patients in totality. When they sit across from me I sense their joy as well as their suffering, the whole spectrum. Everyone has suffering. Everyone. It doesn't surprise or frighten me anymore. I consider it beautiful, a human aspect in need of healing. We contain paradoxes within us—love/hate, hope/despair, strength/weakness—all that the universe holds. Once we embrace this, our life experiences have the ability to transform us. I'm moved by the Yiddish proverb "There's no heart as whole as a broken heart." If we can see even our most profound pain as an opportunity to heal, we can undo the spell of darkness.

Step 1. Notice Your Beliefs

My mother always wanted me to belong to her country club in Beverly Hills. It was, she felt, a "proper" atmosphere, where I'd meet the man of my dreams (in her mind, a Jewish doctor, of course!). I had a problem with this. I wanted to please her. I wanted to fit in. Yet part of me fantasized about blowing the place up. My mother would arrange lavish luncheons, inviting an eligible man—and his parents. She'd be in her glory, talking up a storm. I'd sit there, tongue-tied, mortified. What's the matter with me? I'd think. Of course, there was nothing wrong with my mother's priorities. For her. But I had to be true to my own character. I'm just more of an outsider than part of the crowd. *Now,* I treasure this in myself, wouldn't want it any other way. But it took really trusting my intuition to realize the value of my own beliefs. And then to stand by them.

Your beliefs matter. They will shape how you make sense of your emotional life. What anybody else says is right for you is irrelevant if you don't feel it yourself. We often go years mesmerized by a litany of illusions about who we are—from the media or our parents—that we must unlearn. To counter these I'd like to share with you four beliefs I've found to be empowering. Based on compassion, not convention, they offer a starting point. I practice them, and many of my patients do too.

FOUR EMPOWERING BELIEFS

Your path is perfect. Don't compare yourself with anyone.

Each of us has a unique purpose and path. The details of our lives may differ, but our mission remains the same: to move closer to love. Hold that thought. Make it your mantra. Avoid comparisons. The trap is this: There is always someone who is or seems smarter, richer, funnier, sexier, more spiritually evolved—the list goes on and on. When faced with such a person, how do you react? Are you happy for him or her? Do you want to crawl into the nearest corner? Do you feel stricken? Diminished? Enraged? Welcome to the spiritual training ground, through which all of us must pass.

My patient Robin is a Hollywood producer. Her world worships youth and celebrity. She attends parties with movie stars and supermodels, and relentlessly measures herself against them. Robin, at forty, is a gorgeous woman, inside and out, but she has trouble seeing it. "Don't you compare yourself with other people?" she asked, incredulous. "Of course," I said. "I struggle with it too. Nobody's immune. But in my best moments I can also laugh if I get caught up in it all." I stressed, "The point is trying to love yourself more. You have a choice.

You can judge yourself as better or less than others. Or you can see through that illusion, appreciate the blessings you've been given."

She raised her eyebrows. "That's easy to say. But what about———? He's devious, backstabbing, dishonest. Every year he just gets more money and more success." A perennial refrain from patients and friends, especially in show business. Here, I take a hard line: Real success isn't trading your humanity for power, isn't selling your soul. People who do pay a terrible price, whether or not it appears so, whether or not they know it. If one leads an authentic life, this becomes clear. Very clear. We receive a phenomenal sense of integrity and wholeness. But this is the stickler: Rewards from the external world may or may not follow. Grappling with these issues is at the very heart of what it is to be human.

Feel your power and beauty.

I savor Marianne Williamson's words: "Our deepest fear is that we are powerful beyond measure. . . . There's nothing enlightened about shrinking so that other people won't feel insecure around you." Let this be our model. How often we shortchange ourselves, become invisible. The power I speak of has nothing to do with egotism. It means being proud of who you are, accountable for your strengths. I know how difficult this can be. Over the years one of the hardest things for me has been to see myself as beautiful. It's not that my parents, friends, or lovers weren't supportive—nor was it simply a self-esteem issue. I've come to understand I was terrified of taking responsibility for my power. A flower bursting open is more vulnerable than a hidden bloom. And our beauty—if really seen—has unimaginable dimensions, physical and beyond. In any of us, denying our beauty should never be mistaken for humility. With gentleness we must shift the scales toward valuing what is good in ourselves and urge others to do the same.

So what about when I look in the mirror and fixate on my wrinkles rather than my sparkling hazel eyes? Or when I dwell on a mistake rather than a success? Does our own beauty and power threaten us? Why? When I started lecturing to large audiences, I had an "irrational" fear that I'd be murdered. I understand that it had little to do with the moment itself—perhaps it was a childhood recall of having my intuitions deprecated or silenced, or even a persecution memory from some previous period. Either way, I had to acknowledge this fear to diffuse it. There was a second fear I had to contend with, one that for me evokes the myth of Icarus. You remember—he was flying and he soared too close to the sun. So much power, and then . . . death. It may be that all of us want to fly but are afraid that if we do we'll get burned. Perhaps Marianne Williamson was speaking of just such things. We're rarely taught how precious our light is or how to manifest it. To shine, to be joyful, this is a passage to strength we all must take.

Each of us has a unique timetable for healing.

As a psychiatrist I was taught there are developmental stages through which humans must pass: giving up the breast, toilet training, puberty, and separating from parents, to name a few. These categories imply an orderly progress. The healthy person keeps moving right along; the "neurotic" is mired somewhere in time. It turns out, however, that life is more complex. The other day a patient of mine, the CEO of an international bank, came to see me. He was embarrassed: Only now, at fifty, was he ready to deal with his overbearing mother. "I'm way too old to be going through this," he protested, laughing but almost in tears. I was pleased to tell him that it was neither too early nor too late. We all have an intuitive and spiritual timetable that cannot be forced. Take what appears to be a cruel truth: Sometimes, seemingly prematurely, young children must cope with the death of a parent. But each of us has a unique path; there's nothing to gain in wishing it otherwise. We must embrace what we're given, find its meaning. In addition, there are layers of learning. You think you've dealt with your mother, but *poof!* there she is again. This need not imply failure, past or present. There's just more! For me, it's vital not to feel shame. Intuition teaches us simply to accept what presents itself compellingly—when the time is right.

Go with your emotions—surrender is not defeat.

As a little girl I lived for those Saturdays when my friends and I would go to Pacific Ocean Park, an amusement park in Venice Beach, to ride the Gravitron. A round, rubber-padded, windowless room, it would spin so fast we'd scream as we were glued to its sides by centrifugal force. Then came the best part: the floor dropped out, a good twenty feet below us. From experience my friends and I knew to relax and go with it. Those who didn't? Well, they grasped and groped, sliding downward in a humiliating struggle, ending up plastered against the walls in some contorted, compromising position—the kiss of death for any kid trying to look impressive. It was the Gravitron that introduced me to the virtues of surrender.

Surrendering to emotions doesn't mean being defeated by them. It's the difference between riding the wave and fighting it. Befriend your emotions. Intuitively listen for their voices; they will tell you how to heal. Blend with emotions; don't resist. Blending reduces tension. A patient recently said to me about his anger, "I'm afraid if I even talk about it, it'll consume me; I'll spin out of control"—a not unusual concern. But as a psychiatrist I'd like to make one point clear: Those ever-so-polite, churchgoing housewives turned ax murderers snapped from repressing anger, not from mindfully exploring it. Flowing with emotions is a dance. Be gentle with yourself. Always go at a comfortable pace.

QUESTIONS FOR REFLECTION

- What can you learn from your emotions? Are you ready to view the more difficult ones as teachers, not tormentors? How can this view make you strong?

- Do you believe it's possible that you can heal no matter how hurt you've been? Are you prepared to revisit areas where you've felt stuck using traditional techniques and make an intuitive breakthrough?

- Are you ready to acknowledge your full power and beauty, radiate it out to the world? What's standing in your way? Which old ideas are inhibiting you?

Having a solid emotional belief system—a strategy for dealing with ups and downs—in place is more than just a lesson in survival. For me an emotional belief system is a coherent understanding that all experience is meant to impart knowledge. Such belief provides a way to flourish no matter the situation. The kindness of this approach and your unconditional self-compassion will enable you to handle anything. Opening the heart; if this is the core of your philosophy, it will never fail you. It is the alpha and omega of healing. Take time to formulate a well thought out, intuitively sound foundation that works for you. Then, should the sky grow dark, you'll already have lit a circle of candles.

Step 2. Be in Your Body

In early spring, when the wild yellow mustard blooms in the Malibu Hills, I climb to my favorite spot overlooking the Pacific Ocean. Sitting cross-legged on a warm rock that knows me well, I reevaluate my life, according to my body's truth. If my energy is high and I'm secure and happy, I trust I'm on the right track. If I'm disturbed, irritable, or "off"—stomach in knots, shoulders tense, soul restless—these are warnings. I have to address them. I'm a big fan of periodic emotional housecleaning. If you continually attend to your emotions, they won't fester. I've made a vow to myself: I'm never going to get stuck in a life that doesn't feel right. In this I am unyielding. For example, should my work (my greatest passion) ever stop giving me pleasure, I'm prepared to open up, say, a Chinese restaurant!

To remain in touch with yourself, you must feel. Remember the 1970s movie *The Stepford Wives?* That sinister small-town tale of American husbands fiendishly transforming their wives into automatons to ensure they'd be compliant? Those poor women, all dressed so perfectly, shopping for groceries, always smiling like plastic dolls. Stand forewarned. The antidote to such a fate is letting your emotions come alive in your body and learning from them. This is the meditation: Fight against being cut off, numbed, merely existing. You deserve more.

You may think, I agree, but emotions can be painful, exhausting, aggravating. Very possible. That's often phase one of the work. I promise, though, if you stick with it, things will change. Or you may believe, There's too much to deal with. I'm not up to it. Untrue. Just take one step at a time. You'll get there. Here's where your body's messages may be deceiving. For instance, you're ready to deal with your anger. Suddenly, you feel oh so heavy, like you're moving through molasses, dragging around a lead weight. Don't be discouraged. These are not bad signs. Your inner troop of change-phobic gremlins are slamming on the brakes. They'd rather stay angry because it's familiar, known territory. The unknown can be scary; let them adjust.

What if the volume is turned up? You've been buried under the covers all day, paralyzed by depression. Or you're breathing into a brown paper bag in the midst of a full-blown anxiety attack. Why stay in your body when it's so miserable? What can you gain by listening? There's an intuitive subtext to every symptom. The sensation itself contains the key to its cure.

My patient Debra would panic whenever her father came to town. He'd arrive; like clockwork I'd get a call. Typically she'd come in wringing her hands, pacing, beside herself. I'd be supportive, which helped, but she was afraid to get near the panic itself. Finally, Debra agreed to try to stay with it. "Your body's giving off signals," I said. "Let your intuition interpret them." I asked her to close her eyes, remain as still as possible. Then, with Debra focused on her body's discomfort (it's like holding a tone), we slowly explored her panic together. "Notice any images, sensations, or knowings," I advised. "Don't worry about what they mean. Just let them surface." Over a few sessions a memory emerged. The flash of a bedroom door. It opens. A suit coat, trousers, socks scattered on the floor. A flimsy purple negligee draped on a bedpost. Her father's naked body. A strange woman with him. *A woman.* Who? Why? Shutdown. This is what Debra was blocking out. Her father had been having an affair. At eight she'd walked in on him. Now we had a starting point. Her body held the key.

Our bodies are responsive to sensual cues from our environment. Take seasonal depression ("winter blues"), afflicting over 10 million Americans. In light-deprived winter months, levels of serotonin, a brain hormone, are believed to drop, causing depression. Storm patterns, cloud cover, and latitude are all factors. The treatment? Phototherapy. For a serotonin boost, instead of Prozac your doctor may recommend you bask in the rays of a fluorescent "light box" or wear a nifty light visor-cap an hour a day. You might feel foolish but then, voilà! Your mood improves. Of course, other external forces register on us every day: electrical storms, tides, and, powerfully, the moon. It's well recognized in emergency rooms that the full moon brings chaos—suicide attempts, auto accidents, heart attacks, psychotic breaks, crimes of passion, werewolf sightings! You name it, it happens. What about you? Does your mood change? How does your body respond?

Even in infancy the body reveals so much. I've been privileged to be present at many births, both as a medical student learning to deliver babies and at the side of my patients when their children were born. It's undeniable that a baby's face speaks volumes from day one. Some babies look like wise old souls; others appear new to it all, unguarded. Some seem to be exuding joy, others carrying a heavy burden. Not that either is better, though, not surprisingly, most parents prefer happy infants. Such a bias is understandable, but it does not illuminate any one human's path. In *The Soul's Code* the psychologist James Hillman writes,

"Every person is born with a defining image," connected to something before his or her beginning. This quality is special in each of us, sets the tone for how we can grow spiritually. Recognizing it gives compassionate insight into our own hearts and so into the hearts of others. To best grasp what I'm speaking of, take out some baby pictures of yourself. As neutrally as possible, see if you can read the essential expression on that infant's face: the ineffable essence of character.

Throughout life our bodies change, our beings evolve. It's thrilling to view aging with intuitive eyes. Ordinary thinking tells us we mature from infant to elder, leave the past behind. Not so, says intuition. All experiences are equally alive, equally accessible. I delight in once more being five years old, just as I can again relish age thirty. Time shifting: embodying all of who we are simultaneously, whenever we like. On an inner level you sacrifice nothing. You just become more. One returns to earlier moments, high and low, with the same immediacy but also with earned maturity. Imagine being ten, running on a hillside, rainbow kite lifting in the breeze. Recall, too, a grandmother's last hug. These days are always yours. Realize how timeless you are, despite your body's chronology. Remember everything, ecstasy and sadness. Nothing of the heart is ever lost.

Step 3. Sense Your Body's Subtle Energy

One moment in psychotherapy stands out for me most: when I first meet eyes with a new patient. There's a sublime silence between opening my waiting room door and the words that follow. No intellectual explanations. No social formalities. A time when invisible energy is exchanged and I can intuit what is unspoken. Those few seconds often tell me more about a patient than weeks of analysis.

I've always loved the silence, when noise and clutter disappear. A place of wind, of breath, of light, where we can communicate not with vowels and consonants but with energy. I want to show you ways I use energy to work with patients so that you can learn to do the same. Reading energy will allow you to be more sensitive to your own emotions and see how the moods of others affect you.

Picture this scene. Alex's first appointment. There he sat on my waiting room couch. Armani suit, blond hair impeccably blow-dried—a suntanned advertising executive, about forty. Surfaces: what typically catch our attention, outer layers easily peeled off. I've learned not to make too much of them. Click. Click. Click. Alex's appearance and body language registered. Then I sensed beyond them. His energy, a finely vibrating wave passing from Alex into me. I felt it in my solar plexus (my third chakra)—a sadness that penetrated, a yearning for what was past. A thought came too: Why can't I lead the life I imagined? In a split second all this emerged. Before we shook hands, before we said, "It's nice to meet you," Alex's energy had given me a head start on knowing him.

My job was to help Alex be more real. It didn't matter that he was top in his profession. It didn't matter that he'd come in because of "a problem with my girlfriend." It still amazes me how clearly energy conveys our hearts' desires, though we may be the last to know them. But even with this data about Alex, I went slowly. My style has never been to force things. During the next few sessions I listened to Alex. I waited. My intuitive process is this: First, I tune in to the energy. Then, I tune in to when it's appropriate to share. Timing is everything. I feel like a fox, sniffing around, waiting to make my move.

One day Alex's eyes pinned me down. "Have you read Rilke's *Letters to a Young Poet?*" he asked. "Yes," I said. "It's brilliant." Well, that was all it took. Alex began to replay a previous life. College at Berkeley, 1978. Devouring everything Rilke had written. Madly composing poetry in his garage apartment late at night. Then business school, the pressure to conform. Next, job offers. So many perks. Two decades flew by. Now, here we were. I jumped at the opening and shared my intuitions. Alex was ready for them. We agreed: For him to be happy, his passion for poetry had to be rekindled. Did Alex quit his job and choose the artist's life? No. But he did start reading again, scribbling verse, and dreaming. This made all the difference. It's not surprising that during our sessions the pangs I'd felt in my solar plexus were gone. Alex's energy had shifted. I felt it. He did too. Sensing energy is not of the mind but of intuition.

I'd like you to get in the habit of reading people's energy. It will make you more aware of subtle influences around you. Though frequently not perceived, energy is an envelope of light surrounding the body. It contains input that can be intuited as emotion, thought, physical sensation, image, or instant knowing—all increasing your empathy. You can practice sensing energy everywhere. The bank line, the movies, the grocery store checkout line—all are golden opportunities. You may do this exercise alone or compare notes with a friend to get an instant cross-check of your reading. Sensing energy is exciting, always new. Experiment. This exercise will allow you to detect a range of emotional variations.

SENSING EMOTIONAL ENERGY IN DAILY LIFE

1. Choose a location, say, the food court at the mall, and get settled. Take a few deep breaths. Center yourself. Become still. Then scope out the scene; choose someone to read. Don't overthink it. Be spontaneous. It could be anyone. A little old lady. A gangsta' rapper. A father with his son. Drop preconceptions; looks can deceive.

2. When you're ready, edge closer to your target. Energy is easier to sense at a distance of two feet or less. Try not to be conspicuous. Stay cool. Now, for at least thirty seconds, see what your intuition tells you. Your body is key. Watch for changes. Any sudden waves of emotion? Do you feel happy? Depressed? Overwrought? At peace? Are you charged up? Exhausted? As you move away from your target, do these sensations decrease? Typically, the farther you are from people, the harder their energy is to feel. Note your response. It may surprise you.

Try this exercise with as many different kinds of people as you like.

In the beginning it's important to get comfortable sensing energy in others. Then, with that baseline, you can notice minute shifts in yourself. Emotions have strata. They can be broken down into components of energy just as physical symptoms can. The secret of preventing full-blown turmoil is identifying signs that preempt it. This entails learning to hear the quieter notes you play in yourself. Consider depression. Let's backtrack and pinpoint some potential early warnings, imbalances that are telling. Remember, the essence of energy is pure vibration, which the mind interprets. This makes it easier for us to understand. I'm asking you to delve beneath the obvious in search of what may seem elusive: feelings under feelings, encoded messages. They could appear as a progression or a single sign. For instance, look for the following:

- A hollow ache inside
- Vague melancholy
- Edginess or irritability you can't shake
- A sense of disconnection from other people

• A nagging stuck feeling, like you need to do something, say some-thing, but what?

At first you might miss such nuances, but with practice you'll spot the ways energy expresses itself. Here is your advantage. If you pay at-tention, uncover the origins of these signs, they can resolve. How often we become too tolerant of ongoing subliminal states that drain our en-ergy. Don't allow it. Intuition can transform your emotional life. Why wait until depression or anxiety rages to intervene? Before a crisis hits you'll detect something's off and act on it. The art of intuitive listening is reading your body as a lover would, sensing the intricacies of its moods and physical variations. No change is too small, no discomfort without value. It doesn't matter if there's "no good reason" for any of it. Trust even what seems infinitesimal but feels authentic. In yourself or when reading another, these are the intuitions to follow.

I'm very aware of how patients' energy affects me and the entire room. It can accumulate. When patients do intensely personal work, remnants of energy inevitably are left behind, a very real buildup in the environment that must be cleaned out. It's only fair. My patients deserve free and clear space. They sense if it's not—many call me on it. For this reason I always meditate for a few minutes between seeing patients. By generating positive energy I center myself and also purify my office. Then my patients' connection with themselves and me is optimal.

Energy colors all interactions. It also functions as relationship radar, attracting to you people with whom you're most in sync. For instance, a therapist. What is realistic to look for? Above all, make sure there is chemistry. You can feel it. Electricity. Excitement. Movement. A sense of "Yes, I'm in the right place." Chemistry is more than intellectual com-patibility; it's how your subtle energies relate. The wonder of two peo-ple clicking makes therapy take off. I depend on it. Ideally, you'll have chemistry with a therapist from the start. Sometimes, though, you may not be sure, or you'll be out of touch with your feelings. In those cases I suggest giving it a few weeks. Then, if you still find nothing much is happening, you might consider that you and your therapist are a mis-match. Without chemistry therapy can be painstaking for you both, like pushing a boulder uphill. I've tried it with patients. I know. I'm not sug-gesting that you always have to agree with your therapist, or that you'll never reach an impasse. But if that silent bond of energy is there, you can more readily overcome blocks and achieve the best in you.

Berenice learned this well. A kindergarten teacher in East Harlem, she was assigned to a class so unruly that a brigade of previous teachers called it quits after a few weeks. Seventeen students, all out of control. A teacher's nightmare. The first several days Berenice noticed a pattern. There was a pivotal moment about ten minutes into the morning when the kids would go berserk. In unison they'd start screaming at the top of their lungs, throwing Tinkertoys and finger paints, tearing around like little maniacs. "Calm down," Berenice would say, trying to reason with them. "Everyone return to your seats." But no one would. Berenice realized that to get through to these kids, something more was called for.

She started with Manuel, a tall, gangly boy with horn-rimmed glasses who was suspected of being retarded. Berenice tuned in to his subtle energy. Her intuition told her Manuel was intelligent, yet he held back. How did she know? "It went way beyond empathy," Berenice explained. "I felt a part of him. I sensed in my body what his needs were. I was responding to something invisible both around and in Manuel." A non-verbal communication went from him to her: He needed to be accepted. So, instead of disciplining him for racing around the room, (the expected response), she'd tap him on the shoulder when he whizzed past. "Manuel, you're such a good runner," she'd say. Berenice kept this up for a week. In another circumstance this might've been inappropriate. But she was certain Manuel would respond. Her intuition was predicated not on what he said or did but on his energy. Further, her attention to him raised Manuel's status with the other kids. They started including him in activities. This marked the beginning of his transformation.

One by one Berenice listened to what each child's energy told her, changing that Harlem classroom. By semester's end the class would take field trips to Central Park and museums in Manhattan, all getting along. It wasn't that the teachers who came before Berenice weren't empathic. But Berenice's sensitivity to the unspoken turned the situation around.

This brings us back to how energy affects us. Our emotional fluctuations are more than products of deranged brain chemicals or environmental stress. When you can't figure out what's happening to you or why, consider the subtext your subtle energy communicates. It may provide a missing piece. Or if you already have a handle on your emotions, subtle energy can lend depth to self-knowledge. There are many more facets to healing than traditional medicine suggests.

Step 4. Ask for Inner Guidance

While on a book tour in Germany, I had the honor of meeting Mother Meerha, a renowned Indian spiritual teacher, a present-day avatar who embodies the sacred feminine. It was dusk. As the village steeple bell chimed, hundreds of people from all over the world gathered in the medieval town square. We were led down a cobblestone path to her simple home. There, one by one, we received darshan. Darshan: a silent blessing, a transmission of guidance from teacher to student that awakens. No words. Pure knowing.

Each person had arrived with his or her individual concerns and questions. Sometimes general, sometimes specific, the guidance she offered was crafted to our particular needs. When my turn came, I sat before her. Meerha: appearing quite youthful but perhaps thirty-five—a Hindu woman in gold sari, waist-length black hair, brown eyes gleaming. My eyes connected with hers. They were impossibly gentle, imparting love. I was so close I could feel her breath. Across from me Meerha radiated light and the soundless communication that my body was strong, my path correct. I absorbed all this, and bliss too, in what seemed like seconds.

I want to impress upon you the power of silence. It is open space, the quintessential intuitive realm. Seek it out. An array of blessings reside there—guidance of many kinds, if you just stop and request it. Take time to be still. Look inside. Not with expectation but with your heartfelt questions formed, and the faith to leave the silent place unfilled until that moment when answers come. The proper posture? Ask, then wait. Ask, then wait. No straining for answers.

My patient Tamara practiced such letting go. The abandon it required, the mystery of answers seemingly materializing out of nowhere, appealed to her. This time it was while picking gladiolas in her grandmother's summer garden in Maine. For so long—really ten years of marriage—she'd wrestled with how not to be decimated by her mother-in-law. A brittle matriarch from blueblood society, she'd expected Tamara to wait on her every need. Tamara did her best in a difficult situation. These days her patience was wearing thin. Change had to come. But how?

Sitting in the garden, Tamara posed the question and meditated. Slowly an image appeared. Her mother-in-law's mansion: the front door was ajar. Tamara peered in. It was vacant—no furniture, no light, room after room musty, desolate. Only a single tumbleweed eerily blowing through. Then a voice, "This is what your mother-in-law feels like inside." Flash. Here was Tamara's message. Never had she seen her nemesis in this way. Such loneliness—an intuition that pierced through her, easing Tamara's anger, making room for compassion. "I suddenly understood her differently," Tamara said, moved by the truth of her realization. "I still fully intend to set firmer limits and to say no more often. But now I can be softer with her, rather than snapping and picking fights." Sometimes it's not so much what you do but how you do it. The gentleness Tamara showed—which arose from this guidance—slowly but surely helped the relationship with her mother-in-law improve.

Throughout the day I have ongoing inner dialogues requesting direction. You can try this too. A situation may baffle you. While in the midst of it, ask your intuition, What can I do to get through to this person? How can I turn this interaction around? Then await the response. Let's say you're furious at your husband or wife, about to blurt out something you know you'll never hear the end of. Pause a few seconds. Breathe. Become quiet. Tune in to the bigger picture. See what your inner voice says. Then follow it and notice the results. Remember, pay special attention to guidance that comes through with compassion, as Tamara's did, or insight that feels neutral, without an emotional charge—reliable intuitive markers.

As a physician I frequently seek inner guidance. It articulates what the mind cannot: how to melt resistance, design new strategies if therapy is at a dead end, inject humor and love into my work, make contact with a patient who is withdrawn. Predicaments that seem unsolvable, people who can't be reached, may then be seen with a fresh slant.

Not long ago I received an emergency page from a frantic mother: "My son, only eight, is having visions and wants to kill himself." So young—and thoughts of suicide. My heart ached for them. "Our HMO doctor prescribed Valium and antidepressants. All that medication!" she exclaimed. "He's a little better. But I know you understand these things. Can you check him out?"

The next day Uri came in. Somber, with hundred-year-old eyes, he just stared at me, refusing to speak. From an Orthodox Jewish family, he wore a yarmulke, his sideburns in traditional *payot* curls. A week before, on Yom Kippur, in front of all his relatives, he'd pointed his finger at his aunt and announced, dead serious, "You're going to have a bad car accident." Nostradamus couldn't have done it better. Everyone was aghast. Soon after she got rear-ended, injuring her back. Learning this, Uri became suicidal. Now here he was.

Clearly Uri couldn't or wouldn't talk to me. I sized him up. So tiny, and bearing the weight of the world. There had to be a way for me to reach him. I inwardly asked, Please show me how. I waited. Seconds passed, maybe a minute. Then guidance came. I knew what I had to do. I looked him right in the eyes. Then, for the rest of the hour, I told him my story: How I made predictions as a child—and thought I'd caused them, but I hadn't. How, if you're intuitive, it's easier to pick up "negative events" in the beginning because they give off louder signals. Uri's brown eyes grew large. I saw he was taking it all in. Still, there were no other signs of acknowledgment. At the end of the session he said nothing; his mother, probably more confused than ever, thanked me. And off they went.

Three months later I got a call. "After Uri left your office, he refused to take his medication," his mother said. "So we stopped giving it to him." I gulped, braced myself for the worst. Uri's situation was severe. I never would have suggested this. His mother went on: "Uri started improving. Since then a lot has changed." I breathed easier. I couldn't wait to hear more. "I decided to take him to a Cabalistic rabbi who teaches Jewish mysticism," she said. "He understood about Uri's visions, told him he had a gift. Now the rabbi has taken Uri on as a student. Between you and the rabbi, Uri doesn't think he's crazy. And his depression is gone!"

Healing is enigmatic. With Uri, I had no idea what the outcome would be. I knew only what my guidance told me in the moment. That was enough. I followed through. I broke the rules. Contrary to Freud's "tell me what you're feeling" approach, I talked the entire session, intent on both addressing and relieving Uri's fear. A seed was planted. I did what I could. I find great solace knowing I played a part in preventing a child from being overmedicated or stigmatized by a system that would've branded him psychotic. If I hadn't intervened and if his mother hadn't found that rabbi, Uri's life could have been quite different.

The guidance I seek in therapy is often deliberate. Before I meet patients I routinely tune in to their names. I use the remote viewing technique I suggested you try in Chapter 3 for choosing health care practitioners. It's unimportant that I've never said a word to the person. Intuition allows us to sense one another without external cues.

Here's what I do:

1. I shift my awareness from the sights, smells, sounds of my environment and empty my mind.

2. I focus passively only on a patient's name, remaining open to intuitive impressions: images, body sensations, emotions, knowings, an inner voice, or a spontaneously emerging poem, book, or song. I note them all.

3. When my patient and I meet, I correlate what I picked up with information he or she shares with me.

My patient John offers a good example. Before knowing his history, his likes, dislikes, or occupation, I did a remote viewing of him. Whoosh. The ocean was everywhere. I smelled salt water. I felt the easy rocking motion of a boat. He was sitting on a wooden deck, a rugged-looking man in his sixties. I thought of lines from Coleridge's "Rime of the Ancient Mariner": "Alone, alone, all, all alone, Alone on a wide wide sea." I felt John's longing for solitude. It was beautiful for him, not loneliness but fulfillment and contemplation. That was all I got.

John came to me with a dilemma. Nearing seventy, for four decades he'd owned his own produce business. He'd built it up from scratch and was proud of what he'd achieved. He'd supported his family, sent his son to law school. Now he was thinking of retiring. "But what will I do every day?" he wondered. Year after year, six days a week, he'd been up before dawn, manning his stand until nightfall at the downtown produce mart. Now John had several fears: having time on his hands, feeling useless, losing his identity.

"Have you ever dreamed of doing something else?" I probed, going on a lead from my remote viewing. Tentatively, John said, "You know, I've always dreamed of living on a houseboat. But it seemed so impractical. And now, at my age?" Ahh. There it was. I realized my role was to see John through the transition of retirement, support him in negotiating this change with his wife (she turned out to be thrilled) and in living his dream. Simple things. Priceless to have a wish come true, as

John did. I am gratified that by listening to my intuition I could be of service.

You can use remote viewing to access guidance too. If you're considering a job change, try tuning in to the name of your potential boss before you meet. Within yourself form a question: What will it be like to work together? See what you get. Do you feel excited or flat? Does something in you quicken or shut down? Are you pulled toward this person or repelled? Log your reading. Then integrate it with your face-to-face impressions. Similarly, you can tune in to a friend, coworker, or relative if you're having a problem communicating. Names are sacred vibrations, readable by your intuition. Don't think it can't be done. You simply need practice. Value such input. Let it influence your choices. The mix needs to be there: intuition, intellect, intuition, intellect. Always strike a balance.

Invoke guidance from your heart and it will come. It could be a word, a picture, or an affirmation about how to proceed. Never undervalue even a simple response. Have faith that if your request is sincere, you'll be given exactly the insight you need.

Step 5. Listen to Your Dreams

When you want to understand what drives you emotionally, dreams can clarify. How? Let's appraise two versions of the same event. The waking you: At work your supervisor is demanding; everybody suddenly wants something from you. You feel pressured, irritable, but you're able to shrug it off and go on with your day. The dreaming you: You're captured by a household of vampires, bloodsucking creatures on the prowl. One has your father's expression. His baby blue eyes fixate on you. Breathless, you run, but he chases you, gaining fast. This is a recurrent nightmare you've had since childhood. How do your two selves relate? What is your dream trying to tell you?

There are layers of consciousness, and they trigger one another. You might conclude, My dream was a creative way of dramatizing an energy-zapping afternoon at work. True, but only a sliver of the picture. Your supervisor's a problem for sure, but what else is true? Your dream is signaling, Look again. Vampires? Who else do they evoke? Your father from childhood? What about your relationship? Perhaps he undermined, weakened you, although he appeared supportive. Did the opposite of nourish your spirit. I'm suggesting you do the hard work of consciously thinking this all through. Retrace your tracks on the trail. Let the years recede and reveal whence the vampires came. Answers from the past can liberate you in the present. This is the gist of dreams with psychological themes.

In my practice I've found that most dreams are aimed at sorting through our emotions. Let's start here, then discuss dreams that are predictive or intuitively guide. Don't be fooled into believing that psychological dreams are less "sexy." They'll take you to the epicenter of how you've grown and accentuate areas in need of healing. I revere these dreams. I'm always grateful for the chance to observe my anxieties and fears (no matter how spine-tingling) unmasked. What a relief to put a name to darkness. What a relief to lift the darkness with awareness and love.

I'm fascinated by how similar our unconscious imagery and psychological agendas can be. Take our triumphs. Have you ever dreamed that you're giving birth or watching someone give birth at a time when your life is thriving? A project comes to fruition, a relationship prospers, you graduate from school. How about having survived a typhoon, a sudden stomach-churning fall, or a ravaging war? Such outcomes are tributes to your inner strength, bold reminders to believe in yourself. In everyday terms they may mean you've ended a tumultuous love affair, left a dead-end job, or beat depression. Whatever the specifics, you've shown courage.

Other dreams graphically portray our insecurities. How about the one where you're standing buck naked in front of a group of people who're all pointing at you? Or you're running the last lap of a race, desperate not to falter before you reach the finish line? Another classic hair-raising scenario: being stalked by a malevolent presence. There are so many forces within us that need to be tenderly reckoned with. Will I make it? Am I good enough? Will I be accepted if seen undisguised? How much of myself is safe to reveal? Am I strong enough to slay my demons? All common threads woven between us—dreams illuminate the humanity and vulnerability we share.

To me there is no such thing as a "bad" dream. Even the most harrowing nightmare, the kind from which you wake up drenched in sweat, your heart pounding, is intended to alert. It points to areas in your psyche that require care. By listening to such dreams you can grow. Emotionally intense, amplifying your conflicts, such dreams can be cathartic.

THE HEALING ROLE OF NIGHTMARES

A sure way to exorcise a nightmare is to deal with it. This is how: identify its intent and apply the wisdom it offers, then you'll be able to move on. Are you ready to try an experiment? Think back on a dream that has rattled you. It could be one you've been having since you were little or a newly choreographed meet-your-demon fest from last night. Put aside at least ten minutes of uninterrupted time. When you're all set, curl up or meditate in a safe place. Close your eyes and re-create the scenario.

Notice the following elements:

- *The landscape*—its contours, colors, smells, temperatures, textures
- *The characters*—their expressions, words, or insinuations
- *Your emotions*—building slowly at first, get used to how they feel. Then gradually let them gather momentum and become raw, primal, unguarded

  Now you can confront your adversary. At the right moment stop and take a close look at what or who is threatening you. If you're really brave, meet eyes. Don't back down. Your purpose is to materialize and disarm that rascal who represents your fears.
- *Your mantra*—Remember that your love is more powerful than fear. *Your love is more powerful than fear.* Stand up to what pursues you and be free.

Let me show you how this works. My patient Megan, now forty, had been verbally denigrated by her alcoholic mother when she was a child. Nothing Megan did was ever good enough. For years she had a recurring nightmare:

Enemy planes are shooting at me. I'm on a sheer cliff, an open target, and there they come. I have no idea who they are. Machine-gun fire ricochets inches from me; I barely escape.

Each morning Megan would wake up spent, sweating. I suggested, "During our sessions why don't you re-create your dream? This will help us locate your fear." Though anxious, Megan agreed. Over the next month, each week we repeated this exercise. I told Megan to summon as much detail as possible. While meditating, eyes closed, she was finally able to give her enemy a face: It was her mother. Then our work had a focal point. With time she recounted the horrors of being a child of an alcoholic, saw she wasn't to blame for her mother's irrational rage. As Megan developed compassion for herself and worked toward forgiving—not justifying—her mother's failings, she grew stronger. With mounting self-love and respect she was able to reenter the dream, actually see herself on the cliffs, but the gunfire was becoming more distant. With each effort the planes receded, eventually disappeared. Love had given Megan the power to banish them.

I relish *The Wizard of Earthsea,* by Ursula Le Guin. It tells of a great wizard who's studying the magical arts in school. Suddenly an ominous shadow starts to trail him. In terror, he abandons his wizardly studies and flees. For years he runs. Finally, sick of running, he turns and confronts the shadow. And it turns out to be cast by himself. So, with this aspect of the self accurately acknowledged and integrated, he returns to school to become the most powerful wizard in the land.

The wonderful thing about dreams is that they'll give you continual opportunities to surmount fear. Not to worry. If you don't get the message at first, it will come again. If you keep missing it, the volume will be turned up until you do get it. This is the function of repetitive dreams or nightmares. I emphasize: They are not meant to punish. Dreams are compassionate; they are persistent because they want your attention. They want you to unburden yourself and walk toward the sun. Let them help you.

Shedding areas of unrest leads to a sharpened intuition. Many people start therapy saying, "I want to have dreams that predict the future. I want to find my guides." That's fine—but often the way to achieve this goal is first to dissipate blockages. Then your psyche, now unshackled, becomes transparent, and deeper dream-intuitions can materialize.

By dreaming you can travel vast distances. There's a second kind of dreaming that intuitively elevates your perception of the world and how you cope. It includes dreams of instruction prompting your growth and foreknowledge. I hope you begin to open yourself up to these messages, whether unexpected or sought. They are solution-oriented, practical yet mystical—a storehouse of understanding.

For years my patient Lenny drove a taxi in New York City. A streetwise native of the Bronx, he was a virtuoso in navigating Midtown traffic jams. Not so with his emotional life. He pretends to be a tough guy, though he's a softy inside. "Lenny, please talk to me about your feelings," his girlfriend begs. At forty, it's hard for him. He doesn't know how. That's why he's come to me. To augment our work together, I advise, "Lenny, ask to be shown what to do in a dream." I know how vividly he dreams—something he doesn't share easily (it goes against the macho image). So he promises, "I'll try." He does.

The next time he sees me, Lenny reports his dream:

> *I'm sitting at a table with a carved wooden music box on it. I reach over, open the lid. Instead of music, I hear a woman's sexy voice. "Lenny," she says, practically purring. "I'm watching over you. If you ever need anything, I'm here. For now, just be more affectionate with your girlfriend. That will do."*

Silent for a moment, I marvel. A former taxi driver and a music box. I'll just never be fully prepared for the distance between surface and essence. I'm still shaking my head when Lenny interrupts my train of thought. "Who was she?" he asks, not unreasonably. "A guardian angel or what?" "Could be," I said, grinning. "But, bottom line, did you follow the advice? Did it work?" I could swear Lenny blushed. "Just between you and me, yes. Like a charm. But I got to tell you this—I feel really silly about it." Nonetheless, a beautiful relationship with his dream guide began.

Not that everyone in the world hadn't been telling him for years to open up—but this time Lenny listened. Perhaps the woman in his dreams was the passion goddess Aphrodite. Or maybe she was what the psychiatrist Carl Jung termed anima, an "inner feminine figure who plays an archetypal role in the consciousness of man." Regardless, in dreams she spoke to Lenny, training him to become more sensitive.

Whenever you're in emotional quicksand, dreams can rescue you. Answers arrive in many forms: a voice, a person, a knowing, an instinct to go forward or stay away. Notice any insights or physical sensations that give you a better grasp on your life. It may mean going far back before language, when there was only primal sound. The music of the spheres: I've heard it once—notes, octaves, and tones so heavenly they heal and wordlessly transmit wisdom. Think of Pavarotti's golden tenor times the speed of light cubed. If you experience such music in dreams, relish every moment. It is a blessing. Whatever the interventions your dreams present, record them. Your vigilance in transcribing sleep-time messages, especially in a crisis, can be the impetus that'll save you.

Now what about the dreams that contain foreknowledge of events to come? How do these work? First, remember that the dream world can't be linearly defined. Winds of hyperspace blow here. Past, present, and future are all within reach. Here's a way to work with these dreams. Before going to sleep you can request to be shown aspects of your future (though such previews do sometimes come spontaneously). An intriguing prospect, but be aware that what you learn isn't always immediately a consolation. Be accountable for what you ask. Make sure you have a good sense that the information will benefit you. Does it feel right to know? I always check this out in myself. Generally I prefer to just let life unfold, though I have sought predictive dreams at certain crossroads in my life. My intention was to gain solid footing during emotionally shaky times by further defining my direction. You too can utilize dreams for this purpose.

I'd spent twenty years in medical training and working in private practice before *Second Sight* was published. Forty hours a week, I'd sit with patients in my office, one to one. I felt privileged to do this; it gave me pleasure. Occasionally I'd present talks at Los Angeles hospitals where I was on staff; otherwise I did little public speaking. Then came the book—and the prospect of giving workshops to large groups. A natural introvert, I wasn't sure if I could. So I consulted my dreams. Here was the response:

> *It's twilight. I'm speaking to a crowd from a balcony overlooking acres of lush park. Suddenly, people start pointing at the sky. At first I pay no attention. But everyone is so excited, I look up. I see the moon, and beside it a second moon, a smaller but radiant orb rising. It has never been there before. I'm told it is my "birthmark," that as it comes closer it will grow large. I fall to my knees in gratitude, crying tears of happiness.*

This dream was delineating my future path. The moon has been my spiritual companion since I was a little girl. In private moments I'd gaze at it, sketch it, talk to it, feel its comfort. What is most me, the moon represents. In this dream a second moon appeared on the horizon (my new direction). There was a fatedness (the birthmark) attached to it, fulfillment more than I have ever known (the joyful tears). My inexperience in public speaking aside, I knew it was to be my future. How fortunate I now feel to have witnessed the realization of my dream.

Answers, though, are not always so poetic or complete. At a point when anxiety was getting the better of me in a stressful love relationship, before going to sleep I asked, Shall I go ahead with it? What will it be like a year from now? That night I had a dream.

My friend Don, a Zen master and rabbi, came running up to me, laughing. "I have a message from God for you," he exclaimed. Wow, I thought. "What is it?" I couldn't wait to hear. Don said, "God told me to tell you, Good luck!"

I woke up, confused. Good luck? I thought. Very funny. What's that supposed to mean? Doesn't God intervene a little bit more than that? Well, not always. Here is the wisdom: You can inquire about your future, as I did, but sometimes you just have to live life to find out. It isn't always better to know. Don't get me wrong. God wishing me well meant a lot. It brought a sweetness and levity to my predicament that saw me through. I've come to have faith in the rightness of the messages I receive. Even if your dreams don't spell out this-is-what's-going-to-happen and this-is-what-you-do, see how their advice applies.

Believe in your dreams. Let them work for you. If you ride out your emotions—fighting not to shut down—dreams will never dry up as in Bob Dylan's "Mr. Tambourine Man," in which he sings of "ancient empty streets too dead for dreamin'." Nurture your intuitions so your dreams won't wither. Take advantage of their wide-ranged solutions.

EXTRAORDINARY INSIGHT into practical problems is what intuition provides. Let the tools I've outlined frame your emotional journey, all its phases—your epiphanies, your lows, everything in between. There is spiritual meaning to what you experience. Our vision must be all-encompassing, defined less by struggle than by the capacity of spirit we possess. There is no separation between our biochemistry and God, our emotions and what is holy. No part of our makeup doesn't belong. These precepts drive my work with patients and how I see myself.

At a recent talk to a group of physicians I was asked, "What is the appropriate boundary between the role of psychiatrist and that of priest?" My answer: "Each one of us must trust where we are drawn. If we're pulled toward spirituality in how we practice medicine, we can use it to assist patients." No conflict. Healing knowledge is more than academic. It is inspired. Moment to moment, if we dignify the intuitive impulses that move us, physician or not we can't go wrong. That any of us would consider squelching a hunger for the spiritual is untenable. How could it ever foster our well-being to cut off such a vital life force?

Intuition, spirituality, a return to places of innocence within—this is our path. The *I Ching* speaks of innocence as a state in which the mind is "natural and true, unshadowed by reflection or ulterior design." This is in no sense a naive position but one based on unsullied truth. Innocence leads us "to do right with instinctive sureness." No matter our wisdom or accomplishments, here is where we must begin. Every minute, every second seen anew.

Aptly, the first workshop I ever gave on intuition was in a nursery school classroom in Temescal Canyon Park in Pacific Palisades. Forty of us gathered amid piles of alphabet blocks, neon-colored hula hoops, and miniature wooden chairs. Glamorous, no—but the perfect setting. I was nervous, unsure of what I'd teach or how. The magic of that room initiated me into the best of what teaching can be. Though I still had and have so much to learn, the spirit of innocence that day will always stay with me.

Seeing the events of your life with innocence will enable you to better cherish them. The simplest things—the sun warming your shoulders, that home run you cheered for in Yankee Stadium, your grandfather's smile. Or milestones—the first time you cradled your newborn son, graduation day, your promotion. It took me years to allow the wonder of earning an M.D. to fully sink in. My 1975 acceptance letter to medical school (which my mother had laminated) just kept gathering dust on my office shelf. I didn't even see it. Only recently did the miracle of this letter hit me. It documented my opportunity to become a doctor. A doctor! Suddenly the blessing penetrated.

Innocence slows time down so we can savor life. It's often hard to truly acknowledge our growth. We wanted it, yearned for it. It came. Sometimes before our success can really touch us we're already on to the next goal. Innocence will open your heart so you can accept what is due you. Allow those sweet summer days that lasted forever when you were a child to return. Your emotional cycles will continue. You'll encounter fresh earth and brambles, dark forests and heights. Learn from them. Take it all in. Treasure everything.

7

Centering and Protection

Whoever can see through all fear will always be safe.
—Tao te Ching
(trans. Stephen Mitchell)

I was staring down the barrel of a .357 Magnum. And, unbelievably, it wasn't a dream. There the pistol was, aimed straight at me. At us. Six skimpily clad women taking an early morning aerobics class in a gym in Venice Beach. We froze, too terrified to make a sound. The gunman had rushed in off Lincoln Boulevard. Partially concealing his face with a ratty pink towel, he trembled like a leaf as he screeched, "Strip! Now!" Dear God, I thought, a rapist. A murderer. Fear. Panic. And then my intuition kicked in. To my amazement I was able to ask myself, in this terrible moment, How can we all make it out of here safe? An inner voice replied: "Calm down. Undress, do what he says, but as slo-o-o-wly as you can. You will be rescued." Okay, I thought, taking a very deep breath. I hope I can do this. I got up my nerve. I centered myself. More breathing. I reached down, clumsily undoing the wadded up triple knot I'd tied in my shoelaces. I didn't look up. I was determined not to make eye contact; I instinctually knew not to. The shoelace: my only focus. Then . . . *Smash!* A door flew open. A pumped-up bodybuilder from the gym next door ran in, yelling, "Hey, what's going on here?" The gunman freaked. He charged like a crazed bull at our hero, pushing him aside but—what a miracle—not shooting him. Then, dodging traffic, gun in hand, the assailant fled across the street and vanished. Another morning workout in L.A.

Centering and protection. The posture you take is significant. As was true for me, in-the-moment choices may not allow the luxury of analytic thought. One . . . two . . . three. That's all the time you have to tune it. If such moments arrive, it's good to be prepared. The gunman episode could've been far worse. What if I'd screamed? What if I'd tried to make a run for it? My intuition may have spared me and us some dreadful consequences.

Every day we make decisions our intuition can inform. It delineates right action in both extreme and ordinary circumstances. Now I'll show you how intuition can optimize ways to center and protect yourself. *Centering* means finding the still point inside, no matter what is happening. *Protection* means the strength you can intuitively summon to counter negativity or threat. Why do we need these skills? In dire situations they can be the difference between life and death. In the daily world they also have potent ramifications. Dealing with an angry husband, an intrusive mother, a manipulative boss—imagine being able to center yourself, become unshakable. You tune in, see right through them, know exactly what to say or do to bring out the highest good. Or how about learning to protect yourself from people who drain your energy (aka energy vampires)? Wouldn't it be a relief not to be so susceptible? Inner stability plus intuitive vision are a commanding pair.

High winds blow in different seasons. Be like a sturdy tree, roots firmly planted in the earth. Then when storms—emotional, physical, spiritual—come you won't be knocked flat. For years I was too easily derailed by difficult emotions—depression, anxiety, envy. You didn't like me. You criticized me. You didn't respect my boundaries. You yelled. Any of one of these might've put me down for the count. It could've been months before I got back on my feet. No more. These days when I fall—it's inevitable for everybody—I can pick myself up pretty quickly. Now I want to share with you the techniques for centering and protection that have benefited me. Practice each one. Adopt those that best fit your temperament. They will help you grow strong.

Step 1. Notice Your Beliefs

Each of us has our own special power. It waits to be awakened. Call it your inner self, your spirit, or light—however conceived, you must meet and come to know your core essence. The source of all intuition, it is your fiercest ally and advocate against danger. Here is the premise I build on: By connecting with this part of yourself, you'll build confidence, feel more safe in the world. Then whatever or whoever crosses your path—even the Devil incarnate—will be no match for your resilience.

I want you to flush out beliefs that divert you from your power. Begin by asking yourself, What in my life throws me off center and why? I'm referring to everything from a stranger flashing you a dirty look to dealing with someone in pain. In what interactions does your energy dim? Where are your weak spots, points that need securing? And what about negativity? How do you deal with yours, or another's? If a supervisor says, "You'll never be successful," or an ex-lover announces, "You're incapable of a healthy relationship," do you buy into it? We all have our triggers. The basis for centering and protection is grasping where we get caught, then disengaging the trigger.

FOUR COMMON BELIEFS THAT DRAIN POWER

1. *I'm not strong enough to protect myself.*

As children many of us aren't taught to believe in the full power we contain. Yes, our parents may support our intelligence, talents, physical attractiveness—even teach us sound ethical values, the difference between right and wrong. But what happens to our inner self? Might even devoutly religious parents fail to realize it's there, in us, in them? Our starting point is to recognize that we possess a very real internal source that enables us to see and know deeply. Yet when something goes wrong frequently our first impulse is to look outside ourselves for someone to "fix" us. We get sick; we rush to the doctor. We become depressed; we call a therapist. We're in pain; we take a pill. It's fine to seek expertise—but we have it backwards. We need to look inside first. Really, it's not a big blank in there. Then act on what our wisdom tells you.

What stops us? A likely culprit is the vulnerable child each of us carries within. Mogul or mailman, mother or monk, this aspect of our psyche yearns to be taken care of, protected; it's unequipped to do it alone. He or she pops up in the darnedest circumstances, reducing us to helpless tiny tots. Of course we must tenderly acknowledge the needs of this child within, but we also have to know where to draw the line. Would you want a baby running *your* boardroom? Your life? Remember: Your inner self is more than your inner child. Far grander—capable of ministering to all your needs—is the radiance of your spirit. Feeling this, knowing this, is the best protection of all. You must become your own champion before anyone else can. When you believe in yourself, no one else can diminish you.

2. *Other people's negative thoughts can harm me.*

In my workshops I'm struck by how worried participants are about being thwarted by other people's negative thoughts. Such concerns need to be addressed. On an intuitive level ill intentions or feelings can affect us, creating anxiety or physical dis-ease. We must train ourselves to deflect them. What is negative energy? Any force antithetical to well-being. How does it turn up in everyday life? Let's start at the lower end of the spectrum. Your neighbor doesn't approve of you. A friend puts down your plan to start college at forty. Your ex-boyfriend's girlfriend is sending you bad vibes. Now let's really amp it up. A business competitor—the one who's always double-crossing you—has actually hired a witch doctor to stick pins in a doll made in your image. Or the real topper: An evil spirit, sent by a detractor, is inhabiting you. You're possessed! What do you do?

Follow these broad strategies (more specific techniques will follow):

- Don't lead a lifestyle based on assuming others are out to get you. This perpetuates fear.

- If someone is sending you negative thoughts, avoid dwelling on them. The more attention you pay to negativity, the more influence you give it.

- Focus on the strength of your inner self; this is the best defense against negativity, no matter how dramatic its manifestation. If you are solidly connected to yourself, nothing can get you.

3. *I'm too sensitive for my own good.*

The archenemy of intuition is lack of sensitivity. Know this: There is no such thing as being overly sensitive. To grasp this concept you may have to reconfigure old ideas that have been drummed into your head. When parents or teachers said, "You have to toughen up" or, especially with boys, "Only sissies cry," unknowingly they were undermining the crux of your intuitive tie with the world. Male sensibility in particular has been bludgeoned by such rigid conditioning. But, for both sexes, to break down childhood armoring requires extraordinary commitment, trust, and resolve.

I'm not speaking of simply expressing your emotions. Sensitivity is learning, at your own pace, to remain wide open to an intuitive realm—being one with the wind, the moon, other people's joys, sorrows, the continuum of life and death. From this oneness comes an intimate ecstatic bond with all of existence, exactly what you *don't* want to protect yourself from. Sensitivity turns against you only when you feel overwhelmed. But how do you stay receptive and not get obliterated by the intensity of such input? I'm going to teach you how to remain vulnerable *and* feel safe. The answer is never to shut your sensitivity off but to develop it as a creative resource.

4. *It's my job to take on the pain of others.*

We're trained that as bighearted people we must try to relieve the pain of others. A homeless person holding a cardboard sign—"I'm hungry. Will work for food"—at a busy intersection, a hurt child, a distraught friend. It's natural to want to reach out to them, ease their angst. But many of us don't stop there. Inadvertently, we take it on. Suddenly we're the ones feeling desolate, off kilter, bereft, when we felt fine before. This loss of center is what I want to address. It does not serve us. I am adamant about this: The most compassionate, effective route to healing people is to be a supportive presence, not to attempt to live their pain for them. Moreover, suffering sometimes has its own cycle that has to be respected, hard as that may be to witness.

We must lay to rest the old metaphysical prototype of the empathic healer. Typically these were grossly obese women (carrying extra weight, they mistakenly argued, was the only way to stay grounded) who cured patients by absorbing symptoms with the technique of laying on of hands. The result? Patients would leave feeling better; the healers would be sickly wrecks. These women were convinced such sacrifice was necessary to lessen the suffering of others. As a young physician I almost got snagged in the same trap. During my first months of private practice, I used to drag myself home and flop into bed half dead from everything I'd absorb: a sure path to burnout. This tack wasn't good for me or my patients.

I've learned the value of being a catalyst for people's growth without compromising my well-being. Patients themselves have taught me I can't do the work for them. Nor is that my job. Or yours. Keep this in mind: It is not our business to deprive anyone else of his or her life experiences. I understand the impulse to want to make things better. Compassion and the desire to console are human. But there's a fine line between supporting people and trying to do it for them. No matter how well-meaning or heartfelt your intentions, doing too much is an act not of love but of sabotage. You can be caring and honest with others yet still let them be. Don't equate honoring their growth process with abandoning them. A practical philosophy of healing must include preserving your energy as well as serving others. Striking a balance is essential.

QUESTIONS FOR REFLECTION

- Do you look to authority figures (gurus, psychics, teachers, family, friends) for answers before you seek them in yourself? Why?

- Are you easily thrown off by other people's moods or opinions? What will it take for you to center yourself?

- How can you turn you sensitivities into a plus, let them work for you?

Step 2. Be in Your Body

Envision your body as a grounding rod. Everything you think, feel, see, do, intuit is processed through it. The more solidly you inhabit your body, the less you'll wobble when adversity arrives. Webster's dictionary defines a ground as "an object that makes an electrical connection with the earth." Similarly, your body is of the earth and binds you to it. Elements intermix. You inhale oxygen, exhale carbon dioxide, metabolize sunlight into vitamin D, derive sustenance from food, eliminate toxins. These are just a few of the miraculous functions you must remember you have. Anything you can do to increase your body awareness will make you more sensual and centered.

When you're in jeopardy your body reacts. It's designed to protect you. The instant you feel threatened—a colleague lashes out, an intruder breaks into your home, a wild animal attacks—your biochemistry rallies. Suddenly you're hyperalert; adrenaline, the "fight or flight" hormone, surges through your system. Eyes dilate. Heart races. Breathing quickens. This evolutionary adaptation has only one purpose: survival. But the body's ingenuity doesn't stop there. Science has recently tracked it one step beyond our instinct to recognize and counter imminent threat.

Dr. Dean Radin at the University of Nevada, Las Vegas, has shown that the body can intuit danger even before it hits. His discovery was based on measuring the physiological responses of subjects when viewing a series of randomly ordered slides—some calming (a serene mountain lake), others hideously violent or pornographic (mutilation scenes, pierced genitals). Radin found that seconds before seeing the disturbing images, subjects' heart rates and respirations dramatically increased, whereas before pleasant slides no change occurred. I'd like you to take this away from these findings: Your body is so in touch that it can anticipate harm. Its signals provide a survival mechanism you can depend on.

Living fully in your body is centering. Not living in your body may leave you prone to harm. I'm fascinated by the Native American belief that malevolent spirits hover around bars because alcoholics are more susceptible to their influence. Why? Day after day, drinking relentlessly, alcoholics weaken their flesh and their access to the divine. Their bodies become vacant, nonreceptive. So these spirits target their prey, claim them.

How do you center yourself? As a general rule, do anything that brings you closer to your body or the earth. Exercise. Hiking. Dance. Yoga. Making love. Hugging a tree. Listening to music. Taking a luxurious bubble bath. Getting a massage. Stretching out naked on a warm rock. Going barefoot. Beating a drum. Being around animals. Planting a garden. Relishing a scrumptious meal. Do whatever makes you feel more present and alive. Let your body articulate its needs.

More specifically, I'd like to share with you some easy centering approaches I practice and suggest to patients. When my mind is swirling, if I feel scattered, fatigued, or sick, I come back to my body employing one or all of these methods.

TECHNIQUES FOR CENTERING

Watch your diet.

Notice what foods feel good, what foods do not. Your body will tell you what it requires. Usually, denser foods—meat, chicken, fish—have more of a grounding effect than grains, vegetables, or fruit. I'm not a big meat eater, but if my body announces, I need a hamburger, I will devour one. Listen to your body's signals. Notice how they fluctuate.

Do mundane tasks.

Mindfully concentrating on everyday chores can bring you back to your body. Grocery shopping, paying bills, chopping vegetables, washing clothes, taking out the trash, or cleaning the yard can be grounding. These activities anchor you in the here-and-now by drawing on the luminous nature of the ordinary.

Practice anonymous service.

Do something nice for someone without taking credit for it. Hold the elevator for a little old lady. Let someone go before you in line. Serve food to the homeless. Give a charitable donation. Anything that shifts the focus from you to others. No deed is too small. The act of giving—especially when you're most frazzled—opens your heart and is regenerative.

Spend time in nature.

As the poet William Wordsworth put it, civilization can be "too much with us." People, cars, the news, telephone cables matting the sky, all can keep us from our bodies, divorce us from what is natural. Regularly take at least a few hours out from your routine. Visit the beach, a forest, a canyon, a river. Choose a spot that moves you. Aboriginals seek out windswept plains for purification. Native Americans go to fresh streams to clarify their inner vision. (Any water source, including a bath or shower, can cleanse and purify.) Tibetan monks make pilgrimages to mountaintops. Allow yourself to draw on the earth's primordial forces. Savor the beauty of a twilight, sunset, or dawn. Let all these things nourish and restore you.

Meditate.

Sitting in meditation is a lifeline to your center, to the earth. By calming the mind you can realign with your essence. Close your eyes. Focus on your breath. Then gently extend your awareness downward to strata, bedrock, minerals, and soil. From the base of your spine, begin to feel a continuity with the earth's core. Picture having a long tail that roots in that center. Allow the earth's energy to infuse your body and stabilize you. Whether you meditate for five minutes or an hour, this is sacred time.

I suggest you put these centering techniques into immediate action. Whether you live in a fortieth-floor Manhattan apartment or a hut in the Sonoran Desert, these earth-grounded practices will reinstate your relationship with your body. Your success in centering doesn't ultimately lie in any one action. It encompasses an entire lifestyle—for instance, the way your home feels to you (mine is filled with plants and books, which ground me) or your willingness to improvise according to your body's instincts (when I'm insecure, my body likes to rock back and forth, so I go with it). These sensibilities, when clarified, set a nurturing tone for your life.

Step 3. Sense Your Body's Subtle Energy

When we were growing up, my girlfriends couldn't wait to hit the shopping malls and go to parties, the bigger the better—but I didn't share their excitement. I always felt overwhelmed, exhausted around large groups of people, though I was clueless about why. "What's the matter with you?" friends would say, shooting me the weirdest looks. All I knew was that crowded places and I just didn't mix. I'd go feeling just fine but leave nervous, depressed, or with some horrible new ache or pain. Unsuspectingly, I was a gigantic sponge, absorbing the energy of people around me.

Thank goodness, as my intuition matured, I had a life-changing revelation. From conversations with other healers and from working with patients, I realized I was experiencing intuitive empathy: the ability to sense what's going on in others both emotionally and physically as if it were happening to me. Amazing at times but also challenging. Let me explain the dynamics of intuitive empathy: The more people per square foot, the more our energy fields intersect—thus the tendency to become overloaded in high-density areas. This aspect of intuition is the most neglected and misunderstood.

I'm not referring to ordinary empathy—for instance, when you sympathize with a friend whose fiancé left her or share your brother's joy on the birth of his first child. Intuitive empathy goes way beyond. It's the capacity to energetically merge with others and, for the moment, see life (positive and negative) through their eyes, sense the world through their feelings. If this describes you, it may be impossible to distinguish these sensations from your own, throwing you off center.

I know. I've been there. That my intuitive empathy has become a gift is mind-blowing—and a tremendous relief. Many of us never get to the good part of empathy because we're not shown how. What ails us eludes even our doctors. We go in for care, but it's like the blind leading the blind. No one know what's going on. Empaths can unintentionally make even a good doctor's life hell. They manifest such a barrage of "unexplained," treatment-resistant symptoms that frustrated physicians write them off as hypochondriacs.

Empaths are notoriously misdiagnosed. Patient after patient has come to me labeled agoraphobic or with panic disorder, having received only minor respite from traditional treatments such as Valium and behavior therapy. Some were nearly housebound. They'd all say, "I dread being in crowded places where I can't make a quick escape. Forget department stores, busy streets, elevators, subways. I avoid them like the plague." Sounded very familiar. So I decided to take a history of how these people processed subtle energy in the world, something all healers must be trained to assess. Voilà! I found many were undiagnosed empaths. For me this changed everything. My job then became teaching my patients to center themselves and deal more productively with the day-to-day nuances of energy.

In my workshops I always inquire, "How many of you have intuitive empathy?" It's astounding. Hands shoot up from at least a quarter of the room. Of those people nearly everyone concurs, "I had no idea how to describe my feelings, let alone cope with them." Then they'd dangerously conclude, "I thought something was wrong with me for being 'overly sensitive.'" I want to dispel this myth, illustrate how you can utilize this form of intuition in daily life. From telephone calls, letters, and feedback I receive during my workshops, I've seen how widespread such empathy is. How do you know if you have it?

ARE YOU AN INTUITIVE EMPATH?

Ask yourself the following questions:

- Have you ever been placed next to someone at a dinner party who seems pleasant but suddenly you're nauseous, have a pounding headache, or feel drained?

- Are you uncomfortable in crowds? Do you even go out of your way to avoid them?

- Do you get easily overstimulated by people or prefer being alone?

- When someone is distressed or in physical pain, do you start feeling it too?

If you've answered yes to one or more of these questions, it's likely you have experienced intuitive empathy. Responding yes to every question indicates that empathy plays an active role in your life. If you're still unsure, take some time to notice how you relate to people one to one or in groups. This may require slowing such interactions down to become more aware of your style of processing energy. Give yourself time to listen to and weigh your body's signals. Don't write any response off. Notice if you're a chameleon. For instance, if a friend feels ill, do you also start feeling ill? Or if someone is sad, do you become sad too? When you are learning to center yourself, seeing how you assimilate this information is essential.

How can you deal constructively with intuitive empathy? What practical methods can you employ to avoid becoming overamped or depleted? Try the following strategies. See which ones are appealing and, most important, work for you.

FOUR WAYS TO AVOID ABSORBING OTHER PEOPLE'S ENERGY

1. *Walk away.*

Let's say you're chatting with a man you've just met at a conference and your energy starts bottoming out. Here's how to tell if you're being zapped: Don't hesitate to politely excuse yourself; move at least twenty feet from him (outside the range of his energy field). If you receive immediate relief, there's your answer. Most people are oblivious to how their energy affects others. Even energy vampires—people who feed off your energy to compensate for a lack of their own—aren't generally intending to sap you, yet they still do. Obnoxious or meek, vampires come in all forms. Watch out for them. For years, reluctant to hurt anyone's feelings, I needlessly endured these types of situations and suffered. How many of us are so loath to appear rude that a raving maniac can be right in our face and still we don't budge for fear of offending? Whenever possible—if your well-being feels at risk with an individual or group—give yourself permission to make a tactful and swift exit. In a spot, physically removing yourself is a sure, quick solution.

2. *Shield yourself.*

A handy form of protection used by many people, including healers with trying patients, involves visualizing an envelope of white light (or light of any color you feel imparts power) around your entire body. Think of it as a shield that blocks out negativity or physical discomfort but allows what's positive to filter in. For instance, your sister is on the rampage. She's about to blow up; you don't want her anger to shatter you. Now—take a deep breath, center yourself, engage your shield. Picture it forming a fail-safe barrier around you that deactivates anger, negative energy simply can't get to you. Shielding is a deliberately defensive technique aimed at guarding your feelings, not repressing them. It works by establishing a perimeter of protection around you that doesn't permit harm.

3. *Practice vulnerability.*

One tenet of my spiritual practice is to remain as vulnerable as I can to everything; not to shield, the antithesis of defense. Some people prefer my strategy, some don't. Use it if it succeeds for you. Here's the premise (not madness) behind this practice: If we solidify our bond to our inner self, we'll become centered enough not to need to defend. Thus, the best protection turns out to be no protection—a stance that initially alarmed me. It didn't seem possible I could do hands-on energy work with patients who had cancer or depression, for example, without absorbing their symptoms myself. But it was. What could be more liberating than to find I could hold my own *and* remain open! Too often we're taught to equate vulnerability with weakness. Not so. I like being vulnerable and also strong. This disarms people. To me the appeal of such an approach is that it's a nonfear-based way of living in the world. It requires that you increasingly harmonize with whatever you confront, let it flow through you, then recenter again, stabilized by your own resilience. Pace yourself. A vulnerable posture will feel safer the stronger you get. It is a choice and a lifelong practice.

4. *Meditate.*

To cement your inner bond and hold your center in any situation, I recommend a daily practice of meditation in which you focus on the spirit within. Doing so gets you into the habit of connecting with yourself. Start with a few minutes, then gradually increase the duration. The technique is simple: Follow your breath and explore the silence. It is not void or empty; that's the mystery. As thoughts come, and they will, continue to refocus on your breath—every inhalation, every exhalation. The spaces between thoughts are where your spirit waits to be discovered. There is something real in there worth finding. My spirit feels like a core of head-to-toe warmth, aligned through the center of my body. Imbued in the warmth is an intelligence and intuitive responsiveness to my rhythms and questions. It speaks only truth, which resonates like a chiming in every cell. Silently become acquainted with your spirit. Notice how it manifests itself, which may be very different from my experience. You can return to your spirit to reinforce who you really are—not just the self you present to the world but that part of you that is timeless. Make room to pursue it.

These four methods will increase your ease when relating to anything—computers, bossy people, heights, barking dogs. What's particularly gratifying is that with your earned sense of security often comes the desire to be more generous. Less to defend, more to give. To keep your energy high, it's worth deciding on a mode of giving that feeds you. In the process realize there's an enormous difference between codependent giving and giving from the heart. Codependency is taking inappropriate responsibility for the emotions or behaviors of others—sometimes caring so much for people that you forget to care for yourself. The old joke is that when a codependent dies it is *your* life that flashes before her eyes. Not good. This kind of giving, often spurred by guilt or obligation, can leave you feeling put upon, unappreciated, sucked dry. In contrast, giving from the heart is never forced, makes you happy, is restorative. In terms of empathy, to ensure your energy stays at its peak, try to avoid getting hooked in by codependency issues. The classic book on this subject I recommend is Melody Beattie's *Codependent No More* (see Selected Reading).

As an empath you must remain as conscious of your motivations as possible. A clever therapist once pointed out to me, "The qualities you take on from other people are those you're not clear about in yourself." Of course, I thought. Fear, for instance. It can creep up on me unnoticed or linger subliminally. If I'm out of touch for too long, my intuitive empathy notifies me by cranking up full blast. I not only begin to sense other people's fear more vividly but also become a magnet for it; everyone suddenly seems to be afraid of something, and that cacophony resounds in me. Ugh. But once I uncover the root of my own fear, the "hook" vanishes. I'm no longer as sensitized to this quality in others and do not empathically take it on.

By staying on top of your emotions, you can avoid attracting what you're unresolved about. Regarding intuitive empathy, memorize this principle: Rage attracts rage. Fear attracts fear. Kindness attracts kindness. Don't allow resentments or insecurities to accumulate. What you are you will summon toward you. For this reason among others, over the years I've been in and out of psychotherapy. Here's my rationale: If I have no buttons to push, empathy can't drain me. I may sense someone's discomfort and think to myself, Aha, isn't that interesting, but as long as I remain a channel, not resisting or engaging the feeling, it doesn't glom on. Thus the importance of self-awareness, so you can enjoy the thrill of being intuitively alive.

With a firmer feel for what empathy is and how it affects you, you're free to explore its nuances. For me empathy invokes a oneness, a brotherhood and sisterhood each of us can embrace. Acknowledging this unity brings about deeper compassion, a truth the Beatles captured in "I Am the Walrus": "I am you and you are me and we are all together." Really living this means an inescapable encounter with love. Love, every second, every minute, every hour. You'll see it glowing from faces of strangers and family, from animals, stars, and flowers. No life-form is exempt. Empathize with such goodness. Soak it up. I do.

Once you've established a comfortable philosophy of giving, and gotten used to setting boundaries with others, empathy can become a seamless extension of your heart. In my workshops I have a privileged perspective, sometimes looking out on rooms filled with hundreds of people. All that love. I wish everyone could experience the wonder of this sight. It's rare now, only when I'm overtired or need time out, that I incorporate untoward energy. This is a miracle. If I can accomplish such a feat, you can too.

Step 4. Ask for Inner Guidance

No matter where you are or what you're doing, intuition will protect you. From out of nowhere you're fired. Your teenage daughter storms out the door. A suspicious character eyes you in a darkened parking lot. In the heat of the moment, as panic starts to well up, *stop*. Guidance is available. Take a big breath. Center yourself. And this is critical: Remember to ask for assistance.

But who are you asking? Or what? Consider the possibilities. It could be that you turn to intuition as a wise part of you that surpasses the mind. In emergencies you need to act fast. Intuition is quicker, surer, more masterful than the laborious machinations of logic. Even if you don't believe in a higher power or anything remotely celestial, your intuition will produce the guidance you need. However, you may be ready to concede there is something more. I have a patient, a mailman who's certain he's being watched over by his great-aunt Ida. From photos he'd always felt close to her, though they'd never met. If he's in a fix, while meditating, he calls on her. What should I do? he asks. Ida answers. He listens. A writer friend of mine believes she has a guardian angel. My neighbor, a landscape designer, communicates with a spirit animal, a black bear she calls her protector. Just for now, why not yield a little skepticism? Whether you call on an ancestor, angel, or guide, I encourage you to go inside and investigate if such forces are real. Try to access them. I'm convinced you'll find you're never alone.

Where to start? Say you haven't done this before. First, allow that anything is possible. Set aside the voice that says, This is silly, unscientific, or, worse, What if my mother could see me now? Be a child again, full of wonder, testing the world to discover what's true. No one is watching. Don't hold back. Just see what happens. Give yourself time. You may need to practice this meditation on a few occasions before your guide comes.

CONTACTING YOUR GUIDES

1. Relax yourself. Concentrate on the rhythm of your breathing as you quiet your mind. Immerse yourself in the silence.

2. When you're ready, ask your guide to appear. There's no need to actively visualize or attempt to manufacture one. Let your guide enter on its own. Notice any images, voices, lights, memories, people, or beings you spontaneously perceive. If it seems fuzzy or distant, ask your guide to speak more clearly, come closer. You may specify whom you'd like your guide to be. Of course, it's up to your guide to respond. Don't despair if you secretly hoped for a lone timber wolf but your deceased uncle Sidney from Queens arrives. Beware of overromanticized expectations.

3. Appraise your guides fairly. How do you know they're the real thing? Audition them. Start an active dialogue. See if their advice works and if they protect you. Your guide is a faithful support to enlist whenever you're in need. Value this relationship.

Make it easy on yourself. You may initially want to call on a spiritual figure you're familiar with—Jesus, Buddha, Adonai, any holy teacher you revere. One of my guides is Kuan Yin, goddess of compassion in China. The story goes that she was the youngest daughter of a cruel father. He tormented and eventually killed Kuan Yin, who'd always been filled with compassion for animals and people. In heaven her goodness transformed her into a goddess. She was told, "Your suffering is over. You can go anywhere, do anything you want." Kuan Yin replied, "I want to be sent back to earth to help people." And so she selflessly vowed not to leave until the last human being was free from pain. I aspire to emulate such love. For years I've worn a green jade pendant of Kuan Yin for protection and to open my heart. The psychiatric resident I supervise at UCLA spotted this pendant and started to wear one too. Kuan Yin is a guide who touches us both, enhancing compassion for patients and ourselves.

I'm a big believer in the power of sacred objects, such as my Kuan Yin necklace, to inspire and protect. They're tangible reminders of the greater spirit to which all guidance is addressed. For instance, Native Americans carry talismans and fetishes, small stone carvings of animals intended to keep their owners safe—the mountain lion, fortifying courage; the fox, embodying cleverness; the eagle, a bearer of higher truth. Perhaps these speak to you. Or you can choose any object—statue, stone, jewelry—that evokes your guidance source. When you really need to pull yourself together, hold it close; let its strength flow through you.

Another protective practice I recommend is burning the sage plant, *Salvinia apiana*. Traditionally it's called on by many cultures to rid a physical space of negative energy. In California purple sage grows wild in the coastal canyons, where I love picking it in the spring. Another form of sage, the "smudge stick," is available in New Age stores. Over the centuries smoke and incense have been prized for their properties of purification. The Catholic Church blends frankincense and myrrh. Tibetans burn pine boughs to exile wandering ghosts. Mayans use herbs and copal when cleansing temples. I choose sage for purification.

My patient Greg and his wife recently moved into a new home. It was everything they dreamed of: tucked away in the woods, skylights, with a barn for their horse. "Why doesn't it feel right?" Greg wondered. "There's a heaviness, an anxiety in the air we can't shake. The people who lived here before went through a horrific divorce. Could that be it?" I knew Greg's marriage was in good shape—I didn't sense his discomfort was a projection of difficulties in their relationship. This ruled out, I explained, "Sometimes negativity from the past can lodge in a house like an afterimage. It just needs to be cleared away." So I suggested that we sage the place. Greg and his wife were game. That week I visited them. The three of us, burning sage in hand, covered every inch of their home. Between the pungent smoke (an aroma that soothes me) and the prayers we said to lift lingering negativity, the ritual did the trick. From that day on the house felt lighter, the discord was gone.

You may think of eliciting guidance as a prayer. A reaching out to love and those forces in the universe that will do all they can to protect you. Irene, a therapist, was in the fourteenth hour of grueling labor. The baby's progress was excruciatingly slow. Then she remembered our spiritual teacher saying, "During labor, repeat my name several times. It will speed things along." In a prayer Irene did—her daughter was born soon after. Whenever I'm in an airplane and turbulence hits, I inwardly focus on my teacher's name. It centers me, and I swear conditions stabilize. Is this simply magical thinking? Feel free to put it to the test, like any good rational soul. Whenever you're in a dicey situation, try invoking your teacher or guide. Does it make a difference? Change may be subtle or dramatic. A small shift may be all you need to gain a surer sense of self.

Don't hestitate to pray. I do it all the time, sometimes at many points throughout the day. Flash prayers: short, quick, effective. If I'm thrown off I pray, "Please let me feel centered again," when frightened, "Please let my courage return." This approach can bring impressive results. Or perhaps you find that you want to care for someone and, for whatever reasons, there's not much you can concretely do, a frustrating scenario that can leave you feeling helpless. Remember, you can always pray for that person's well-being. Such an act has significance. Prayer travels. Put it out. It will target its destination. Have faith that good will be accomplished. Healing can occur in the most unexpected ways.

To really know you are protected, allow yourself to picture heaven.

Not necessarily the way storybooks paint it but a vision straight from your own heart. See what's there. Try to sense the personalized support available; there's never a shortage of time or love. This perspective will provide you a certainty of refuge. Your guidance can help you experience heaven. What's there is here if you make it so.

Step 5. Listen to Your Dreams

I'm prepared to remain awake each day only sixteen hours max. For me that's it for linear time and the mundane world. My safest place is in my dreams. There I become centered. I inhabit a form that feels more fluid, and I effortlessly replenish myself with images, energy, tones that are a bigger stretch to assimilate otherwise.

How you sleep, where you sleep, with whom you sleep will determine if your sleeping environment is protected. The softness of your sheets, weight of your blankets, room temperature, circulating fresh air, and quality of light all make a difference. When you sleep you're most exposed. All those hours your body lies there as you travel to other places. You want everything about sleeping to feel safe.

My bedroom is right on the Pacific Ocean. Every night I hear the surf breaking on the shore. Even when, in dreams, I'm light-years away, I feel it, rhythmically caressing me. Wave motion is to dreaming as our heartbeat is to life. Vibrant dreams come from living by the water. I have a low wooden table next to my bed. On it sits a small blue vase with a single fresh rose. I like every variety, every color of rose. That rose is the last sight I see when I go to sleep and the first sight that greets me when I awaken. These pivotal moments are too often ignored. They set a tone of beauty and awe for anything that follows. Also, my rose has become a signal for me to remember my dreams and write them down. I suggest you find a similar cue. Then, before you think of anything else, your dreams will be there. So, between the water, the rose, the gentle breeze (I always leave my porch door cracked open), the moonlight streaming in, and how cozy I feel beneath my beige down comforter, I'm as cocooned as I can be when I sleep.

Your bedroom must be uniquely suited to you. This is not just about redecorating. I'm talking about the subtle feng shui (energy alignment) of dream dynamics. You don't have to live in a castle or on the ocean to dream well. Wherever you live will do, if you make the effort to make it feel good. How you arrange your home has to be a reflection of your sensual and spiritual preferences. Even the direction of your bed can alter dreaming. North, south, east, west—try them all. Be unconventional enough to know the value of finding a position of your own.

This brings us to insomnia, a cruel condition that plagues the nicest people. One night of tossing and turning, staring at the clock, can push the sanest person over the edge. You feel like you don't fit anywhere. So what is insomnia about?

Is it just that we're so obsessed with daily worries that we can't shut our minds off? Sometimes that's true. But insomnia can also echo a deeper subconscious fear of loss of control, even death. No one teaches us how to fall asleep. No one teaches us what happens afterward—the leaving-the-body part. As children we need to be trained how to make this transition. For those who have a hard time going from material to nonmaterial form (though you may never have defined it this way), falling asleep can be problematic. The terror of surrendering to the unknown. Is there something there? Will it be benevolent? How will we know? Who could fall asleep with these concerns? One problem is, they are rarely voiced in this language. But they need to be. When you get down to it, our ease in falling asleep depends on our comfort level with what we'll find in sleep.

In a sense sleep is a wonderful preparation for death. The only difference is that in death we leave this body and don't return. It follows that anyone with a fear of death might be an insomniac. I work with numerous patients on this issue. In fact, fear of death taints many aspects of our culture, precludes us from fully experiencing the span of life we are given. Letting go. Death. Supposing this is our subliminal association, who in her right mind wouldn't hold back when falling asleep? If this seems familiar, don't be alarmed. Many people never put two and two together. But if you struggle with insomnia, you may be defending against what you're not even aware of.

I promise: Dreams are safe. Some are even protective. They can offer key imagery for solving potentially perilous situations. My friend Lisa, while camping outdoors in the Mojave Desert, was startled awake by such a dream. In it she was explicitly told, "An enormous dust storm is about to hit. Find cover." Though there was no sign of it, she alerted her bewildered friends and gathered them into their van. A few hours later, eighty-mile-an-hour winds began whipping through the desert and lasted until dawn. Fortunately Lisa listened to her dream. Let yours protect you too. When you are faced with physical or emotional danger, these dreams can be your way out. Lisa's was offered without prompting, but you can actively enlist protective dreams. All you have to do is ask.

Here's what my friend the anthropologist Hank Wesselman suggested to a girl who came to him plagued with fears. She'd been in traditional therapy, but it didn't seem to make a dent in them. Hank wanted to give her additional tools. So he told the girl a story about a Chumash medicine woman. When afraid the woman would visualize a large blue egg, then picture herself climbing inside, where nothing could touch her. The girl liked the egg idea and started applying it to her own fears. Soon after she had a dream: While window shopping she noticed a gang of scary-looking teenage boys skulking around. To her horror they edged closer, then started chasing her. She ran as fast as she could, trying to escape. Suddenly, rounding a corner, she noticed a blue VW Bug at the curb. The blue egg! She looked—the key was in the ignition. She jumped in the driver's seat, locked the doors. The boys surrounded the car, pounding on it, but couldn't get in. Impervious, she started the car and drove away.

Protective images, grand or unassuming, will get the job done. The secret is to excavate and claim those you resonate with. If the blue egg appeals to you, it's yours. Then again, you may prefer seeking refuge in an enchanted forest. If you're swooped up by an Arnold Schwarzenegger–like superhero or your guide appears, that's fine too. We all have our champions, special places. Waking imagery can filter into dreams. Only a gossamer veil separates sleep and waking. Protection from dreams imbues ordinary life. Make the most of this interchange.

CENTERING AND PROTECTION are intimately related to our views of war and peace. The stand we take has global as well as personal implications. Between countries or in your own living room, war is a state of antagonism, a struggle between "us" and "them." People who go to war have enemies. People who keep weapons have something to defend. Peace, by contrast, is an agreement to end hostility—politically, with others, or inside the self. This may result in both an end to violence and freedom from disquieting thoughts, oppression. Enduring peace has no duality, no enemies, no victims. The *I Ching* says it is "a time in nature when heaven seems to be on earth." Bull's-eye: the epitome of centering. How can we move toward peace, inner and outer? What stands in our way?

We all can acknowledge that there are real threats to our safety. And surely we have no lack of capacity to respond to them with force, troubling as it may be to do so. Equally troubling, however, is our apparent inability to establish when we are safe enough, when peace could be of our own making. Mahatma Gandhi, Martin Luther King, and John Lennon weren't just "dreamers." Daily life is experimental ground, a place to practice centering. War or peace? Always a choice to be made. All kinds of day-to-day situations conspire to push you to your edge. You may not know what to say or how to handle them. Let me make it simple for you. I believe that, when you get down to it, there's a bottomline answer: If in doubt, come from your heart. Then you can't go wrong. Ever. It's a process. Sometimes you make large gains, other times not. But victory lies in your commitment to a heart-centered goal. That's your real haven.

In ancient Chinese lore the best way to cure a haunted house is to move a happy family into it. The agreement between landlord and tenant goes like this: In exchange for living rent-free, the happy family has to put up with the inconvenience of the ghost's shenanigans—which sent former residents running. Strange sounds, objects whirling around the room, apparitions, they're all part of the package. This doesn't bother the happy family. They just go about their business. Loving. Steadfast. True. Exactly what is needed. Little by little, the ghost is driven away. Their centered energy works wonders.

Ghosts and goblins. Demons and shrews. Don't get discombobulated by the havoc they engender. Do as the happy family did. Cultivate an ongoing sense of inner peace and resolve, strengths that come forth invisibly. There's nothing like a little centeredness to counteract even the biggest, baddest, most unsettling calamity. Have confidence in your own power.

8

Finding Light in Darkness

The darkness declares the glory of the light.
—T. S. Eliot

*E*very year, in the depth of winter, my friend Rabbi Don Singer takes more than a hundred Jews and non-Jews to visit Auschwitz. These Bearing Witness Retreats are five days of on-site learning from the bleakness of the largest Nazi concentration camp in Poland. People from the United States, Israel, Poland, Western Europe; children of survivors; children of the Wehrmacht and the SS; priests, nuns, rabbis all gather in this radical meditation on peace.

The season is dreary—bitter cold, snowy, the sky's insufferable grayness ever-present. Prayers are said in the ruins of the crematorium: Jewish, Christian, Moslem, and Buddhist services conducted simultaneously. Can you see it? Faces of many colors and ethnicities filled with compassion, yearning for a hidden light that transcends rational explanation. These people travel to Auschwitz in the dead of winter not just to memorialize atrocities committed there but to seek a clearer view of human darkness.

Many of us share their deep need to know. The insight they gain isn't only about Auschwitz. It's about themselves—their own lives, their own capacities. How to confront impulses from anger to self-hatred, which, if repressed, may cause us to act out our worst aspects, put us unspeakably far from realizing joy. Don says, "Healing comes from knowing you don't have to run from darkness. You must go into it, eyes open, and discover your own strength."

We see human beings everywhere doing terrible things. To better understand why, Don explains, "An aim of these retreats is to view others as yourself." There is no quality in anyone that we don't contain, in fact or in potential. As Lenny Bruce once said, "I am part of everything I indict." Accepting this gives us a chance to clean house, to make sure we never inadvertently turn into the people we abhor. I know some of you are going to balk at Don's extraordinary faith and argument: He sees all of us as more similar than not. I must tell you I agree with him. It's a hard truth but an inescapable precondition for healing.

Think of something closer to home—hate crimes, the unconscious projection of rage and fear onto others. Freedom begins with comprehending our place in the continuum of this dynamic. Only then can we hope to transcend it. In our lives we recapitulate the evolution of the species. Not just biologically but in struggling through the long process toward actualizing peace. The aspiration is to create something finer.

Following the example of Don and his coleader, the activist Buddhist Roshi Bernard Glassman, this chapter will plunge into darkness. The worst of the worst. Depression. Suicide. Addiction. Psychosis. Not pegging them as adversaries but rather seeing them as vehicles for self-knowledge and opening our hearts. The principle is this: The pain wounding us will inevitably escalate, whether it manifests as self-destruction or mass destruction. Thus, our task is to eliminate the distance between ourselves and the emotional danger within. To heal, we must know what we're dealing with, learn from it, and cultivate compassion. Before 1942 there was no Auschwitz, but human history has always been mired in violence. It's up to us to break the pattern. In dark periods, yours or another's, be especially kind.

Truth is light is love. Even if it's difficult I prefer to know the truth about myself, darkness included. But remember, life isn't always as it appears. Even in the most painful circumstances there exists a possibility for magnificence and connection to spirit. For me, either personally or when treating patients, this means both nurturing and preventing the loss of life force during stressful times. My persistent ambition as a doctor is to stop the hemorrhaging of the soul.

Step 1. Notice Your Beliefs

Scientists recently saw the first sign of so-called dark matter when . . . an ordinary star suddenly brightened. Unlike ordinary matter, which may comprise 10 percent or less of everything in the universe, dark matter cannot be seen directly because it does not emit radiation. But it has mass, so it exerts gravitational pull on everything from stars to the light emitted by stars.

—*Los Angeles Times,* 1993

Dark matter, another cosmic surprise we're still just documenting. There to be seen the whole time, if only we knew how. Scientists say that when a clump of darkness comes between the earth and a star, the star's light bends: it appears brighter. What a paradox! Darkness illuminates. Perhaps such new physics can brighten our understanding of the psychology of light.

Black emotions. How do traditional psychiatrists conceive of them? Let me give you some insight into how they think. Psychiatrists have a Bible—the *Diagnostic and Statistical Manual of Mental Disorders (DSM-IV).* One might call it the complete book of human darkness. This eight-hundred-and-eighty-six-page volume is arranged according to "pathology," an encyclopedia of all "mental disorders" known to humankind. Included are everything from zoophilia, "the act or fantasy of engaging in sexual activity with animals," to psychosis, an inability "to maintain adequate contact with reality." Chances are when you go to a therapist, he or she will be sizing you up according to the criteria of this book. You will leave that day slotted in a category—too often it's easier for your therapist and insurer to deal with labels than with people.

I'm a board-certified psychiatrist, a credentialed member of the medical tribe. Why do I have a problem with this picture? Here's my concern: This particular Bible pathologizes experience, assuming that "abnormal" behavior falls neatly into specific symptoms with assigned numerical codes. It doesn't reflect the whole person. I value the *DSM-IV* for providing our profession with a common language of guidelines and a starting point for organizing a breadth of emotional states. However, from insurance companies to hospitals, the instant a code gets slapped on you, it determines the amount of money providers get paid and creates expectations about treatments to offer and how you'll respond. Even doctors who don't mean to get pulled in, do. This is the training model for all medical professionals.

I want you to be aware of the advantages and limitations of the system. I want you to see yourself as far grander than its categories. The new model I'm suggesting includes spirituality and intuition, not just clinical signs. A wider path through the darkness. I combine my mainstream education with what the mystery teaches me, moment to moment embracing it all. If you come to me with panic attacks saying, "I hyperventilate. My heart is racing. I'm jumping out of my skin," here's what I'll do. First, as a traditional psychiatrist, I'll consider the *DSM-IV*—but I'll go further. I'll intuitively tune in. Flash. Images, impressions, or knowings will surface. I'll sense your subtle energy, request added insight from remote viewing and dreams. All this information, linear and intuitive, creates a richer portrait. Just because two people share a diagnosis doesn't mean their treatments should be identical. The great strength of intuition is its ability to honor the individual, making generalizing impossible. I cherish its inability to be regimented or pigeonholed. I reject the cookie cutter approach, value a person's uniqueness, let it speak to me.

Your essence can never be labeled. Still, if you're anxious and a good friend is anxious, you may share some aspect of experience. You can learn from each other, lend support. This is not the same as being stereotyped. One of the surest ways to gain compassion is to have gone through something yourself. In retrospect, I'm thankful I've had so many ups and downs in my life. There's not much patients can tell me that I can't identify with. This helps me to help them. In your life move toward people and professionals who can see beyond psychiatric labels and offer you a range of treatments. Insist on care that is personalized. What matters most is you: your needs, your reactions, interventions that make your life feel worthwhile again, cause hope to return.

Old models die hard. For years working in hospitals I had to search for like-minded peers. The one safe harbor I found to treat patients in our spiritually phobic medical system was on chemical dependency units. There the Twelve Step Alcoholics Anonymous program viewed substance abuse as having a spiritual (not religious) solution. I was in heaven. I'd found a secret society where both staff (most were in recovery) and patients talked openly about finding a "higher power," relying on a soberly grounded intuition to guide their lives. Conventional medicine tolerates such an approach mainly because not much else works for addiction. The psychosocial model alone, including therapy and medication, is often insufficient. However, when it is combined with the Alcoholics Anonymous approach currently practiced by over 2 million people worldwide, success is significantly greater. From the merger of these techniques, I saw how a more integrative form of medicine was possible.

Today all kinds of spirituality—the twelve Steps, meditation, contemplation, conventional religion—are increasingly being accepted in psychiatric training programs. I'm supervising Meredith, a twenty-eight-year-old UCLA psychiatry resident who is hungry for it. I'm thrilled that my alma mater is supportive. So supportive they've okayed Meredith to assist my workshops around the country to study how to apply intuition and spirituality to group dynamics. The participants love it, I love it, she loves it. My dream has always been to blend the way I work with traditional medicine, not function on the periphery. It's coming true.

The dark night of the soul. How to navigate it? I suggest you adopt an attitude of nonconformity to view this passage with fresh eyes. In Los Angeles there's a group, Poets Anonymous, that places quotations on billboards to inspire urban travelers. These windows for reflection provide a pause to remember light is there. I was driving through the intersection of Fairfax and Melrose, in the center of West Hollywood, and right above me was a quote from the poet Charles Bukowski: "What matters most is how well you walk through the fire." It made my day. Such reminders keep us from going numb, instill courage to persevere.

When it comes to your emotions, discard the strip-mall mentality of mental illness; watch out for the pejorative labeling I've described. What you're going through is not explicable only by science or psychology. There is a spiritual significance to your experience. Even if it eludes you now, give it time. The Western approach to life is, Understand it, then do it. The Eastern approach is, Do it until you understand. Try something radical. You may not know where you're going, but see what you will find. All the while, aim for modest gains, not ambitious advances. These will be the most enduring.

QUESTIONS FOR REFLECTION

• Are you ready to accept all of you, light and dark, learn from both how to heal? What resistances do you have? How can you get through them?

• When under emotional duress, do you give up on your intuition? Or will you keep listening for it, though it's hard to hear?

• Are you prepared to search for both the psychological and spiritual meaning of difficult emotions? How can this practice serve you?

Step 2. Be in Your Body

What makes emotions spin out of control? Freudians implicate repressed sexual impulses. Behaviorists, traumatic conditioning. Chinese medical practitioners believe it's a blockage of energy flow. Psychopharmacologists, a new breed of psychiatrists, attribute certain kinds of severe depression and anxiety to imbalanced brain chemicals, called neurotransmitters. The treatment? Medications that correct the deficiency.

A few of many theories, no single truth. Still, whatever mode you choose must be geared toward returning you to your body. When you're stressed the focus of your awareness shifts, out of your body into your mind—a type of shock reaction. It can be hell staying stuck up there, fears blaring, no escape. For sanity's sake you must reverse the process. How? Very gently. I was once treating a schizophrenic teenage boy convinced he was being stalked by the FBI. Grounding himself in his body didn't mean dwelling on his paranoia. Rather, while sitting with him, I'd ask, "Tell me, how do your fingertips feel? Your toes? Earlobes? How about your belly button?" Hot, cold, tingly—it didn't matter. My goal was to refocus him at least temporarily, while keeping a lighthearted tone. Body awareness provides a healthy counterpoint to an overworked mind. When tension mounts it can extinguish a flame within you. By rekindling your senses you bring the flame alive again.

Also vital to keeping that flame alive is awareness of what you put in your body, particularly medication. I often get asked, "What is the role of traditionally prescribed medications in emotional healing? Should I use them? If so, how can I most benefit from them?" I want to present some pros and cons and offer an intuitively oriented system of deciding if they're for you.

Such medications during dark periods can be lifesavers for some, unsuitable for others: there's no absolute right or wrong. They could be your first choice, or you may initially want to try alternative methods, including herbs and homeopathy. It troubles me when people make sweeping judgments, positive or negative, about traditional medications. Don't get snagged by some common misconceptions: "I'm afraid

I'm putting poison into my system," "I'm ashamed," "I've failed spiritually if I take a pill," "I should be able to feel better on my own." These
are all understandable concerns, very human, but my own view differs.

Let me explain. I believe God was in the laboratory when medications from vitamins to Prozac were discovered, just as God is everywhere
else. Taking them is neither inherently spiritual nor inherently unspir-
itual. What matters is discerning their use and the spirituality of your
approach. For instance, in certain people the body's chemistry goes out
of whack, resulting in crushing depression, panic, or psychosis. This
may happen even if they meditate, even if spirituality abounds in their
lives, or even after they've exhausted alternative medical options. As in
diabetes or heart disease, medications that correct a biochemical imbalance can be a compassionate, intuitively sound solution. In this instance it takes strength to opt for them; doing so need not be a cause
for shame.

Sometimes, not always, good medicine entails prescribing medication. For me it's a fact-based and an intuitive call. Take my patient Gracie, a brilliant financial analyst found gallivanting naked at 2:00 A.M. in
front of the dinosaur museum at the La Brea Tar Pits—in the throes of
a manic high. The psychiatrist in me knew she needed lithium. During
mania adrenaline soars, at times causing simultaneous euphoria and
horrendous judgment—hardly something to fool around with. Lithium
could equalize Gracie's biochemistry and restore her balance. It's not
that medication is how I most want to solve any problem. If I can get
away with not using it, I will. But with Gracie it was necessary—my assessment was medically founded and also felt right. Sad to say, this was
regardless of Gracie's opinion or intuition. In such a state she was out
of touch with herself and would gladly have roamed downtown Los Angeles baring all. In mania and other kinds of psychosis, I must step in.
It's a judgment, and I have to make it until my patient's clarity returns.

Depression presents similar choices. Peter, a camera operator, came
to me pale, gaunt, in the depths of despair. He said, "Nothing specific
really set it off. But for the last month I can't eat. I can't sleep. I can't
make decisions." Even washing the dishes was a Herculean effort.
Depression ran in Peter's family. His mother had it, his maternal grandfather too. A classic profile of biochemical depression, versus less
debilitating types, which are usually sparked by specific events—for example, bankruptcy, your mother dies, a project falls through—storms
often best weathered without medication. In these "situational" depres-

sions by generating inner strength you can emerge more whole. With a biochemical disadvantage such rallying may not be possible. If you or your doctor suspect a biochemical imbalance, it's reasonable to consider antidepressants.

Should you take them? How do you know? Sometimes the answer is clear-cut: You've had previous biochemical depressions. You're in one now. Antidepressants have worked for you. Or maybe you've never considered medication. You're too muddled to think straight or hear your intuition. Your therapist says, "Do it." You figure you've tried everything, alternative and mainstream. You have faith in her. Here, listening to advice is reasonable. Preferably, however, you're presented with facts and your intuition tells you whether to proceed. Finally, it may be that both you and your doctor agree medication is not necessary, that your biochemistry is okay. In this case you'll gain by facing feelings on your own, riding the wave through. In healing everything from loss to low self-esteem, it's important to identify and respect those times when your own resources are sufficient. It's equally important to respect those times when your doctor's recommendations have more clarity than your own.

Antidepressants (and other medications) can be a first step, getting you over a hump that appears Sisyphean. A cruelty of depression is that it strips beauty, hope, and stamina from you. No matter how you try, you can't reach them. But the apparent failure of spiritual tools isn't cause for self-reproach. Even the devout are susceptible to emotional pain. Think of Job in the Bible, a man of faith who's tested to the limits. Finally even he slowly reaffirms his faith after harrowing loss. Now you may ask, Did Job use antidepressants? Answer—no, but perhaps they would've helped. Still, he didn't have that choice. You do. Can you use them without doing violence to your spiritual practice? Always a hard decision. However, with intuition you may conclude that informed assistance will spare you unnecessary anguish. Also, you may need only a short respite to recenter. Or, if you've suffered lifelong depression, medications can offer an initial glimpse of well-being. Then, when you're ready to discontinue them (always under your doctor's supervision), you'll know what to aim for. Remember, though, depression is partially a spiritual dis-ease, a dis-ease of longing for connection. No pill can single-handedly reverse that.

Taking any medication is a start, not the whole answer. We want to avoid the risk of indiscriminate pharmacology—fifteen-minute session, prescription is written, and out. Not only do I recommend psychotherapy but I always encourage my patients to meditate, develop a continuing spiritual practice. Why? There's no clear separation between body and spirit. From what I've seen in psychiatry, making an intuitive connection between the two can build deficient neurochemicals (such as serotonin in depression), enhance subtle energy, speed recovery. The result? Many of my patients have lowered their medication doses and minimized side effects. Others have discontinued medication completely. Some, however—for example, those with chronic psychosis, a tormenting disorder with no perfect solution—require long-term medication to counter an inborn imbalance. It's always a question of weighing the side effects of drugs like Thorazine (which regulates dopamine, implicated in psychosis) against the hellishness of the disease. Even so, once someone is stabilized the benefits of a conscious link with spirituality and intuition are within reach, bringing increasing faith and understanding.

In every case I relentlessly advocate that my patients listen to their bodies, work with them. Native Americans believe each illness has a spirit. Similarly, each chemical substance, although inert, has a spirit we must consult. In intuitive terms everything has life. To overlook this is to make a great omission. At best therapy is a collaboration, an ongoing tuning in: I tune in to my patient and the medication. My patient tunes in to the medication and herself. It's a three-way conversation. The moment you swallow a pill, you enter into a relationship with it. The goal is to harmonize. I seek to match the energy of the medication with the person. I'm looking for an affinity between the two, a resonance where the tone or frequency of the medication, as I intuitively perceive them, will enhance the body's functioning.

Mind and body aligned make miracles. Dr. Carl Simonton's pioneering studies of cancer patients show that by picturing wellness you can help create it. His accounts are truly inspiring. Visualizing their radiation and chemotherapy treatments as well as their white cells in a positive way, many of his patients experienced reduced side effects; some went into remission. I'm advocating this kind of intimate participation with medication and taking it further: Visualize the best possible outcome and partner with the spirit of the substance you're taking. Then you're on the front lines of your healing.

This only works when there's clear communication. I'm treating a new patient, a doctor who'd been taking Valium for sleep disturbances.

After our first visit, perhaps too accustomed to being in charge, he abruptly stopped the Valium without checking with me. This caused a violent, unnecessary impact on his system. Physically it was wrenching; spiritually he had not respectfully disengaged from the substance. He'd acted before we even discussed these issues. I recommend patients both invoke the spirit of a substance before use and take leave of it with care—bowing with respect going in and going out, working with their physicians closely through the process. Otherwise one is building a house without asking permission of the land. As some native traditions believe, no good will come of such an attitude. Nothing is simply technical, or mechanical. Never stop any medication without telling your doctor.

Tuning in to medications allows you to take part in your health responsibly. All medications—for emotions as well as for pain relief, cancer, or any physical ailment—are amenable. There's an intelligence to be addressed, not just a conglomeration of molecules. Get to know your medications, including herbs, homeopathic remedies, or other alternatives. Interact with them, pose them questions, listen for a response. Then you're more than a passive recipient of some strange substance, inhabiting your system, doing what it will. You must be in sync with your medications to maximize their effect. And you must work hand in hand with your health professional.

Here's an exercise I recommend to patients and practice myself. It allows you to have an active relationship with what you put in your body. Address each medication individually.

INTUITIVELY TUNING IN TO MEDICATIONS

1. Find a relaxed position and close your eyes. Place your attention on your body. Hear what it says. Ask yourself, Does the medication feel good in me? Notice if it blends with your rhythms, feels natural, if your energy is high. Also pay close attention to any feelings of discomfort. Are you revved up? Dragged out? Tense? Irritable? Establish a baseline for your reactions. Then you can go on.

2. Let's say you're concerned about dosage. Address the question directly to the medication. Am I taking too much, too little? Don't force anything. Let it answer you. You may get a simple inward sense of yes or no. Or your answer may be an image: a pot bubbling over, a glaring light, or a traffic jam, suggesting too high a dose. In contrast, sensing

you're not full enough or being hungry for more may indicate a boost is required. Stay alert to how your needs fluctuate. Feel free to ask anything at any time. Both intuitively listen to your body and query the medication. Open up a dialogue.

This exercise will make you more sensitive to your body. Practice it. My patients do. I need to know what they're feeling. They need to know. I take their intuitions seriously, depend on them to inform our choices. The dance we do—a doctor prescribing, patients taking a pill to help heal—is predicated on the intuitive truth of their experience. What they say or feel fits into the scheme, even without the confirmation of a medical text. I accept what they tell me, integrate it. Such attention also guides the process of ending medication. Overreliance can rob people of their power. Knowing when to stop is critical. I've had patients say, "Judith, it feels like it's time to get off." This isn't a question of side effects; it's about a sense of completion. Responses from patients are at the heart of my medical practice. My mandate is to hear and respect them. Yours is to find a healer who values your intuitions.

Such conversations between you and your doctor are especially essential because medications kill 100,000 people annually. The *Physicians' Desk Reference (PDR)* has many benefits—specifying dosages, side effects, actions, uses. The problem is, the *PDR* comes to be cited as scripture, capable of leading a doctor to disregard what a patient's trying to explain. You can be turning purple. If it's not in the *PDR*, your doctor may ignore it or, worse, imply It's all in your mind. This does incredible human damage. Where does it leave you? Doubting what you know to be true. Further, the *PDR* fails to take into account subtle energy. Nor does it adequately point out that some people are overwhelmed by even small doses or require a fraction of what's recommended. I'm a living example. On the rare occasions when I take Tylenol, a quarter of a pill does the job. Over the years doctors have relentlessly tried to prescribe larger doses of medications than my body tolerates or needs. I've had to learn to insist that the *PDR* may not know everything about me. My doctors have come to agree.

My patient Marge takes a sliver of Prozac for depression. It's not supposed to work, but it does. How do I know her reaction isn't a "placebo effect"? On this tiny amount Marge exhibits the same benefits and some of the liabilities the standard dose should give. Taking more only overloads her system. Marge is a meditator; she's cultivated an intuitive awareness of her body. This may contribute to her being a "quick responder," someone on whom medication acts faster than the *PDR* expects.

Whatever the *PDR* says you must tune in to how medication affects you. With antidepressants, for example, there can be real problems from side effects. Are you more cut off from your emotions or sexuality? Does it take forever to have an orgasm? Are you gaining unwanted pounds? Do you feel remote from your spirituality or intuition? If you answer yes to any of these questions, your physician's job is to finely calibrate the medication with your special needs. Doing so can take time and effort but will help you achieve true balance.

Finally, it may be that you can't tolerate a given drug at all. Forget dose, forget duration! The point then is to find another strategy, perhaps a different formulation or medication, or herbs, acupuncture, energy healing, homeopathy. But always this is an interchange based on listening to your body, being informed about substances you're ingesting, and having free, thorough discussions with a sympathetic doctor.

Whatever the course you must believe in it. Scientific research has shown that if you have faith a therapy can heal, it can. Such response confounds prediction. In a landmark 1950 study pregnant women debilitated from morning sickness were given syrup of ipecac, a vile concoction known to cause violent vomiting—but were told it was a new nausea cure. Their symptoms of morning sickness decreased. If your intuition tells you a medication will succeed, the strength of your belief affects how your body responds. This is not simply a question of belief in the therapy, as the Harvard cardiologist Dr. Herbert Benson has written. In his studies, those who felt the "intimate presence of a higher power" made better recovery and gained improved health. Sensing that presence, and feeling it imbued in the medication, can itself be a blessing.

Step 3. Sense Your Body's Subtle Energy

I recently met Ed, a sweet-natured Beverly Hills dentist who specializes in "dental-phobic" patients—people prone to panic attacks while cranked back in the dentist's chair. The high whine of drills, the mere thought of a needle with Novocain, has been known to throw them over the edge. But not with Ed there. Patients fly from Asia and Europe to see him. The secret to Ed's success? Subtle energy. He explains, "Root canals are the worst. Patients come in trembling. From the moment they sit down, I run my hands about two inches above the length of their body, sensing what areas need to be balanced. Then I send them loving energy. My patients immediately relax. They tell me, 'I'm less afraid' and 'It doesn't hurt so much.' " Miraculous, coming from panic sufferers. Ed adds, "Energy work makes less anesthesia necessary, and postop pain is reduced."

Energy is a variable that can revolutionize your recovery. It speaks to the essence of intuition, that which is often only sensed, a substratum of your emotional upheaval. By mobilizing energy you're going straight to what spirit is composed of. You're acknowledging, "Yes, something real is there. And, yes, I can contact it to heal myself." Whether a teacher facilitates this or you practice it alone, you'll be able to touch even hidden places. For me energy work is like planting roses that bloom in the midst of unhappiness and confusion. In darkness their fragrance is ubiquitous; with it the light comes. Subtle energy is light. We just have to know how to find it.

Simple acts can be lifesaving. For instance, placing your hand on your heart chakra. If you're upset rest your palm midchest, two inches above your diaphragm. Hold it there for a few minutes. Meanwhile, conjure up love. Love of the sky, your fluffy white kitten, your two-year-old daughter, Buddha himself—anything that allows your heart to open. Love is a balm that can soothe the nastiest wounds. Being able to channel it from your heart through your hands is an instant transfusion. For me it's become an instinct, a reliable mood stabilizer.

In my practice energy is indispensable. I have a wonderful velour couch in my office. You might assume I analyze my patients there. *Au contraire.* This couch is where I do energy work. My patients remove their shoes, lie there, eyes closed. I prefer complete silence, in contrast to a Russian healer I know who loves working to the music of Benny Goodman's band. To each his own. Kneeling on the floor, I say a silent prayer, let my hands be shown where they're needed. If someone has a migraine, and I get pulled to her knee, that's where I'll go. Energy centers have little voices. They say, "Come here," or "Go there." I just do as they suggest. I don't think about it. My function is simply to be a vessel though which love travels.

Patients come to see me in all sorts of states. Some are composed; you wouldn't know by looking what they're feeling. Others can barely contain themselves, wringing their hands, sobbing. Then there are those who are depressed, not quite in life, not quite out, slow like turtles and quiet. How beautiful everyone seems to me. In each case I do the same thing. I send loving energy to them, trust their bodies will utilize it well. Then I wait for the roses to sprout. Sometimes it's right away. Panic melts. Eyes sparkle. A workshop participant wrote, "When you put your hand on my chest, my spine started to tingle. I've been depressed for years; almost instantaneously that was removed. Even my doctor commented on the sudden change." More often, though, improvement is a gradual brightening that comes with balance. Its rate is not up to me; each person has his or her own timetable.

My purpose is twofold: to relieve suffering and to program my patients' bodies to access their own healing energy, in a way similar to biofeedback. I am a catalyst. Once they know what energy feels like, they can find it again. A jump start is often all they need. I teach my patients to heal themselves. It's never just about me doing it. The point is always for them to apply what they've gained in our sessions to their lives. This doesn't guarantee problems will evaporate, but it does ensure they'll have plenty of coping tools.

For you the first step is to find a skilled energy healer. This may or may not be your doctor, depending on her training. In either case, energy work is compatible with both traditional medicine and psychotherapy. As with physical pain, there are cycles of emotional turmoil that must be broken. Even with just the right doctor, you don't always succeed. No amount of talking will get you there. Energy work provides a missing ingredient. Healing can be like ordering from a Chinese menu, mixing and matching to find the best blend.

Not everyone agrees. Consider a 1998 article in the *Journal of the American Medical Association (JAMA)*. It reported a study concluding that therapeutic touch practitioners were unable to perceive a "human energy field" greater than would be expected by chance. This was "unrefuted evidence that claims of therapeutic touch are groundless." The "news" made the front page of *The New York Times*. But let's back up. What was really established? The experiment itself was conducted by a nine-year-old girl whose mother, a registered nurse (and the article's coauthor), was from a group called the Questionable Nurse Practices Task Force. The statistician analyzing the findings was from Quackwatch Inc. As the study was designed, there was a partition, through an opening in which the healers inserted their hands. The girl would then place her own hand over one of theirs. It was found that the healers correctly ascertained the location of the girl's hand—and so detected her energy field—less than half the time.

Oh, the scientific method! Where to begin? First, does belief predetermine outcome? Medical research itself amply documents the power of belief to affect results. Thus, the researcher's affiliations give one pause. Could the spirit of this experiment be neutral? Knowing the vehemence of skeptical groups, one has to ask. Attitude is communicated; negativity, unconscious or unexpressed, can impede energy flow. Second, these researchers assumed that when you place your hand over another's, energy can always be felt—a large assumption. Even if the girl was scrupulously trying to be neutral, she could have inadvertently held her energy in. Celebrities, for instance, well know how to be visible but also are deft at being invisible to avoid being hounded. How we project energy often determines the way people perceive it. In any experiment energy can be influenced by a multitude of factors.

Despite my reservations about the *JAMA* study, I'm always excited to hear of research in this field. I do hope, however, that its premises and methods will be accurate and balanced. I know it's imperative to question things. I also know it's imperative to trust your own experience. I decided to discuss this study to demonstrate the controversy in medicine about subtle energy. But what I or anyone else argues is irrelevant unless it rings true for you. Real life is an ideal laboratory in which to draw your own conclusions.

As my patients do, you must be prepared to act on your feet. Panic or depression doesn't care if you're at a company Christmas party when it strikes. You need immediate damage control. Don't just stand there and suffer. Here's a trick I teach patients: Go to the bathroom and lock the stall door. There and then, hold your hand over your chest; get your heart energy pumping. It doesn't matter what anyone is doing around you. Just concentrate on yourself. Stay calm. Take a breath. Then another and another. It will bring you back to center. Unpressured, you can decide if you want to return to the party or leave. When I'm in public and feeling off, this is my favorite strategy. I feel subversive meditating in that bathroom stall, summoning the mysteries of the universe. See how you can cater to your emotional needs in any circumstance. Be an adventurer.

Energy deepens how we perceive ourselves and others. Ordinary communication dictates that people must talk for us to understand them. Not so with subtle energy. Intuitively speaking, words are the least of it. We're used to them, but you must realize they aren't necessary. A bridge must be spanned. As a psychiatrist I appreciate that some people in profound psychic pain may not feel like talking, nor are they always capable of it. Or, as with schizophrenics, they might be in another reality altogether. What then?

I envision what I do as slow dancing. Not imposing my step on you, but seeing what your step is. This may entail careful watching or listening, sensing where my body is pulled. I could gravitate to a chair ten feet from you. Or perhaps I'm drawn to sit very close on your hospital bed. These are all energetic considerations that matter. I feel energy as waterlike, wave motions I must attend to. It also articulates an intuitive language. If something in you says to me, "I am lonely, I am lost," I hear it. Your energy may flash before me like a strobe. You're ten years old. Your father's beating you with his cowboy belt. You're terrified, can't even cry. Afterward he storms out, leaving you crouched in a corner, so alone. I see what happened. I sense in myself that anguish you've been carrying. You know I know, though the awareness may be unconscious. It brings us closer. In silence your world came to me. Therein lies the birth of our intuitive bond.

All this, and no words. Of course, there comes a point when with the aid of therapy and/or medications, the words will return. Along the way I file my intuitions. I'm not in a rush to mention them. As always I tune in for the proper time. But before talking resumes, realize that soulful, nonverbal interactions are possible and real. Don't ever assume that muteness, or even coma, precludes accessibility. To penetrate these states requires us to shift gears.

Goldie, an eighty-year-old patient of mine, slipped into a coma after a stroke. I visited her frequently in the hospital, meditated at her bedside, read her poetry. I felt a little funny, being a psychiatrist—after all, she was unconscious, couldn't talk. I admit I closed the door so the nurses wouldn't see in. I'm sure they didn't know what to make of me, but they didn't push it. Those moments with Goldie were not to be missed. When she became conscious again, she said, "I sensed you were near. I'm glad you were with me." In my mind healing isn't just caring for people when they're alert. It's caring for people always. Words or not.

Unresponsive people are a challenge. Imagine a schizophrenic's point of view. Some sinister voice is warning you, "Don't touch that food. It's poisoned." Or "Don't talk to that doctor. He's the devil." Then here the doctor comes, sauntering down the shiny hall of the locked psychiatric ward, grinning. You think, Oh, no. He sits down next to you in the cafeteria, pointing to your uneaten plate of rubbery-looking "mystery meat." "D-o-n't y-o-u w-a-n-t t-o e-a-t t-h-a-t?" he asks, elongating each syllable, as if enunciating words for a child. In this position what would you say? What would you do?

We all have our ways when it comes to energy. As you continue to be intuitively open, respect these innermost expressions of feelings and styles of negotiating life. Notice your patterns; observe others. When energy is activated in you, it will bring added fortitude. Consciously awaken this human attribute. Draw on it to build emotional resilience.

Step 4. Ask for Inner Guidance

I know a nun who's a recovering alcoholic. In her drinking days she'd sneak bottles of Scotch and hide them under her bed in the convent. She thought she was fooling everyone. Her guilt was enormous, the pain inside raw, unrelenting. "I had no faith, no guidance to turn to," she told me. "You see, I never really found a God of my own. I acted as if I had faith, but I didn't. So I drank, too ashamed to say anything, not daring to risk censure. It took going into recovery—honestly grappling with my doubt—for me to finally discover a spirituality that feels real, to have available an enduring source of guidance."

This courageous nun plummeted into hell to find the light. All that pressure to be of God, to believe, the deadening months of isolation. An impossible situation without someone to comfort her and say, "You dear one. You must try to find your own spiritual truth. Be kind to yourself." The path to connection is worth forging. Watch for turns in the road that may divert you from what is most authentic within. There is no point in pretending or trying to strive for someone else's ideal. It's important to fess up to how you really feel and work with it.

Intuition offers the voice of sanity and spirit in emotional conundrums. If ever you needed to hear your inner guidance, it's now. What it says will direct you. Even if friends and family are supportive, check in. If you're on your own, intuitive guidance is always there. The appropriateness of any action is confirmed by such advice. I know when you're not feeling your best intuition may seem distant. These are times when the art of quiet listening is invaluable. Just because your emotions are churning doesn't mean your intuition isn't present. You simply must go deeper.

Whatever you're up against, try this remote viewing technique to clarify right action. A timesaving, in-the-moment intervention, it utilizes a simple yes or no format.

FINDING SOLUTIONS:
USING REMOTE VIEWING IN AN EMOTIONAL PINCH

Take a few minutes to breathe deeply and calm your thoughts. When you're relaxed, formulate a specific question to illuminate your situation. For instance, "Should I go into psychotherapy?" Then, while gently visualizing yourself in therapy, notice how your intuition responds. A "yes" often feels like a quickening, a waking up, chills rushing through your spine, joy, safety, relief, your heart opening. Affirming images could be a bouquet of flowers, the moon rising, a gull taking flight, any picture signifying abundance. Or lively music may come to you: a Mozart concerto, a spiffy show tune, any upbeat piece. In contrast, "no" may be a shutting down, numbness, inertia, or sense of dread. Negative images such as an ominous storm, an airless room, or maybe a snippet of a somber Brahms requiem can signal beware. Whatever your symbols, let them inspire you to choose the right course.

When you're emotionally vulnerable it can be much more difficult to trust yourself. How can you be sure of your inner voice? I want to reiterate that pure intuition comes through in two main forms: (1) information conveyed without an emotional charge; (2) information conveyed with compassion. If the guidance you request is tinged with any intense emotion, it obscures the picture.

As a psychiatrist I know all kinds of voices other than their inner voice populate people's heads. The familiar lineup includes fear, anger, insecurity. The ones that say, "I'm not good enough," "I'll never get better," "I'm not deserving," "Why try?" Intuitive guidance these are not. Negativity can also escalate. I often get asked, "What's the difference between a psychotic voice and an intuitive voice?" Easy. Psychotic voices are cruel, paranoid, destructive. They'll say, "The CIA is out to get you—hide in the closet with a gun" or "You're cursed." At their most diabolical they'll say, "Kill yourself" or "That man is a threat. Kill him." Be clear: This is not intuition. Your intuitive voice, in its neutrality or compassion, is always protective of who you are.

Psychosis, though, is not simple. It has elements traditional psychiatry fails to address. In medical school at USC, I treated chronic, hardcore psychotics on a locked county ward, many with symptoms straight out of the *DSM-IV*: hallucinations, delusions, bizarre behavior. One purple-haired man explained about himself, "I'm radioactive. I'm being invaded by an alien force," and I naively tried to talk him out of it. For him this is how it was—end of story. The only treatments I know capable of making a dent in such fixations are drugs like Thorazine. I wish there was another way, but in such dire cases I haven't found one. "Medicate psychosis": in psychiatry, this is the rule. However, what complicated the picture during my training were psychotic patients who'd also say, "I feel God," "I have visions," "Energy currents are rushing through me." For such people these were not pleasant perceptions. Being uncentered these people couldn't integrate what they felt. Typically, psychiatrists clump such "symptoms" with psychosis and go no further. But there were undertones to these experiences I needed to understand.

The intriguing work of the psychiatrist Stanislav Grof filled in the missing piece. He observed that certain people, particularly those with acute psychosis, were undergoing spiritual emergencies. They'd have an onslaught of visions, wild fluctuations of subtle energy, and realizations of God—behavior that in many cultures is deemed divine. Over the years I've had the privilege of caring for such patients. Their passage into wholeness requires special attention. Typically they'll say, "I'm terrified," "I'm afraid I'm going crazy." As with anyone in the midst of psychosis, I first help them regain balance. My mantra is always "Ground. Ground. Ground." Sleeping, eating, reducing anxiety are the priorities. Then, when they are on more stable footing, we can begin to go deeper.

Psychosis must be appreciated from a wider view. I've seen people with biochemical instabilities who benefit from medications despite their drawbacks. For others, though, a spiritual awakening is also occurring. A mystical door opens, but too much floods in—a mishmash of delusion and intuitive clarity that must be sorted through. Transpersonal psychologists, trained in the spiritual dimension of mental health, are equipped to intervene (see Resources). I hope physicians can begin to dignify this aspect of psychosis too. Simply medicating can do violence if spiritual factors aren't sensitively approached. When supported rather than judged by conventional standards, patients with spiritual crises in the guise of psychoses can open to a truer appreciation of authentic intuition.

When you're feeling down or off, discerning reliable inner guidance can be tricky. Beware also of being seduced by the voice of despair. You know, the one that intimately whispers your name when hope is waning. You're depressed, the push to keep going just seems too much. "Come to me," despair murmurs. "You deserve relief." Hmm, you think. Suicide. Why not? If ever this option starts to feel good, *stop and regroup.* You may not be able to see a solution, but you must search for it. There is *always* help available.

In *Darkness Visible* the Pulitzer Prize–winning author William Styron concludes about his devastating depression, "It is not the soul's annihilation. . . . It is conquerable." He writes: "Return from the abyss is not unlike the ascent of the poet . . . at last emerging into . . . the shining world." I believe in the power of life to conquer despair—with patients and in myself. Intuition is life-preserving and will provide a map to navigate turbulence. I've seen it happen time after time.

I used to think suicide was a viable option. I assumed, If things get tough enough, everyone has the right to check out. Now, except possibly with terminal patients in unrelenting physical pain, I no longer feel this way. As I explored intuition more deeply, I came to realize that considering suicide as a card I could play was keeping me removed from the essence of daily life. A commitment to being in my body, through thick and thin, was a prerequisite for living fully. I made an affirmation: "I believe in the wisdom of what my days bring, and I'll do my best to embrace it." Thus, each moment I could be more present.

Suicide has many faces. I was touched by how it was depicted in the film *What Dreams May Come.* The story is of a wife who kills herself after her beloved husband dies. In heaven he hears of this and, despite being warned against it, searches for her to the reaches of hell. Her hell, though, isn't what you might think. Not fire and brimstone but rather confinement in a barren house, alone with her fear, without any memory of loving him. Seeing this, he knows she doesn't recognize him— yet his love impels him to stay. Such love, of course, can vanquish fear, and it allows them both to find heaven.

From what I intuit of the other side, who you are here is who you will be there too. Just leaving this body doesn't relieve you of your spiritual challenges. I don't mean this in a punitive sense. I am merely saying that your soul's growth will continue. Sooner or later you'll have to confront the matters at hand. I figure, Why not now? For those who believe in past lives, confronting the self is inevitable. Whether immediately or in a thousand millennia, you must do it. This is good. This is purifying. It makes your spirit bright.

I've had patients attempt suicide. One succeeded. He was a tattooed heavy metal rocker whose megasuccess could never console the relentless sirens in his head. When he died I hadn't seen him for months, but I grieved his loss. We had been close. I did everything I could—but he was on a crash course. I realized this, yet still I railed against my powerlessness to save his life. I'll always miss him. I remember those mornings I'd visit him after a previous suicide attempt. He was on a locked psychiatric ward, along with others who were suicidal, homicidal, or psychotically deranged. To me it's a travesty to put people struggling with depression in with that group. I wish I could've sent him to a serene place with gardens, trees, and sunlit halls. But our mental health system isn't set up like that. Those needing intensive supervision all go together. So I saw him there until he was no longer suicidal. Against my advice he went on tour too soon. I feared for him. Then I got the news: He was gone.

It's the exception that suicide is inevitable. More often, with savvy interventions it can be averted. I know many people—including those on a spiritual path—who in low moments have considered suicide. It's nothing to be ashamed of or to suppress. But I also know the strength gained from walking toward the sun, trusting your intuition to see when the eye cannot. Discovering this truth is a revelation.

There's an adage: You're never given more than you can handle. It may not seem that way at the time. But I believe it is true. Our higher power asks a lot of us. It used to get me mad. Some situations seemed too terrible to face. I'd protest, "I can't do it. I don't have it in me." But I did—and I had to see that. So must you. What your mind says and what your inner guidance relates may conflict. For that reason, look beyond the mirage of walls and detours. Don't be hoodwinked by how daunting they seem. My spiritual teacher says, "Heaven is not a dead-end road." I promise, there's always a path there. With intuition you will find it.

Step 5. Listen to Your Dreams

I'm nine years old. My mother and I are sitting on the bench of our baby grand piano in the living room. A fire is blazing. She's teaching me to play Beethoven's

"Moonlight Sonata." I follow her steady fingers, one by one, memorizing each note and chord. I'm entranced by how she smells, how she concentrates so intently. But somehow the music, in its wistful beauty, is taking her from me. I feel and see my mother—yet I have the horrible sense I'm losing her. As I play, as she listens to me, an icy panic wells up in my chest. I fight back tears, determined to complete the piece.

For months after my mother died of cancer, I had this recurring dream, a mix of grief and childhood memory. I resisted writing the dream down or even thinking about it. I didn't want to remember those days when after school just the two of us would spend hours together at our piano. I didn't want to remember the way her eyes lit up as she taught me the music that so transported her. Especially our favorite, the "Moonlight Sonata." After my mother's death I could barely stand to hear it, afraid of loving her so much I might explode. Those first weeks I longed not to feel anything—and still this dream came. And came. The truth of it kept calling out. Finally, I let my guard down, allowed it to touch me. My dream was helping me understand that the music my mother and I shared (our relationship) continued beyond life into death. I felt she was urging me to let my guard down, allow feelings of loss to touch me—yet not intuitively lose touch with her. The dream, in its wisdom, burst open my sorrow so I could begin to heal.

Dreams are your path out of darkness, a built-in survival guide to life. From preventive premonitions to instructions on how to get through everything from depression to stress, dream messages are liberating. Not just because of their intuitive foresight or their uncanny capacity to cut to the bottom line, but because of their unerring, compassionate, personalized intent. In dreams *you're* in the spotlight. Paramount is *your* happiness, *your* healing, *your* peace of mind. When you are floundering or in the pits and a dream comes—as mine did—make the most of it. Or before you go to sleep, pose a question; invite dreams in. Unbeatable problem solvers, they can both warn of emotional tumult and lead you through rocky phases if they arrive.

How can dreams convey trouble before the fact? The trick is to stay alert for your predictive symbols, which may be unique to you. I train my patients to look out for them. You can too. Watch what I mean. Jill, a workaholic architect, is prone to fits of rage that scare others. Before such a fit, Jill typically dreams she has forgotten to stock up on canned food for her sweet bulldog, Max, who ends up neglected and ravenously hungry. Translation: Jill is being told she's been ignoring her own needs for tenderness and self-care, which must be fed. If she listens, she often can avert the episode. If not, it comes in full force.

I'd like you to pin down your intuitive alarm signals. Be aware of recurring dream symbols that foresee distress—especially regression to an unsettling phase of life, being out of control, or abrupt loss of financial, emotional, or spiritual support. Here are some common themes:

- You're trapped in a house where you used to live with no way out.
- You lose your wallet and are stranded without credit cards or cash in a dangerous neighborhood.
- Your car is careening down a steep hill. You wildly pump your brakes, but they've given out.
- You ask for your familiar dream guides, but they don't come. You feel alone, lost.

We are creatures of habit: symbols foreshadowing difficulty tend to repeat themselves. Like clockwork, when problems loom, there they are. For example, every time my patient Jack, a recovering heroin addict, has a "slip" dream in which he mainlines the drug, he tells me. In the past he didn't; he'd go out and use. Many recovering addicts and alcoholics have slip dreams, in which they see themselves using drugs or drinking again. These dreams are typically upsetting—always reminders of the tenaciousness of addiction and possible indications of relapse. They need to be analyzed and understood. Realizing the significance of a slip dream, Jack and I could work together to safeguard his sobriety.

The language of dream-intuition can save you. Stay aware. Know your vocabulary. Act quickly on messages you receive. Doing so buys you time. Get to the crux of what's off kilter before it has a chance to manifest. Whether adversity is better prepared for or entirely averted, you'll come out ahead.

What's marvelous about dreams is that you don't have to be on an even keel to query them. Your clarity while awake and your clarity while asleep can be radically different. No matter how down you feel in ordinary reality, in the dream realm all is well. It may be useful to think of human life with its turmoil as of the earth and dreams as of heaven. The good news is that information is constantly being channeled to us. Spiritual guidance for the material world. This is all the more reason to turn to dreams when we're at a low. Sometimes the process may feel like blindman's bluff—your eyes are masked, you have no idea of direction—yet invisible forces carry you. Indeed, some dreams can point to a positive outcome long before it seems possible. They give assurance in face of current troubles that specific solutions will be found. Our minds or emotions may be kerflooey, but our intuition, the stuff of which dreams are made, will save the day.

When in doubt you can always ask a dream, How can I feel better? That's a simple beginning. As usual, the posture is to put out your request, then await the response. Being sincere is the most you can "do." Attempts to force or actively visualize results will stymie intuitive flow. Try not to worry about whether an answer will come. Just go to sleep; see what happens. The next day write your dream down. Try this for a week. Whether you get a one-word answer or an elaborate rehabilitation plan, welcome what you're given and go with it.

My patient Lois had chronic depression. She wasn't much interested in anything. She'd get a little better, then she'd get a little worse. In therapy we didn't seem to sustain progress. Then I said, "Maybe your dreams know more than we do. Why don't you see what they have to add?" Lois was as halfhearted about dreaming as she was about everything else. But she did her best and consulted her dreams. The results surprised even me. One day she came into my office weeping. "In my dream I saw the face of a child," she reported. "She was lost. I know that girl. I know who she is." Then more tears—a breakthrough for someone so cut off. Puzzled, I asked, "Who is it?" "My daughter!" Lois exclaimed. "Daughter?" I wondered. Lois was single, nearly a recluse.

Here's where dream magic entered. Lois told me, "In 1962, at sixteen, I got pregnant. I felt so ashamed. My parents sent me away to have the baby; we put her up for adoption." A painful chapter closed, or so she thought. In Lois's dream it resurfaced like gangbusters, starting her on an amazing journey to locate her daughter. Through a combination of detective work and good luck, they reunited five years ago. Mother and daughter: that union anchored the axis of Lois's life. For so long there had been only depression, a vague, numbing fog. During a lifetime birth can happen more than once. Lois's dream had been the midwife for such change.

At times dreams are able to heal more than medical science can. They offer fresh air and open space. Whether your dream says, "Take a break from your girlfriend" or "Meditate an hour a day," or predicts, "Don't worry. Your depression will lift soon," I'd take the message seriously. It could be that you just wake up "knowing" you must nurture yourself more. Or that it's high time you deal with your anxiety. Accept this input at face value. The loveliness of dreams is that your relationship with them is continuing. They are a resource that forever grows.

HEALING INTO WHOLENESS is taking full advantage of approaches that best fit your needs. It requires a measure of logic and intuition, setting blinders and prejudices aside. If you're hurting and come to the situation intuitively open to the possibilities of what can help, healing will flow organically. If, however, you have a mind-set fixed in stone, never pausing to tune in to your intuition, you'll deprive yourself of the creative instincts nature has given you to surmount crises.

On this note I recently received an all-too-true e-mail from a friend that made me smile. I want to share it with you. Aptly, it is entitled "A Brief History of Medicine" (author unknown).

2000 B.C.E.: Here, eat this root.
1000 C.E.: That root is heathen. Here, say this prayer.
1850 C.E.: That prayer is superstition. Here, drink this potion.
1940 C.E.: That potion is snake oil. Here, swallow this pill.
1985 C.E.: That pill is ineffective. Here, take this antibiotic.
2000 C.E.: That antibiotic is artificial. Here, eat this root.

Healing has come full circle over the centuries. What's in one year is out the next—then it's back again. Our task is to reconcile extremes, recognize every method with merit, treat the whole person. To understand your emotions, explore all that will contribute to your growth. There is no one way. Talking therapy, medication, meditation, herbs, homeopathy, energy healing, spirituality, dreams—a rich tapestry of alternatives that can elegantly interact. What matters is which one moves you. There is spirit to any path you choose. Remember to align with it.

Emotional wholeness has many variations. One scenario is that your depression or anxiety completely lifts. Another may entail living with some imperfections. This is a matter of courage; it doesn't represent defeat. A schizophrenic man at one of my workshops told me, "I still hear occasional voices, but they're more distant. I have a strong spiritual practice, meditate every day. It's allowed me to really reduce my medication." How incredible! This man doesn't sit home all day and worry about his voices. He gets out in life and lives it. The fact is that, despite your efforts, some discomfort may remain. You then have a choice. You can focus on the 90 percent of you that's better or the 10 percent that's off. If, for now, you can't get rid of every symptom, try amicably coexisting, a strategy different from just "learning to live with it." Your meditation then becomes harmonizing with your discomfort, no resistance, continually refocusing on your strength within.

Some of us carry a deep-seated sorrow that is often misread as a deficit. I've had it as far back as I can remember, whether I'm happy or down, whether my life is going well or not. What I've come to understand about this sorrow is that it's neither depression nor what's commonly perceived as grief. In fact, it's a soul-quality—a form of empathy that allows us to penetrate people, attune to a collective sadness that longs to be quelled. Some sorrow, like fresh rain, purifies, expands the soul. Appreciating the positive qualities of what once seemed to me a negative emotion, I now trust it, believe it lends integrity to the intuitive process. If you identify, try to view such sorrow as a mystical linkup with the world, not as a trait to fear or eliminate. Many seers—including my own best teachers—have described a similar feeling. Allow it to teach you compassion and be of service to those in need.

A blessing of emerging from the dark is using what you've gained to help people. The schizophrenic man I mentioned earlier shows others with schizophrenia how to meditate, a pivotal aspect of his recovery he wants to share. Who could better address the spiritual nature of their experience than he? I also have a friend, a recovering alcoholic, who teaches meditation to men at a homeless shelter, many struggling with alcoholism. Every Wednesday at 6:00 A.M., in a rickety trailer in a parking lot, a group of men gather to tune in to themselves. Sacred time. Guidance involves both receiving and giving back. To think of it this way keeps the cycle of healing renewed.

Learning about darkness and light is our challenge as humans. The dynamic of this pairing is stunningly mirrored in the night sky. During workshops I have participants meditate on the interplay of starlight, the moon, and the vast backdrop of blackness. Why? To see how radiant it all is. Last summer, on a remote island in western Canada, conditions were ideal. In the midst of the spectacular Perseid meteor showers, I sent sixty-five people out in silence to experience them. My only instructions: "Take it in, all of it. And remember to make wishes, as many as you want." So there they went, some swimming in the bay, others snuggled in sleeping bags in the pine forest, watching shooting stars galore. Bursts of white light arcing across the sky. The next morning people said, "There were so many I used all my wishes up!" Can you imagine? No wishes left, everything in the heart spoken for! Don't forget—wishes in the dark have power. In trying periods remember to make them. Angels are dancing all around. You will be heard. In *The Inferno*, when the dark time is gone, the poet Dante writes of light as the ultimate victor:

> *E quindi uscimmo a rivider le stelle.*
>
> *And so we came forth, and once again beheld the stars.*

9

Honoring Relationships

The love you make is equal to the love you take.
—The Beatles

*L*et me tell you a story of true love.

My friend Arielle had been single all her life. A feisty, truth-telling, statuesque book publicist, at forty-four she longed for her soul mate. None of her boyfriends ever lasted more than three years. The apparent problems varied: fear of commitment, intimacy issues, perhaps her fierce independence. A successful professional, Arielle was also a spiritual seeker. Her teacher came from India, was famous for giving darshan—blessings of many, many people. During a retreat Arielle whispered to this woman, "Please heal my heart of everything that's stopping me from finding true love." That night Arielle had a dream: She heard the sweetest voices singing, "Arielle is the one who comes after Beth." What's this? she thought when she woke. Is the man I'm looking for in a relationship with someone named Beth?

Three weeks passed. Then, during a business meeting out of town, Arielle met Brian. Here is her account of what happened. "When I saw him, I instantly felt happy. He was attractive in a preppy way, but not my type. Still, I heard the words inside my head saying, This is the person you're going to spend the rest of your life with!" Dumbfounded, Arielle thought she was losing it. For all she knew the guy was already married. But, as the meeting ended Brian said to her, "I know this sounds amazing. But I've met you in my dreams." Arielle was speechless. What was going on? Worse, never had she experienced such an urge to kiss someone. Just then an associate yelled to Brian, "Why don't you ask Elizabeth to join us for dinner?" Arielle's heart sank.

All was not lost, however. Beth turned out to be Brian's girlfriend, though they were in the process of separating. That evening, as Brian drove Arielle to the airport, they talked so easily, they could've known each other for years. Already both were certain they'd get together again. Two months later they became engaged. And one year to the day after they met, Arielle's spiritual teacher married them. It's not that their marriage has been without the usual ups and downs. But all along they've been clear they're meant to be together forever. The sense of connection and comfort they felt that first afternoon has not failed them. As Brian said, "We're here to nurture each other and share a magnificent love."

THIS CHAPTER IS DEVOTED to love—how to achieve it, what's stopping us, and how to find the faith to risk with all our relationships, from lovers to colleagues. *Namaste—"I respect the spirit within you"*—is the common greeting in India. I want *namaste* to be the point from which we always begin, when it comes to others as well as ourselves. Relationships are a holy meeting ground that teach us to love. This is true even if you don't like someone! Especially with difficult people, we must search for the highest part of them and speak to it. Only such effort liberates us from being mired with people at their worst. From an intuitive viewpoint all relationships impart valuable lessons. The art is not to repeat destructive patterns.

Our focus will be on ways to develop intuitive, spiritually attuned relationships versus the 1950s paradigm of uptight values. We're talking about two different universes. For example, many people say that passion in a thirty-year marriage is doomed because of familiarity and predictable routines. I'm saying that in an intuitively alive relationship, there's no such inevitability. The reason? Through intuition you see differently, bringing renewed wonder to the known.

I'm suggesting we keep what traditionally works about relationships and discard the rest, take our best models and build on them. Love, trust, commitment—these are the basics. I'll show you how you can use intuition to strengthen these bonds or forge them. By listening to your inner voice, you can shape your own fate, attract healthy people to you, recognize danger signals. From beginning a relationship to all the way onward, this careful attention will ensure you find the highest ground. Plus, it engages a magic available only when you invite the mystery in.

If you want passion in all your relationships, an immediacy that being in the moment brings, intuition is the catalyst. Welcome to a world of synchronicities, moments of perfect timing when fortuitous events just seem to fall into place: You can't stop thinking about an old friend and you run into him, or you miss your plane and on the next flight you sit next to someone with whom you fall in love. Thrilling, too, is the experience of déjà vu—a striking sense you've known someone before, though you've never previously met. Where these serendipitous linkages take you can enliven your life. With intuition you can also communicate beyond words. You'll discover how to "read" people so you can better reach them. Or, like Arielle and Brian, you could even have matchmaking occur in a dream! The promise of such intuitive openness is having relationships that are mystical, practical, and fun. It's a way of loving more completely in every aspect of your life.

Step 1. Notice Your Beliefs

I believe in true love. I believe in bonds so deep you can feel the universe rush through them. This is as true in Peoria as in Paris, accessible even in the nitty-gritty fabric of daily life. At the breakfast table your mate smiles at you, and that light is there. Your best friend shares concerns about her child—you're right by her side, sisters throughout time. I'm not talking just about emotional epiphanies. I'm referring to quiet, ordinary moments. The pleasure of being with people—lovers, friends, family—not out of obligation but because it feels right. This doesn't imply things will always go smoothly, but it does guarantee your soul won't wither from longing for sustenance. Even if such intimacy feels far from your reality now, it's worth cultivating and fighting for. These are the relationships I recommend you strive to achieve.

How do you find such heartfelt unions? With intuition, not just the mind. Typically, in friendships or romance, the old model of relationships goes like this. You meet someone you like. You may notice this person is nice looking, intelligent, kind, talented, trustworthy—or in the case of romance you might have a wild physical attraction. So everything appears fine. Off you go. Now here's the new way: You may observe all of the above, but you see more. Ask yourself: Does this person feel familiar, like a member of your tribe? Does your gut say, "Go ahead. This will be great for you." Or is it cautioning, "Halt." Do you feel an affinity that transcends surface connections? Along with sexual excitement, does your heart energy open? In the new way what looks good on paper is meaningless unless an intuitively authentic bond is there.

The relationships I'm speaking of have specific components that set them apart from what is usually expected. The following four qualities fuel ongoing passion and commitment. I make them central to all my relationships, from undertaking business interactions to falling in love. Radical departures from the status quo, they can bring new life to any pairing.

FOUR FOUNDATIONS OF AN INTUITIVE RELATIONSHIP

1. *Spirituality as a priority*

A relationship is never just about two people. It's also infused with a spiritual force. Whether god or goddess, the majesty of nature, or a benevolent intelligence, there is more at work than you and your partner. No matter if you tap into it through meditation, traditional religion, or peaceful moments alone, it empowers, sustains. How extraordinary when each of you has your own direct line to spirit and brings that to the relationship. This way no one is empty upon arrival. No one is alone. Nor will you ever be. Thus, whether you're single or attached, fear of being alone can no longer hold you hostage in a situation that's harmful or one that you've outgrown. I encourage you to view all relationships as divine, parts of an ever-deepening meditation about compassion and growth.

I've seen many people in long-term relationships who are resigned to being bored. "We've known each other too long," they say. "It's to be expected." Often these couples are in a comfortable rhythm—nice kids, nice house, their lives logistically functioning well—but the kiss of death is that a shared excitement—the ongoing intuitive capacity to see the miraculous in small things—which puts the juice into things, is missing. With this element nothing is "boring." This is more than "attitude change." It's a perceptual shift that comes from the depth of intuition. It makes the mundane—getting the children off to school, lounging together on a Sunday afternoon, having sex for the millionth time, luminous. Little by little, as you try, you can sense such spirit too. It changes everything by revealing what was always there to see.

2. *A mutual honoring of intuition*

Trusting the wisdom within takes faith of the highest caliber. One person living this is remarkable. Two people living this together is sublime. Everyone needs support. No matter how self-sufficient you think you are, the words of a close friend or partner affirming, "Wow. Your dream is fantastic" or "I trust your gut feeling. Go for it," feed the soul. Such support is a world apart from someone saying, "Are you nuts! Making a decision on what?" I've seen patients in the tender stage of discovering intuition get ripped to shreds by a skeptical partner's insensitive comments. It's very different to feel someone is on your side. Very different not to have to defend every instinctually informed act. Others don't always have to agree with you or support what they perceive to be a harebrained scheme. What's crucial is engaging in a kind-spirited dialogue, not an adversarial collision of beliefs. If, however, your partner knows little about intuition, he or she might need to be educated. Then it's up to you to gradually, gently convey what you know. Do this by modeling, not by hitting him or her over the head. Meditate. Tune in. Use your intuition to find just the right words that can dissolve resistance and improve the relationship. Embody the strength of your convictions.

3. *Respect for the power of the feminine*

From ancient times intuition has been equated with the feminine. The *I Ching* speaks of the feminine as the "receptive," "primal," and "yielding" yin element, versus the more I-can-fix-this-problem, control- or action-oriented masculine, called yang. Yin does not combat yang but completes it. To ignite intuition in our relationships, the feminine must gain more of a role than it has been given. Male or female, we all possess a masculine and a feminine side. Denying either we eclipse our own nature. Often, though, the feminine is the first to go. Men fight it by becoming macho, women by becoming "masculinized," either all suits and briefcases or looking like stick-figure fashion models. Why? A burly man, proud of his machismo, recently gave me his view: "You want me to be a wimp? Are you crazy?" Many women also mistake yin for weakness. For that reason I want to make this clear: If you're a man, accessing your feminine side doesn't imperil your testosterone level. If you're a woman, the yin in you imparts strength. Both sexes realize their full selves—and are open to intuition—only by embracing the feminine as part of their balance. This isn't at all to repudiate the yang, but that's hardly the danger in our culture these days.

In relationships giving the feminine its due is an antidote to complacency. Here's the principle: When you're receptive, intuition flows—your body comes alive; creativity and passion heighten; your heart opens; loving solutions come through. How can this be bad? Electrifying all interactions, not just sexual ones, our feminine side is the well-spring of the visionary in us. Our female predecessors were burned at the stake as witches. But unlike all the women over the centuries who were suppressed or destroyed, we—men and women—can revel in our yin to build love.

4. *Being mirrors for each other*

Why is it that we are often most difficult with people we know best? This is true at work, with friendships, and in the home. Often this is because we know we can be; these people will "take it" from us, accept and forgive us, warts and all. In addition, though, the closer you are to someone, the more you'll be his or her emotional mirror—both positive and negative. Spiritually speaking, this is part of the job description: We reflect to others emotional issues they need to heal; they do the same for us. It's a rewarding though demanding process both people enter into with awareness. In relationships problems inevitably come up. This is no surprise, but your attitude is critical. A patient of mine is wrestling with fear of abandonment. It's only escalated since she's had a boyfriend. Though she "knows better," she gets insecure, tells him, "You're going to leave me for another woman." Her fear gets hard for him to take. Still, he knows she must confront it; he's committed to supporting her effort to evolve emotionally and spiritually. For better and for worse, he's her mirror. I'm impressed by the mindfulness of their approach, their commitment and courage to see it through. This is what's required, as opposed to relationships in which the tendency is only to become irritated, to deny, or to blame.

How is conscious mirroring related to intuition? How can it facilitate a strong relationship? Preferably you have an aware counterpart. If not, accept your responsibility in the dynamic; focus on the issues yourself, with a friend, or in therapy. Mirror yes, project no. Unlike mirroring, projection is unconsciously attributing your unrecognized feelings to someone else—a costly distortion of a relationship, the mistake my patient almost made. Seeking mutuality with another human being, strive for your own reality check, not to read in others what isn't there. Otherwise, your intuition cannot be brought to bear, a loss for both of you.

WHEN PRACTICING the four foundations, I want you to watch out for a major glitch: power struggles. They come up all the time. Even good-hearted people get drawn in. Power struggles are a spiritual dilemma. To transcend this no-win game, we must have an intuitive understanding of the part we play. The setup is predictable: You think you're right. The other person thinks he's right. Neither of you intends to give in. How extreme can such a standoff get? Here's an actual radio conversation released by the chief of naval operations in 1995:

No. 1: Please divert your course 15 degrees to the North to avoid a collision.
No. 2: Recommend you divert your course 15 degrees to South to avoid a collision.
No. 1: This is the Captain of a U.S. Navy ship. I say again, divert your course.
No. 2: I say again, you divert your course.
No. 1: *This is the aircraft carrier* Enterprise. *We are a large warship of the U.S. Navy. Divert your course now!*
No. 2: This is a lighthouse. Your call.

This humorous story contains hard truths none of us is a stranger to. But where to go from here? Often the question is, How can we bring ourselves to yield? It's no simple task. We get locked into the contest. It may help to ask yourself in any escalating exchange if you are the lighthouse or the *Enterprise,* or both. Also practical is to manifest some yin, some yielding. People are surprised by it, become disarmed. This isn't defeat for either side but a voluntary reduction in aggression. Then change is possible. For instance, your mother is adamant: "You're quitting your sales job to enroll in art school? Don't be ridiculous!" Well, you could go down the "you don't understand me; I won't do it your way" road *or* you could intuitively dance with her. I suggest the following approach:

- Do not engage in battle, but remain firm. Recognize your anger and hurt if they're there, but choose not to let them drive you. Never counter force with force.

- Channel as much heart energy as you can. It melts resistance, shifts people into their better selves. In a loving tone say, "I know you're worried about me. But here's why I feel as I do." Addressing her concerns as you present your position makes her feel heard, an ally. By simply "being right," you lose.

- If you aren't making progress, employ "nonaction." That is, be the mountain (or lighthouse!). Know when to sit tight. Allow her to absorb the situation; see if she comes to you. Not pushing can do wonders.

The grace of communicating is embodying both yin and yang. The best scenario: Whoever you're dealing with will respond to the heart-centered energy you're sending and soften, appreciating your point of view. Worst scenario: He or she won't. Even so you've created the most positive environment to sustain a relationship despite differences. In an impasse knowing when to change the rhythm is an intuitive choice. As John Lennon said, "Peace is here if you want it."

All of us hunger for relationships that really count. The other day I was in a doctor's office filling out the information form. I got to the part about who to contact in an emergency. I paused: I'm single; my mother is dead; my father was too ill to qualify. I thought of my close friend Berenice, but doubts crept in. I wondered, Would she actually be there for me? When I asked Berenice later, she beamed. "Of course," she said, not hesitating an instant. I was deeply touched. I ask you: Who are your true friends? Even if you have none now, guided by intuition you can begin to gather a loving circle around you.

QUESTIONS FOR REFLECTION

- Do your models for relationships include spirituality and intuition? How can these qualities allow you to be more caring?

- In heated moments do you consult intuition before reacting? Do you use it to help resolve power struggles instead of staging a showdown?

- What's your track record in choosing relationships? Do you listen to your intuition *before* getting involved?

Step 2. Be in Your Body

When I was a little girl I sought refuge in books. For hours I'd curl up in the den, lose myself—alone with the stories that lifted me from my body into other realms. I took special pleasure in those moments— not having to relate to a single other soul. Today I still crave solitude; I have a side that can do without people (or a body), yet I also yearn for the warmth and bonding of human intimacy. I've had to work to balance such competing needs.

I savor how Peter Beagle's *The Last Unicorn* addresses this dilemma. It tells of a unicorn who lives happily by herself in an idyllic forest, believing she's the last of her kind. Then one day she learns from a butterfly that there are more like her—but they've been driven into the sea by an evil power. Suddenly the unicorn longs to find the others, to set them free. This means she must leave her forest and take on human form to keep from being recognized. Becoming a woman, embracing the depths of being human, she liberates the exiled unicorns. And so the miraculous is restored to the land.

Like me, some people are powerfully drawn to the clarity of time alone. This is a domain of purity, but the full spectrum of human magic makes itself known only in the world of people. The starting point is always the body. Its signals can inform who you fall in love with, who you choose as colleague or friend. It's counterintuitive to be cut off from such input. From the first nanosecond you lay eyes on someone and throughout a relationship, your body registers intuitions. All organs go on alert. Stomach, muscles, heart, skin, lungs—each chimes in, will tell you if it's comfortable with someone or not. How a person smells, feels, moves, speaks, holds energy has impact. Your body responds to these sensual cues. I'd like you to begin to attune yourself to them, trust what you perceive.

Here's a general guide to body-based intuitions. Some will give a go-ahead in relationships, relaying a state of openness, well-being, expansion. Others will issue warnings, trigger a protective shutting down. You can use this checklist—correlating it with other telling images, knowings, or premonitions you perceive at a first meeting or troubleshooting problems if you're already involved.

POSITIVE INTUITIONS ABOUT RELATIONSHIPS

- You have a feeling of comforting familiarity; you may even sense you've known the person before, as with déjà vu.
- You breathe easier, your chest area is relaxed, receptive.
- Your shoulder muscles are loose, your gut is calm.
- You find yourself leaning forward, not defensively crossing your arms or edging away to keep a distance.
- Your heart opens; you feel safe, energized, excited.

NEGATIVE INTUITIONS ABOUT RELATIONSHIPS

- You have a sick feeling in the pit of your stomach or increased stomach acid.
- Your skin starts crawling, you're jumpy, you instinctively withdraw if touched.
- Your shoulder muscles are in knots, your chest area or throat constricts; you notice aggravated or new aches or pains.
- The hair on the back of your neck stands on end.
- You feel a sense of malaise or being drained.

Optimally, you'll be able to pinpoint these signs, factor them into your assessment of a person. Particularly with warnings, I'd pay rapt attention; weigh even one seriously when embarking on a relationship. But the more specific signs you notice, pro and con, the clearer your body's advice. What may cloud the picture, however, is anxiety. If you can't separate the jitters about first meeting someone from "beware" messages your body sends, you may want to give the relationship time. Typically, as you come to know someone better, early jitters dissipate, but your body's instincts persist. By contrast, the anxiety that comes from being afraid of intimacy may be ongoing; it might even instigate a Woody Allen–like onslaught of physical symptoms. The closer you are to someone, the worse it gets. Then your task becomes sorting fear from fact. As always, through breathing and meditation get in the habit of centering yourself. This will train you to "see" from a calm, more neutral position.

Intense sexual attraction is also notorious for obliterating intuition. My patient Amy, a successful stockbroker, was a textbook case. When she met Scott, he could do no wrong. Everything he said or did thrilled her. "That's nice," I'd respond. "But what is your body's intuition telling you?" She'd attempt to tune in but felt only turned on. I'd advise, "In meditation, try to find a neutral state—then scan your body for any discomfort." (Positive intuitions are less dependable here because they often coincide with sexual attraction.) My work with Amy was to help her learn to practice detachment. Not exactly what anyone in the heat of passion wants, but essential to understand how the body, apart from sexual desire, really feels. Just the fact that hormones are raging doesn't mean someone is right for you.

During the O. J. Simpson trial I spoke at a benefit for Denise Brown's Alliance for Women. My talk, "How Intuition Can Be Used to Prevent Domestic Violence," focused on showing women how to identify and act on the body-intuitions I've described. The body knows. The body senses potential for kindness and for violence. Many women who'd been in abusive relationships admitted, "My body initially told me something was wrong—but I ignored it." The pattern was consistent. They'd say, "I'd meet a man. At first he'd be charming, sexy, sweep me off my feet. The electricity between us was amazing. I'd write off the little voice in my gut that whispered, 'You better watch out,' as fear of getting involved. It was so subtle anyway. When the abuse began I was already hooked." Some body messages, though, are anything but subtle. On a first date one woman landed in the hospital with an IV, retching from "psychosomatic" abdominal pain. But did that stop her from seeing the guy?

Reasons for tolerating abuse include violent family history, low self-esteem, fear of one's own power—all tyrannizers of intuition. In every case inner strengthening is required. Without it the body's signals are puny compared with the hurricane force of these negative drives. The good news is that such strengthening is possible. From these women we gain a real-world lesson: No matter how enthralling someone appears, close attention to your physical self will enable you see beneath exteriors.

A special kind of body-based intuition that can guide your relationships is the experience of déjà vu, a cellular memory of having known a person at some other time or place. Such a meeting is not an introduction but a reunion. (This sense of inexplicable kinship differentiates déjà vu from physical chemistry, though both are compelling.) Déjà vu may be positive or negative, sudden or slow; it will be more significant with some people than others. Always, however, it's telling you to "stay aware," perhaps to complete what's not yet finished. Whether instances of déjà vu are explained by a memory of a dream, a premonition, or a past life recollection, they draw you closer to mystical alliances.

All my most meaningful relationships have begun with such a gut-level connectedness. The first few minutes with people, I'll know if we're going to be close. It isn't that I associate them with someone else or that their traits are simply appealing. Rather, my body and soul relate to them not as strangers but as spirits with whom I have an earned trust and shared history. The timelessness of this rapport is missing with other acquaintances and friends.

I've come to rely on the integrity of my intuitions, but I've taken a lot of flak for it. Particularly about guys I date. "Why don't you give him a chance?" well-intentioned family members and friends would urge. I felt they might have a point. Okay, I thought, maybe I'm being unreasonable. Could I have been sabotaging my fondest wish, to be in a relationship? I needed to know. So I decided to try spending time with men I liked but where an instant connection was lacking. Without fail it never worked out. Every deep romantic involvement I've had has started with a feeling of déjà vu. I'm not saying a relationship can't succeed without it. With a positive or even a neutral take on someone, you may want to investigate. Good things can come of it. But if ever you experience déjà vu, don't let him or her get away. Explore the bond. Whether you spend minutes or a lifetime with this person, there are lessons to be learned.

Some instances of déjà vu mark auspicious beginnings. Think back. Have you ever been chatting with a woman you just met at a business lunch and suddenly it hits you, Aha. Here's an old friend. It's obvious: You're both just continuing where you left off. Other instances of déjà vu are protective. In potentially dicey situations, they caution you to halt, separate friend from foe. The instant a screenwriter patient of mine walked into a meeting to sell a project, he cringed. One look at the potential buyer, whom he'd never even spoken to before, and every cell screamed, "I know him. Get us out of here!" Luckily, my patient listened. Soon after this man was indicted for fraud. Either heralding a good omen or veering you away from harm, déjà vu is your body's way of taking care of you.

A repository of intuitive wisdom, your body is your champion in every aspect of relationships. To stay healthy, some people, like myself, can't get away with letting anything slide. If something's off our bodies give us instant feedback. This is good. It motivates us to address what needs tending to. Like clockwork my stomach gets tied in knots if I don't say no enough; my friend Jan's back aches when she's harboring a grudge against her husband; my patient Phil's eyelid twitches when he doesn't trust someone. I'd like you to notice how your body reacts to others. Big pains, little pains, hot flashes, spasms—the quirkiest reactions count. By following their lead you can quickly resolve issues with people close to you.

It's so much nicer to be involved with someone your body likes. Then you're not always guarding against a basic suspicion or incompatibility. You must give yourself permission to listen to your body if it says, "This person is perfect for you. She will be a blessing." In real life the old line "I'd never belong to a club that would have me as a member" isn't funny. To be happy, take a risk, go for everything you deserve. Joy is part of it.

Step 3. Sense Your Body's Subtle Energy

What's most important to me in people is their capacity to love—a quality of heart emanating from them like the sun's rays. Love is a distinctly felt energy, a warm glow that makes you happy. It can't be feigned. The kinder you are to yourself and others, the stronger your connection with a spiritual source, the more love you exude. All kinds of people say all kinds of things about their spiritual and emotional capacities. If you want the real scoop, just stand beside them; you'll sense the truth. People's presence never deceives, nor does the integrity with which they lead their lives.

Take Ruben. He's spent eleven hours a day for twenty-two years in an office building as an elevator operator, an almost extinct breed in our automated culture. Ruben considers his job a calling; he has never missed a day of work. "I was born to go up and down," he said with a mischievous grin in a *Los Angeles Times* interview. Tenants adore him, look to him as philosopher, role model, guru. One tenant reported, "I was full of questions about my film career. . . . Then I met Ruben. . . . He had that inner peace we're all searching for." Ruben's energy was so striking it prompted this tenant to produce an award-winning documentary on Ruben's life. This ability to inspire people is a testament to

216 • EMOTIONS AND RELATIONSHIPS

the love Ruben embodies. Regardless of profession or training, love is a transmittable energy with real effect. More than any other factor, it can transform relationships.

Your energy influences people; theirs influences you. Consider this before you commit yourself to any long-term involvement. Being with someone, whether boss or mate, day in, day out, entails intimately interacting with his or her energy. You might like the person, but also be sure you respond positively to how he or she "feels." When my patient Fran married, she didn't realize what she was getting into. She told me, "I'm in love with my husband. But I'm being demolished by the constant anger he gives off." In arguments it wasn't just his harsh words that got her. She also described "a toxic force field" around him that was draining. "Am I doing that?" he asked, bewildered. It must've been horrible for him. Devoted to his wife, he felt helpless and to blame. Like many people he was oblivious to how anger tenaciously lingers as energy. Even in calm moments or in sleep, Fran empathically felt it. The situation became so intolerable she started sleeping in their second bedroom.

It was then they consulted me. When we met I wanted to see if I shared Fran's perception of her husband's energy. Using my body as a litmus test, I'd gain an idea how to proceed. So, as they were talking, I first tuned in to him. On the surface he was delightful. But in my solar plexus the intensity of his anger gripped me like a clenched fist. I've grown accustomed to such discrepancies between surface and depth. I filed the information. Next I tuned in to Fran. It was clear she had no clue how to center herself, absorbed her husband's energy like a sponge, and became depleted by it. My job was to show him ways to resolve his anger and to teach her meditation techniques to ground and shield herself. Utilizing a mix of psychology and energy awareness, Fran and her husband were able to rekindle their love.

There's an art to salvaging relationships (always eliminating those that have persistent physical or emotional abuse). Even if you've grown apart or vehemently disagree, the ability to read energy can prompt reconciliation. To know if a relationship is worth fighting for, you must sense an underlying bond of respect and love. You may feel it as a fullness in your heart, a timeless or core-felt connection. It has nothing to do with guilt or obligation, transcends the specifics of your fallout. If, for the two of you, this reciprocal tie is present, you owe it to yourselves to try to mend the relationship. The effort can open your hearts.

My patient Jim was estranged for years from his dearest childhood friend. "We're both actors," he explained. "We started competing for the same roles. He'd get one—I didn't. I'd get one—he didn't. It was crazy-making." But the closeness they'd once shared suddenly started tugging at him, as if possessing an energy itself. Because of the love compelling his intuition, when Jim asked, "Shall I call him?" I advised, "Yes." The heart has its own agenda. Jim's making the first step, yielding, not finger-pointing, opened the door. Then the specifics of their break could be addressed, allowing a friendship to resume.

But what happens if your heart has been broken? What if you've been betrayed? Some relationships are irrevocably undone. Lies, abuse, disloyalty—something in you knows it's over. But is that reason never to fall in love again or risk being vulnerable? I am well acquainted with the anguish of heartbreak, the feeling of being trampled so horribly the damage seemed irreparable. What I didn't understand for so long was that this wasn't merely an emotional loss. On a subtle energy level an actual injury occurs, a tear in the veil, an icy wind rushing through. For some people that's it. "The pain's unbearable," they say. "I'll never love again." And they don't. But I ask you, What's the cost? That wind that makes us shiver so, does it disappear? I think not. As energy it implodes, freezes our passion.

Personally I couldn't bear this. I'm thankful that over the years my pull toward love has always outweighed the risk of pain. To me the mere hope of loving someone sustains. A hidden gift of surviving heartbreak is that the love in us (apart from any relationship) reconstitutes our essence. Your heart breaks only to become more full. But to get to that point, you have to go through the pain, all of it. Let yourself mend. Then, purified, deepened by the strange alchemy of loss, begin again. And again. True victory is to love others more madly than ever, not to shut down. On the path toward loving, you live and you learn. Bear in mind, too, *you can never lose something that doesn't belong to you.* You'll be given the relationships you're meant for. Some are short-lived but help you grow; others are enduring and help you grow. Either way, in the most profound sense you receive what you need. Have faith in that, even though it will not always be easy.

Some people, though, don't buy this pro-relationship philosophy. My patient Pat at fifty prefers to have nothing to do with the human race except when absolutely required. She works as a librarian, then comes home. It's to her ten dogs, all small—Lhasa apsos, Chihuahuas, toy poodles—that she gives her heart. As a psychiatrist of course I felt it was my duty to encourage her to socialize, to uncover emotional blocks precluding her from making human friends. We did uncover quite a few, the most glaring a withdrawn mother who stifled her. Still, the only relationships Pat wanted were with her animals.

Whether or not it matches society's standards, Pat's way of opening her heart was through her dogs. So in our sessions I treated them as family. From Pat I came to know each one, grew fond of them. Together we went through their deaths, illnesses, the joys of companionship and play. She showed me the virtues of nonhuman partnerships, opened my mind to the attributes of such energetic bonds. While I would've preferred she venture human involvement too, I couldn't force her. What I could do was support Pat in expanding her capacity for intimacy with the relationships she could tolerate.

Can it be that we reflexively think of relationships as only human? From an energetic perspective rich interactions are possible with all of life. I learned this early on—many children do. When I was a little girl, trees were my friends. I'd sit under them, talk to them, dream about them. Nestled in the shady hollow of the trunk of my favorite oak, I absorbed its energy. I'd feel freshness rushing through me from head to toe, hear a subtle vibration much like a fairy's song. Throughout my life particular trees have been my mentors and companions. Their spirits are as alive to me as yours is. I'll close my eyes, seek their advice. Or when I'm worn down by the world, I'll snuggle beneath a tree's boughs, drift off in the invisible arms that surround me.

We all could benefit from having friends such as trees, flowers, and animals. They possess intelligence, kindness, healing power. The joy of exploring intuition is that you learn to converse with nature and its creatures, cultivating what the ancients called a sympathy for all things. The language of energy is universal. Trees speak it, you do too. This may be an intuitive leap, but it is one that will restore your sense of wonder. Being in an adult mentality is fine, but a special chemistry happens when innocence mixes with maturity. Then you "see" you're part of everything, experience life flowing through you. Thinking yourself there won't work. You must feel it. Flow is spontaneous, waterlike, free. To meld with it, let go, allow yourself to be carried.

The epitome of flow is a relationship born of synchronicities: golden moments when human energies align. You're in the right place at the right time; opportunity knocks. This can't be planned, nor does living in a "small world" explain it. Synchronicities result from an attunement (conscious or not) to a pulse surpassing sound. Imagine it. *Lub-dub. Lub-dub.* Your rhythm synchronizing with all others' and the earth's. That makes for a pretty impressive magnetism. Lives crisscross—then suddenly he's there: your husband-to-be, your future employer, an investor who believes in you. The Swiss psychiatrist Carl Jung called such synchronicities "a meaningful coincidence of outer and inner events . . . not causally related." These coincidences can portend a good pairing. Or not. Some can announce, "He's trouble," or reveal critical reasons why not to pursue an endeavor. In either case they are evidence that mystery is alive and well.

The more your life intuitively flows, the more it will be studded with synchronicities. You want this. It can spare you a chaotic day-to-day existence—a truth I keep relearning. For example, the other day I needed an electrician to repair a broken fixture in my home. I was rushing. As usual, I had too little time, too much to do. Here's what happened: I tried to call him. Got his voice mail. He called back. Missed me. We went back and forth for a week. Flash forward, a month later. Another outlet needed repair. This time I was relaxed, not frantic. I called him, left a message. Then I leisurely went down to the garage to get my mail. Eureka! The electrician appeared, heading to my neighbor's place.

Ordinary life is filled with cosmic lessons. How energy flows is evident in the tiniest acts. If you wonder why your soul mate hasn't shown up, look to interactions with *your* electrician, bank teller, or grocery checker. The daily details of your life bespeak the greater picture. Notice patterns. Are you prone to rushing around? Chronically under pressure? Curt, brusque? Realize that by trying to push the river you're clogging vital energy. At all levels you'll accomplish less, not more. Synchronicities build when you slow down; rushing undermines the best-laid plans. Being a student of the mundane world will teach you volumes about energy.

Large or small, don't dismiss synchronicities. They'll often nudge you in the right direction, say "go for it" when your mind is hedging. One patient of mine is a writer who lives a quiet life. Friends wanted to fix him up with a high-powered CEO, a total extrovert. He figured, "We're complete opposites. What's the use?" Sounded reasonable. But even so he asked me, "Why do I keep bumping into her?" On the street, at a restaurant across town—he even discovered her son happened to be roommates with his friend's son. My patient wondered, "What's going on? What does it mean?" I suggested, "Why don't you go out with her? See if these synchronicities are telling you something's there." He did; there was. My patient was lucky—the universe kept tapping him on the shoulder until he could accept the gift.

For synchronicities to become a regular part of your life, you must prepare for them. Much of intuitive training is about setting a tone. Cleaning house, so that your window is transparent when the sun comes. Whether you're craving passion, a family, or a chance to get up onstage and sing the blues, ask yourself, What's standing in my way? Then methodically clarify and remove the obstacles. Envision this effort as a clearing of energy so that nothing keeps you from your dreams.

Step 4. Ask for Inner Guidance

The night before I was to give a talk in San Francisco, I'd planned dinner with a friend. At the last minute he canceled. I thought, Great. Free time. I'll go pick some things up at Nordstroms. Heading through Union Square, every few feet I passed another homeless person, someone hungry, someone wanting work. I'd been here before, knew how overwhelming it was to see so much misery. Guarding against my vulnerability, avoiding all eye contact, I'd just keep moving. This time, however, my eyes were drawn to one particular man. To my amazement a voice in me said, "Why don't you take him out to dinner?" I was shocked. A stranger? And what would he make of it?

But the voice returned. "Don't miss this opportunity." Opportunity? I'm essentially shy, value my privacy. So what to do? Well, that voice had power: I got up my nerve, invited him to join me for dinner. Actually, I thought he might decline, but he smiled and simply said, "Sure." So we sat at a table in a nearby restaurant eating vegetable soup and turkey sandwiches. We chitchatted, people-watched; we shared a meal, then parted. Strangers, yet not entirely. I don't want credit for my actions—this wasn't what I'd planned. But I did listen to my guidance. As a result I partook of a small but good moment with another human being, something surprising to me that never would've happened if I didn't follow my intuition. Something at least as valuable for me as for him.

I want to emphasize the necessity of going beyond convention, acting on what's inside. Many of us have intuitive impulses about people but don't follow them; we deprive ourselves of magic that could be. I urge you to respond not to fear or inhibitions but to the spontaneity of guidance. Listen moment to moment, relinquish preconceived agendas. Otherwise we shrink the universe time after time, diminish ourselves. The goal isn't to be reckless. Safety and courtesy are essential. But convention can also strangle, preclude the excitement of discovery.

Guidance not only surprises; it can arrive just in the nick of time. I have a friend whose family arranged a lavish wedding ceremony for her. There she was in the synagogue—parents, colleagues, aunts and uncles she hadn't seen in years, all present to celebrate the happy day. Walking down the aisle in her white-trained gown and veil, a perfect moment. Except that a voice suddenly screamed inside her head, "Don't do it! Don't do it!" The organ playing the wedding march. Her mother smiling ear to ear. My friend thought, This must be typical. Last-minute jitters. Struggling for control, she repeated these words to herself but knew they weren't true. Nonetheless, all those people; approaching the rabbi, it was too late. The wedding proceeded. One very, very difficult year later, she divorced.

Guidance advises what to do, what not to do. Is there some help my friend could've received before so final a moment? Before the invitations were sent out? *Yes.* Before meeting someone, and during a relationship, you can use remote viewing to tune in. Consider it a preventive measure, to get to the heart of the situation. This keeps you on track, lends newness to your perceptions. No matter how taken I am with someone, initially I'll allow a few minutes to "read" him or her, then do periodic intuitive check-ins along the way. To stay on top of your relationships, you can try this too.

USING REMOTE VIEWING TO READ PEOPLE

1. Close your eyes. Spend a few minutes meditating. Slowly quiet your thoughts and open your heart.

2. While meditating, focus gently on a person's first name. Let it hover in your mind, never straining. Remain as neutral and assumption-free as possible.

3. Notice any images, impressions, knowings, sights, smells, sounds that come to you. Notice also your body's response. Whether you have one intuition or many, trust that what you're given is exactly what you need.

4. Do not analyze the intuitive input. See how it fills in the blanks later.

Refer to this procedure as a model for how to tune in to everyone from a blind date to your mother-in-law. People present a certain face to the world. Sometimes their outer and inner selves coincide; sometimes not. Remote viewing gives you a peek into the whole person, to offer a more balanced view. With this advantage in sizing people up, you'll have an edge on choosing relationships that will flourish.

Take my patient Milton, an endearing but high-strung software designer who would drive himself crazy analyzing every decision to death. Recently, when he was considering taking on a business partner, the pros and cons bedeviled him. "I can't sleep," he told me. "Should I? Shouldn't I? Who?" Milton had two people in mind, a perfect predicament for remote viewing. During a session I suggested, "Intuitively focus on each person's name for a few minutes. Don't force it. See what you get." Relaxing has never been easy for Milton, but with encouragement he managed to let go. While he was tuning in to Candidate 1, a sense of calm came over him. "It's strange," he said. "I feel at peace, happy, like I want to celebrate." Then, flash—he saw an image of a sparkling jewel. Shifting gears, Milton moved on to Candidate 2. He started squirming. "Ugh," he groaned. "I'm getting nervous, queasy. I keep seeing this annoying little black bird pecking me to pieces." There we had it: two people, two different readings. With these intuitive cues Milton had more to go on. The verdict? Even though both candidates were impeccably credentialed and enthusiastic, impelled by his remote viewings Milton went with Candidate 1—a choice marking the beginning of a trusted partnership that has stood the test of time.

You want relationships that are harmonious with your spirit. You want to be with people who smile when you fly. Remembering this, begin to live your life differently. Intuitively, not just from the mind. For example: You meet a guy who sweeps you off your feet, but when you read him, despite no external cues, you sense he's conflicted about his sexual identity. Before going ahead, weigh this information. Consider yourself forewarned. By contrast, if on a first date you think, She's a little boring but nice, also see what a remote viewing tells you. If you sense a real fire in her belly, think twice about writing her off. You could be missing out on a good thing.

The closer you are to someone, the harder he or she may be to read, especially family. But it can be done. Learning to become neutral takes practice. If you want to get to the bottom of why people behave as they do and to change unhealthy patterns, neutrality breeds the compassion to see clearly. Ah, Mother! She'd always know exactly what to say to infuriate me. After forty years you'd think she would have tired of pressing my buttons. Never. My boyfriends were her favorite topic: "He's too old." "He's too young." "He's not Jewish." That did it. I'd grab the bait; off we'd go. It took every ounce of restraint for me not to get locked into the same struggles. Remote viewing was my secret weapon. It showed me that beneath my mother's proud, commanding exterior was a gaping wound that flared if she felt threatened. This image emerged whenever she was itching for a fight. It is what allowed me to say and mean, "I love you, Mother. Let's sit by the fire and drink some tea," instead of spewing venom that poisoned us both. Letting love transform your relationships comes from seeing who a person is from the deepest place.

Remote viewing can take you many places. Time and space do not confine. I remind aspiring parents of this. Intuitively speaking, it's possible to tune in to your child before he or she is conceived. If you concede that spirit has enduring intelligence, why not try? I suggest that my patients who want to get pregnant—both parents—sit quietly in meditation and invite the spirit of their child in. This is a respectful thing to do, an honoring of that soul who will soon be entrusted to you, a hello before the fact. Whether you sense an essence or see the details of your baby's face, acknowledging the eternality of your bond before conception gets the parent-child relationship off to a positive spiritual start. For my patients who are having difficulty conceiving, extending such an invitation can act as a homing device. It's a way of communicating, "I am here, this is how you get to me." Think of it as emitting a signal your child can recognize so he or she knows the coordinates of where to land.

Similarly, remote viewing enables you to tune in to loved ones who've passed on. I was struck by how natural doing this can be at a workshop I gave in South Carolina. We met in the clapboard-churchlike structure where Martin Luther King wrote his "I have a dream" speech. The building was the first post–Civil War free school for blacks in the area. African-Americans now living there had tremendous pride in their ancestors, revered their ongoing presence. We in the room were privileged to feel it too.

Given this, I tried an experiment. Typically when teaching remote viewing, I say the name of a living person (offering no other facts) and ask the group to intuitively tune in. Then everyone shares intuitions; I offer feedback about accuracy, a process that shows participants what they're capable of. This time I chose Elizabeth, an elderly friend who'd just passed on, though the participants didn't know that. They had only her name.

The group's responses impressed me. Describing Elizabeth, they said: "I'm gazing at a vast ocean." "I see an angel." "I see brilliant white light." "I keep wanting to look up at the sky." "I think she's dead." "I hear Dorothy in *The Wizard of Oz* saying, 'There's no place like home.' " "God is near." "I'm filled with awe." Each person unknowingly offered a vision of heaven.

Intuition stuns: it allows us to know the unknowable. Most people at the workshop were novices to remote viewing. Yet nothing stopped them from going further than this life to connect with Elizabeth's spirit. I stress: There is nothing supernatural about sensing those who are gone. However, don't assume that being on the other side makes any-one smarter or more powerful than you. They just don't have bodies. Aunt Martha is Aunt Martha, here or there. Relationships do continue. Remote viewing can be your connector.

Whenever you seek guidance about someone or something, your heartfelt intentions will elicit heartfelt response. It all comes down to love. Relationships are the training ground. It's okay to ask for help. Every time you pray, "Please guide me. I want to love, but I don't know how," your reaching out makes loving all the more possible. Maybe that's the point.

Step 5. Listen to Your Dreams

Hiking in the mountains of Big Sur last winter, I struck up a con-versation with a feisty seventy-five-year-old woman I met on the trail. We got to talking about family. I am single. I live alone, sometimes more in contact with the moon and clouds than with other people. I long to find the right man, but I haven't yet. I keep waiting and watching. Unlike me, this woman had been happily married for over fifty years. "Any kids?" I asked. Smiling, she explained. "In the beginning we tried and tried, but no luck. That is, until I saw my eldest son's face in a dream. I'll never forget it." She told me this story:

I'm at an elementary school playground. The children are lined up in one row; their mothers are paired with them in another. Watching from a distance, I spot a little boy down the line I recognize as my son to be—but he's matched with another mother! Devastated, I freeze, not knowing what to do. Suddenly the mother starts madly waving at me to come over. "Thank goodness you're here," she exclaims. "I have to go. Can you take my place?" Thrilled, I say, "Sure."

"Wouldn't you know it?" the woman continued. "The next month I got pregnant! *Amazed* couldn't begin to describe my feeling. That was the fall of 1948. Six children and three grandchildren later, here we are." Winking, she added, "Honey, don't worry. If a relationship is supposed to happen, it will come to you. It's never too late." I must say, I walked away with my heart uplifted.

A marvel of dreams is the relationships we have in them. We're conditioned to consider these people products of our unconscious, not "real." But what constitutes a real person anyway? Must we encounter real people only in daylight hours when we're wide awake? Or, as was true with this woman, is love so determined that it knows no physical bounds? During sleep a mother and a son found each other. Special relationships take on special life. I always go out of my way to honor such situations. Occasionally I've dreamed of patients I don't yet know— then they call. To me it's a sign we're intended to work together. No matter how packed my schedule, I'll make room for them. Without exception these relationships have a meant-to-be quality and turn out particularly well. I'm telling you this to open your mind to possibilities. If you notice someone in a dream who later shows up in your life, jump at the chance to know him or her. Whether it's your mail carrier, a five-year-old down the block, or a lover, explore the unique significance of the relationship.

Dreams also spotlight day-to-day relationships. Compassionately, they don't let you hide from your true feelings. The most poignant nuances of inner yearnings get enacted in dreams so you may see them, so you may mend the hidden parts of yourself, work toward being free. The psychological meaning of dream images is sacred, never mundane; it can ease you through transitions in a relationship.

For nearly two years I witnessed my father's Parkinson's disease strip him of all sense of control. Once a radiologist who took pride in running his own practice, he became incontinent, requiring diapers safety-pinned around his waist. Unable to feed himself or walk unassisted, he relied on an attendant for every move. One day I asked, "How are you doing, Daddy?" Oddly, he looked surprised by the question. Then his face lit up. "Judith, I love life. I love life." I just melted. My father: He was the one who knew the secret. His body was disintegrating, but his soul was bright. At that moment all I could think was, You brave man. I'll never bear losing you. Daddy, don't leave me. That night I had a dream.

> I'm with my father in the care facility where he lives. He's ebullient, robust. Beside him is his brother, my beloved uncle Sidney—a Bogart look-alike who died years ago. My father beams at me. All is well. I sense it. I kiss him good-bye, then head up to his room to get my shoes. But instead of leaving, I crouch on his closet floor, huddled beneath his suitcoats, jackets, and slacks. The very sight of his clothes soothes me. So safe I feel in this small space. The sweet scent of my father is everywhere. I breathe it in, let it fill me. I want time to stop. I want to be here forever.

My dream was a portent of the future. No matter how incapable I felt of living without my father, I was being prepared for that inevitability. It's funny what we remember about our parents. When I think of my father, what stand out most are the little things. The way he called me darling, the fragrance of his cologne, the softness of his cashmere sweater when he hugged me. They are the hardest to relinquish. No wonder I longed to take refuge in his closet. Holding on is often necessary before we can let go.

Dreams are offerings from spirit. Mine was about change, ebb and flow. Yours may be about climbing the highest mountain, the mix of struggle and reward entailed. Or it could be your abusive boyfriend is chasing you around like a maniac with a stick. Then, in waking life you have a choice. To continue the relationship or to say, "No, I can't tolerate this anymore. Either get help or leave." Remember, dreams are on your side. In relationships they always cheer you on. Whether you wake up angry, sad, or more in love than ever, study the themes in dreams and benefit. Healing is the mission. Let dreams pinpoint and release your fears and resentments, making you more available to loving others.

FIVE WAYS DREAMS ENLIGHTEN RELATIONSHIPS

1. Dreams define emotional patterns that need healing.

2. Dreams ease you through difficult transitions—deaths, separations, breakups.
3. Dreams facilitate problem solving (ask a question before you go to sleep. The next day, record your dream and look for the answer).
4. Dreams present a vision of the future in your relationships (including warnings if someone's in danger).
5. Dreams acknowledge how you've grown.

Dreams inform all dilemmas. They access a creative universe that dwarfs logic. Relationships push you to your edge. They're supposed to. Opening your heart, they permit spiritual evolution. No relationship is without conflicts. Turn to dreams to resolve them. Say your husband's snapping at you. You point this out, nicely; he shrugs it off; the behavior continues. Don't resort to nagging. Try a different tactic. Ask a dream, "What's going on?" If, for example, you dream you see his boss berating him, it's a clue. Feel out your husband about the climate at work. (You can mention your dream if he's receptive.) Give him room to respond. A nudge, based on your dream's cue, may be all that's needed to uncover the root of his edginess.

Not all dreams need to be dreamed at home. Whenever my patient and her husband fight, he heads to a remote cave in Malibu Canyon—his sacred spot, where he cools off and dreams solutions to their struggles. She is supportive; she knows that's where he goes to find clarity. I believe everyone could benefit from having a sacred spot, whether it's a meadow of wild yellow mustard or the gardening shed in the backyard. A special dreaming place, yours alone, where you close your eyes and await answers. Just knowing it's there is power enough to enhance your dreams.

Also consider this: You may ask a dream for a solution and receive an exaggerated response. Once my friend dreamed her mother's life was threatened. She awoke distraught and confused. Was this real? What should she do? Before she had a chance to act, the phone rang. "You'll never believe what happened," her mother said. "I just slipped in the kitchen. I think I broke my arm." So my friend's premonition was accurate yet slightly off. Particularly in the early stages of developing intuition, your fears often amplify intuitive facts. You sense danger and your mind immediately leaps to death. With practice you learn to discern the gray areas in between.

Another dream-related phenomenon to watch for occurs right as you're going to sleep. Drifting off as a little girl, I'd often hear a chorus of background voices in my head—as if I'd tapped into a party line, eavesdropping on fragments of trivial conversation. "I have to go to the store to get a Mars bar." "Let's meet at the bus stop." "I can't forget to call my sister." A blurred montage of random thoughts unrelated to me. Was I going crazy? Hallucinating? No. I've come to believe there's a transitional stage between sleep and waking when some of us tune in to a collective frequency. On a mundane level we pick up other people's thoughts. This is an intriguing intuitive state you need not be frightened by. A buzz, that's all. If this happens for you, relax. Consider such ability to blend with the collective a sign of your mounting sensitivity.

How sensitive we can become! How much we can grow! Some dreams highlight our progress in relating to others and ourselves. Savor their affirmations. As I've explained, one of my biggest hurdles has been achieving an enduring romantic relationship. Related concerns include how I am with men in general and how I balance the male-female aspects of myself. These are vulnerable areas for me. Often I need encouragement. A dream offered it.

> *I'm standing by a shimmering bay, breathing in the freshest air. I'm alone. Off-shore a pod of dolphins is playing. I stoop down in the sand, trying to make eye contact with them. I do. One comes close. She's white like a pearl, smaller than the others but crowned with a pair of strikingly noble ram's horns. Swimming out of the water onto the beach, she lets me touch her. So silky, so glorious to stroke. Then she speaks—aloud in English—"I have to go get my husband. I'll be right back." I patiently wait on the water's edge for her.*

The next morning I felt delightfully whole, somehow more put together. My dream's message? This dolphin was a fantastical blend of masculine ram and utter femininity—inner qualities that had merged. I felt blessed. The dolphin spoke to a fuller beauty I'd always resisted. But from her, how could I not accept it? Not that my growth was complete. Her promise was of a deeper union, when she returned with her mate. Perhaps I, too, will meet mine. But surely the melding of male and female in myself, an alchemy I've longed for, is under way.

Your dreams will celebrate you. The images you cherish will flow forth, saying, "Your work has paid off! Now's the time to recognize it." Whether you dream of winning a marathon, breaking through a barrier that separated you from a friend, or you and your husband soaring like eagles—a victory has occurred. Bravo!

There is strength in exploring vulnerability. There is reward in revealing yourself. So many layers to be fathomed. Dreams know what's required, how much to expose, when. The upshot is, who you are reflects what your relationships will be. You'll come to know yourself and feel secure. You'll be shining. Shining.

RELATIONSHIPS IN YOUR LIFE are impeccably paced according to your needs. The matchmaker behind the scenes divining these introductions is no fool, has method, motivation. I picture her as a gourmet chef wearing a tall, puffy white hat and spotless white apron. Pots are boiling on the stove, steamers hissing, delicious aromas wafting through the air. There's no rushing this chef. She's a genius at work. It would be beneath her to present a meal half-baked.

So if you pray, "Dear God, I'm lonely. Please send me my soul mate," and this person doesn't instantly show up, don't despair. Try to see it from God's point of view. Once I was given that opportunity! In a psychodrama exercise at a workshop I was attending, each actor was assigned a role. I got to play God (my big chance). The others were people on earth with a variety of problems who prayed to me. You'd think I would've been glad to answer their prayers. When I could, I did. It was an intuitive call. Some requests felt right, some didn't. Surprisingly, I also began to appreciate the compassion it takes not to grant a prayer. At least for the time being. The moment had to be perfect.

When I turned forty my biological clock was about to explode. I yearned to have children; I prayed for them. Even so, the right man hadn't materialized, and to be a single mother felt too overwhelming. So I grew angrier and angrier with God. I wasn't getting what I wanted. Defiant, I declared, "I'm not going to believe in you anymore." So there. But try as I did, I felt God's presence even more. This got me thinking. Children or not, maybe there was a plan in store for me that surpassed what I'd conceived. Although different from my own vision, it too was good.

On the origins of our physical universe, the physicist Stephen Hawking writes, "Even if there is only one possible unified theory, it is just a set of rules and equations. What is it that breathes fire into the equations and makes a universe for us to describe?" In the sphere of relationships such spiritual fire is the guiding force. If you can feel it, trust it, live it, your relationships will unfold naturally and thrive.

Forgiveness inevitably figures in: the openheartedness you must

strive for to release injuries and pain others have caused or you've in-
flicted on yourself. The Indian sage Maharaji taught, "Don't put anyone
out of your heart." When you do you also exile yourself. This isn't to say,
however, that if someone close betrays you, you're not entitled to be enraged, devastated, even to decide to leave a destructive situation. But if
anger is all you ever have, healing can't occur. Forgiveness is a process;
it doesn't happen overnight. You'll need to express your feelings and,
as time passes, purge them. Reasonably enough, you may protest. "Forgive? Why should I?" Forgiveness is a way of lifting resentments, more
for you than anyone else. Understand also: forgiveness refers to the
actor, not the act. Not the offense, but the woundedness of the offender. No argument, you were wronged. But forgiveness arises from an
intuitive empathy for the depths of other people's wounds. The desire
to transcend hatred is a summoning of light. A choice to seek higher
ground. You can't force forgiveness. It's a state of grace, an answered
prayer.

In World War II my friend Louise's father was in the U.S. infantry.
To her mother's dismay, he mailed home a Japanese flag he picked up
on a battlefield. It belonged to a dead soldier. A good luck banner,
signed by everyone from his village. In retrospect, Louise's father, a
man of conscience numbed by the kill-or-be-killed insanity of war,
deeply regretted his action. Fifty years later, after his death, Louise felt
compelled to travel to Japan and return the flag. A friend asked,
"What's driving you?" Louise, who valued intuition, searched herself.
She said, "The flag had taken on a life of its own. I was simply following
its story."

After months of searching, she finally located the soldier's family.
They agreed to see her, initiating Louise's pilgrimage. She imagined
knocking on the door of a tiny house in a rice field—the family and her
alone in a room with the flag. Instead, amazingly, the entire village
showed up to greet Louise! The mayor announced, "We are all so
touched that you have come from far away." Introductions and
speeches were made. Then the flag. The soldier's brother-in-law pulled
it out. People gasped. They cried. Then touched it, some finding their
names where they'd originally signed. Following was a banquet and celebration. For all, a day of emotional release and a step toward healing.

One miraculous result of such a mutual honoring despite very different points of view is the spiritual perspective it lends to seemingly irreparable situations. Of course, the villagers didn't have to open their

arms to Louise. But they accepted the flag, understanding her efforts to respect her father and make individual amends for the barbarism of war. As for Louise, she was able to do something her father never quite brought himself to set straight. Perhaps too she was able to acknowledge the dehumanization he suffered in combat. How glorious this tapestry has become! Woven with threads of compassion, not bitterness, a tribute to the best of relationships.

Forgiveness offers a radical template of loving to build on. It may not ensure that your resentments dissipate totally. But it does guarantee that bit by bit they'll be supplanted by the freedom of seeing beyond them. When someone hurts you, I know how easy it is to assign blame. But that doesn't have to be the end point. In both small and large interactions, reach beyond your pain toward something greater.

The status quo of how relationships are conducted is too limited for my taste. I rail at the narrowness of convention, crave more authentic, innovative forms of relating. As I do, you may get the wildest flashes. Once while I was eating breakfast at a diner in Manhattan, it suddenly occurred to me, Why don't you leave five dollars in the bathroom? Someone will find it and feel lucky. Then they'll believe anything is possible. I figured, Okay. Why not? Now, whenever I have the impulse, I leave a dollar here, five dollars there. Not much, just enough to get people thinking. I receive a lot of satisfaction from this. Plus, it's fun. Why inhibit yourself? In relationships be brave; follow your intuition. Let love shake up your world.

10

A Final Good-bye

The moment of change is the only poem.
—Adrienne Rich

*R*elationships carry the whole universe within them. They can be everything, nothing, here, then gone. One moment, loving someone makes you shine; the next, it feels like matter and antimatter colliding. The glory of loving a person over many years is learning his or her individual phases—and blending together, watching who you both become. But in all relationships—with parents, children, lovers, or friends—one thing is assured: Our time on earth has limits. Between even our dearest ones and us, letting go is inevitable.

Letting go? I couldn't conceive of it as a child. To me my parents were larger than life. My mother, dressed in Chanel, intense and iron-willed, locomoting through her days, savoring each moment. My father, handsome and strong, always there. The three of us eating yet another dinner: it seemed we'd be together forever. I wasn't so far off, really. I've discovered, though, forever has many seasons. In this life and beyond.

I'm no stranger to letting go. I've had my share of loss. In 1993 my mother died from lymphoma. Then five years later, at 6:00 A.M. one chilly November day, I was shaken out of sleep by a call. "This is the intensive care unit at Brotman Hospital. Your father had a cardiac arrest. He's in a coma, in critical condition." Grief clenched my chest. Oh no. The day had come. It was expected. I knew that. But how could I ever really be prepared to lose my father? Being by his side the past two years as he succumbed to the devastation of Parkinson's disease had bred a tender intimacy between us. No masks. No hiding. Father and daughter: together through it all. Shivering, I jumped out of bed, dressed hurriedly, and rushed for the hospital.

This is the story of my father's death. I want to share the wonder of it with you. To pay tribute to the process, and also to convey the indispensable role intuition and dreams played when my world was crumbling. As compassionate guideposts they gave me bearings. It seemed that years of spiritual practice had culminated in this moment. I was primed to see clearly, act fast. Death opens a doorway of perception. If you watch carefully, secrets of the spirit will be revealed.

I WANTED MY FATHER to have a gentle passing. I'd done everything possible to plan for it. The staff at his care facility knew he had chosen not to have his life prolonged by extraordinary measures. Yet, wouldn't you know it? When my father's heart stopped there was a paperwork snafu. So the paramedics came, resuscitated him, placed him on a respirator. When I arrived there he was: unconscious, brain function gone, tubes in every orifice, a machine breathing for him.

One look at my father, and I nearly came undone. Despite the horrific conditions, he seemed so beautiful lying there, like a child sleeping. I prayed, "Please give me the strength to face this." It came. A realigning of myself, arrowlike, determined. Then an awful scenario flashed before me: a drawn-out legal battle over withdrawing life support. Instantly I rejected it. Not us. Not that. "There's been a huge mistake," I told the on-call physician, explaining the details. Fiercely protective, I further insisted, "Take my father off the respirator. Now!" The doctor bristled. "Do you think it's that easy? We'll have to follow the proper protocol, go through the medical ethics committee." This couldn't be, I screamed inwardly. A committee deciding my father's fate? In response an inner voice suddenly came: "Don't worry. Things are going to work out fine." From past experience I knew to trust it (although nothing about the situation suggested an easy resolution). I calmed down, waited. Within an hour I watched a potential nightmare tangle of red tape miraculously unravel. A woman from the committee hugged me, apologizing, "I'm so sorry we had to put you through this." I stood beside my father as the respirator was withdrawn. It would be a matter of only hours.

In circumstances like these we learn our own strength. I had no family in Los Angeles; they all lived on the East Coast. Friends would've come, though I didn't call them. It was just me and my father in that room. Whatever doubts I had about being up to helping him die quickly vanished. Seeing his sweet face, feeling the love between us, I intuitively knew, I can do this alone. I was being shown how far my heart had come, what it was capable of, a gift I'll never forget. In the end, though, I wasn't alone. Minutes later a nurse brought the phone to me. My father's caregivers, a husband and wife, had tracked me down. "Honey, we want to be with you. Do you want us to come?" Oh yes. Yes, I did. So two angels appeared to support me. To support him.

Over the next few hours, sitting by my father's deathbed, I had many thoughts. I remembered the last night I had visited him. He was incontinent, in pain, thrashing around. But, as always, despite the indignities of his disease, I saw a God-force around him. Now a powerful but delicate white light was emanating from his broken body, assuring, All is well. It was beyond paradox—such a sense of protection even as he was in the most extreme jeopardy. For the first time I was honestly able to say, "Daddy, I want you to know, whatever happens, I'll be all right. You don't have to worry." Instantly he quieted down, just looked into my eyes. Then he started repeating, almost chanting, "It's good-bye. It's good-bye. It's good-bye." Tears welled up, streamed down my cheeks. I kissed him on the forehead whispering, "I love you." Still he kept saying, "Good-bye. Good-bye," as if there were no other words left for him. A few hours later his heart stopped.

Strange synchronicities. It seemed my father had intuitively waited for me to feel secure enough not to need him anymore. I never felt pressured to reach that point. Though he didn't articulate it this way, his spirit appeared to be fully prepared to endure the wrath of disintegrating health until I got there. But once I had he was able to be freed from his failing body. I recalled a dream I had soon after my mother died, speaking to the nature of my father's devotion.

My parents and I are driving west toward my condo in Marina del Rey. My mother announces about halfway there, "Here's where I get off. I have to go." Then she looks at my father impatiently. "Well, Teddy, aren't you coming with me?" Shrugging, he quietly shakes his head and replies, "No, dear. I'll have to catch up with you later. I need to make sure Judith gets all the way home."

All the way home. My father brought me. Now, at his deathbed, I was able to help get him home too. So precious are these last moments, when the body winds down and spirit takes hold. But for my father (as is true for many people) the transition started months before the moment of death—a gradual lifting off, dissociating from this life, connecting to another.

Until his illness my father never believed in anything "psychic." When friends asked, "What do think of your daughter's work?" he'd say proudly, "Personally I've never experienced what Judith has. But if she's doing it, it must be good." For many years we left it at that. Then one evening at dinner, casually he began: "Judith, last night I could've sworn your mother was sitting next to me on the bed. I was scared, didn't dare look out from under the covers." Amazed, I listened, gently answered his questions about what I thought was going on. I kept it low-key. I wanted his experience to feel as natural as I knew it to be. Soon after, in synagogue, while Kaddish, the prayer for the dead, was being recited, he elbowed me. "Do you feel Mother?" I did. "Do *you*?" I asked. He looked excited, even proud. "Yep, I do too." As the Parkinson's disease progressed, his conception of linear reality loosened, allowing him to perceive differently. Boundaries blurred. My mother's spirit was becoming more palpable.

In my father's case dementia led to expansion, but it also has other faces. True, a demented person is downright confused about certain things; synapses don't quite connect. I was reminded of my father's seventy-eighth birthday a month before. His caregiver was a radiant woman from Belize he affectionately called Bubeleh (Yiddish for "little doll"). She and I gave him a German chocolate cake and were singing "Happy Birthday." Learning what kind of cake it was, he snapped to attention and yelled, "Bubeleh, the Germans are coming. Run and get your gun!" He was so earnest, we laughed and cried at the same time.

Funny or disturbing, dementia also sometimes heightens intuitive clarity. I saw my father start to talk regularly with people on the other side. He received repeated visits from a couple named the Blooms. "Who are they?" I asked. He'd patiently explain. "Mr. and Mrs. Bloom are not from here." I was fascinated. "From where then?" "They're dead," he'd answer matter-of-factly. It was obvious, he'd become available to extraordinary experiences. The night before his best friend Elizabeth died, he called Bubeleh to come closer. "There she is. It's Elizabeth. She's wearing a black mourning shroud, sitting in my armchair." My father wasn't simply confused, pointing his finger at nothing. He'd seen her, as she was about to pass on, a good friend coming to say good-bye.

Good-bye. Now I had to say it to my father. We all gathered around his bed—Bubeleh, her husband, and I, just taking him in. Synchronistically, my spiritual teacher happened to be in town; I'd planned to meditate with him that day. My father was stable, so I'd decided to slip away for an hour. During my meditation the clearest memory surfaced.

> *I'm nine years old. My father is teaching me to bodysurf at Sorrento Beach in Santa Monica. It's late afternoon. The sun glistens on the ocean. "Just go with the wave," he tells me. "Let it carry you." I push off from the sand, feel the swell lift me, lift me—and I fly. Jetting across the curl of the waves, my father and I ride them one after another until twilight turns the sky violet. We're tired out and happy; it's time to go. Driving home, my father picks up a hitchhiker. He winks at me. "Don't tell your mother. She wouldn't approve."*

I came out of the meditation weeping. Purifying tears, cleansing me. These were the most joyful days I'd ever spent with my father. They hadn't crossed my mind for years. Why now? Was it simply an attempt to remember him, remember us? To pin down our history? I lingered for a while, talked to other people about it. Then my teacher urged, "You'd better get back to your father. He'll need you soon."

When I returned I became mesmerized by my father's breath. The breath of the dying is distinctive, unforgettable. A raspy, labored effort, hungering for oxygen, mobilizing every last ounce of strength to claim it. Cheyne-Stokes respiration is the technical term. I think of it as getting revved up to cross the great river. My head resting on my father's chest, it lifted up and down, each breath barely sustaining his fading life. I breathed with him. I listened to his heart. His heart. Just one more beat.

Then something in the room changed. I sensed a conclave of spirits encircling him. One by one they glided past me, wisps of energy, the softest breeze, but more dense than air. I heard a distant, high-pitched tinkling, a symphony of triangles rung by wands. Could these be angels? I felt compelled to hold my father's head, placing my hand over his crown chakra, our connection with spirit, where white light pours in. Without knowing why, I began to recount our bodysurfing days. "Daddy, remember when we used to go to Sorrento Beach . . ." We were there again together. The sun glowed golden on the water, illuminating the hospital room. At the end of the story my father took his final breath. A gasp. A grunt. A long, long sigh.

I watched in awe. Pieces started falling into place. Only a few hours before, during meditation, I'd been given my father's death image. I hadn't understood it as such until the moment came. That didn't matter. Without planning, something inside me intuitively knew when to present it. My father passed over as we were riding those waves, a natural evolution. Water became air became breath. His last breath, a cherished gift of life he gave me. How special to have witnessed it. Not everyone gets the chance.

Nor does everyone get the chance to spend time with a loved one's body after death. I chose to. Typically, the family is whisked out of the room (without being offered the decision). What a blessing that the hospital staff knew not to intrude. "Take as long as you want," a nurse told us. I needed to be with his body. I needed to hold him, stroke his skin, his hair, his cheek. I fought to etch his body in my memory so I wouldn't forget. The irony was, he'd never really enjoyed being touched. Shooing me away, he'd always say, "Judith, don't do that." But here he was. I couldn't help myself. On some level I feel his spirit orchestrated the scene—and prolonged the circumstances of his death—out of respect for me. Because of the "foul-up" at the care facility, I received the luxury of saying good-bye in my own way.

More than an hour passed. During that time Bubeleh, her husband, and I reminisced. My father's quirks, tastes, sensibilities. The beauty of the moment was that there was no fear in the room. Not of death, not of his body. Slowly, given this time, I began to disengage the subtle energetic link I had with my father. A spool of yarn unwinding—as it must—bringing to an end our physical tie. I mourned freely, accompanied by people who understood. It's not always so with the loss of a loved one: fissures erupt between families; the fear of death in relatives and friends may stifle the flow of grief. Instead, I was privileged to have the space and support to feel only love.

When a parent dies a portal opens, the winds of the universe blow through. Two days later at the funeral, standing by my father's open casket, I heard them howl. How strange, how magnificent to see my father's face, wrinkleless, all signs of disease erased. So cold his body was, I hugged him unashamed. My warm tears fell on his icy forehead. Then a vision came: a gorgeous infant being born feet-first out of the crown of my father's head. The same spot I'd touched as he was dying.

I marvel at what I'm afraid of. Not death—no, never. But about his funeral, I was frightened no one would come. My mother had all the friends—four hundred people to mourn her. My father was a loner. Too proud to have friends see him sick, he'd withdrawn from them. Bubeleh offered a touching perspective: "Honey, if it's just the three of us holding hands in a circle around your father's grave, it will be perfect." What had I been thinking? Funerals aren't popularity contests; they're to memorialize a life. But as it turned out there was a lovely gathering of twenty, some of my friends, some of his. Everything he would've wanted.

Winds of grief continued. I spread my arms wide, planted my feet on the ground, held on. No matter how difficult, this was passion, this was raw primal force. I couldn't miss a minute of it. That week of the funeral I was scheduled to speak to a group of five hundred people. I did it, adrenaline pumping as always when I teach. But this time the adrenaline numbed me, separated me from my grief. I canceled further lecture engagements, just let my sorrow come. The portal stays open only so long, then the nature of grief changes. This was holy time. The waves of exhaustion I felt, my body coiling into itself, hibernating, my endless tears, were prerequisites for healing.

We are not alone. Spirit is always with us. Our relatives, though, may not comprehend this fact. They want to console, but their anxieties often intercede. "You're alone. You're alone," one uncle "helpfully" reminded me. Others kept using the word *orphan*. Orphan? Weren't they forgetting something? True, I was an only child whose parents had gone. But, bottom line, my primary relationship was with God. Now my spiritual task was to make that real on every level, put my beliefs to the test. Of course, panic had its say. "Who's going to take care of me?" the little girl within sometimes cried. The answer? Spirit will. To intuit such an absolute reality dissolves fear. Deepening this intuition is my ongoing meditation.

The circularity of human love. In many kinds of bonds we find ourselves caring for those who once cared for us. Parents can regress to children we're entrusted with. Roles reverse, transformed. Daughters become women; sons become men. There's a purpose for everything, an intuitive intelligence to support you through life's ups and downs, imbuing them with radiance, with heart. You gain multidimensional sight; understanding replaces illusion. I hope you'll embrace intuition in all that you do, especially in the worst of times.

Life wants us to become brighter, better, more. Being there for my father as he died, grief sweeping me through space with no known destination, wasn't just about letting go. It was about becoming. I wasn't anyone's child anymore. I've since discovered a larger identity. Something lost, something gained. A ripening. Lately I've noticed changes in myself. I'm growing softer, more womanly. I go barefoot every chance I get. I crave the warmth of earth between my toes, ancient waterfalls, the cool moisture of dew. After a bath I study my body in the mirror, the sensuality of its curves, its tones. The woman in me rises, longs to be seen. I can feel her awakening.

PART THREE

Sexual Wellness

11

Passionate Sex, Deep Spirit

The secret of secrets is in me again.
—Anna Akhmatova

*R*ecall the most perfect summer day you can remember. Breeze caressing your skin, sun warming your shoulders, sweet scent of fresh-cut grass. There's a softness to everything. Nowhere to go. Nothing to do. Looking around, you feel both fully yourself and part of the world. Your body, the tiniest leaves on branches fluttering, people passing—a melding with it all. In these instants of sensual at-homeness, life washes over you; you're bathed by pleasure. So simple it seems, but you've touched the essence of passion.

You deserve to live passionately. You deserve to savor each moment. Passion is your birthright, very much within reach. With sexuality and every other area, it's waiting for you to embrace it. But how? The secret: If you "see" with heart the light in all things—from hoeing your petunia garden to making love—passion radiates. If you "see" with just your mind, radiance recedes. It's a choice. Your vision of the world depends on you.

We are wising up. We are growing more intuitive. Dissatisfied with cultural stereotypes, we are ready to begin to view sexuality in a new way. What we've been traditionally taught—by our parents, teachers, popular magazines—doesn't honor the gorgeous beings we really are. I want to present sexuality from an intuitive and spiritual (not to be confused with religious) point of view. Commonly it's been defined as physical love, how you feel in your body or bond with another's. That's wondrous but only a fraction of the picture. More empowering is to understand sexuality as fueling an intuitive style of being in the world, en-livening everything about you. A means of sparking an energetic open-ing in yourself, with others, and God. Oddly, for Westerners, God is often construed as punitive in regard to sex, a notion we must correct. In fact sexuality goes beyond a physical act. It becomes a force of heal-ing that can be holy.

Such fullness. Such connection. From experience I know these are worth fighting for. Even so, I've found the path to awakening sexuality can meander. As a woman I've had to get used to the idea that I could encompass many facets of myself safely. It took time. Intuition, sexual-ity, spirituality—little by little, they've begun to be woven into a won-derful braid.

It hasn't always been so. As a psychiatric resident in my late twen-ties, I'd often go dancing on nights off. No white doctor's coat. Dressed head to toe in black, my shoulder-length auburn hair as curly as I could make it, I'd drive to a funky after-hours club in downtown Los Angeles. A mix of the bohemian, the hip, it was my place just to be. No one there knew I was a psychiatrist—I couldn't risk those passion-paralyzing I-know-it. You're-going-to-analyze-me looks from men. Instead, I became a secretary, artist, waitress, whatever I pleased. Led Zeppelin and Aerosmith blasting, psychedelic strobes lighting up the Art Deco ballroom floor, I shimmied hard, dancing until dawn.

In those days I didn't know how to be both psychiatrist and woman. I compartmentalized, never mixing the two. Somehow it felt dangerous or inappropriate to embody it all. I've since discovered that, to be whole I can, I must. The secret was to integrate parts of myself, not split them off. True for me, true for you. Over years, with my intuition maturing, I've experienced spirituality and sexuality blending, unconflicted. A tremendous liberation.

I had a lot to learn. I began through my interest in Eastern philos-ophy. My spiritual teacher explained that our bodies are composed of subtle energies, from psychic to sexual. Spiritual balance entails acti-vating them all, above the waist and below. The goal? To wed our many sides. This made sense. I could feel, meditating, that what I'd imagined to be a "spiritual" experience was very much of the body. Erotic force is a component of a larger continuum. What appealed to me was that I didn't have to hold back; being spiritual meant expressing my total self.

To achieve this, for you or for me, requires sexual healing. That is, personifying sexuality in a natural way, not running from it, fighting it, or overcompensating for a lack you feel inside. A body-centered realization that spirit is the source of ecstasy, your physical form its channel. In numerous cultures the gods are right at the center of human eroticism, a root truth that can't be ignored. Consider Dionysius, Greek god of passion. According to the myth, when he came to a certain city, the king, representing law and order, disrespected him. As a result the entire city was destroyed. The gods, who have a great stake in human passion, must be given their due. If we acknowledge this, then sexuality becomes a spiritual union between another and oneself. Imagine that the next time you make love. But so much interferes. For many sexuality is unawakened, traumatized. You may have walled it off completely. You may know you have it but may be afraid; perhaps you were hurt. Here's where intuition can intervene. It's a laser, illuminating what debris of the past needs to be cleared away. Also it mends wounds, gives you courage to realize your sexuality, whether in a relationship or not.

Such change requires tenderness, care. No rush. No pressure. But if something in you is curious, inquire. Don't assume it's beyond you, that you don't have the time, space, or peace of mind. The type of sexuality I'm speaking of has no prerequisites. Stay receptive. Be easy on yourself. You'll feel tension releasing, energy rising, in the words of the novelist Michael Ventura, "a great rush of wind, as though all the locked doors and windows within have been thrown open, and body and spirit can finally breathe again."

Step 1. Notice Your Beliefs

Your beliefs about sexuality frame how you perceive it. A tenet of quantum physics is that the act of observation inevitably alters physical systems. Heisenberg's uncertainty principle says that two people looking at the same event will see it differently. I suggest you try to see sexuality in both ordinary and nonordinary terms. The ordinary has the vocabulary of the physical and emotional, techniques and gratification. Important, but limiting. But a nonordinary appreciation of sexuality includes another dimension entirely, the spiritual. This becomes real when we use the intuitive's magnifying lens.

We widely accept as true only a sliver of what's possible. Typically, sexuality is equated with intercourse, sensuality with heightening of the senses. I'm saying, not only that they enhance each other but that, when catalyzed by intuition, intimacy in lovemaking increases because it is a more spiritual experience. What's more, such receptivity invokes a fuller world. Nature itself is filled with ecstasy, contains a literal erotic force we can tap into. It's alive. We're alive. We connect. This may be surprising for you, but paradigms do shift. The unthinkable becomes thinkable. Even in terms of yourself. I want to show you how to broaden your vision, experience aspects of sexuality you may not have considered before.

INTUITIVE BELIEFS FOR A NEW SEXUALITY

1. *Sexuality and spirit are related.*

Get ready for a mind shift. When you let go sexually, you enter an open, intuitive state, permitting a greater force to flow through you, similar to the way artists are moved by creativity. Your consciousness changes. Ordinary boundaries fall away. With or without realizing it, you're encountering the transcendent. Pure bliss. Picture yourself a conduit. Something to strive toward, an evolving process. Awareness quickens it. You cultivate the practice of inviting spirit in—which, in turn, triggers your body's neurochemical pleasure response. Many of us misperceive these sensations as self-generated. We've got it backwards. Passion of the body is ignited by the passion of heaven. Knowing this is the beginning of knowing bliss.

2. *You don't have to be in a relationship to be sexual.*

I can't tell you how many times I've heard, "When I'm not in a relationship, my sexuality goes on hold." The premise? You need another person to feel sexual. How disempowering, and untrue. If sexuality derives from a spiritual energy apart from any human being, what's to stop us? Begin by asking each day during meditation, "Please let my sexuality blossom in me." It will. All over. Tingles. Rushes of warmth. Tactile sensitivity. Notice every change, whether in your belly, genitals, or breasts. Be as aware as you can of your body. You're exploring. Then extend your sensuality further. When jogging I delight in tucking a sprig of the night-blooming jasmine growing along the trail into my blouse. Its delicate star-shaped petals and pungent scent excite me. The flower and I become one. Try allowing yourself to feel the erotic aura of the earth, the sky, any aspect of nature. Even if you're never in a relationship again, know that your sexuality will be there. However, if you choose to be with a partner, you won't arrive empty-handed, nor will you expect him or her to kindle a passion you already possess.

3. *Sex can improve with age.*

Robert Heinlein's novel *Time Enough for Love* is about a romance between a man who's immortal and a woman who's not. One of my favorite scenes is when she plucks out a gray pubic hair to hide from her lover the fact that she's growing old. Even reading this at twenty I well understood. Sexuality, beauty, passion—how we fear they will dissipate with age. Does some timer go off, and suddenly we're not sexy anymore? No. No. No. With age the body does undergo change, but hormones aren't everything. View it this way: To compensate for hormonal shifts, look to your spiritual life to increase energy. Shakti, or chi, it's called. The more you consciously draw on it through meditation, sacred movements such as t'ai chi, or prayer, the more energy you'll mobilize, sexuality included. By nurturing your vital force, you can't help but become sexier with age. I'll offer techniques, but you must know this about yourself. Celebrate it.

4. *There is no such thing as casual sex.*

Sigmund Freud wrote, "We ride with our ancestors on streetcars. We are carriers of all the relationships we have." By this he was saying that we are psychologically shaped by our heritage and all the people we are close to. Presences continue to dwell in our psyches. And, I suggest, in our energy fields. Of course, this fact has various implications in daily life. Remember, when someone touches you—even a single time— energy is communicated, energy received. There's no way around it. We affect one another. Now extrapolate to what happens when you make love. Energy implodes, explodes, spirals around you, through you, imprints itself invisibly. The more you love someone, the more intense it becomes. But even with limited emotional involvement, some intuitive merging occurs. Though you may not be aware of it, making love (one-night stands included) can influence you in subtle ways.

Sexuality is an oasis for nurturing our spiritual selves. How can you prepare to get to such a place? Specifically, what's there to do? You may well begin before the actual moment. Sometimes getting ready means not having sex but doing other things: spiritual housecleaning or finishing a project. You're creating space for change. The timing has to feel right. Rushing is pointless. Sometimes I get impatient, want to push this area of my life along. One night I dreamed I was stranded at the end of a long line that was barely moving. Aggressively, I barged up to the front. There I saw a woman beginning to set up an enormous sun-lit room. She smiled at me quizzically. "Honey, you're too early. We're not ready for you yet." A dream reminding me that I can't hurry my growth—nor can you. But we can prepare ourselves by doing everything possible to ensure our hearts are open when the time comes. And it will.

QUESTIONS FOR REFLECTION

- On a daily basis, are you in touch with your sexuality? Or is it submerged? If so, what keeps it there?

- Would you like to explore how spirituality and sexuality relate? What beliefs from your past are inhibiting you? Do they make sense anymore?

- What would it mean to nurture your sexuality, not just with a partner but as part of how you intuitively relate to the world? How could this improve your quality of life?

Step 2. Be in Your Body

The elegance of our bodies can be appreciated through the eyes of sexual biology. A knowledge of your microworkings enables you to intuit primal forces. These aren't just facts. You're being shown spirit in action as it enlivens the physical. Men. Women. How are we the same? Different? What draws us to each other? What holds us back? To better understand, I want to show you how the psychology of sexuality is enacted in our cells.

Take the sperm and the egg, living organisms with a shared destiny. To pin down exactly what happens between them, I recommend an award-winning *Nova* video, *The Miracle of Life,* the first filmed record of human conception. You're right there; you view everything. Envision it: During lovemaking, 2 to 3 million sperm plunge into the vagina in a spectacular wave. They're all programmed for one thing: to find the egg and penetrate it within forty-eight hours, before they die. How astonishing—an army of sperm, tails whipping, urgently propelling themselves; we hear their rumbling like the background drone of a large city. The vagina's defense system attacks, protecting itself from invaders. Just a few sperm survive. Then they spot it: the egg. Vastly larger than every one of them, a white, luminous orb, so still, radiating. One tiny sperm reaches the egg's membrane; it's drawn inside, dissolving in her essence. This is conception.

What can this teach us about the dance of intimacy? Demonstrating the compelling instinct men and women have to join, conception is the blending of aggressive and receptive elements. The purpose? To create something new together; complement, not combat. Also identified are the things that impede. First, from a female perspective (imagine yourself the egg): fear of domination, invasion; perceiving male energy as alien, incongruent with her own—feelings I've heard women commonly express. Next, male (be the sperm). Simply ask yourself, How would you feel if you were about to be absorbed by a massive, undulating orb, unsure what happens next? You'd have your share of fear of commitment too. A man in one of my workshops admitted his apprehension: "I'm afraid if I fully surrender to a woman, I'll become female myself." Ah! Feminine energy is powerful; it can threaten to overwhelm. My point is that whenever men and women mingle—especially during sex—these intuitive dynamics unconsciously activate. To love with abandon it's essential for you and your partner to be sensitive to and establish a dialogue about them.

In addition, as we get to know the masculine and feminine aspects of ourselves, the opposite sex seems like less of an enigma. No one is just male. No one is just female. With everyone there's a balance, much as the larger culture still tries to deny it. For example, both sexes produce testosterone (the "male" hormone responsible for libido in men and women), as well as estrogen and progesterone ("female" hormones increasing tissue health and elasticity), though in varying proportions. Integrating both energies—becoming neither effeminate nor overmasculinized—is a form of sophistication you can practice. Doing this widens our range, completes us, helps us love each other, makes for better sex. What we accept in ourselves we don't have to guard against in others. Then, while making love, we can surrender and feel safe. If we're part of a same-sex couple, we can better appreciate the interplay of the masculine and feminine sides of each other.

Our physical form! A multitude of sizes and shapes. So many different feels—warm, moist, cool, soft, wrinkled, rugged. Sometimes we're tentative about being touched; sometimes we can't get enough. Our bodies are barometers of our moods and cycles of sensuality. You're only given one body. It deserves to be catered to, adored. Don't let anyone tell you otherwise.

Sadly, popular culture dictates a myopic version of physical beauty. It's vital that you rethink this. Sense what's sexy from an intuitive position, not from what's propagandized by Madison Avenue. I once came across great advice from Mary Smith, a Chicago newspaper columnist: "Don't read beauty magazines. They will make you feel ugly." Sexual energy is mysterious, huge. How could it ever be confined? We mustn't be stymied by stereotypes. They don't tell the whole truth. Let's use intuition to enlighten our vision and learn to love our bodies more.

We carry such shame—about weight, age, hair loss, complexion, the shape of our toes or our nose . . . the list is endless. So unrelenting, in fact, that many of us can't even bear to glimpse our bodies in the mirror, or turn the lights on when we make love. To heal shame, we have to look lovingly at our bodies again. Gradually embracing every curve, crevice. I recommend you start slowly. There's no need to push through resistance. Let it melt on its own. Rediscover yourself in phases. Try this exercise.

SEEING YOUR BODY WITH INTUITION

For a few minutes each day, stand in front of a full-length mirror. Completely dressed, begin by focusing on the safest parts of your body. For instance, your hands, your hair. What do you see? Feel? As comfort grows, over the next weeks slowly reveal more—face, neck, arms, stomach. Then, when you're ready, bare your breasts, buttocks, genitals. At each stage, say, "I am beautiful. I am sexy." Treat yourself with kindness. To counter critical voices, visualize light radiating around and through every inch of you. Let yourself go. Imagine being composed of many brilliant colors exuding sexual vibrance. There is passion there. Now's the chance to feel it. This is you! Try to take that in. Spirit loves you completely, doesn't intone, "One part is beautiful, one is not." It thinks you are the sexiest thing in the world. This perspective is what matters, what allows you to see yourself clearly.

Elements of beauty continuously unfold. Each of us has a special allure. Make no mistake—the bodies we've been given, whether voluptuous or thin, are perfect for us. Of course we want be at a healthy weight, eat wisely, care for ourselves well. If they appeal to you, makeup, facials, experimenting with hair color, and pedicures can also be glorious. When we nourish our physicality, passion grows. I'm not asking you to convince yourself of something you don't believe. I'm simply advising, See differently. Deeper. Then decide. Body type doesn't dictate sexuality. How we perceive ourselves does. Attitude is everything.

Step 3. Sense Your Body's Subtle Energy

A book I can't get enough of, Marion Zimmer Bradley's *The Mists of Avalon,* is a retelling of the Arthurian legend from a feminine perspective. She refers to the "glamour" of the goddess, an energy priestesses summon to present themselves. It has nothing to do with physical qualities. Rather it's an aura they exude, a calling forth of sensual power. As accessible for men as for women, this is the essence of sexuality.

My patient Julie, a therapist, has learned to read energy. "Often I don't even notice a person's appearance right away. I can meet the most handsome man, but if his energy is off, I'm not attracted. How could I be?" Julie's feelings are relevant. Once you discover how to sense energy, your perception of sexual attraction shifts, there's no avoiding it. If someone's energy isn't sexy, isn't loving, he can look like Sean Connery (I'm wild about him!) and nothing will happen. Without energy to back them up, physical features seem a facade, can't possibly satisfy. As we begin to perceive essence, not surface, we won't settle for less.

In the same way you learned to sense your heart chakra, I want to teach you how to read sexual energy—where to start and how to continue as relationships progress. At this point I'd like to refer you to the Miniguide to the Chakra System in Chapter 2. To refresh your memory about the locations and functions of the chakras, take some time to review the chart. Practice finding each chakra in your body. Throughout this section I'm going to focus on the sexual energy centers: the first chakra, at the genitals, and the second chakra, midline, about two inches below the belly button. Both project outward a few feet like spotlights. I specifically sense this energy in all my patients and new acquaintances (including men) from the instant we meet. Energy transmits information beyond words. I don't consider sensing it as intrusive, any more than noticing a person's scent, touch, or tone of voice would be. Sensing energy imparts a better feel for someone. It gives you more to go on when choosing relationships.

For me as a psychiatrist, part of knowing my patients is reading their sexual energy. This doesn't require touching them or even talking. Here's how I do it: A new patient is sitting in my waiting room. I open the door. For the first few seconds I make it a point not to say anything. In that silence I quickly scan his or her body. I'm not obvious—I do it in a flash, focusing on the person's sexual energy. I can feel it transmitted to my own first and second chakras, registering how my patient carries sexuality. For instance, in our culture both men and women often lead with sexual energy, whether they are aware of doing so or not. Wham! In certain people it's intense, overbearing, not respectful of boundaries. I'm bowled over and get an inkling of how others must react. This is vital input. I think, Aha. Part of our work will be about balance. In contrast, there are those who emit hardly any sexual energy; when I'm with them my chakras register a blankness, numbness, withholding, even discomfort. Here an awakening is called for.

In my psychiatric residency I was taught to take a sexual history based primarily on what patients would tell me. How my own body reacted sexually was to be strictly controlled. My teachers were concerned that inappropriate sexual feelings would pollute treatment, not to mention worried about the danger of "acting out." Of course, it's well known that many therapists have wrongly crossed this ethical and legal line. However, what I'm speaking of is a more thorough history-taking approach using intuition. Doing this, my body becomes a kind of litmus paper or seismograph. Listening to how it responds to my patients' energy gives added insight into them.

When you're learning to read sexual energy, it's best to practice with both male and female trusted friends, the more the better. Then you can compare similarities or differences. Your agreement is that the two of you have permission to observe and sense each other's energy. You do this fully clothed. We typically look at a person only from the neck up. Not here. To check out your friend's energy, you must concentrate on the genital and second chakra areas, see how they connect to the rest of the body. In my workshops I always tell participants to look each other up and down. Not like mothers often do when they're taking inspection, but with a real eye for separating energies and naming them. When you catch on, keep going. Try reading your spouse, lover, or a first date. Out of respect for people who don't know they're being read, you'll need to be more subtle than in practice sessions.

FOUR TIPS FOR READING SEXUAL ENERGY IN EVERYDAY LIFE

1. When you first meet someone, take a few seconds to tune in. (Think of it as a loving pause.) Notice how your entire body reacts. Are you attracted? Repelled? Neutral? Rejuvenated? Fatigued?

2. Next, get more specific. Briefly notice his or her first and second chakras. Don't make a big deal out of it or stare. Try to sense the person's sexual energy in your body.

3. Ask yourself: How do my first and second chakras respond? Warm? Cold? Shut down? Aroused? Suddenly pulsing with energy? Next, focus on the intensity of what you feel. Is it too much? Just right? Too little? Overall, are you comfortable with his or her sexuality? If not, do you feel put off or unable to connect?

4. When you are spending time together, do your impressions sharpen or change? Include this in your assessment. It will provide clues about your compatibility.

You are the receiver. Signals come in. Get accustomed to reading them. Sometimes they're subtle, sometimes they're not. Always evaluate if a person's sexual energy is a good fit for you—not solely a romantic consideration. When you're in sync with others' energy, you constantly feel it on many levels, even if others are oblivious to what they're emitting. In all partnerships—at work, at home, or in social settings—sexuality enters the picture, has a definite intuitive effect. You want to be with people with whom you feel at ease.

Sensing sexual energy is important, though it's just a beginning. The real victory is to link passion with the heart. It's one thing to have a strong first or second chakra. But to take sexuality higher, you must be heart driven. The wham-bam-thank-you-ma'am macho mentality of lovemaking is prehistoric by comparison, being stuck in first gear when you can travel at warp speed. Your heart lends a spiritual dimension to lovemaking, fueling eroticism. So in a partner look for heart and sexuality combined (an antidote to the genitally focused sexuality of our culture). You'll feel both manifest as energy in your body. An exquisite synchrony occurs. Your heart and lower chakras come alive.

Around the world I'm seeing a new prototype for being a man, being a woman, a movement toward blending heart, sex, and soul. We're sharing what's best in us—have the courage to express it. Our passion is enormous. We're entitled to experience our full scope of energy. We yearn for it. What's to stop us? Why not be it all?

Step 4. Ask for Inner Guidance

One summer I was on retreat at a remote spa in New Mexico. Wrapped in a thin white towel, getting a facial, I could hear gusts of late afternoon wind whipping across the desert. It was so wild it carried me as the facialist's fingers softly stroked my forehead, my neck. Pure pleasure. Then a vision came. I was making passionate love to a man I'd known only casually from New York—but with whom I had a business appointment in a few days. What a surprise! I'd never thought of him in that way. I soon discovered my vision had signaled the beginning of our romance.

Sometimes guidance can be offered to us about love. As mine was, its tone can be extremely erotic, a news flash showing me what my ordinary senses had missed. I was alerted to see this man differently, and I did. Often how we view people is a matter of perception. Inner guidance, offered spontaneously or sought, can recalibrate our sensitivity, make us receptive.

More than in any other area, I depend on guidance in sexual issues. This is where I—and many people—get the most befuddled. Unlike with other types of energy, with sexuality I'm at greatest risk of losing my center. Maybe because it feels so good. Or because the promise of merging heart and sexual passion has such seduction that reason and intuition often go out the window. My lessons are to keep my center without caving in; to see a man clearly, sharing the bliss of sexual intimacy while still expressing my needs. In the past I've been torn. I'd immerse myself, entranced in an erotic world with a partner—a kind of fantasy I feared too much reality would shatter. But in recent years the draw of a practical life with a man has been strong; I long to incorporate it with the erotic. As a wise friend advised, "Keep remembering Toto in *The Wizard of Oz*," the scruffy little dog who pulled the curtains on the all-powerful wizard, revealing he was just a man. A man in all his humanness! This is the real magic.

Sexual attraction is notorious for blurring good judgment in the most sensible people. Why? First, it's an altered state of consciousness programmed by primal urges. Passion intoxicates. But there's also a spiritual incentive: The ecstasy of lovemaking can reflect a profound connection between two people and God. Once you are in this zone, it's hard to leave. You're exhilarated; you'll make the craziest sacrifices, not all wise, to stay there. Confronted with dual desires of such magnitude, naturally we may lose our footing. Still, our task is to maintain our center no matter what we encounter. This needn't pull the plug on passion; being grounded accentuates wholeness, amplifying pleasure.

How can you keep your presence of mind, stay sufficiently centered to receive intuitive guidance? The key is to invoke the Buddhist principle of detachment. Though it may sound exotic or foreign, it's something we can all do. The gist of it is to experience a situation without clinging to it, for at least a few moments, as if you were the sky watching clouds pass through. I'm not saying to shut down emotionally but to actively seek neutrality, a state in which you can step back, temporarily disengage, and intuitively evaluate your choices. Detachment takes practice, patience, motivation to *see* with new eyes.

To find detachment and receive guidance about sexuality, try this exercise.

CENTERING YOURSELF WHEN YOU'RE ATTRACTED TO SOMEONE

1. Settle in a comfortable position to meditate.

2. Take a few minutes to breathe with awareness and calm your mind. If thoughts come, keep returning to your breath for centering.

3. Set your intention or pray to be as neutral as possible (a state of grace that can be sought but not forced). Picture yourself observing the situation from a distance, as if watching a movie.

4. Once you are quiet and relaxed, inwardly formulate your question about sexuality in general or a specific relationship. Listen for any intuitive impressions, body knowings, or dreams you receive.

Your intuition is on call twenty-four hours a day. Particularly with sexual issues, don't hold back. You're turning to your highest self, not your mother. No dilemma is too small, too complicated, or forbidden.

The more specific your question, the better your chance of getting a specific answer. First, ask—then let go and wait for a solution. It may come quickly. If not, keep at it. What circumstances are amenable? Here are some common examples:

- If you don't have a sexual partner but want one, ask: "What's blocking me? How can I remove it?"
- If a relationship is turbulent, ask: "Please tell me what I can do to improve communication, make peace."
- When choosing a partner, ask: "Will this person be good for me? Will he or she be an exciting lover?"
- If something's precluding you or your partner from surrendering sexually, say: "I want to know what it is. Please show me what's holding us back."

Answers come in many forms. Some are straightforward. You'll be sitting in meditation and get an aha feeling, a knowing or a scenario that explains. For instance, a patient asked, "Why is it so hard for me to fall in love?" Her answer was a horrifying vision of her father strapping her hands behind her back with a rope. Voilà—a place to start. At other times answers are conveyed more indirectly. A friend once confided, "My husband and I haven't had sex in months. Whenever I bring it up, he just changes the subject." So, while meditating she asked, "How can I get through to him?" Still, she drew a blank. She didn't know what to do, but she didn't have to. Outside intervention occurred. A colleague, without realizing the problem, invited them both to a weekend yoga retreat. Her husband loved it and began to practice yoga regularly. This renewed his link to his body, sparked his desire to make love again.

Intuition involves listening. And listening again. When it comes to sexuality, answers may evolve. Keep tuning in as you progress. It's a process of connecting the dots over time. One intuition builds on another, keeping your inner dialogue current.

You may encounter the paradox that receiving guidance doesn't guarantee you'll act on it. You want to know. You pray to know. The guidance comes. Even so, you don't listen. I've seen this happen time and time again with patients. Human nature comes into play. Regardless of intuition, you go down some path. Still, my spiritual teacher says, "There are no wrong decisions, only different lessons to learn, some more strenuous than others."

My patient Jill is a perfect example. A single mother who badly wanted a relationship, she came into my office beaming. "Judith, I have a new boyfriend. Could you tune in to him?" Ordinarily I would've hesitated. I'm well aware that what most people seek in a reading is good news. But since Jill and I'd been working with intuition—and I had a strong instinct it would be of benefit—I did. Unfortunately, what I picked up was not consoling. However, because she'd specifically inquired, I shared my impressions. "I see an intensely sexual but difficult relationship filled with heartache and legal problems." Jill took this in, even believed me. But because of her attraction to this man, she didn't listen. So my job became supporting her through a hellish year. Besides having a vicious temper, her boyfriend was arrested for tax fraud; she financed his defense. As a therapist I go where my patients take me; I don't condemn their choices. Of course I couldn't help thinking, Stop! You'll get hurt. But it was Jill's call, not my own.

Sexuality is fraught with land mines; intuition will show you how to avoid them. For better or worse, in the arena of love I've always learned the hard way, though I'm not recommending it. The soul knows best how it needs to grow, even if the path is painful. Ultimately, though, from failing to listen, I've discovered how mandatory listening is. We all come to trust intuition differently. Whatever your style, guidance is an ally waiting in the wings. When you're ready, it will be there.

Step 5. Listen to Your Dreams

Sleeping is a sensual experience. You take your clothes off. You may wear a silk negligee or comfy pajamas, perhaps nothing at all. Nestled under soft blankets and sheets, a womblike environment, you breathe quietly, close your eyes. How luxurious, those first few moments drifting off, cares of the day receding, something else entering. You let it take you. You want to go. And you do.

Who lies next to you all night affects your dream life and well-being. Sleeping can be more intimate than making love. Your mind stills; intuitive senses elevate. Unarmored, for hours you and your partner blend; energy is exchanged. You may pick up his or her dreams, emotions, thoughts—a potent interaction to consider, whether you're with someone one night or many years. It's fine to consider sexual compatibility, but focus also on your sleeping compatibility. These go hand in hand, since you usually sleep with people you're having sex with. With both you must be at ease. Before making a long-term commitment, I recommend you experience the sleep-state with your partner. Notice how it feels. Do you wake up replenished, rested? Or are you antsy, tired, off kilter? Sleep is not an area where you want surprises. Make sure spending all those hours with a partner feels right.

Dreams care about your sexual life; they will excavate and liberate it. As with your physical or emotional health, dreams about sexuality may be spontaneously presented, or you can turn to them for explicit advice. Most important, record dreams—no matter how graphic—right when you wake up. Your memory can be selective, particularly with sexually charged material. Write these dreams down fast; don't leave details out. The sexual censor in society and your everyday mind doesn't exist in dreams. Dreams are about freedom, awakening, higher truth. Accept such messages in the healing spirit they are intended.

My patient Tess's intuition was strengthening. At work, at home, with friends, it was there. She said, smiling, "I feel like roses are sprouting everywhere." This appreciated rejuvenation included her body waking up. The body can tolerate being disregarded for a long time, though it's not advisable. At age forty Tess's was coming out of hibernation. "I feel flashes of sexuality, then they're gone," she said. "Why can't I hold on to them?" Tess asked a dream. That night a single image stood out. She reported,

"I see myself. I'm a beautiful girl, about fifteen, paralyzed from the waist down. Frustrated, I want to walk, but I don't know how."

Tess's dream was time-specific, pointing us to the stage at which her sexuality shut down. Her adolescence was a conglomeration of traumas (from being overweight to being snubbed) that we needed to discuss. Sometimes preparing for sexuality requires emancipating energy from your past so it's available in the present.

Dreams can also deliver information about your love life, surprising you with their predictive accuracy. A friend had been suffering a three-year dry spell in relationships. Then she had a series of erotic dreams. Every night my friend was making love with a different man. Monday, rolling around naked on a windswept Caribbean beach. Tuesday, on the pillowed floor of a rustic mountain cabin, fireplace blazing. And so it went. "What's going on?" she marveled. "Am I so starved for love that it's coming out in my dreams?" Yes and no. A week passed. Then at a party she met the man to whom she's now been married for five years. My friend's dreams were readying her for the encounter, saying, "Don't worry. Your sexuality's still alive. Get set. Love is coming." And so it did.

Whether dreams steer you to your past or herald your future, pay attention. Notice the context and quality of your sexuality in dreams. What you feel mirrors the energy you have in you. If your sexuality is strong, if it's weak, no matter. Work with what's currently yours and build on it. As erotic energy surfaces, either asleep or awake, let it feed your body. You may even have orgasms during dreams; in this realm you're more fluid than ever. With your defenses down, ecstasy courses through. If this happens, greet it as a blessing.

Dreams are interested in your romantic choices. Their special talent is intuitive matchmaking; they'll relay precise data about who is good for you, who is not. You may welcome such input or ignore it. That's up to you. But I've got to tell you that, in reviewing my old journals, I confirmed that my dreams were rarely wrong about men. When it came to sizing people up, they had an impressive track record.

Today I listen to my dreams about relationships, but I didn't always. I get a good giggle when I look back at my journals and see what I chose to ignore. Once I went on a date with the nicest man, though I wasn't physically attracted to him. That night I dreamed:

> *He squeezes me a fresh glass of grapefruit juice. It tastes sweet, invigorating, delicious. I know he will nurture me.*

Did I go out with this man again? Nope. By contrast, I met someone I was wildly attracted to, but he wasn't emotionally available. Soon after I dreamed:

> *I'm standing on a busy street with him. Suddenly a blood clot goes to my brain. I crumble on the sidewalk. Roaches are crawling everywhere. He just keeps walking.*

Did I see Mr. Unavailable again? Yep. As you might deduce from my dream, the relationship, though richly sexual, was filled with peril.

I offer you these blatant examples of me not listening to my dreams in the hope that you will. It's human to veer in the wrong direction when sexuality is involved. But dreams aren't bamboozled by the lure of mere sexual attraction. Their overriding concern is your welfare, who will make you happy, secure. The trick is to translate such intelligence into everyday relationships. To believe in your dreams so much that you defer to them. But perhaps you're stubborn, like I've been through the years. You make mistakes, sometimes over and over, until you learn from them. That's all right; the time will come when you'll tire of this. Then you'll be ready to give intuition your hand and find freedom.

Patterns do change. Not long ago I had this dream:

I'm hugging the actor Danny De Vito (I think he's unbelievably cute). He couldn't have been more excited to see me. It's a sexual embrace. We're both enjoying the feeling, grooving on each other. Then I notice he has a big piece of food stuck in his front teeth. Instead of putting me off, it makes him look even sexier. I pull closer to him, thrilled we can be human together, not always perfect. Realizing this blasts my attraction for him off the Richter scale.

In the morning I felt relieved of an obstacle to intimacy. With men and in all of my life, I want to be myself—to be accepted. I also want to accept those I love, shortcomings and all. But I could never quite believe that someone would love me so much that I didn't have to look good constantly or remain upbeat to be considered sexy. Perhaps I also doubted I could totally accept a mate. My dream demonstrated growth. Idealizing a man, seeing only a portion of him, was not the appeal. The real turn-on was the authenticity Danny and I shared (symbolized by the food in his teeth). Our humanness and mutual ease, mixed with physical chemistry, was the most powerful aphrodisiac of all.

Be honest about what's confounding your ability to find love and sexual fulfillment. Then you'll have hope of attaining them. Whether you're single or attached, dreams provide clues about igniting and sustaining sexuality. There's no reason for sex to fizzle permanently in a relationship if love is there. It's never too late to rekindle passion. But at times you need to supersede what you rationally know, seek other solutions. Intuition and dreams have answers with light in them that your waking mind may miss. Knowledge about sexuality is revealed in dreams. Take full advantage. The puzzle does come together.

IT REQUIRES BRAVERY and readiness to explore your sexuality. As you do you'll access an extraordinary reservoir of energy, benefiting every endeavor. In sacred Hindu art sexuality is often depicted as a mighty serpent, called the Kundalini, coiled tightly at the base of the spine. When it awakens, energy rises in the body, nourishing it throughout. Vitality increases; stress dissipates. Spirituality becomes sexuality becomes love. The grace of heaven and the passion of our bodies are synergized. Then, inevitably, lovemaking encompasses more than any single act. We're setting a course into the mystery.

What intrigues me most is to cultivate a total sexuality. If you yearn for such wholeness, this is a chance to find it. We're only on earth for so long. Our bodies are transitory. Make the most of them. Let them unify us with everything that is and will be. They can teach us about pleasure, about love. Always love—the ultimate connector in sexual universes and all others.

My spiritual teacher was once asked, "What is love?" He just smiled, pulled out a piece of paper. On it, letter by letter, he wrote a formula:

L = love is life
O = nothing is everything
V = souls coming together in union
E = throughout eternity

I keep looking at this simple diagram, learning more. To me it speaks of relationships. With our souls. With all souls. With life. With passion. Nothing closing. Only arms spreading wider in union with everything imaginable. As I intuit more about this, I find myself overcome by irresistible urges: to roll around in fields of flowers, skip barefoot on the sand, or climb trees whenever the impulse moves me. You might have similar urges. The passion in your soul will be drawn to the passion in all things. And to your beloved. In response, he or she will recognize the passion in you. Love doesn't disappear; it multiplies. The great mandala spins in the shape of a heart throughout eternity.

12

Awakening Sexual Power

Like the universe coming into existence,
the lover wakes, and whirls
in a dancing joy.
—Rumi
(trans. Coleman Barks)

*F*rom the time when my memory begins, I've always felt a blue wind blowing through me. It howls deep inside, through canyons and ravines of night, thunderous. Haunting yet enthralling. As a little girl I'd curl up behind the azalea bushes in front of my grammar school, aware of this wind in me, wondering, Why is it so strong? So lonely but still soothing? And such a wonderful blue? A color not of earth but of home, of essence. For years I associated this wind with a solitary, spiritual presence—never with people, certainly not with sex. Then, when I was an adult, my scope of intuition increasing, the wind took on more dimensions—erotic, passionate, primal. Astounding: I realized the blue wind was my sexual source. Feeling it stirred each of my senses, arousing the woman within.

Sexual awakening means coming into your own erotic power. How each of us does this may differ. Conventional wisdom teaches you to clarify your sexual needs, then learn to communicate physically and emotionally with a partner. Of course, both are essential. The promise? You'll become a great lover and, according to popular literature, have night after night of fantastic sex. Maybe you want to enter such an Olympics. Maybe not. Sexuality is neither a marathon nor a sprint. Nor is it competitive! You must find your own sexual rhythm and style. The kind of awakening I'm describing includes the psychological and physical, but intuition offers other erotic options. I'm going to present ways to uncover what truly moves you, not by conforming to other people's or societal biases but by making your own path. Sexuality is as compellingly personal as spirituality.

This chapter is about how to mobilize the erotic side of intuition and spirituality. Sexuality radiates from many places: your physical body, your body's subtle energy, inner guidance, dreams. And if learning from the natural world appeals to you, I'll show you how to identify your element in nature—earth, water, fire, air. You have inside you something analogous to the blue wind I've known for so long. In addition, I'll share other intuitive exercises for locating sexual vitality that doesn't fade with age. Don't worry if you're currently out of touch with your sexuality. Prepare to play. Expect the unexpected. You'll have plenty of options. Choose the ones that make you curious or excite you.

Start over again. Honestly ask yourself, Am I happy with my sexual life? What works? What doesn't? No judgment. Only truth. Then you'll know what you're dealing with. You don't have to answer to anyone but yourself. You may want to explore a complete process of rebuilding. Or perhaps you'll embrace the good, discard the rest. Remember, though, with intuition, nothing is static. It keeps changing, growing, honing your awareness of every moment. Isn't that the nature of passion? There's no end point; it continually regenerates itself. Passion can't die if intuition thrives. Use the ideas and techniques I offer as a foundation. Fine-tune your sensibilities. Discover your sexuality in the living of it.

Step 1. Notice Your Beliefs

Teaching workshops throughout the country, I see a radical shift in what many of us want for ourselves sexually. Tolerating months or years slipping by without sharing a real connection in a relationship no longer seems feasible. Couples long to relate more closely, even if they don't know how. Awakening sexuality requires intimate expression. Partners must talk, explore, dream, intuit, make mistakes, make amends, overcome strife by returning to the heart again and again and again. We're all learning together. Your triumphs are my triumphs; they have a collective ripple effect on everyone wanting intimacy. Conscious sexuality, founded on spirituality and intuition, requires four building blocks.

264 • Sexual Wellness

FOUR BUILDING BLOCKS FOR CONSCIOUS SEXUALITY

1. *The Erotic Power of Common Values*

Sexual relationships become more erotic when people share basic values. It's a balancing of forces. Resonances harmonizing. For instance, imagine you and your partner making love. If you both believe this act is sacred, your bond will strengthen, your ecstasy increase. Spiritual values differ. After my mother died my father, then seventy-five, went out on a few dates with the same woman. "Is it romantic?" I asked him. "She's nice," he said. "But I could never sleep with a woman who didn't give to charity." I was startled by both his frankness and his priorities. For my father charity and intimacy were related. What traits do you associate with intimacy? Two people don't have to agree on everything. Harmony is the melding of simultaneous notes in a chord. But when it comes to what counts—the merits of the heart, spirituality, a desire for passion—be on the same page with your partner, or at least striving toward it. You may have to take the initiative to gently educate him or her, but it's the worth the effort. Developing common values builds safety and trust. Then, during lovemaking, you'll feel freer to surrender.

2. *Passionate Communication*

Being intuitive with a partner doesn't mean you can always read each other's minds. One of my patients, a corporate executive, couldn't get himself to communicate his sexual needs. His fantasy: "If a woman and I are sexually in sync, we should know how to turn each other on. Talking about it kills spontaneity." Why? When we got down to it, the difficulty was that he confused being direct with being corrected or criticized. We can all profit from this, expressing preferences as positively as possible. For instance, telling your partner, "I really like it when you touch me softer here, harder there," "Going slower feels great," or "Please do that again." If this is the tone between two people, tougher subjects can also be broached. A sense of appreciation of your partner and a sense of humor keep passion going. In relationships communication must stay open in all areas. People drift apart when resentments mount. Passion is built on interchange, not guessing games. The extraordinary range of feelings that surface together, including aesthetic preferences—taste, smell, texture, sound—have to be honestly discussed.

Beyond emotional communication, as you and your partner become intuitively attuned all kinds of wild subjects may come up. When making love you could see colors, feel energy shoot through your spine, experience intuitive flashes about how to bring your partner closer. This can all be very erotic. Don't hold your experiences in or think they're weird. Agree to talk about what's happening, push the envelope, see where you're being taken sexually. This is what intuitive lovers do, what makes sex so exciting.

3. *Making Love with Spirit*
The writer Alan Watts said, "When you're in love with someone, you see them as a divine being." The divine is ecstatic, at times erotically so. Many spiritual belief systems fail to make this association. Typically God is portrayed as love unrelated to sexuality. I'd like to amend this; I believe we must include God in our sex lives too. Take a simple approach. If you've never experienced spirit as sexy before, while making love ask, "May the divine flow through me" (a sacred, not sacrilegious request). Then stay aware of what happens physically, focusing on your erotic response. Slowly let it spread from your toes through your genitals to your head. Spirit gravitates to where love flourishes. Your body is the instrument it sensually plays.

During sex you also become sensitive to collective forces. Once, in the middle of lovemaking, I inwardly heard the awesome Bessie Smith's voice wailing the blues. I'm not talking about fantasy or visualization. It was her! We generate so much positive energy when sex and spirit mix, the essences of people who've lived their passion, past or present, are drawn to us. Passion elicits passion even across space and time. Let your imagination go. Whether spirit manifests as a tantalizing warmth rushing through you, a vision of Isadora Duncan undulating in a diaphanous gown, or an orgasmic communion with God, allow it in.

4. *Letting Go of Shame*
Let's aspire to viewing our entire bodies as luminous. For the purposes of society, we wear clothes. But beneath layers of pants, sweaters, skirts, mufflers, coats, slips, hosiery, and underwear, we are all naked. This is our natural state, though it's not mentioned much. The words *vagina* and *penis* embarrass people. Except between lovers they're rarely used in our vocabulary. We are a culture of shame. But sex is nothing to be ashamed of. A patient told me, "My girlfriend has the sweetest

breath, but she always gargles with mouthwash before we make love, takes a shower right after. 'Why do you do that?' I asked her. I didn't want to be hurtful or make her mad." My patient was at home with his body, adored hers. In contrast, his girlfriend had been raised to believe that sex was dirty, something to "wash away." Her answer: "I didn't want to offend you." From childhood shame insinuates itself into our thinking. You may not even recognize it.

Sensing the beauty of the body with intuition lifts shame. Respect your particular aesthetic sensibilities, but also be ready to examine which ones are based in shame. Touch. Scents. Sounds. Positions. Techniques. No shame—instead of being so quick to erase the primal traces of sexuality, move intuitively with them. There's no need to inhibit yourself. D. H. Lawrence wrote, "Be . . . true to your animal instincts." Don't hesitate to allow earthiness in. Experiment with what feels natural, pleasing. Identify areas of shame and heal them.

QUESTIONS FOR REFLECTION

- Are you satisfied with your sex life? Or is it nonexistent? Routine? What about your sexuality would you like to awaken?

- When making love, do you hold back? Why? How would your life change if you let your full erotic and spiritual power shine?

- In what ways can intuition boost your sexual awareness and strengthen your spiritual bond with a partner? Would you like to try?

Step 2. Be in Your Body

I once spent an afternoon with Bengal tigers. I was invited to an animal park in Northern California by a man who used intuition to help train these gorgeous creatures. He could sense and dream the animals' needs. Sleek white tigers with thin black stripes, prowling silently on open grass. Close enough, I watched, captivated by their agile sensuality. At dinnertime, back in locked cages, the tigers were thrown giant slabs of juicy raw meat. As they devoured it I heard them growl. Resonant, guttural explosions, strangely comforting. Ten tigers in unison: My body knew that sound from an ancient time. Wild cats courting their mates under the stars, ravishingly sexual. The growl is within me—and you too—we just need to recognize it.

Feeling the primal power of the tigers got me wondering about its role in our sensual world, how it colors our notions of attraction. Of course, when we're erotically drawn to someone, physical, emotional, intuitive, and spiritual elements all come into play. But to better understand what constitutes sexual attraction, I'd like to focus first on the primal as a springboard and use a survival-oriented lens. Then we'll construct a more elaborate picture.

Evolutionary biologists tell us that humans, like other primates, evaluate a mate's attractiveness in terms of reproductive potential. Basically, we have built-in visual radar for the best gene pool. What do both males and females look for? Symmetrical face and body features (according to a 1998 *American Naturalist* review of over forty species). And the anthropologist David Symons, in *The Evolution of Human Sexuality*, cites numerous reports that attractiveness reflects the averaging of physical characteristics. It is interesting that there seems to be this composite of shape, not beauty, which nature reads as optimal.

Further, scientists identify traits having particular allure for the opposite sex. Keep in mind these findings were of people viewing photographs, not responding to present human beings. Research in eighteen cultures suggests men are attracted to an hourglass figure; a narrow waist-to-hip ratio may indicate estrogen production and fertility (*Journal of Personality and Social Psychology*, 1993, 1995). For example, the beauty icons Marilyn Monroe and Audrey Hepburn had different body types but a similar waist-to-hip ratio. Women, scientists argue, are attracted to a T-shaped body above six feet tall and a thick head of hair—evidence of healthy testosterone, suggests the Harvard psychologist Nancy Etcoff. In *The Survival of the Prettiest: The Science of Beauty*, she proposes that Madison Avenue doesn't create but exploits these "universal preferences."

Reviewing this literature, I had to remind myself to breathe! Can we really be reduced to physical stereotypes, biologically or culturally conditioned? Do evolutionary motives dominate our sexual drive? I believe that even where evolutionary impulses exist, our evolution has hardly stopped. The human instinct to procreate is worthy of awe. But evolution, even as construed by these scientists, continues day by day. We may have a sense of where we've come from. But where are we going now?

Let's rethink visual cues in terms of intuition, which allows us to look beyond the surface. Appearances can deceive. On a primitive level nature may program people to equate certain hormonally visible signs of fertility with sexiness. Youth-focused fashion magazines, intentionally or not, reinforce such associations, conditioning our tastes. The danger is that our self-worth gets tied to this incomplete reading of beauty, making both aging and adolescence treacherous. If an unconscious link exists in our brains, between fertility and sexual attractiveness, what can we do about it? Here's where consciousness and intuition can extend our appreciation of beauty to many ages, shapes, and sizes. Building on techniques from the previous chapter, I'll show you how to intuit sexuality more completely, to sense energy beyond appearance.

My friend Marty, an Air Force sergeant in the Vietnam War, was blinded at twenty-eight during combat. He told me, "Before my accident I was a macho slave to sexual stereotypes. I dated only women who looked like models. Gradually, after losing my sight, my concept of sexiness changed. With outer cues reinforcing my preferences gone, I had the opportunity to separate from earlier visual conditioning." This, plus embarking on a spiritual path that developed his intuition, shifted Marty's idea of attraction. Now he says, "A woman's sexuality is palpable, an intangible erotic energy she gives off. I can feel her comfort with her body, as well as her insecurities and withholdings. When I'm hugging a woman, shape alone won't arouse me if a genuine warmth and sexual vibrance isn't there." The essence of a person—what he senses, not sees—is what makes sexuality real for Marty.

I asked another male friend, "What do you consider true sexual beauty?" His answer: "At first I went for starlet types. That's what we men are taught to do. But after a couple of them, I found that what initially caught my eye seldom kept my interest. The truth is, unless a woman's sense of self comes from something more substantial, the end is near." I've heard many men express this realization; it's good to hear. But given the positive changes I've seen in many men over the last decade, it computes. As we increase intuition our vision of sexiness shifts; external beauty can't sustain itself without an inner radiance.

Many body-related factors enter into sexual attraction. How a person tastes, smells, feels, skin texture, tone of voice, quality of eye contact must be physically appealing to you. See if you're compatible with someone in these areas. Our bodies' chemistry can have a dramatic effect. Consider pheromones, for instance. A 1999 article in *Psychiatric*

Annals discussed the recent discovery of these invisible, odorless sex attractants, secreted under the arms in men and women. Even at a distance another person can sense them and be aroused. When pheromones were added to the cologne of both sexes, experiments showed an acceleration of romantic attention and sexual activity. Eureka! Cosmetics companies quickly capitalized on this, making pheromones available in over-the-counter fragrances.

I have to admit I went out and bought a bottle. You can try this too. I wore the pheromone for six weeks, as the instructions said. During that time I did get more attention from men. But whether it was from the pheromone or not was hard to tell. Whenever I dabbed the vanilla scent on my body, I felt sexier. Though the pheromone ultimately didn't bring romance my way, it helped me fall in love with myself, reconfirming my own attractiveness.

Awakening sexuality can occur at any age. The belief that sexuality must wane after the reproductive years is obsolete. Intuition doesn't know a time line. If your sexuality starts flowing in later life, that's the right sequence for you. Since the typical human life span has doubled since 1900, this becomes a relevant concern. I recently gave a workshop in which a surprising number of participants were in their eighties. One couple, madly in love, had just married. Another woman, eighty-two, confided that since meditating she'd begun to feel sexual again. "I'm too old for this!" she exclaimed. "I haven't had a partner for years." "Well, maybe you're ready for one now," I replied. She just glowed. I have the feeling she took my response under serious consideration.

Joyce, an attractive, accomplished performance artist, put on a provocative one-woman show at age sixty-five. Wanting to make a statement about how sexuality needn't die with age, she sensually danced onstage in revealing costumes. Wrinkles, sagging parts; little was concealed. This offended some of the audience, particularly men. "It's revolting," they'd tell her. "For God's sake, you're over the hill. Why do you want to show your body like that!" Months after the show closed, Joyce continued to get hate mail. What she'd encountered was the violent ageism of our culture, a backlash of self-hatred many people feel that was projected onto her. We carry sexiness throughout life. It's a travesty if we can't endeavor to see that.

I hope I've shaken up your ideas about attractiveness a little. I hope you'll want to love your body more. Regardless of our physical measurements—or what society preaches—it's up to us to elevate our sexual consciousness. One person at a time we can change things, representing a richer sexuality others can emulate.

Remember the great scene in *Star Wars* at the interplanetary bar? Life-forms from different galaxies all socializing together. Physically very diverse. But nobody seemed to care. Someday our species may intermix with other intelligent life in the universe. What then? Ponder the impact of this on the parameters of desire. Hopefully, by that point our spirits will say yes to loving, intuitively recognizing beauty and sexiness in everyone. With such bigheartedness will come the promise of peace.

Step 3. Sense Your Body's Subtle Energy

I want to take you to another place and time. Back several thousand years to India, before Jesus, Buddha, or Mohammed walked the earth. A rebellion stirred against the repressive moral code of the Brahmans, the Hindu priesthood, who believed sexuality must be denied to attain enlightenment. In response, Tantra, a spiritual system that views sexual love as a sacrament, was born. *Tantra,* meaning "expansion," refers to more than a hundred ancient books on sexual practices and meditations. Topics range from physical positions to orgasm, all leading to enlightenment. It's fascinating to imagine these volumes being recorded, mystics by candlelight writing for our ancestors as much as for us. Tantra also offers a complete plan for life, including making sherbets, performing gymnastics, studying astronomy. But of its sixty-five sciences, the noblest is considered the art of sexual love.

How can Tantra, so multifaceted, enlighten us? My focus will be on its capacity to consciously combine sexuality and spirituality through knowledge of our bodies' subtle energy. A gorgeous erotic pleasure comes from this awareness—not only physical release but a joy so profound it feels like God is laughing through you. You revel in it; your partner does too. A touching of hearts and bodies, arousing you to the point that ecstasy continually redefines itself.

Tantra tells us how to achieve this experience by mobilizing subtle energy. Millennia ago it revolutionized ideas about sexuality, introducing the concept of chakras. As we've already discussed, these seven major energy centers are located down the midline of the body, from the genitals to the top of the head. For our purposes I'm emphasizing

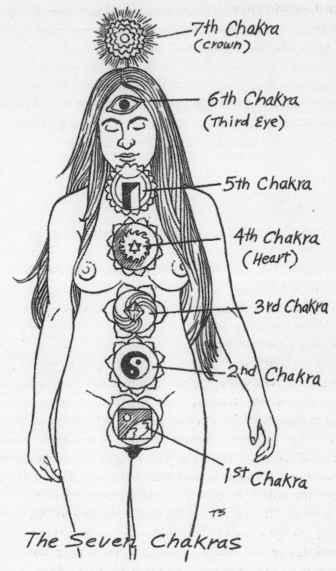

7th Chakra
(crown)

6th Chakra
(Third Eye)

5th Chakra

4th Chakra
(Heart)

3rd Chakra

2nd Chakra

1st Chakra

TS

The Seven Chakras

Figure 1

these chakras, although there are others, including on the palms of our hands and soles of our feet. Each chakra has a physical location (penetrating your body and radiating outward), a color (which at times can be intuitively seen), and a focus (see Figure 1 for placement of chakras in the body).

Using the chakras as a reference point, I'm going to show you ways to direct your sexual energy. To prepare for this exercise, take some time to locate your first and second chakras before you're with a partner. Sitting quietly, eyes closed, spend a few minutes sensing each one. Try to notice the flow between them. Pay attention to any heat, cold, tingling, holdings, expansion. Once you locate this energy in your body, you can intentionally channel it in your erotic life. Practicing the following exercise, you'll learn to activate sexual energy in your genitals and train it to rise as ecstasy replenishes your entire body. This is a sublime sensation, caressing every inch of you.

AWAKENING SUBTLE ENERGY IN LOVEMAKING

1. *Create a sacred space.* Compose an environment that's sensually and spiritually uplifting. A bouquet of wildflowers. Your favorite incense. Candles flickering. Perhaps oils to rub on each other. Phones—and pagers—turned off. No interruptions. No hurry. The effort will set a mood.

2. *Hold each other.* Spend as long as you like in each other's arms before you go further. Exchange love through your eyes. For a few minutes slowly breathe together, synchronizing inbreath and outbreath, becoming intuitively attuned. Next, each of you focus on your own chakras; attention activates them. Take your time. Then, embracing, the chakras of both you and your partner aligned head to toe, feel their energy blending. Sense your mutual colors and heat. Let go. Allow the joy of such intimacy in.

3. *Feel your energy rise.* When you're ready, go on to intercourse. During penetration be aware of sensations in your genitals, but also try to feel energy ascending the spine to the crown, stimulating each chakra. Do you notice colors? Emotions? Does your heart open? As you reach orgasm, energy amplifies. With practice you can feel its upward movement as sexual energy unifies with the spiritual. You might see flashes of white light. Bliss mounts as you and your partner become one.

4. *Relax together.* Savor the moment. Don't be too quick to get out of bed. If it feels right to be silent, fine. If you want to talk with each other, do. Cherish the spirituality of the experience.

An appreciation of your body's energy reveals how large love can be when you share it physically. This exercise is meant as an ongoing meditation, a seed that will bear future fruit. Sometimes you may even trigger a revelation in your partner. After a workshop I gave one woman recounted, "When I got back home my husband was asleep. I woke him up; we enthusiastically made love. As I was having an orgasm he exclaimed, 'White stars like the Milky Way are shooting out the top of my head!' He's a mainstream man. He never heard of chakras, yet he was in pure bliss." Such a response to your intuitive growth is the kind of good news I'm talking about.

During lovemaking energy has different manifestations. It can be emitted through the eyes; the sensuality of how you look at someone travels across space, arousing him or her. Also, when energy rises emotions may be liberated; it's natural to feel them as your heart opens. Sometimes this causes awkwardness, discomfort. Many men have told me, "When we're making love, my wife often starts crying. I feel helpless, like I've done something wrong. I want to do the right thing, but I don't know what it is." For the future, understand: Commonly, in both men and women, crying (or laughing) is an energetic release, an indicator of passion, not something that needs fixing. Ask your partner to confirm this so you can be at ease. Unless he or she says differently, there's nothing "to do" other than flow with it.

The act of lovemaking itself changes the overall quality of energy you exude. In *Sexus,* Henry Miller described the dramatic phenomenon of women being especially drawn to him right after he's been with a lover, as if they detect something different, compelling. This experience rings true for many. Both male and female patients have sworn, "I attract more people if I'm in love myself." When you are sexually active, your chakras wake up. Get used to sensing the change in yourself; notice the reactions of others. Be conscious of the vibes you give off.

Though everyone carries sexual energy, it's not just human—it's also present in nature. With this in mind, you can innovatively use the energetic import of Tantra. Next time you go to the ocean or the woods, sit quietly; try to feel the exuberance of these places in all your chakras, paying special attention to chakras one and two. Hear nature talking to you through energy. I first received communication in this manner quite unexpectedly.

It was on the north shore of Kauai, 1986. I'd gone there to attend a women's workshop on spirituality. Before three days of silence and fasting, I walked through a tropical forest to the ocean as the sun set. While a light wind rippled though my short cotton dress, I rested my back on the trunk of a fragrant plumeria tree. Feeling the moist, soft air caressing my skin, I was mesmerized by how it made the leaves flutter; their lilting movements seemed to be gesturing to me. I began to feel sexually aroused. The wind: what was it doing? To my amazement I sensed it pulsing waves of heat through the bark into my body, shooting from my spine to my scalp. I glued the slope of my back to the trunk, afraid if I moved or analyzed what was occurring it would cease. For once, thank God, my mind cooperated. The erotic energy accelerated; my whole body burst into orgasm.

That twilight in Kauai introduced me to the ecstatic forces of nature. Over the years it's become clear that the air element is my personal touchstone to nature's sensuality. Now, whenever I get even a glimpse of wind it makes me smile, brings out my sexuality. I know this by how my body reacts. I know this because, even though it may seem far out, I've given myself permission to listen. Often I deliberately tune in to the wind for a sensual refueling. I watch it, sense it, let it enter my body. Wind has the quality of human touch but more so. Before Kauai I'd always depended on a man to ignite my erotic side. When I was single I felt less feminine, almost invisible as a woman. Realizing that sexuality originates in myself, and in nature, has been life-changing.

Sound improbable? Think of things that give you pleasure. Butter melting on fresh bread. The fragrance of a rose. The light of an evening star. We all recognize such palpable beauties but, alas, understate their effect. A marathoner I know would snort with derision if I suggested his daily miles—dawn breaking, breeze fresh in his face, tank top clinging to torso—gave him sensual expression! Why deny the miraculous? As I did you can find the element—air, fire, water, or earth—for which you have the most erotic affinity.

For instance, sit next to a roaring campfire or by the fireplace at home. Take a few breaths. Center. Lose yourself in the flames. Remain receptive sexually, focusing on your first and second chakras. Notice if the fire excites them. Are they vibrating? Warm? More alive? Even orgasmic? If so, you'll know. It's all right. There's nothing strange here, just another sensual outlet to enjoy. Similarly, experience the other elements. Test out water: go skinny-dipping in the ocean or a swimming pool. Just you and the water. What do your chakras feel? Next, go to earth. Lie naked on the grass, walk barefoot, hug a tree (the hippies were on to something). Soak up the energy the earth gives. Then continue with the wind. Let it blow over you. Is your body stirred? Ultimately, the element that's yours is the one you'll have the strongest reaction to. You can rendezvous with it whenever you please. Never tell a soul unless you choose. Make it your special secret.

So you can see energy has many applications to sexuality. Let yourself investigate beyond what I've discussed; map out virgin territory. Soon you'll be astonished to realize how much of the sexual world previously eluded you. Erotic opportunities utilizing energy present themselves. Ordinary vision is unequipped to take you on this adventure. Intuition can and will.

Step 4. Ask for Inner Guidance

It's a chilly midwinter night in a candlelit loft in New York City. I'm part of a spiritual circle of ten women who meet regularly. A colorful mix, including an erotic filmmaker, a sex therapist, a magazine editor, a real estate broker. We call ourselves the Goddesses—to inspire us to remember our inner wisdom, so easily muted by an externally fixated world. Silence fills the room. Everyone holds hands, joining forces. A current buzzes through us. We let it energize our bodies, drawing on it to increase intuition. In this heightened state we *see* solutions for ourselves and for one another. A little intuitive help from your friends does wonders.

Flickering flames softly illuminate the women's faces. We go around the circle, each sharing a dilemma we want to resolve—a prayerful summoning. Surprise: top of the list is often love and sex. Tonight a few of the requests are, "How can I get through to my husband?" "What can I do to have a sex life again?" "What's stopping me from being a more responsive lover?" Our collective intent makes magic happen. Outcomes that may seem impossible to achieve alone, the group facilitates through the power of being honest, the grace of asking for help, the invocation of a spiritual force to intervene, our intuition combined.

Such support from a loving group can amplify inner guidance for both men and women. Sometimes people stay stuck too long, not perceiving the benefits of reaching out. Of course, when it concerns romance, first you must tune in yourself. But there are times, when we are blinded by desire or emotion, that a group is handy. In our culture we've lost the mystique of the village fire. Ancients gathering, moderns awakening again. Try it. Be the one to initiate a group. The intuitive journey is not about isolation; it fosters peacemaking, a soulful coming together as trust mounts. These groups may be small or large, male, female, or mixed. Choose what feels best.

Inner guidance about erotic matters is imperative. There's how your partner presents himself or herself and also what he or she feels inside. Sometimes the two don't jibe. This can be confusing. One method I use to read a partner better is psychometry, the technique of holding an object that belongs to him—such as a set of keys or piece of clothing—and seeing what images or knowings arise.

I recommended psychometry to my patient Brad. Ordinarily he and his wife had excellent sexual communication. But in the past few months, he said, "When we make love, she seems somewhere else. She goes through the motions, but her heart isn't in it." All kinds of fears surfaced. Had she stopped being attracted to him? Was she having an affair? Brad had spoken to her about how removed she seemed but had gotten nowhere. I suggested, "While meditating, hold one of your wife's favorite objects. Pose a question such as 'What is she feeling?' Then, over the next few minutes, notice any intuitions." So one afternoon Brad sat calmly tuning in to an antique pearl bracelet she treasured. Here's what emerged. A memory: her mother's funeral, which they'd attended exactly a year ago. A voice: "I'm afraid of getting ovarian cancer like my mother." A knowing: Lovemaking aggravates this fear.

The bracelet containing his wife's energy revealed to Brad the crux of her struggle. How tender he could now be—as opposed to letting his fear of rejection drive him. Slowly but surely they talked her concerns out. After a short time she was present more than ever in their lovemaking.

"Inanimate" objects have an intuitive life. Energy gets absorbed into what we touch, what we love. That information can be gleaned if we respectfully request it. There's a spirit to all physical things. They have voices, eyes and ears too; they can tell you about people. Use psychometry to empathize with your lover. There's no need to feel silly. The secrets of the universe can be found in the tiniest pebble if you know how to look.

Science is only fiction if we don't understand it. Psychometry has other purposes as well. It allows you to tune in to a partner whether he or she is in the same locale or not. For many years I was in love with a man from New York. Too frequently we were separated by an entire continent. One Christmas he gave me a luxurious plaid cashmere scarf that had been his. I wore it all winter, adored wrapping it around my body to feel closer to him. I gave him a small ceramic box that had belonged to me. The objects had special meaning for us.

Some nights we'd synchronize times, hold these objects, and sense each other. Then, over this great expanse, we'd make love. I'm saying that we both projected our energy across thousands of miles. He'd think of me; I'd think of him. Then we'd visualize our bodies joining. The gifts we'd given each other acted as erotic homing devices, seemed to transmit energy. It's incredible what you may feel. Something enwrapped me, like a warm blanket tingling. Our smells, our tastes, our desires were right there. Not fantasy but genuine contact. He and I kept in sensual touch this way, different than the usual but satisfying too. If you and your lover are apart, see where psychometry takes you. It creates a bond that transcends space and time.

We have the ability to affect people erotically without touching or speaking. Sexy thoughts can be intuitively conveyed. I'm reminded of a mind-blowing scene in the film *Cocoon*. A man and a woman are flirting at opposite ends of a swimming pool. She, we know, is an Antarian, an extraterrestrial. "How do Antarians express affection?" he coyly inquires. Smiling, she emits a golden ball of light, which jets around the room, then orgasmically melts into his body.

New possibilities for a new time. I'd like you to evaluate, not rashly dismiss them. All this, of course, in the spirit of love and exploration. Do you realize that with the unaided eye we can gaze at the night sky and see 2.24 billion light-years away? Or that with a telescope we can see 14.5 billion light-years? Our capacity to see spans an incomprehensible distance. Don't dwell on what can't be done. Envision what's possible. Inward. Outward. And beyond.

Step 5. Listen to Your Dreams

I'm going to share with you some dreams about erotic awakening and how to work with them. Remember, if you want advice about sexuality, all you have to do is ask. Before going to sleep use these secret passwords: "Please show me how to grow and where I'm unclear." Then, if you keep asking, keep listening—open sesame: dreams will devise the most telling sexual scenarios with you as the star. For at least a week record them in the morning. See what you get. Don't just wait for the ones that come unbidden. Get used to being the initiator. Be deliberate about your requests.

My patient Ruth, at age thirty a successful marketing executive, wanted to let go sexually but couldn't. In therapy she admitted, "I'm angry at men. It's hard for me to trust them." This sentiment stemmed from her father's rages when she was a child. To armor herself, she'd inadvertently come off as icy, remote—even with her boyfriend. Especially during lovemaking he was feeling shut out. Ruth wanted them to be closer, yet she felt stuck. So, to augment our psychological work, she turned to a dream: "How can I be more emotionally and sexually vulnerable?" Soon after an answer arrived.

> A handsome, elegantly dressed Egyptian man about fifty approaches. Untypical for me, I instantly trust him, sense we've known each other forever. Warmly, he says, "I want to teach you about sexuality." I marvel that I don't resist. His mix of gentleness and strength is comforting. Then he hands me a golden liquid to drink. Without hesitation I swallow every ounce—it tastes sweet, refreshing. Suddenly, sexual feelings well up in my groin. As the liquid takes effect, my body gets hotter and hotter. I'm transfixed by the kind beauty of his face, feel his maleness opening me. He winks in acknowledgment. I'm filled with gratitude.

Who was Ruth's exotic visitor? According to Egyptian mythology, male energy is embodied by the sun god, Ra, creator of the world and all that "comes into being." Not the distorted masculine of her angry father but a pure, potent essence. Drinking in the sun—the golden liquid (one of her associations was semen) offered from a man's hands—nourished her sexuality in a dream. Sometimes you need to return to the archetypal origins of eroticism to realize what can be done here and now. Though Ruth was not conversant with Egyptian lore, her dream invoked a mythic guide she'd respond to. The masculine had never seemed as palatable before. Ruth now had a healthier model to go on. With her boyfriend she could aim for such union, see the safety in it.

Awakening is the specialty of dreams. They rally when you say, "I am afraid to be intimate," "I don't feel sexy, never have." They can give you strength if you let them. This doesn't mean you'll be without doubts. All that's required is an openhearted request. Cosmic ears perk up. Universes will hear.

During recent years I've been growing more at home with my sexuality, feeling freer to share it with a man. Positive changes do occur. A dream explained:

> I'm attending a wedding. Everything is of impeccable quality. A close friend of the bride and groom informs me, "Each part of the body has significance in terms

of the marriage." He asks, "What is your favorite body part?" "The baby-soft un-
derside of the forearm," I respond. "What does it symbolize?" He lights up, an-
swers, "An inner life." I'm surprised and pleased that I connect an inner life
with marriage.

In the past my biggest apprehension of being in a sexually intimate
relationship had been sacrificing an inner life. The "alone time" I require, the consistent internal focus that rejuvenates me, I feared would
be gone. I didn't know how to assert these needs with a man, make
them a priority. Instead, I'd become immersed in our sexual bond but
lose another important part of myself. Inevitably this would backfire.
The only way I knew to reclaim my inner life was to end the relationship. That's not so now. Happily, I've seen that sexual passion and an
inner life can coexist. As my dream emphasized, balance is attainable.

Dreams abhor claustrophobia. They'll assist you in removing anything that muzzles your spirit, including a sexual rut. You might not
know how to regain passion in a relationship—even believe it's beyond
you—but dreams can explain.

My patients John and Pam had lost the sexual fire in their marriage.
For twenty-five years their main thrust had been raising three children,
though they were still very much in love. Now that the kids were in college, an opportunity to revamp their sex life presented itself. John's
dream instigated this:

I see a conservative-looking man in a three-piece suit locked in a suburban tract
home. Frantically he struggles to escape, but the doors and windows are glued
shut. I can feel his panic; there's also sexual frustration. I notice the man has
an erection. He tries to hide it, but I know it's there.

Sigmund Freud pointed out that one way to interpret dreams is to
see all the characters as yourself. John's sexual conflicts were being
dramatized for him to observe. "I hesitate to tell my wife about the
dream," he said. "It's been so long. What if our sex life is unfixable?"
Can you predict the fate of their relationship if he had masked his feelings? In similar situations out of fear many people do, and they suffer a
withering of their life force. I told John this, urging, "Be honest.
Thoughtfully convey your needs. Trust the love between you." He did;
his respectful approach allowed his wife to hear him. Their sex life
gradually changed. The twist was I introduced them to Tantra. A sub-

urban couple practicing Tantra, ancient lessons for contemporary living. Everyone can do it. I believe John's dream—and his willingness to act on it—saved their marriage. No matter how many years have passed in a relationship without an erotic tie, if love is there, sexuality can be awakened.

Some committed couples I work with have taken their dreaming to another level. As mutual intuition matures, lovemaking may also be experienced in dreams. Our sensual geography can be extended. Think of it as making a dream-date. Enlarging on what you've already learned, this is a finer adjusting of intuitive focus. It's for couples with good rapport who are ready to be playful and practice.

If the exercise interests you, here's what to do: Before you both drift off to sleep, set your intention, inwardly saying, "Let us be together in dreams and make love." Kiss, then go to sleep. The next morning compare notes. Did you see each other? If so, wonderful, a great accomplishment in itself: the first goal is simply to meet. But was there more? Did you talk? What was said? Did the interaction go on, become sexual? Don't worry if all this doesn't happen immediately. Get used to the idea of relating in dreams. As you progress it may lead to dream lovemaking—exceedingly fulfilling, surpassing the material. Pay particular attention to dreams in which guides appear. Listen to instructions given about the erotic: positions, attitude, technique. Expertise from the dream realm can go a long way in this one. Make the most of it.

Sexually, dreams will keep you on your toes. Start to conceive of them as sexy and they will be. Set aside the linear self. Take a break from the A + B = C mentality; see how much further sexuality can go. Awaken here. Awaken in dreams. Awaken always. There's nothing better than this.

WHEN SEXUALITY becomes a spiritual quest, evolution occurs. Webster's dictionary defines *evolution* as "a continuous change from a simpler to a higher or better state." How to get from here to there is through awareness and intuition. Then sex can be seen as physical pleasure but more: as energy, as light. The problem with the unawakened eye is that it misses so much. I hope you don't want to miss a thing. No matter your background or notions about your limitations, it's time to move on.

We must create evolved sexual role models: Women who love their bodies and can impart this love to their daughters. Men who are intuitive, sexy, and strong so their sons can see how to be. If we don't embody the change we long for, who ever will? *Nothing* is more convincing than exemplifying your beliefs, living a life founded on the joy you've discovered and radiating it. Children are not fools. They know how to tell phony from real. When you've found an authentic life—sexual and all else—your children have a model to imprint. Generations will continue to improve on what you've started. This is how humankind evolves.

Sexual awakening necessitates balancing masculine and feminine aspects. If a man feels, I must be macho, or Vulnerability makes me weak, that balance teeters. Similarly, if a woman feels, I have to squash my intuition so I don't threaten men, a kind of death is under way. Awakening is about seeing how multidimensional we are rather than sexually polarizing. It's not that men are more powerful than women or women more powerful than men. True power comes from internalizing both qualities.

I was struck by a recent article in the *Los Angeles Times* telling of a small island off the coast of China run entirely by women. Stereotypical roles are reversed—men assigned menial tasks, women in charge of major decisions. Women take lovers but have no desire to marry, wanting to maintain independence. When one woman was asked, "What do you think of the men?" she confessed, "We really don't like them very much." I can't tell you how many female friends and patients spotted the article, cut it out, and kept it. I did too. Why? How could we not feel the generations of women throughout history who were persecuted, silenced, or shamed cheering through each one of us? Wielding feminine influence has definite appeal. Yet this island was not the solution. It only perpetuated a deadly split in our nature, as men, as women, that is the antithesis of sexual wholeness. The kind of world I'm suggesting celebrates the male/female in us all.

Imagine making love. You and your beloved in each other's arms. Time recedes. A moment comes where there's no separation between you, no need to defend. The peace of it—a blurring of the edges where you end and your partner begins. In your life strive for such unification, with spirit, with your partner, with yourself. Awaken to the sexual fullness of who you can be.

13

A Return to Beginnings

> He looked at his own soul with a Telescope. What
> seemed all irregular . . . he saw to be beautiful
> constellations . . . hidden worlds within worlds.
> —Samuel Taylor Coleridge

*I*t was the summer of 1965, my freshman year in high school. At fourteen I fell in love for the first time. Andy's eyes were cobalt blue. I'll never forget how they gleamed like the ocean as he surfed Malibu, as I hugged him, salty and wet at sunrise on the beach. And the love letters he wrote—I hid a whole stack in a secret compartment in my bathroom under a shelf of towels so my mother couldn't find them. I read every word over and over. Though we never actually went "all the way," my sexuality flowered with him. During those two years (an eternity for a teenager), Andy was everything to me.

Then one day, without warning, I spotted him kissing another girl— the most popular blond-haired, blue-eyed cheerleader at school. There they were, making out in the backseat of her brand-new red Camaro, not caring that I could see, knowing that I could. Something in me shattered, a part that felt far too tender sexually and emotionally to be disillusioned so soon. Pain, then a horrible numbness. I wanted to cry, but no tears came.

It was so silent as I walked up the staircase to my mother's medicine cabinet. It creaked open. Hypnotized, I reached for a bottle of sleeping pills. I poured the contents into my palm. I watched myself, unreal as it seemed, swallowing them. In minutes darkness began to overtake me. It swirled. It tasted sweet, like chocolate. Then, suddenly, light broke. A voice inside screamed, "No! I don't want to die!" In that moment I was certain. Immediately I found my mother—I knew she was at home—

and confessed what I'd done. Horrified, she whisked me to the UCLA emergency room to have my stomach pumped.

Thank God, I was physically okay. But emotionally . . . it took years to recover fully, to establish an authentic and stable sense of inner solidity. Andy never called, didn't bother to explain. It took two decades for him to contact me. Finally, as he and I were having tea at the Rose Cafe in Venice, I was able to ask him, "Why?" Of course, I relished his response, "It was the worst mistake of my life" and "I did it out of selfishness, wanting to be 'popular.'" Teenage reasoning, I sadly understood. Still, this early betrayal colored my romantic attachments, making trust an especially delicate issue. In the end, though, I was fortunate. What happened with Andy set me on a healing path. My intuition grew; my spirit strengthened, revealing that love is worth everything it entails (except the loss of life—no, never). For me there is no greater gift.

Our sexual histories—traumas and celebrations alike—affect us today. Formative experiences set a tone for future relationships. Every breakthrough and disappointment is encoded in your body's intuitive memory. Thus, a thoughtful return to beginnings is called for. The last thing you want is a phantom running loose in your consciousness. Psychic specters can tyrannize by wedging themselves between you and your partner.

Love and sex are spiritual catalysts. The higher the stakes, the more to lose, more to gain. Even if you've had repeated heartbreaks, betrayals, or sexual abuse, you can take the initiative to heal. The most difficult experiences can lead to self-confidence and heart. You have a choice. You can view adversity as defeat, even punishment, or, in the name of love, surmount the obstacle. Never does something happen for no reason. When we're wounded we can hear the angels sing, in the depths remembering a few more bars of their songs.

I'm a big advocate of opening Pandora's box. What resides there is not intuitively unexpected. According to the Greek myth, Pandora, the first woman created by the gods, was sent to earth. Succumbing to temptation, she looked into a forbidden container. Innumerable plagues were unleashed into the world—sorrow, envy, revenge, many others. However, the point often neglected is that Pandora also liberated one more spirit imprisoned in that box: hope. Reexamining your sexual life doesn't mean needlessly probing old wounds; the purpose is to release you from them, to see yourself into being again. Compassionately review and profit from it all. Then you can reenter the present, not the same but more whole than before.

Step 1. Notice Your Beliefs

Who you are with your lover can reflect who you've been with your family. To have a richly abundant sexuality, you must look honestly at generational patterns. Grandparents, mothers, fathers: Freud once said, "We are never alone in the marriage bed." There are both psychological and intuitive implications. Your bloodline, from the primal horde onward, echoes through you. Hence, the importance of honoring the messages your predecessors send. Some you'll adopt, others you'll reject; it's your decision. Locate where you stand in the bigger picture.

What beliefs did your parents have about sexuality? How did they communicate them? I remember, as a teenager in the sixties, when I finally got up the nerve to ask my mother about sex, she quickly dismissed me. "It's too early," she said. "We'll have this discussion when you're twenty-one." That was that. My girlfriends and I learned by swapping stories, bumbling through erotic initiations on our own.

It's funny; I have no recollection of even once hearing my parents make love when I was growing up. My bedroom was right next to theirs—we slept on either side of the same wall—and not a peep ever gave them away. Except for an occasional peck on the cheek, they rarely showed physical affection in front of me. Years later I was surprised to discover from my parents that all along they'd had an active and satisfying (albeit quiet, from my point of view) sex life. Who could've guessed?

How your mother and father carried their sexuality served as your example. Children are like ducklings imprinting their parents' every move. If your parents were at home with their bodies and expressed a natural sexuality, you were in luck. But most people don't have such good fortune.

Typically other scenarios transpire. Toxic sexual perceptions are handed down, sometimes wordlessly, from one generation to another. Your grandmother is ashamed of her body; she imparts a negative self-image to your mother, who imparts it to you. Or, if your grandfather was a womanizer and your father becomes one, you might internalize identical behavior. The same principle underlies the perpetuation of sexual abuse. Families are unconsciously programmed to keep reenacting violence. They may not conceive of it this way or intend to inflict harm—yet they do. If your father or mother abused you, you're at risk for abusing your spouse or children. You may also develop uncanny radar for locating partners who abuse. When such incessant dynamics remain unaddressed, they will continue.

Intuition is a trance breaker; it can let us escape the ghostly palace of our predecessors' wounds. Increasingly I'm seeing patients and friends refuse to enact destructive family templates. It's a fascinating phenomenon, as if individuals are being singled out to shift an entire lineage's fate. They are the brave ones. They'll do whatever it takes—psychotherapy, family therapy, intuitive and spiritual work—to break the spell of the past. By saying no to abuse, no to the suppression of the robust sexual energy you hold, you heal yourself *and* future generations. If your children observe in you a healthy sexuality, they'll emulate it. Reach for something better and be one of the heroes of our time.

Mothers and fathers are the innovators of sexual change. Children being taught well are beautiful to watch. My patient Carrie, a talented playwright, came from a family that instilled guilt in her about sex. During therapy she worked hard to heal, not wanting to mimic the same message to her eleven-year-old daughter. When Carrie first spotted my statue of the goddess of compassion, Kuan Yin, she immediately went out and got one. As I've explained, Kuan Yin represents a gentle aspect of the feminine; often with women who want to delve into sexuality, she's a good place to start. Carrie's daughter also took to Kuan Yin and told all her friends about her. The whole group, in fact, became so enthusiastic they arranged a trip to Chinatown in central Los Angeles to buy statues of their own. This piqued the girls' interest in reading about other goddesses. They went on to sew a goddess quilt—each square depicting a feminine quality, from the hot-blooded Aphrodite and Diana the huntress to the kindhearted Kuan Yin.

Mothers and daughters discussed the goddesses, and sexuality too: how to be a woman, what femininity means, the complex depth of the female spirit. (Men have equivalent positive male archetypes to draw on, such as the powerful Zeus, the wise Solomon, and the mighty Hercules.) As I looked at a photo of the goddess quilt Carrie showed me, I couldn't help feeling envious. If my mother had introduced me to being a woman in this way . . . who knows? What I do know is that mothers and fathers have the wherewithal to heal their sexual past and offer a glorious vision of manhood and womanhood to their children. If we all did this, how different the world would be.

QUESTIONS FOR REFLECTION

- Are unproductive ideas about sexuality still being replayed in your love life? How can you remove them?
- Do previous hurts or betrayals prevent you from expressing or receiving affection?
- How can you demonstrate a balanced, optimistic sexuality for children and adolescents? What would you do the same as or differently than your family?

Step 2. Be in Your Body

Dancing—I first felt its power as a teenager. I used to lock my bedroom door, Otis Redding or the Beach Boys blasting, and move in front of a full-length mirror, the sexier the better. I'd watch myself: my body had changed, was changing still. Every day something new—a sense of command younger girls don't experience. At times while dancing I'd play an intuitive game. I'd start to concentrate on a boy I wanted to go out with, attempt to psychically connect with him. A kind of conjuring. Guess what? It often worked. I was just beginning to appreciate the intuitive reach of my sexuality.

Puberty is a transition that needs to be intuitively and spiritually reframed. Reflect on how your body felt during this stage. Too often puberty is dealt with clumsily by parents and peers, breeding shame, not awe, about sexuality. Instead we must see our shifting hormones as harbingers of the wonder of romantic love and reproduction. In girls hormones surge, developing the vagina, ovaries, uterus, commencing cycles of ovulation, menstruation, and birth. In boys there's accelerated growth of the penis, enhanced sperm production, and sexual drive.

Ideally puberty is a time of circles forming. Grandmothers and mothers around daughters. Grandfathers and fathers around sons. Questions answered, the body spoken of by elders with reverence. No eyes looking downward; no crude locker-room jokes, rather, an exuberant message: "I am a loving, sexual man or woman. You can be too."

This is not the rule in our society. Though puberty rituals, such as the bar mitzvah or bat mitzvah in Judaism and its Christian counterpart, confirmation, exist, their primary aim is to welcome the child as a full member of the spiritual community, equal in matters of religious law. Typically there are no sexual tête-à-têtes, sharing of dreams and intuitions as the Mojave Indians do, or intergenerational dialogues about the body's changes. (To explore empowering puberty rituals for our contemporary world, I recommend *The Joy of Family Ritual* by Barbara Biziou.)

Like many teenage girls, I wasn't told much about menstruation. When I got my period my mother gave me a brief talk about Tampax and personal hygiene. Though supportive, perhaps even pleased, she made no mention of the holiness of this process. It was my first spiritual teacher, Brugh Joy—a man—who first did so. During a woman's workshop in Hawaii, Brugh asked, "So, Judith, how do you honor your menstrual blood?" "Honor?" I responded, shocked. I'd rarely even look at it, simply flush it away. But consider the alternative, viewing menses as sacred. The moon, the tides, rhythms of nature and a woman's recurring physiological preparation for bearing life. What could be more basic, more true? By noting these intuitive interconnections, you can't help but appreciate the mystery of the female body; and you and your partner will come closer.

Did you realize, for instance, that when women live in close proximity, their menstrual cycles intuitively synchronize? (It goes beyond pheromones—natural, odorless chemical communicators that women respond to in one another.) This pattern wasn't unnoticed by Sigmund Freud. He went so far as to chart the cycles of women in his household, noticing a tendency among women "affectively linked" to menstruate simultaneously. The biologist Martha McClintock confirmed this when studying female lifeguards. During the menstrual time an intuitive rapport between women increases. To be sensitive to a woman's disposition, men need to know this. Sympathy between the sexes depends on such understanding. And to maximize the nurturance of female bonding, women need to know this about themselves. They may then want to gather to foster intuition and common strength.

Although legends of ancient matriarchs suggest menstrual blood was once sacred, historically it has mostly caused loathing. Superstitions abound. People feared it as a toxin that could destroy crops, shatter glass, dull swords, drive dogs insane. To Orthodox rabbis, it was God's curse for Eve's original sin. Canonical law forbade menstruating women to be in the company of men; when their periods ceased women had to take ritual baths. Freud believed these myths stemmed from a "blood phobia," a primordial human terror.

My patient Reva was no stranger to such thinking. Raised an Orthodox Jew, for twenty years she'd been the wife of a renowned Hasidic scholar whom she deeply loved. Reva told me, "When I was thirty I went through menopause. In my heart I know it was my body's intuitive defense against how my religion views menstruation." I empathized, although clearly such an abnormally early menopause demands a physician's review to rule out organic problems. I respect different religious traditions, but the reaction of Reva's body could not be ignored: her hormones had shut down. This scarily confirms the drastic repercussions negative projections about the body may have. I still flush my Tampax away, but I have reflected often on the gifts menstruation brings along with the inconveniences. Redirect your focus.

In men and women misconceptions originating in puberty can impose themselves on adult lovemaking. Freud believed that "quantitative disharmonies" in people cause neurosis. To dichotomize bodily functions into good and bad only works against us. Loving a man's body, loving a woman's body depends on seeing the marvel of all its phases. Make it simple on yourself—strive to see your body as perfect. Adore it.

Boys, too, face roadblocks to achieving sexual ease during puberty. For one, the common attitude about genitals, specifically, penis size. In locker rooms boys are constantly comparing. "Large penises are better" is an illusion we must dispel, even if, as in Robert Mapplethorpe's photographs, people find them visually compelling. The evolutionary purpose of a large penis is thought to be its ability to get closer to the cervix to fertilize the egg—a theory that may or may not be true. What's indisputable, however, is the psychic pain boys—and men—undergo when they perceive their size is lacking. In a recent workshop I gave one gutsy man volunteered, "In a public bathroom, when I notice another man's genitals are larger than mine, I feel so threatened I can't urinate." Nearly all the men present had experienced this too. It was a real eye-opener for us women (many of the husbands hadn't told their wives), deepening our empathy for the male sensibility.

Equating size with sexiness diminishes the masculine, implies that arbitrary measurement defines the alchemy of male character. Nonsense. How lovers relate is a result of numerous factors—chemistry, aesthetics, intuitive and spiritual communion, as well as physical fit. For men and women the size that feels good to one body may not to another. Compatibility of bodies is extremely personal. Generalizations are irrelevant.

During puberty our delight in the body can be tarnished by callous attitudes as well as traumatic events. It's important for you to pinpoint wounds, by word or deed, and begin to undo the damage. Sometimes just sharing with someone you trust works wonders. A close woman friend confided, "When I was twelve—and starting to feel my sexuality—I was walking to the drugstore to buy some candy. On the way I passed a church. I saw an elderly man, partially hidden by a bush. Suddenly, he jumped out and exposed himself. I was terrified. I'd never seen an erect penis. It looked strange and scared me. *He* scared me. I bolted. Never looking back, I ran all the way home." My friend didn't tell her mother, afraid she'd panic or get mad. My friend learned to associate fear with the male anatomy just as she was discovering boys—an alarming mix she's had to reprogram.

Scour your past for sources of awkwardness about physicality. Discomfort can slyly intervene. I have a friend whose lover is a gynecologist. When they started being intimate, he'd ask her with a perfectly straight face after sex, "Do you have to void?" Ah, medical school! This man's uneasiness with the human body didn't start there—but science gave him a convenient vocabulary as disguise. What does your discomfort or embarrassment stem from? I've emphasized puberty here, but scan your entire life. A lover's insensitive remark, disappointing comparison with the swimsuit model, a harsh reappraisal of your body after childbirth or aging have made their marks. No troubling occurrence is minor if it's significant to you.

Step 3. Sense Your Body's Subtle Energy

The first time you ever made love: certain passages in life are unforgettable. This is not solely a physical or emotional initiation; it's an energetic one too. If, early on, we'd been taught to view sex as a sacrament, we'd have been prepared when the moment came. Our parents might've shown us illustrations of the Kundalini serpent, embodying sexual life force in the Tantric view. We'd have realized that having sex would breathe fire through our being. Alas, few of us are told this or realize the imprint our first encounter leaves. In terms of energy we are moldable as fresh clay. Subtly, our first lover will always stay with us.

Let's rewind time. Same people. Same places. Different perspective. Now, filling in the blanks—with your eyes today—you'll see how intuition and spirituality enter in. No matter how you felt, whether your first sexual encounter (assuming you were a willing participant) was an epiphany or a disaster, a wider world opened. Initiations are ceremonies, sometimes ordeals, giving status or role to a member of a society. Not always graceful, erotic initiation marks a milestone. Dormant energy from sexual chakras comes alive, flows. How could the gods and goddesses keep from smiling?

Recall when you first made love. What was it like? Who was it with? What do you remember? In detail, set the scene—songs, sights, smells, textures, feelings. Attempt not just to relive it but to resee it. This includes, of course, the unheroic—mosquitoes, fear of pregnancy, sand in your bathing suit. It's true also that for some people first sex is simply something to have done, or gotten over with. They're almost too busy achieving it to experience the energetic openings I'm speaking of. Even if you were unaware, try to see them now. Zoom in on your reactions. Some may have been temporary, others enduring. Notice: Did your sense of sight, smell, or sound grow more acute? Were there new sensations around your genitals? An opening? Tightness? Warmth? What about your heart? Did it expand? Constrict? You may feel as if a curtain lifted, somehow making life more real. Whatever your responses before and after first sex, consider how your body and general outlook changed.

My first sexual experience was at sixteen. The winter of 1968, a period of torrential rains in Los Angeles. I'd worked hard to put Andy in the past. My new boyfriend, Art, and I were hippies. I, in tie-dyed silk tops and holey jeans. He, a sweet, bearded bear with a beat-up old Datsun. Every weekend we'd hang out with friends in a funky clapboard house on a walk street in Venice Beach. Wild times.

One evening Art boosted me on his shoulders into the attic. We climbed into a secret room. It was dark; we had only one small candle. Outside the waves thundered in the midnight storm. We crawled into a soft sleeping bag, zipping it up tight. Art and I'd been together a year. We knew each other's touch, taste, smell. But that night we went further. "Is it okay if we make love?" Art murmured, hesitant. "Is it okay?" Meltdown. A choice that is far more than a choice. A ripening before the act, I went from girl to woman as "yes" floated from my lips. Mostly, I recall longing to be closer to someone than ever before. I was scared, but I was ready.

For me this experience was a good one. Fitting together: we both had to figure that out, went through our share of fumbling. But more, something freed inside. The next morning, eating cinnamon rolls with white icing together on the Venice boardwalk, I felt strangely, unexplainably whole, as if my vision had keener focus. My body was a whirling universe of diverse sensations, an enlivening of crevices I didn't even know existed. Further, my heart and Art's joined in the kind of union intercourse can accentuate. This was true, even as I felt his complicated mix of attentiveness, pride, and insecurity. A shadow of too much obligation taken on. I couldn't quite admit what it mirrored in me. What had we gotten ourselves into?

In hindsight I realize that, apart from our fears, a yin-yang interchange had occurred, a masculine and feminine merging. Bound energy replaced by energy released. I was lucky to be loved. Art's gentleness and our mutual affection were pervasive. Even so, we weren't able to express any kind of spiritual consciousness about what we'd shared. I wonder how making love would've been different had that been articulated. A mutual acknowledgment, "I know this is sacred. I want to honor the sacredness in you." I don't believe that such an awareness is beyond teenagers—if they're savvily educated in simple, heartfelt terms, without preaching. I do believe it adds integrity.

Memories are tied by mystical cords. One event relates to another, then another. Your body intuitively records everything. No one's early sexual life is without glitches. Note what you've been given, the gaps too; transform the profane into what's holy. See. Heal. See. Heal. As you do, heaviness will lift.

Part of surveying your past is taking compassionate stock of sexual traumas. Little or big, they lodge themselves in your unconscious, impeding progress. You may want to avoid dealing with them. What you went through may be painful. But if ignored these incidents persist in your energy field, frozen, until you're ready to face them. Intuition isn't capable of denial; its sole function is to see. Whenever you're wounded intuition witnesses. It remembers. At your own pace, for greater freedom, you must too.

Currently it is estimated that millions of people have suffered sexual violence, a range of behavior from abusive sexual touching through fondling to rape. Too often these memories go underground, obscuring the past. For some, large chunks of childhood remain a complete blank. I've worked with numerous women and men who've been sexually abused. A prerequisite to healing is recalling what took place. The process of assimilating it includes deep emotional response—expressing rage, terror, shame among other feelings about the assault and offender or offenders. All of this makes an admirable, necessary start. But to add depth to such psychotherapy, I use energy work. It's especially effective with people who can't access abuse memories or distance them by intellectualizing. Energy is what melts resistance.

Paul, a twenty-five-year-old television producer, had been fondled sexually on numerous occasions by an uncle who used to baby-sit him. One night, Paul's parents caught the uncle in the act and forbade all further contact. Paul remembered but had been unable really to confront what happened. That was why he came to me. We started with talking it out. For weeks we went slowly, simply surfacing the facts. Then he was ready to go on.

So, during sessions, besides our discussions I began sending Paul energy. He'd rest on the couch, eyes closed, lightly meditating. I'd place my hands about four inches above his body, saying, "Notice any memories, knowings, or intuitions that come to you." Initially Paul felt his body as numb, but increasingly sensations returned. One day, when my hand was over his solar plexus (the chakra that is the emotional center), Paul started sobbing. "Tell me what's going on," I softly urged. Voice trembling, he responded, "I see myself. I'm about eight. I'm tucked in, ready for bed. My uncle is standing over me. He's undressing. He's touching himself." Paul continued to cry; a wrenching memory was surfacing. "Stay with it," I urged. No matter how hard remembering was for him, it was an emotional breakthrough.

Sensing energy makes the past real in a way that talking sometimes can't. Activating Paul's solar plexus triggered a memory buried in his body. During therapy I helped him integrate it. For the first time the reality of his boyhood abuse sunk in, marking a turning point in his recovery. Energy was the catalyst. Sometimes if you knock on a door demanding, "Who's in there?" no one will reply. But if you gently but energetically tap on that door with love, it opens willingly. To gain insight into sexual traumas, knowing many languages pays off.

What you know in your mind, you must also know in your body. Reviewing your sexual history, see what presents itself. Whether you experienced physical or verbal abuse, low self-esteem, or romantic disappointments, try to sense if these injuries are energetically still with you. How can you know? Any chronic symptom, physical or emotional, is suspect. Some are specific: stomach problems, spastic colon, headaches, discomfort during intercourse, impotency. Some are less specific: anxiety, fatigue, depression, weakness, pain. Of course, before you assume a symptom is emotionally based, you must eliminate any underlying organic cause.

Whether or not my patients say they're sick, I always begin with a thorough medical history. If I suspect a problem, I'll refer them to an appropriate physician for a work-up. From depression to migraines, sometimes the solution may be medication or other physical treatments. With such intervention the symptom resolves, case closed. At other times, however, it may offer only a partial answer, or none at all. Here I don't hesitate to investigate contributing psychological factors. Whenever you find yourself in a situation where a medical reason for your symptom has been ruled out or adequately treated, your body's subtle energy may hold the key.

Lingering ailments often mask hidden feelings. The following exercise will give you a place to start gaining insight into them. I recommend you try it. In the beginning, if your intuitions seem general or vague, don't worry. With practice they will become increasingly specific. To gather more information about puzzling, persistent symptoms you can repeat the exercise as many times as you like.

IDENTIFYING SEXUAL TRAUMAS LODGED IN YOUR BODY

1. Close your eyes. Take some slow, deep breaths. For a few minutes relax.

2. When you are ready, focus on your symptom. No matter how unsettling, purposely dwell on the sensations you feel—every ache, pain, twitch, spasm, sadness, anger, fear. In your body describe the energy of each. Is it hot? Cold? Tingling? Tight? Do your best to stay with it. First allow these general impressions to surface; they can lead you to the specific insights about healing embedded in the core of the discomfort. Let it talk to you. See what it has to say.

3. Concentrating on the symptom, observe any intuitive impressions or memories that arise. Do you see flashes of faces? Scenarios? Do emotions come up? How are they related to your symptom? These intuitions can lead you to when the sexual trauma first occurred and the cause. Try to piece them together to round out the picture.

Examining old wounds is tender terrain. It's often prudent to ask for professional assistance; if you've been the victim of traumatic sexual abuse, I strongly urge you to do so. Some issues are too excruciating to take on alone. Loving, knowledgeable support is invaluable. Seek a therapist or energy healer who's skilled in both a psychological and an intuitive approach to sexual trauma. Doing this work by yourself isn't necessary, and could be unwise. Know when to reach out. Don't hold back where your healing is concerned.

Even for a therapist, however, interpreting memories is complex. One concern: How can you be sure a patient's insights are true, particularly if they are unverifiable? For example, a gynecologist once asked me to see a patient with chronic pelvic pain. He'd located no detectable physical cause. As I had the patient delve into her pain using the preceding exercise, a strong memory surfaced—of being raped by her elder brother when she was a little girl.

Here's how I worked with what she told me. First, I know that memories held in the body can be activated. I also know memory is mediated by perception. Many therapists get into trouble by taking their patients' memories at face value. This error is at the heart of the current "recovered memory" controversy. Thus, with this patient, as with all patients, I couldn't simply assume she was remembering a literal truth. I had to weigh whether she was psychotic—delusional, seeing what was not there. Or whether the memory was a distortion.

This woman, I concluded, was not psychotic. Thus, my goal was to examine her memory further, to explore her relationship with her brother and see if there was a linkage between her recollection and her current symptom. Inevitably my patient herself asked, "Is what I'm remembering true?" I replied, "I can't know for sure. But right now this is your truth. We need to see how it affects your relationships, health, and sexuality." In other words, I treated the memory as a possible real event. I'd never say, "I think you're imagining it." At the very least I'd want to look into the spectrum of aggression by her brother and its connection to her self-esteem. Her memory was, by the most conservative reading, a metaphor.

In this case it became apparent that over the years her brother had viciously mocked her, put her down, pushed her around. As she and I worked on these issues, her pelvic pain gradually subsided. I want to stress that my patient never was certain whether or not her memory was literally true. She did weigh confronting her brother but decided against it, concluding no clear good would come of it. For me the therapeutic value of the memory was enormous. Whatever its literal truth, from that memory she and I were able to address patterns of emotional abuse that were indisputably accurate.

Energy contains answers. Whether they're uplifting or difficult, they're good to know. Personally, I want to be apprised of anything from my past that's constraining me today. Old baggage, who needs it? Energy allows us to track down what burdens us and release it. Likewise, we can identify the positive and grow. Such effort is worthwhile. Give it a chance and see.

Step 4. Ask for Inner Guidance

Your relationship patterns go way back. Many factors, from upbringing to instinct, contribute to them. Why do you choose relationships that aren't good for you? How can you pick ones that are? Now's the chance to analyze intuitively previous setbacks and successes. Attending to inner guidance pays off, no matter what mistakes you've made or how frequently you've made them. You must identify how, by whom, and why you get seduced off course, then formulate strategies to avoid it. I'm going to zero in on some everyday dilemmas and offer intuitive explanations and remedies you might not have thought of.

Through the years the outer qualities of men I've loved couldn't have been more different. My boyfriends have included a bespectacled computer whiz, a Willie Nelson–type country music manager (he took me on Willie's bus in Las Vegas!), a tattooed, muscle-bound biker-by-night/salesman-by-day, and a high-powered, Armani-clad corporate CEO (when relaxing he wears "khakis," not jeans). Externals aside, it was always chemistry that drew me, easy rapport, and the goodness I felt in each. Fair enough, but I've had to ask myself, Why didn't these relationships last? Was there something I should've seen more clearly? These are some of the places I've gotten snagged, as have many patients and friends. See if you can relate and put into action the following solutions.

FOUR WAYS INTUITION CAN IMPROVE YOUR ROMANTIC LIFE

1. *Know the difference between lust and love.*

You meet someone. Lightning strikes. You feel it. He or she does too. Zap, zap, zap—your body electrifies. All you know is that you want to touch this person, have him or her touch you. It doesn't seem to matter that you're not well-acquainted. You may feel, Aha. I've met my soul mate. Or, God, it's been so long. I've prayed to feel like this about someone. Now here that someone is. Off you go.

With instant passion, however, the place you end up may not be where you'd hoped for. Many of us go wrong by mistaking lust for love. Knowing the difference spares heartache. How to tell? I want to point out some commonsense and intuitive cues for making informed decisions. Of course, whether you dive into a sexual relationship, opt to go slow, or say no thank-you despite a wild attraction is up to you.

When entranced by someone, take a few minutes to meditate on the following distinctions:

Lust
- Sexual intensity exists without other significant emotional, mental, spiritual, or intuitive connecting points.
- A gut feeling announces, "Danger" or "Getting involved doesn't feel right."
- A sense of erotic excitement is present without a sense of safety.
- It's time-limited, will wane after a "honeymoon period" if love is missing.
- Relationships are usually compartmentalized—sex only, without inclusion in the rest of each other's lives.

Love
- Physical chemistry is obvious—but it's associated with your heart opening (an actual warm feeling in the midchest), which signals a possibility for deep, caring rapport.

- Your gut is relaxed, comfortable, affirming, "Go for it! Wonderful things are ahead."

- An intuitive empathy exists. Even from the first you may be able to sense each other's emotions, thoughts, dreams; you both feel familiar, as if you've known each other before.

- You want to learn everything about this person, bring him or her into your life.

- Intimacy blossoms with time, and leads to better sex.

Try to get a good feel for each point to make a reliable romantic assessment. By far the most confusing is how to recognize a genuine heart connection. Many distraught women and men have come into my office saying, "I swore I felt it. But after we had sex I never heard from him or her again. What happened?" Here's the problem: When you're being charmed, whether a person intends it or not, a transient sense of heart may also be communicated. Make certain the other signs of love are also present. If you're not sure—and want a lasting relationship—don't be so quick to jump in. It's wiser to put off becoming intimate until you get a fuller sense of someone. I've known people who've had sex quickly and the relationship has worked out. More often, though, I've seen expectations smashed, hearts broken. There's no need to rush. Let your relationship develop. Time is the best truth-teller of all.

I realize how challenging it is in the heat of passion to pause, find a neutral place, and listen inwardly. When you do, though, I guarantee an arrow will form, aiming you toward love. If your past is studded with short-term relationships, with sexuality your main tie, you may be ready to alter that pattern. Whenever you have sex with someone, a psychic bond is created; then it's harder to be objective or disengage yourself. My advice: in your next relationship, move like a turtle, slowly. Watch with your intuition—then see.

2. *Beware of misreading potential for reality.*

Intuition allows you to sense many dimensions in people. There's who the person is and who he or she has the capability to be. It's common to misread potential for reality. You might spot it, thinking, I can bring out the best in this person. From then on helping to fulfill your partner's "potential" becomes your special project. Avoid falling into these predictable traps: You meet someone who's been commitment-phobic for years and conclude, I know she wants to change. She'll be different with me. Or someone doesn't earn a living now, and you assume, He's so talented. If I could just convince him to go to school and get a degree . . . Another doozy: He's never been very sexual, but if I love him enough I can bring it out. Know this—if people don't want to change, they won't. You may well be intuiting a very real side of the person, but if he or she isn't devoted to actualizing it, you can't do it. Lip service about changing is meaningless; a consistent, observable shift in behavior is essential. Many of us lose years in the pursuit of improving others, a no-win situation.

3. *For a relationship to work, a soul connection must go both ways.*
A befuddling intuitive phenomenon exists. You feel a profound connection with someone, as if you've known him or her before, yet the other person doesn't reciprocate. You might assume he or she will eventually come around. Maybe that person just needs time. But how much? Months? Years? Where do you draw the line? Here's my rule: Continue living fully. Be receptive to other relationships. Never put your life on hold for unrequited love. I've seen sensitive, bright people make that mistake. Don't. Here's the principle: Love that is destined can never be stopped; leaving your options open won't deter it. Relationships take two. Even if the inner bond you're intuiting is authentic, it can remain unrealized. Maybe the other person can't or won't reciprocate, or is simply oblivious. View it as an irony you must adjust to, not fixate on. For a year a friend of mine kept hoping a man she thought was her soul mate would pursue her romantically. He never did. Finally she stopped waiting. A few weeks later she met her current husband. For something new to come, she had to make room. You must too. Don't get lost in the enchanted limbo of unrequited longing. Find people who can love you in return. There's more than one soul connection possible in a lifetime.

4. *Avoid fantasizing about an unhealthy relationship or one that has ended.*
Sexual fantasizing about people keeps them alive—not just in memory but also on your intuitive wavelength. In loving relationships partners fantasizing together can cement bonds, make sexuality creative. In ties that aren't mutually loving, fantasizing works against you, forcing something to be viable that's meant to dissolve. A raising of the dead for no good purpose. Continually thinking about someone who doesn't

share your interest is an intrusion on his or her intuitive space; it also keeps you hooked in. I know how painful it can be to let love go—especially when you didn't choose to. It's human to want to cling to what's lost. Even so, try to catch yourself. Remember Lot's wife in the Bible? Warned not to look back at the burning cities of Sodom and Gomorrah, she still did—and was transformed into a pillar of salt.

Here's a visualization I suggest to help you move on: Envision yourself and the other person linked heart to heart by a ribbon of light. Take a quiet moment to honor your connection. Next, gently—even if it's painful—begin to see the ribbon detaching from each of your hearts, then completely disintegrating. Doing this will sever any invisible cords between you, so no fragments of attachment remain. Say a final good-bye. Then gather all your strength, turn around, and walk away. Focus on the light ahead, not on fading shadows. Move toward the new love that awaits you.

Step 5. Listen to Your Dreams

Picture your lifeline as a golden thread that stretches from the moment of birth to your death. Dreams happen along the way. They are markers of experience. Reviewing them, you'll spot knots in the thread to be untangled. The past is not the past from an intuitive perspective. Ex-husbands, ex-wives, mothers, fathers: harmful messages they've sent about sexuality drone on during sleep. You may finally say, "Be gone. I'm tired of this." Hallelujah. Then, look to your dreams for instructions about healing.

My patient Patrice, at thirty a wife and mother, had never felt proud of her body. She'd always dress in layers covering every inch, preferred lovemaking with the lights dimmed. Her figure was lithe, graceful as a dancer's, yet she'd never show it. "Why?" I asked. Patrice wasn't sure. All she could express was, "I don't like people looking at me. I don't want them to stare." To give us more to go on, she consulted a dream. A snippet came:

I'm in a modern-day concentration camp being herded by Nazis on the beach. One general looks strangely like my cousin, who's ten years older than me. Dressed in a sexy chartreuse leotard and top, I stand out. This puts me in danger. Nazi planes can spot me from the air. I'm afraid of being killed!

"What do you make of the dream?" I inquired. Notice Patrice's associations. Throughout childhood she'd dodged her cousin's eyes. He'd look at her, smile; then she'd hide. Hide-and-seek was her favorite game. Her cousin would find her. Her cousin would lightly kiss her on the lips. He'd hug her, pat her butt. It felt funny. It lasted too long. She didn't like it. Becoming camouflaged was her solution. Her cousin couldn't see or feel too much then. By covering up she protected herself.

As an adult Patrice kept protecting herself, even from people she didn't need protection from. Her husband was a thoughtful, handsome man, yet being naked with him disturbed her. This dream of the past allowed Patrice, in therapy, to differentiate her cousin's actions (never blatant abuse but inappropriate) from her husband's sexual desire. Gradually, layers of garments fell away. Shawls, sweaters, leather combat boots slowly turned into dresses, shorts, sandals, sometimes no clothes at all. Finally, Patrice was ready to risk being seen by the man who loved her.

You might assume that dramatic traumas in childhood—sexual violence, abandonment, emotional abuse—are the most frequent causes of adult sexual dysfunction. True, they exact a toll. But more commonly, I've observed, it's the less obvious insults that shut us down. A teenage boy's body shamed by the class bully in the locker room. A little girl relentlessly teased because she's overweight. Being unpopular in high school. It's no surprise if your sexuality gets off to a rocky start. So, retracing your steps with dreams, be kind to yourself; never minimize how deep "minor" hurts can go. Ask your dreams to reveal anyone, anything, that currently keeps you small.

Dreams about childhood may also comment positively on a relationship today. Utilizing comforting symbols from your past, they can affirm if a romance is auspicious. Take these as signs to advance. Shortly after I met the man I'm currently going out with, I had a dream. I knew I was attracted to him, felt at ease in his company, but the dream signaled to what extent.

My boyfriend takes me to dinner at a magical restaurant. Simple, elegant, with trellises of night-blooming jasmine, it's located at the railroad tracks where, as children, my best friend and I'd relish meeting after school. A wise-looking, friendly woman behind a gift counter is selling St. Christopher medals, which I recognize to be protection for travelers. I think, Wow, I used to love wearing those as a little girl. This woman is also selling endearing tokens from my boyfriend's childhood. She looks familiar. Radiating joy, she seems to know both of us well.

A meeting on the edge of time. In dreams uniting past and present, who appears can be telling. I considered this woman a kind of benefactor giving us her blessing. His childhood, my childhood—as if we'd always been linked. As with my dream, at times you'll encounter a guide you know and who knows you. It's the oddest sense of intimacy; you're sure you've seen this person a thousand times before but may be unable to remember where. No matter. Memories are elusive. Golden memories: When we were ten, my girlfriend and I'd place shiny pennies on the railroad track and gleefully squeal as the speeding trains flattened them. We'd keep these pennies in our pockets forever. Forever is something I want a relationship to be. Dreams as premonitions may take a while to unfold. Maybe this man is the one. Maybe as travelers together we will be fortunate. For now, I'll have to wait and see.

Other sexual dreams may come in the form of nightmares—difficult wisdom that, when learned from, can relieve what binds you. Stifling childhood patterns keep working themselves through. Take my patient Pam. Now forty, she'd had shame about sex all her life. Her background contributed. She said, "I was an outspoken child who attended a Christian fundamentalist school in 1960s rural Alabama. I kept 'misbehaving' in class. As punishment I was forced to memorize the Bible in the principal's office. My father was a minister in town. The rules at home were strict. No dancing, no playing cards, certainly no premarital sex." At sixteen Pam met a man with whom she had a long love affair. Suddenly, the nightmare started. She said, "It was always the same.

I'm shocked to discover I'm pregnant. I panic, break into a cold sweat. Somebody's going to find out, I think. What will they say? My parents will disown me! Before I know it, the baby is born. To my horror, it's a Cyclops! One gigantic blue-green eye, the color of mine, peers from the middle of its forehead. I want to hide the baby, but it's too late. The whole town learns of the Cyclops and shuns us.

The dream evocatively depicts Pam's guilt about having sex, defying her parents, her religion. "I was sure God would punish me," she said. "Every morning I'd swear, 'I'll never sleep with him again'—but still I did." The dream continued until the relationship ended. But for years after the memory wouldn't let go. Pam admitted, "I've never had children. Deep down I was terrified I'd give birth to a monster." How devastating it must've been to have hidden such apprehension. There was only one way to penetrate it: with compassion.

When a person longs for change, the universe cooperates. I did my part, offering Pam a more embracing spiritual context for sexuality. But when one dances with an archetype as compelling as the Cyclops, it inevitably plays a healing role too. One just has to know how to perceive it. What is most scary may contain its own redemption. Many years later Pam learned this at a woman's support group. A new member was telling her story about having given birth to "a baby—a Cyclops—with just one eye." Boom! Worlds overlapped. Pam listened, transfixed.

Although the infant died, the woman had experienced a unique sense of soul, which mothers often pick up from their children. She said, "This was the most spiritual event of my life. I felt graced to have carried such a beautiful being for even a short time." Healing words. One woman's dream . . . another's reality. An extraordinary synchronicity. Pam was being shown how to view her situation differently. Serendipitous growth occurred; sexual taboos (symbolized by the Cyclops) were transmuted. Though the women's situations differed, this mother's compassion for the birth scenario Pam most feared helped Pam forgive herself. A horror, it turned out, might not be only a horror. Even a nightmare vision can be reread in a fuller human context. Now Pam could lovingly begin to redefine the meaning of sexuality.

Dreams of the past, changes now—the two are tied. So when a sequence of your life keeps replaying during sleep, it has purpose. Sexual feelings can possess a delicacy that must be respected. If you're afraid of loving, your body knows. It will recoil from sharing itself. What's disconcerting from your earlier life begs to be healed. What's empowering wants to assert itself. Follow your sexual dreams. Let their wisdom lead you.

INVENTORIES OF THE EVENTS OF LIFE are fundamental. Allow plenty of time for reflection. The sexual beliefs of your family don't have to define and limit you. It's not disrespectful to reevaluate what's gone before; it's simply smart. You are fully equipped for the task. By offering insight to see and compassion to heal, intuition prepares you to meet every chapter of your sexual history.

The journey is both sublime and strenuous. Even when you think,

It's too demanding. I can't do this, take a moment out. Don't try to push through the feeling. A break is called for. Before going further focus on restoring your peace of mind. Whenever doubts or fatigue creep in I like to watch the night sky. Nothing, I find, is more awesome. Something up there smiles through me, restrengthening my resolve. Find your touchstone; call on it whenever necessary. Maybe it's listening to Muddy Waters sing the blues, going boogie-boarding, making fresh vegetable soup, or curling up with a good novel. It's lifesaving to know how and when to refuel. Then, once rejuvenated, keep on moving.

The point of past reflection is erotic liberation. It doesn't serve you to have any aspect of your sexuality marooned in some previous time. My tolerance for the past tugging at me has worn thin. It's unbearable not to be able to fly. If something's in the way, I want to know. I hope you do too. Inner lightness results in an exhilarating erotic life. The heart wants to free itself from anything that imprisons it.

14

Sexual Energy's Healing Gift

Sex is the outward visible sign of an inward spiritual
grace bringing about love.
—Alan Watts

*O*nce upon a time, a real time, when the world hadn't heard of
Judaism, Christianity, or Islam, the priestesses were preparing the temple at full moon. Clad in diaphanous silk robes, polished silver anklets,
and crescent earrings, they exuded musk, the scent of passion. These
"sacred prostitutes," the most highly esteemed of women, utilized sexuality to heal. All over Europe and the Middle East, the Goddess of Love
was revered, the priestesses were her vehicle. Sex with a priestess was
consecrated; it was physically, emotionally, and spiritually elevating.
She'd heal you by transmitting feminine essence, kindling your soul's
spark, rejuvenating your life.

Today more than ever these priestesses can instruct us. But how?
And can people hear? At a talk I gave to physicians called "The Intuitive
Healing Power of Sexuality," I gathered my courage and, toward the
end, snuck in the concept of sacred p-p-p-prostitutes. I asked, "What
can the priestess show us about treating patients now?" I was suggesting
not that doctors have sex with patients, rather that we help them access
a positive sexuality and as physicians be healthy role models. If physicians are comfortable with their bodies, it shows. If we're at ease
discussing sexual issues—when clinically appropriate, never intru-
sively—patients will be put at ease too. But more, when physicians (or
other healers) understand—and embody—the tie between sexuality
and spirit, we can educate patients and be examples for those who desire such integration. On a subtle energy level, when our sexuality is bal-

anced we give off a vibration, much like a tuning fork, that others can sense and emulate.

The message of my talk: The way we carry our sexuality, an attitude and healing energy we convey, can facilitate the health of others. The group's response to this notion astounded me—in particular many urologists and gynecologists, men and women, wanted to know more. "What can I read?" "Who are the leaders in this field?" As one doctor told me, "Drawing on sexuality is both a missing piece in my own growth and a part of patient care I've been searching for."

In our sexual lives we can all be healers. We can all be healed. During lovemaking passion and tenderness have health-promoting benefits for you and your partner. Tension is relieved. Worry dissipates. Vitality returns. These are all rewards of erotic experience. More extensive healing, though, is another possibility. You'll see how pleasure becomes therapeutic by, for example, partaking in the variety of orgasms I'll describe. You'll also learn to direct sexual energy intuitively (on your own or with a partner) to specific organs to lessen symptoms from back pain to depression. The empathic interchange during sex, when focused, can activate the healing system, even help alleviate disease. Allowing sexuality to nurture you on many levels adds exuberance to everything you do.

You are the goddess. You are the gods. So when you love someone, don't restrict that desire. Whether you're male or female, the ancient ways of the temple priestess can work through you. Even in our under-spiritualized world, if you're humble and heart-centered as you consciously direct your sexuality, a millennia-long power is yours. Use it. Savor it. Don't underestimate the goodness and restorative sexual instinct you possess.

Step 1. Notice Your Beliefs

When it comes to sexual healing, consider the many possibilities: the way you smile at someone, how you view your body, your receptivity to passion, your ability to transmit it. Give. Receive. Give. Receive. There's a mutuality—you and a lover, you and yourself, you and God. Passion emanates from all sides. Be a vessel, but know this: You may be a technical virtuoso, but if your heart is missing, you cannot truly heal or be healed through your sexual power.

A film I adore about sensuality as therapy, as art, is Bernardo Bertolucci's *Stealing Beauty*. It describes a girl's passage into womanhood while she is visiting her late mother's bohemian friends in an Italian villa. I love the film because all the characters, no matter what their appearance or age, are presented as sensual—even a male writer (portrayed by Jeremy Irons) dying of cancer. He becomes the girl's confidant, his passion for life her example and inspiration. Portraying a dying man as sexy is revolutionary. Despite his having lost hair from chemotherapy and being on an IV, one is struck by his sensual, caring aura. Healing infusions: As he is fading—in erotically lush countryside surroundings rather than a sterile hospital room—the girl's sexuality is coming to life. Who heals whom and how is a tale of complexity and grace.

The healing attributes of sexuality and sensuality are for everyone—whether you're twenty, forty, or eighty, whether you have an illness or are even reaching the end of the line. To help yourself or others, call on them to soothe or invigorate. With eroticism a little goes a long way. It can trigger intuitions. Did you realize that by simply touching someone you can spark a realization in him or her? Or that a special kiss can make another person's wish come true? Your positive energy can augment another's. Sensual sharing isn't only *what* you do but the love with which you do it.

Sexuality can also energize those who refrain from intercourse, even those pledged to chastity. Once I was approached at a talk by a flustered nun in full habit who'd read *Second Sight*. She said, "After doing the meditations you suggested, my intuition is improving. But I've noticed the strangest thing. I'm suddenly flooded with sexual feelings! What am I to do?" So moving. What a dilemma! I reassured her. "It's natural when opening up in meditation for sexual feelings to arise. But you don't have to act on them. Just let them nurture you and flow through." Understandably, the nun was relieved.

If you believe there's an interrelationship among spirituality, sexuality, and healing, one will evolve organically from another. While meditating, strolling in a fragrant garden, bathing in warm Caribbean waters, or making love, allow your body to absorb each luxurious activity. This is health-promoting—taking in positive energy, letting it transform. How could your immune system resist? White cells breathing in lilacs, red cells swimming in clear waters—healing, like intuition, has an aesthetic. Your delight invites spiritual passion in. There's a wonderful saying in the ancient Jewish Haggadah: "We will be accountable for all the permitted pleasures we failed to enjoy."

The search for ecstasy, however, may be misconstrued. Consider sex addiction. I've treated both men and women who've struggled with this tormenting disorder. Nothing about it is fun. Craving pleasure merely to fill an emptiness, sex addicts obsessively seek partner after partner. Gratification may last seconds or minutes, then it's gone. One patient, at age thirty a successful businessman, would voraciously comb the "massage" ads in newspapers or cruise Hollywood Boulevard for hookers. He'd admit, "I'd be having sex with one woman—and already fantasizing about the next."

Sex addicts are confused. They think they're after sex, but their hunger is really spiritual. If physical ecstasy originates from a divine source, they must first look to divinity to find it. It is not surprising that a widely accepted treatment for sex addiction, Sex and Love Addicts Anonymous (SLA), is a spiritually based twelve-step program. The aim is to give addicts tools to find a higher power of their own, not attempt to be "fixed" by anyone or anything external. Ingenious. By replacing sexual obsession with a quest for spirit, sex addicts refine the search for ecstasy. Once they make the spiritual connection, they can bring that sense of wholeness to the search for intimacy.

Sexual wellness is unity of mind, body, and spirit. When these aspects align you shine like the sun. If one of these parts is split off from the others, sexual experience will leave you dissatisfied, vacant. A nineteen-year-old female patient, a college student, said of a one-night stand, "After we had sex all I wanted to do was go home. An awful feeling, nothing between us." Obsessive, unfeeling, or obligatory sex can never heal you. Healing comes from love alone. So in attitude and act, let it motivate you.

Artists are replacing our stale concepts of sexuality with a more elevated vision. A bold paradigm shifter is the Manhattan-based erotic filmmaker and sex educator Candida Royale. Countering the body-parts myopia of X-rated movies, she defines what's sexy from a spiritual-feminine perspective. Royale explains, "Women want to see sex shown in a way that makes it look beautiful, real . . . they want a buildup of tenderness." No "crotch shots" or close-ups of exultant ejaculations. "Women find these offensive," she affirms. "My films focus on . . . connecting between humans as opposed to a series of mechanical acts." Committed to her own spiritual growth, Royale brings that sensibility to her art and role as educator. Her work has intrigued the medical profession. Her lecture at the American Psychiatric Association, "Creating Adult Erotica That Presents Positive Sexual Role Models from a Female Point of View," was standing room only. Royale's work heals by offering a model equating eroticism with intimacy. Appealing to women, it also invites men into fuller aspects of sexual experience.

I witnessed Royale's work in action. She had invited me to a filming. Fascinated, I wanted to see a nonexploitive (as she puts it, "sex-positive") treatment of male and female sexuality. So there I sat—a tad embarrassed, I have to admit—actually at the foot of the bed, cameras rolling, as a married couple (both of them porn stars!) made love. I saw *everything*. I watched. I intuitively tuned in. I observed Royale set a specific heart-centered tone through her awareness of energy. Not at all the sleazy, low-consciousness stereotype. As director she maximized the couple's erotic chemistry by bringing out their closeness. This high-voltage sensuality seemed intuitively comfortable, right. I stopped feeling awkward and left that day with a sense of being more womanly, more eroticized, more myself—a sign to me that I'd gained something valuable, something healing.

I consider Royale's priorities part of a cutting-edge sexuality, celebrating both the male and the female in ourselves. Balancing these elements creates an axis in the body, firmly planted and passionate. Men and women can enlighten each other. Different or similar, let's understand our mutual makeups as much as we can. The feminine yin traits: receptivity, intuition, flow, moonlike rapture. The masculine yang: a hunger to achieve, penetrate, conquer. We contain them all. Bring your feminine and masculine together; share them with your lover. This is the basis of sexual wellness.

QUESTIONS FOR REFLECTION

- Have you experienced sexuality as healing? What have you found to be the physical, emotional, and spiritual rewards?

- While making love did you ever have predictive impressions or knowings about your partner that were on target? Do you realize that sexual closeness enhances intuitive rapport?

- What aspects of erotic play (videos, props, et cetera) do you find stimulating? Are you ready to experiment with how spirituality and sexuality fit together?

Step 2. Be in Your Body

Erotic zones exist in your body, perhaps undiscovered, waiting. People go a lifetime in the dark. Nobody tells us how to find them. Some even believe they're not there. Over the years feminists and sexologists have debated feverishly. Are they real? How do we locate them? What role do they play? Drawing on intuition and an awareness that the body is spiritual too, I want you to see for yourself. Our focus: the enigmatic realm of orgasms.

What is an orgasm? First, physiology. You feel, see, hear, taste, or smell something that sexually arouses you. Then, if you're a woman, your vagina engorges with blood, lubricates; your pelvis contracts. If you're a man, blood rushes to your penis, making it erect, semen propels outward, sperm ejaculate. Both male and female orgasms are orchestrated by the nervous system; you feel pleasure. Beyond the physical, though, orgasm fills you with divine ecstasy—physiology is merely the conduit.

From an intuitive viewpoint, during lovemaking your orgasm is never just your own. Energy gets conveyed to your partner, affecting his or her sense of well-being and health. Orgasm is a honing and transmitting of life force; its quality has therapeutic implications for both sexes. Here I want to discuss the female orgasm as a chance for men and women to experience the healing sexuality can bring.

The age-old conundrum: Are female orgasms clitoral? Vaginal? Knowing is important; it expands your options for pleasure. But more, it exemplifies how different kinds of orgasms foster health. Female sexuality as transformer depends on understanding the body's capabilities.

What can the historic conversation reveal? Opinions have vacillated, generating confusion. In 1944 the gynecologist Ernst Grafenberg "discovered" the G-spot (named after, yes, *him*self), legitimizing the vaginal orgasm in America. The accepted wisdom from then on, supported by Freud's theories, was that mature women had vaginal orgasms, immature women, clitoral. Enter the feminist movement in the late 1960s. Now the superiority of the clitoris was reinstated; men were accused of promoting vaginal orgasms to keep women dependent. At the same time the scientists William Masters and Virginia Johnson concluded, "All orgasms are centered in the clitoris." It wasn't until 1983 that the primacy of the vaginal orgasm was reborn in the bestseller *The G-Spot,* but this book was attacked by both feminists and physicians. Finally, science has arrived at a consensus. A 1999 article in the *Psychiatric Annals* declares, "Yes, women can experience orgasm as a result of vaginal stimulation." This is currently "fact." But, why are many of my patients still unaware of this fact and its importance for them?

Of course, there was always another way to read the situation. A tradition thousands of years old: Tantra. As we've discussed, this ancient Hindu spiritual system makes sexual love sacred. It details the proper attitude and techniques lovers can adopt to achieve intimate union and erotic ecstasy. I was first shown how to apply these teachings in a weekend workshop offered by Charles and Caroline Muir. Their language itself opened my eyes. They used the Sanskrit terms *yoni* and *lingum*—sacred space and wand of light. What's in a name? Consider the vocabulary in American English. Think of the derogatory slang terms for male and female anatomy. Tantra's nomenclature presumes a very different sexual vision.

In ancient eras students were mentored in the multidisciplines of Tantra and the art of love—everything from kissing methods to the virtues of each sexual position. Westerners, however, seldom receive positive, pertinent erotic education. I remember in junior high seeing a fuzzy 1950s black-and-white newsreel about the horrors of venereal disease. A genuine threat but a stilted truth. We deserve to be informed more about pleasure, about love, not just about sexually transmitted diseases. Men and women can become each other's teachers, be trained to ignite dormant sexual energy in each other. Tantra gives us the start.

Perhaps, like me, you're intrigued by the promise of the discovery of "new" erogenous zones. A highlight of the Muirs' workshop was their explanation of how to find the "sacred spot" (aka G-spot). I'd heard of it but had never experienced a vaginal orgasm. About the sacred spot Charles said, "Every woman needs healing there, no matter how awake you think you are." Caroline added, "Most women have traumas in this region . . . infections or abortions, pregnancy, cancer, sex you didn't want, sex that hurt." Wounds lodge in the yoni, anesthetizing. Thus, one therapeutic benefit of "sacred spot massage" is a clearing of the past facilitated by vaginal orgasm.

Before sending us all home to do the exercise with a partner, Charles and Caroline explained the process. *Mood:* Flowers. Candlelight. Incense. Preparing herself, the woman may soak in a bubble bath, the man sensually washing her, toweling her dry. *Female attitude:* No an-

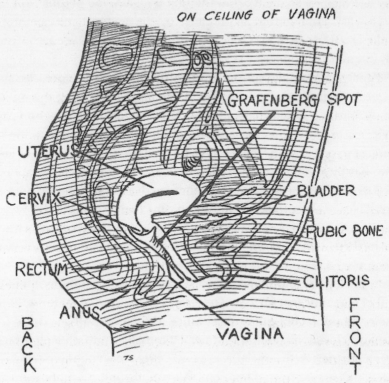

DIAGRAM OF SACRED SPOT (G-SPOT)
ON CEILING OF VAGINA

GRAFENBERG SPOT

UTERUS

CERVIX

BLADDER

PUBIC BONE

RECTUM

CLITORIS

ANUS

BACK

VAGINA

FRONT

FEMALE SEXUAL ANATOMY (INTERNAL)
Figure 2

alyzing. Be fully receptive; let pleasure in. Freely express all emotions. *Male attitude:* Consider this an opportunity to "serve the Goddess." Not to have intercourse but to act as healer awakening the feminine force. Inevitably one man asked, "You mean we don't get back anything?" (Hmm, I thought. Men!) Charles responded, "Try it one night. By giving a woman pleasure, you may receive everything you want and more." The *sacred spot* is situated on the ceiling of the vagina, between the opening and the cervix (see figure 2). A few inches wide, it's an area that can shift and enlarge. The man stimulates it with his finger as the woman relaxes.

This night was a revelation. I went in with doubts. Does such a spot exist? What if I don't have one? What if my partner can't find it? These are natural apprehensions you may share. At first when my partner touched this place, I felt only a vague ache. But my partner was patient;

he kept at it, sensitively feeling his way. Often awakening takes time; it may not happen at once or on the first try. "Are you getting bored?" I had to ask after about an hour. "No," he assured me, smiling. (I could've asked, "Are you suffering carpal tunnel syndrome?" A joke I didn't make.) And so we continued.

Finally, amazingly, a sun began to glow in my core. Brighter, brighter, brighter, the sun exploded, warming everything feminine in me. A spiraling of light pulsing from my genitals throughout my body. Then an expulsion of clear fluid (*amrita* in Sanskrit, divine nectar) thought to originate in the vagina's Bartholin's glands. At this moment I was hardly alone in my awe. Did someone ask, What would be in this for a male? My partner was right there with me. Talk about a contact high! To see the pleasure he'd given and feel it himself. He was the healer; I was the recipient. That night a glorious aspect of my sexuality was birthed, a locus of female strength. Now that I know how my sacred spot feels, I will never forget. Awakening is like that. The hardest part is often getting there the first time.

Let me guide you further. The structure I've described for setting attitude, mood, technique is ideal. Since it's anatomically awkward for a woman to locate the sacred spot herself initially, I advise you to practice with a partner. Activating this area may require someone else's loving touch. Subsequently a woman can more easily find it on her own. During orgasm some women may expel up to a cup of clear fluid; others may not expel any. (Amrita, I must stress, is *not* urine.) Physiologies vary. Each woman must see how her body responds. When practicing, allow at least a few hours. Let there be no time pressure. Here the purpose is to pinpoint the sacred spot, not to have intercourse. Approach the exercise with reverence for the erotic, for each other.

FINDING THE SACRED SPOT

Prepare a setting that's sensual, soothing: soft lights, fresh sheets, perhaps a bouquet of tulips. The woman rests on her back on a cozy couch, bed, or pillows. The partner sits or kneels beside her. Take a silent moment to get in sync. Gaze into each other's eyes. Then, when you're both ready, the partner gently places a well-lubricated finger into the woman's vagina, visualizing light emanating from one person to the other. Then the curled finger goes deeper, touching the vagina's ceiling midway between the pubic bone and the cervix. Softly, the finger massages this two-inch area in a circular motion. It may feel spongy or like a tiny bulge swelling when aroused. Many women have an urge to urinate, even if the bladder is empty—a reaction often soon replaced by erotic excitement. If a woman does have discomfort, the touch must be lightened, but the partner should continue to massage the spot, loosening it up for a few moments. Then release—never forcing it. Note blissful areas, also those that are tender or numb. Experiment with hand positions, pressure. Communicate about what feels good. Enjoy the process. Don't focus on orgasm. When the time is right, a woman may have one or many, often involving her entire being. She may laugh, cry, relive memories. Allow it all to flow. This purifies, magnifying ecstasy.

This exercise is intended to be repeated so it becomes more familiar, playful, a spiritual practice. It enables a woman to discover a part of herself she may not have known existed. It opens a man to the power of the feminine, which heals him too. A rigidity melts in both partners. They feel joy, pleasure, well-being. Go tenderly. An orgasm may bring emotional release, discharging negative energy, flushing out traumas, as well as bringing pleasure.

Partner as sexual healer: We may need to be that for our beloveds. The film *Bliss* chronicles a husband helping his wife recover from early sexual abuse. Enlisting the aid of a Tantric teacher, he learns that sexuality is an honoring of the physical and a sharing of heart. The teacher tells him, "Anyone who doesn't accept the body can't experience ecstasy. Sexual fulfillment is not merely orgasm, though orgasm results in bliss." Devotedly, the husband adopts techniques of bringing sacredness into their lovemaking. Doing so, he erotically awakens parts of his wife's body—and the disturbing memories they hold. Remembering leads her first to emotional pain, then to freedom. His actions catalyze a sexual healing in his wife that traditional analysis alone was unable to achieve.

Conceptualize a woman's body as energy. During orgasm that energy can be mobilized differently. A clitoral orgasm has one quality, a vaginal orgasm another, point and counterpoint. Both are marvelous. Together, through self-pleasuring or with a partner, they can equilibrate a woman's health. If one is missing the bounty of resources in a woman's body are not being used. So the art of female orgasm involves experiencing both, letting their dual expression feed both partners erotically.

Step 3. Sense Your Body's Subtle Energy

Now let's explore male orgasm. I want to give you a new way to think about it—from an energetic stance. Male orgasm holds many secrets; it has therapeutic value for both a man and his partner. It is a sublime spiritual and physical act that transcends society's ordinary definition. Typically, male orgasm is synonymous with virility and sexual prowess. We assume that the more orgasms a man has the better, that the raison d'être of sex is to climax. What pressure to perform! In the West, even if a woman doesn't have an orgasm, she probably believes a man should.

The philosophy of Tantra offers a radical alternative. Male sexual vibrance, stamina, and intensity with a partner can be enhanced, with no need for Viagra. Reorient yourself. Tantra sees erotic energy as a commodity to accumulate, not thoughtlessly expend. We Westerners presuppose a man's sexual reserve is endless. Tantra does not. This isn't a negative reflection on masculinity, rather it is an energy-based recognition of inevitable ebb and flow. Bear in mind a difference between the sexes. Women tend to be invigorated by orgasm; men often fall asleep afterward, spent. Tantra's explanation is that semen contains a man's life essence; when it's expelled he may get drained. Over time if that essence isn't replenished, there's a physical toll. Teenage boys, at the start of their reserve, don't usually have difficulty. But as a man ages he may. It takes longer to get an erection or reach orgasm; the quantity of ejaculation is less; the time before he can climax again increases. Normal signs of aging? Not so, says Tantra. Signs of energy depletion.

Note Tantra's brilliant solution: Men can experience orgasm without external ejaculation. For most of us this just doesn't compute. Is it possible? How often can one do it? What are the advantages? For a moment suspend disbelief. Tantra defines orgasm as an inner burst of erotic energy. Ejaculation is its external release. One needn't involve the other. Thus, if a man shifts his body's subtle energy, he can learn to climax without expelling his life essence. Tantra suggests that during lovemaking a man refrain from ejaculating at least one out of every four times. That's hardly giving up the Taj Mahal! But it builds energy, prevents depletion. The type of orgasm therefore becomes deliberate.

Many Tantric teachers, including Charles and Caroline Muir, propose a specific plan of action. Be patient. Go slowly. As with attempting any new task, allow yourself to acclimate. The technique I'm going to describe can be employed if you're happy with your sex life but want more, or if you're dissatisfied and desire better sex. It's intended to be repeated, polished, and customized to your own chemistry and needs. It's also simple—a very basic version of a sophisticated body of knowledge. Those of you who want to go further can consult the extensive literature on Tantra (see Selected Reading).

HAVING AN ORGASM WITHOUT EXTERNAL EJACULATION

1. *Strengthen Your PC Muscle*
The pubococcygeal (PC) muscle in both men and women supports sexual organs and contracts during orgasm (it's the muscle that stops urination when squeezed). To strengthen your PC muscle, try regularly clenching it while urinating, intentionally stopping the stream. You can also try clenching your PC muscle at times other than urination. Practice for at least twenty seconds a few times a day. For a man a well-toned PC muscle gives a strong erection and the control necessary to separate orgasm from ejaculation. During lovemaking try this: As the man approaches climax, both partners stop all movement. Simultaneously, the man keeps tightening and clenching his PC muscle, remaining still, centering himself.

2. *Control Your Breath*
As orgasm builds, breathing becomes rapid. As a man nears climax, he should slow down his breath, inhaling and exhaling more deeply. This will help focus sexual energy away from the genitals to other parts of the body. Some accomplished yogis can regulate orgasm by breath control alone. The man quiets his respirations; his partner breathes in sync with him, establishing an intimate union, both intuitive and physical.

3. *Bring Your Energy Upward*
The man begins to sense the current of orgasm rising in himself. He pictures it making a U-turn away from the genitals, streaming instead toward the upper body. While he's doing this his partner also visualizes his energy ascending. As bliss spreads the man may feel an overall erotic aliveness, every inch of him turned on—an acceleration toward what

some term "total body orgasm." Ecstasy everywhere, not merely genital. No need to worry, however, if such intensity isn't immediate or if an erection partially diminishes. With practice pleasure often increases in increments. Allow energy to mount and diffuse throughout the body.

My patients who've worked with this three-part exercise have enjoyed it immensely. It's full of surprises. Most mind-blowing for both partners: A man can actually experience orgasm without ejaculating. Precious sensations, illuminating to feel. Health-promoting. Don't ever think it's not possible. Undoing the narrow limits of what's been imposed widens the reach of sexual healing. The energy of orgasm must be distinguished from the form of its physical expression. Such alchemy of intimacy and eroticism offers a fresh context in which couples can relate.

As a psychiatrist introducing this method to Western lovers, naturally I've encountered resistance. One man, a sports newscaster whose wife wanted to investigate Tantra, voiced some common concerns. It's too much effort—why bother? What if I can't do it? I like sex as is. Holding back will ruin things. You expect me to believe I'll get the same satisfaction? These are all fair considerations. In my experience when male patients relax and experiment, many find this kind of orgasm extraordinary, even prefer it. But, of course, it's not either-or. The real proof is in the pleasure of the practice. Don't prejudge. Give it a try. Trust *your* experience. If you have reservations, consider the benefits of regularly alternating types of orgasms. Numerous men who have mastered the technique have reported

- Their erections last longer, are stronger
- They don't feel tired after sex
- They can make love more often
- By extending lovemaking, they can better please a partner
- The risk of pregnancy is reduced (but *don't* count on this for birth control!)
- Pleasure is heightened throughout the body
- A couple's intimacy deepens

There are also definite health advantages. Men who've supplemented their sexual practice with Tantric orgasm often appear more youthful, vital; their sexual endurance extends into old age. By consciously channeling sexuality, men can nurture themselves, distribute energy evenly, maintain physical balance. Men have the right to control their bodies; then orgasm becomes a choice, a form of empowerment. Such self-regulation is essential, especially for those with sexual dysfunction. For men with impotency or premature ejaculation, for example, Tantra can restore active control of their bodies. Tuning in to energy tunes men in to their physiology and how to optimize it. By intuiting nuances of their sexual rhythms, men can determine what's healthy or unhealthy, take positive steps to heal.

Whether you have a partner or achieve orgasm through self-pleasuring, you can learn to direct sexual energy flow. How you respond sexually is unique to you. There's no point in comparisons. Respect your sensual needs; track them as they evolve. Avoid compartmentalizing your power. You possess a brilliant erotic light within. You want to radiate it everywhere in your body, not just below the belt. You can extend your pleasure.

Step 4. Ask for Inner Guidance

The mind-body connection: It starts with a split-second flash of thoughts and feelings (sexual included). These signal your brain's electrical impulses, which in turn signal physical-chemical changes affecting your health. How does this translate when you make love? Follow the progression. Passion fills. You love. You love. You surrender. Energy magnifies. It bursts. Then releases. . . . All that power. Why let it dissipate? Let's see how it can be harnessed for healing.

You can have a say in how you use your sexual energy. The force you generate can be routed to specific parts of the body or aimed at troubling emotions. Here's the principle: First, during lovemaking focus on the pleasure you're experiencing. Notice where it's most heightened. For instance, your genitals? Heart? Second, request it be extended to a physical or emotional area that needs healing. Third, visualize and actually sense the pleasure traveling to a locale or permeating general feeling states (such as anxiety or depression). Doing this is especially therapeutic at the instant of orgasm, sharing bliss with parts of you that need it most.

My patient Sam, a retail grocer at fifty, suffered chronic neck pain from arthritis. Standard medication and physical therapy helped, but not completely. Sam and his wife had a fairly active sex life and were interested in how intuition could intervene physically during lovemaking. These were my instructions.

For Sam: Imagine a pathway running from your genitals to your neck. Get a sense of this point-to-point continuity. Concentrate on the linkage, but don't strain. Simultaneously, feel your sexual excitement as energy intensifying in the body. Then, with intuition, you can tune in to its subtleties and steer its course. During orgasm or before—your choice—make an inner request (a kind of prayer): "Please let pleasure go straight to the center of my pain." Then, without forcing, allow pleasure, fully amped, to shoot up the pathway you've mapped out to its target.

For Sam's wife: Be amorous. Love your husband madly. Gratify both of you as much as you can. The whole time, try to think of Sam's neck pain as the destination: you're sending passion to penetrate and relieve his discomfort.

This exercise is meant to be fun; you can even orchestrate your practice sessions. Sam and his wife opted for the Rolling Stones' "Midnight Rambler." Other patients have picked everything from Tony Bennett to Pachelbel's Canon in D to the Red Hot Chili Peppers. See what inspires you when traversing these uncharted zones. That we can intuitively direct sexual energy to reduce pain, illness, or angst is new for most of us. This newness makes the effort even more delectable. The sky's the limit, as Sam and his wife found. A special tenderness was born between them and is born between all partners who similarly share, one saying to the other: "My darling, I love you so much. I offer my life force to heal you." Inconceivable love, *mutually* nourishing. Love that welcomes the journey to your deepest, darkest pain. Sam and his wife utilized their eroticism for healing. Over time his neck pain decreased. Sam reported, "Judith, you've made a believer of me. Our passion went right to where I was suffering." There's a Zen saying, "My happiness is your happiness. There's no greater happiness in the world." This we can give to our beloved. Bliss, as healer, activates the immune system, improves health.

Beyond such visualization, fantasies can have therapeutic import. At the inception of modern science, Leonardo da Vinci made sketches of the penis. He drew two channels, one for seminal fluids, the other for *pneuma,* the substance of intuition, imagination. In men and women erotic fantasies can be emotionally and physically revitalizing. Who you fantasize about, and how, transmits intuitive messages to your body. My best sense is that positive, loving fantasies create good health; negative, destructive fantasies probably do not. So, if your intention is for sexuality to heal, choose health-promoting imagery and scenarios. Whether you fantasize with a partner or during self-pleasuring, your thoughts set the tone for cellular change.

Regarding your sex life, always double-check with your inner guidance. A part of you might be saying, Awesome! but your intuition is shouting, Hey, I don't like this. Cut it out! I was once consulted by a Manhattan call girl with a very elite clientele who, at age thirty, had been in the profession ten years. She told me, "Since I've been meditating, my intuition has taken off. I can pick up my clients' thoughts and feelings before they tell me. It's interfering with my work!" After encounters with certain men she'd become physically ill, nervous, drained, whereas previously she'd felt fine. I explained, "It sounds like you're empathically absorbing what your sexual partner's feeling. During physical contact there's an inevitable back-and-forth flow of intuitive impressions. When you're intimate with many people, you're exposing yourself to a range of energies, not all pleasant." That's a vulnerable, health-compromising position for any intuitive. This woman's rationale was "Sex is just business," yet her inner guidance was announcing, "It doesn't feel good to do this anymore." I urged her to listen.

Being on the same intuitive wavelength as your partner is a precondition of a nurturing relationship. Who he or she is, who you are together must feel emotionally and sexually harmonious. How can you know? Your inner guidance will tell you. When consulted it's outspoken about preferences and aversions. Even if you're swept away, remember to ask.

Step 5. Listen to Your Dreams

Dreams are passionate, and the object of their passion is you. If you sat the Maker of All Dreams down and asked, "What motivates you? What are you trying to tell us?" I suspect this genius of a being would respond: "I want your spirit to soar. I want you to be happy. I want you to heal." To do this, of course, requires an unflappable commitment to our evolution—not indulging our trepidations but appraising them so we can realize our priorities. The DreamMaker shoots straight from the hip, an unwavering truth-teller, hoping we will hear.

My patient Sue had been announced to me in a dream—within a week she called. I knew to pay special attention. Sue was fearless. A twenty-five-year-old fashion designer, she longed for a more authentic sexual style, eager to match the woman she was becoming. I first saw Sue in my waiting room: She was nearly six feet tall, a chic redhead, stick thin in short-shorts, and with abundant cleavage. She reminded me of a walking, talking Barbie doll. Sexy maybe, but more a caricature of what sexy is supposed to be. She told me, "I want to develop my intuition. I need you to teach me how to interpret dreams."

Sue had vivid dreams and could articulate them. While asleep she was kept busy with ongoing dream-time messages. One stood out:

> *I'm invisible, a guest attending my own funeral. I see myself in the coffin, quite dead. I nearly faint, but, even creepier, my hair and makeup are flawless and I'm seductively dressed in hot pink Versace! I wait. I watch. Months pass. With X-ray vision I observe my body decompose. Then I spot them: my silicone breast implants, intact! They're all that's left of who I was. Two very expensive, rock-hard synthetic mounds, emitting a toxic nuclear glow. I'm paralyzed. Is this how people will remember me? Is this all I am?*

Sue had received an eye-opening vision of her sexuality. I was happy for her. She needed to reconsider what constitutes femininity. Her dream didn't mince images: Trying to live up to some prefab version of a woman she thought men wanted had almost killed her. Sue's days of epitomizing the Material Girl were over. Her dream made sure of that—those death-defying implants were indelible. She said, "They reminded me of cockroaches, so indestructible they even survive the atom bomb." From then on Sue started seeking a sexuality that felt truer. Mirror, mirror on the wall, who's the fairest of them all? I am, Spirit says. Come find me. Sue did. Our first goal was to allow a palpable sense of spirit to emerge in her life. Then we sought to let it manifest in both her inner and outer beauty.

Feng shui is the sacred Chinese art of energy alignment. Though we often hear of it in relation to the locations of homes or furnishings, in my practice I apply it to people. Multifaceted, it sheds light on everything from cosmetic surgery to the structuring of sexual life. When an endeavor has an auspicious feng shui—an optimal conjunction of the spiritual, emotional, and physical—it will succeed. Otherwise, not. Dreams are feng shui masters; they will point you toward constructing an exuberant sexual self. Attend to their communications. Feel their vibes. Healing will ensue.

Gifts of power arrive when you are ready. Another patient, Martha, had such a dream. At fifty, with a harrowing divorce behind her, she made a wish: "I want to recontact my sexuality." Then she dreamed:

> *I'm at a party talking to a stunning woman dressed in fine silk. Excited, she hands me an evening purse, saying, "Treasure this gift." I open it. Horrified, I find two shiny black snakes, one male, one female. I know they're not poisonous, but still I'm repelled, can't bring myself to touch them. Crazily, at the same time I see that the snakes form a living necklace designed just for me, their jaws intended to join in front to form the clasp. A comfortable fit, easy to put on and off. Incredibly beautiful, too, as much as it threatens. I know if I wear the necklace my sexuality will return. But I'm frightened. I wait.*

Martha's profound dream did grant her wish, but its complexities required a fear-finding expedition in therapy. "What disturbs you most about snakes?" I asked. (I almost laughed. Who could pose this question without hearing Freud's Austrian accent?) Martha made a list: "They're slimy. They'll bite. They'll choke me. They'll change me. I'd be a completely different person if I let a snake get close. Besides, no one would love a snake lover." Where did these associations begin? Martha explained, "When I was seven, my older brother put a garter snake in my bed. I nearly died!" All right, I thought, but no doubt Martha's feelings went far deeper. I had much to consider. Historically, the snake archetype has rich meaning. In ancient Greece it adorned the healing staff of Asclepius. In Hinduism it's the mighty Kundalini energy. For Cleopatra the serpent was an attribute of the Goddess Isis, spewing venom at Egypt's enemies. Classic psychoanalysis, of course, deems snake phobia fear of the phallus.

For Martha, sexual healing entailed accepting in herself all qualities of the snake, including its raw primal force. Over time she dealt with various fears: male energy stifling her, being too sexy "at her age," and, most of all, a fear of her feminine power, of all she'd have to change to acknowledge her true self, what such freedom might allow. Still, given her hunger to recontact sexuality, what choice did Martha have but to move forward? It took work, but these days Martha considers the snake an ally. In meditation and dreams she savors a vision of herself wearing the necklace. At ease with the snakes, male and female, she intuitively enlists their wisdom. Foe has become friend, healer. Stimulated by her dream, Martha's sexuality has never been more present in her life. A year later I'm happy to report Martha is in a loving relationship. Such transformation can happen to you too.

We all have fears; some we share. A Sierra Club guide once told me, "In the wilderness what women are most afraid of are snakes. What men fear most are snapping turtles!" There you have it. His words made me smile. One man's observation: see if it applies. Eroticism and the natural world are related. In dreams when an animal, bird, reptile, or combination thereof (including dinosaurs, dragons, or even the herd of winged rhinoceroses a patient of mine saw) appears, the primal within is engaged. Dreaded or adored, these creatures contain clues to your sexual healing.

Intuition invisibly joins us. You dream for me. I dream for you. As a collective we all dream together. When our sexuality is confident and centered, everyone wins, including future generations. The powers that be delight in our achievements. Dreams patch us into their great gladness, permit recognition of our full selves. Recently I dreamed:

I'm awaiting the start of a performance at the Hollywood Bowl. A warm summer evening, crescent moon in the east. The orchestra begins Beethoven's Ninth, the Ode to Joy. The choir, a thousand voices singing, fills the outdoor amphitheater. I look around, see women of all ages, all shapes, as far as the eye can see. Faster. Louder. Faster. Louder. The music peaks, exhilarating. Suddenly, as if on cue, each woman in concert gives birth—to a gorgeous cat! What euphoria! The place goes wild. Everyone applauds furiously.

I awoke as if secure in a new refuge, proud of being a woman. My dream felt epic in scale, granting an understanding that a sensual, feline femininity has taken and is taking form in me. During my forties something special is happening: Sexuality has ripened as spirituality and intuition mature. I feel blessed to sense a distance between myself now and the sexual poverty of my earlier years. This dream also left an awareness of being fecund, fertile. Further, I felt a shared abundance with those around me; together we were prolific, fruitful, life-giving. My dream, then, wasn't just about me. It was about all women, all men. In our fervent yearning to awaken, we are birthing ourselves and each other.

SEXUAL HEALING coheres our many parts. A sacred marriage takes place, a union of the erotic and the Transcendent, heaven and the everyday world. Jung declared it an "earthing of the spirit" and a "spiritualization of the earth." As a result, marriage is inevitable. Perhaps not what you pictured, though surely more far-reaching than you dreamed. The internalized, sensual communion of the masculine, the feminine, and the divine—all this you can bring to a partner or draw on to sustain yourself. The sacred marriage is an event within you, an alliance that prepares you to lead ordinary life in an extraordinary way.

Such a perspective doesn't guarantee your relationships will be perfect. What you can depend on, however, is that you'll live every day with passion. For me, this extends to all that I do. Even the smallest actions are deliciously sensual. I crave to make the most of each moment, feel cheated if I miss out on anything. From washing vegetables to making love, I want to be utterly present. I hope you do too.

Intuition brings you home to your sexuality. At the end of the day, it's imperative to feel good about the person you've become, confident you haven't left a single stone unturned in actualizing your soul. All over the country, with group after group, in city after city, I see both sexes experiencing a renaissance of ideals: poetry, intuition, and spirit are increasingly reconciled with sexual love. Microlayers of haze are lifting. You can dream your awakening again and again. I keep relearning that this process is beyond time lines. It's simple: When you're ready, change occurs. Such growth has no beginning, no end. Rather it's an infinite cycle of becoming. So, as you continue along your journey, think of me. And I'll think of you. Let's travel home together.

Afterword

Total Healing

After the final no there comes a yes. And on that yes,
the future world depends.
—Wallace Stevens

*W*e must ask ourselves, What do we most dearly wish for during our short stay on earth? Embracing the poet Wallace Stevens's words, what is our yes, our deepest affirmation? To affirm means to assert that something *is,* or is true. Apathy deadens. When it comes to healing, we have to take a stand. The well-being—even survival—of our bodies, families, communities, the planet depends on it.

Total healing is a compassionate life agenda. It compels us to let love transfuse who we are, all we do. My daily affirmation is, "I commit myself to a life of love. I'll do everything in my power to achieve it." Throughout the book I've emphasized physical, emotional, and sexual wellness, the basic trinity of self-transformation. Total healing, however, encompasses personal and spiritual as well as global change. A coming into light. *Visibilis* counters *invisibilis.* The impulse to heal is kindled in each individual, then spreads to illuminate social and political systems. As we become whole, the larger world will too.

Intuition is the future. Much of what we currently believe is already being left behind. My prediction: In fifty years medicine will have graduated to a holistic art and science; intuition, spirit, and technology will be seamlessly integrated. What seems cutting-edge, even heresy, today will have become standard clinical practice. I'd give anything to eavesdrop on a conversation among physicians of the future. I can imagine them scratching their heads, wondering, What was that alternative medicine controversy all about? Retrospective wisdom, but why wait for it?

With your health or a loved one's, advocate for—no, insist on—enlightened medical care now.

Total healing inevitably extends to the earth. Our home. The fate of humans, of all species, is contingent on preserving nature's ecosystems. In the intuitive subconscious, when forests are ravaged, we bleed; when oceans are poisoned, our bodies weep. I once dreamed I was orbiting earth in a space module with a group of scientists. One of them advised, "Look down." Awed, I gazed at the lush planet thousands of miles below. I saw vast continents, silken cloud covers, azure oceans. But, strangely, the globe was also emitting a foreboding amber glow. Sickened, I understood. I was witnessing the aftermath of an apocalypse. Our earth, contaminated, dead. I was overcome by a silent wail of loss. A disembodied vertigo as this primordial umbilical cord was severed. My dream's doomsday scenario, I believe, was presenting not fact but warning. Never forget: If the earth thrives, we thrive; if she withers, we will cease to be.

Life, approached as prayer, is a healing invocation for a positive future. To revere the earth, your body, the tiniest ant in a field, personal and collective priorities must be defined. The Haggadah maintains that prayer is meaningless "unless it is subversive," unless it challenges "callousness, hatred, opportunism, falsehoods. True prayer is revolutionary: it seeks to overthrow forces that . . . destroy the promise, the hope, the vision." In this spirit, together, let's offer a prayer for the world.

Total healing presumes that change, small or large, is attainable where the heart is true. In the perspective I'm suggesting, no one is precluded from the possibility of renewal. Intuition bestows new beginnings; it's a knowledge, unicorn-old, with a restorative grace so surprising it cannot be calculated. Trust what life gives. Strenuous or joyful, every interaction is about building soul. Stay focused on the process. Simply engaging in the effort is a job well done.

I adore love letters, giving and getting. So I dedicate this book as my love letter to you. The heart has no boundaries. It is the place from which real power flows. My wish for you is to experience the truth of this, then share it with others. Listening to intuition makes loving irresistible. You just can't help yourself. It's good karma to spread love around. Do it. Again. And again. You'll receive a life of unimaginable wonder.

SELECTED READING

Intuition and Healing

Brugh, Joy. *Joy's Way: A Map for the Transformational Journey.* Los Angeles: Jeremy Tarcher, 1979.
  A classic text by a physician and healer on energy healing and the chakra system, including the best illustrations of the chakras I've seen.

Dossey, Larry. *Reinventing Medicine: Beyond Mind-Body to a New Era of Healing.* San Francisco: HarperCollins, 1999.
  A groundbreaking, scientifically documented look at intuition and nonlocal (distant) healing.

Emery, Marcia. *The Intuitive Healer: Accessing Your Inner Physician.* New York: St. Martin's Press, 1999.
  A psychologist's practical handbook on developing intuition filled with easy-to-understand exercises.

Myss, Caroline. *Anatomy of the Spirit: The Seven Stages of Power and Healing.* New York: Random House, 1997.
  A clear overview of the chakra system and energy medicine, written by a gifted medical intuitive.

Naparstek, Belleruth. *Your Sixth Sense: Activating Your Psychic Potential.* San Francisco: Harper San Francisco, 1997.
  A straightforward, loving guide to developing intuition plus a penetrating study of intuitives.

Ornish, Dean. *Love and Survival: Eight Pathways to Intimacy and Health.* New York: HarperCollins, 1999.
  A presentation of the medical basis for the healing power of intimacy.

Radin, Dean. *The Conscious Universe: The Scientific Truth of Psychic Phenomena.* San Francisco: Harper San Francisco, 1997.
  An encyclopedia of psychic research by a top researcher in parapsychology.

Schultz, Mona Lisa. *Awakening Intuition: Using Your Mind-Body Network for Insight and Healing.* New York: Harmony Books, 1998.

The autobiography of a neuroscientist and medical intuitive with an emphasis on how intuition relates to physiology.

Targ, Russell, and Jane Katra. *Miracles of Mind: Exploring Nonlocal Consciousness and Spiritual Healing.* New World Library, 1998.

A fascinating look at remote viewing and nonlocal healing from the unique perspective of a pioneering psychic researcher and a healer.

Your Anatomy

Gray, Henry. *Gray's Anatomy.* Philadelphia: Running Press, 1978.

The classic medical text detailing human anatomy.

Parker, Steve. *Brain Surgery for Beginners: A Scalpel Free Guide to Your Insides.* Highland Park, NJ: Mill Brook Press, 1993.

A primer on the brain for both children and adults with large print, colorful illustrations, and simple explanations.

Stark, Fred. *Start Exploring Gray's Anatomy: A Fact-Filled Coloring Book.* Philadelphia: Running Press, 1991.

A delightful coloring book that teaches how to visualize the body's structure.

Steinman, Louise. *The Knowing Body: The Artist as Storyteller in Contemporary Performance.* Berkeley: North Atlantic Books, 1986.

A compelling description of the power of the body in performance art.

Dreams

Delaney, Gayle. *Sensual Dreaming: How to Understand and Interpret the Erotic Content of Your Dreams.* New York: Fawcett Books, 1995.

A specific exploration of erotic dreams and how to interpret them.

Freud, Sigmund. *Interpretation of Dreams.* New York: Avon Books, 1983.

A seminal text on Freud's theory of dreams and their meaning.

Garfield, Patricia. *Creative Dreaming: Plan and Control Your Dreams to Develop Creativity, Overcome Fears, Solve Problems, and Create a Better Self.* New York: Fireside, 1995.

A cross-cultural look at the role of dreams in everyday life.

Jung, C. G. *Man and His Symbols.* New York: Laurel Leaf, 1997.

A must-read for everyone wanting to learn basic dream interpretation.

——*Memories, Dreams, Reflections.* New York: Vintage Books, 1989.

Jung's visionary autobiography focusing on his dreams, premonitions, and rich inner world.

Death and Dying

Blackman, Sushila. *Graceful Exits: How Great Beings Die.* New York: Weatherhill, 1997.

Inspirational stories of how Hindu, Tibetan, and other Buddhist masters confronted their own deaths.

Brinkley, Dannion. *Saved by the Light.* New York: HarperCollins, 1994.

A courageous man's account of a near-death experience.

Hoffmann, Yoel. *Japanese Death Poems: Written by Zen Monks and Haiku Poets on the Verge of Death.* Boston: Charles E. Tuttle, 1986.

An exquisite compilation of poems written by monks and poets describing the final moments of their lives.

Kübler-Ross, Elisabeth. *On Death and Dying*. New York: Collier Books, 1997.
A must-read demystification and approach to death and dying written by a
path forging physician.

Levine, Stephen. *Who Dies? An Investigation of Conscious Living and Conscious Dying*.
New York: Anchor Press, 1982.
My Bible in compassionately understanding the death and dying process,
how to deal with physical pain, and, most of all, how to live fully.

————. *A Year to Live: How to Live This Year As If It Were Your Last*. New York: Bell
Tower, 1997.
A yearlong meditation on how to make the most of every moment.

Rinpoche, Sogyal. *The Tibetan Book of Living and Dying*. San Francisco: Harper San
Francisco, 1992.
A stunning guide to the Tibetan approach to life and death.

Sexuality

Anand, Margo. *The Art of Sexual Ecstasy*. New York: Jeremy Tarcher, 1989.
A practical step-by-step introduction to Tantra with useful diagrams and exercises.

Angier, Natalie. *Woman: An Intimate Geography*. New York: Houghton Mifflin, 1999.
An exploration of female sexuality from orgasms to menopause by the
Pulitzer Prize–winning *New York Times* biology writer.

Borysenko, Joan. *A Woman's Book of Life: The Biology, Psychology, and Spirituality of
the Feminine Life Cycle*. New York: Riverhead Books, 1996.
An accessible, scientifically grounded, and spiritual description of the female
life cycle.

Dunas, Felice, with Phillip Goldberg. *Passion Play: Ancient Secrets for a Lifetime of
Health and Happiness Through Sensational Sex*. New York: Riverhead Books,
1998.
Sexual healing from a Chinese medical practitioner's point of view.

Moore, Thomas. *The Soul of Sex: Cultivating Life as an Act of Love*. New York:
HarperCollins, 1999.
A poetic, articulate look at how the soulfulness of sexuality can extend to all
of life.

Muir, Charles, and Caroline Muir. *Tantra: The Art of Conscious Loving*. San Francisco: Mercury House, 1989.
An easily understandable summary of Tantra by two of the finest teachers in
the field.

Watson, Cynthia Mervis. *Love Potions: A Guide to Aphrodisiacs and Sexual Pleasures*.
New York: Jeremy Tarcher, 1993.
A holistic guide to enhancing sexuality from herbs to homeopathy written by
a physician.

RESOURCES

Referrals, Training, and Information

American Holistic Medical Association
6728 Old McLean Village Drive
McLean, VA 22101
703–556–9728
www.holisticmedicine.org

American Holistic Nurses Association
2733 Lakin Drive
Flagstaff, AZ 86004
800–278AHNA
www.ahna.org

Barbara Brennan School of Healing
P.O. Box 2005
East Hampton, NY 11937
800–924–2564
www.barbarabrennan.com

Colorado Center for Healing Touch
12477 West Cedar Drive, Suite 206
Lakewood, CO 80228
303–989–0581
www.healingtouch.net

National Institutes of Health
Office of Alternative Medicine
P.O. Box 8218
Silver Spring, MD 20907–8218
888–644–6226
http://altmed.od.nih.gov

Nurse Healers Professionals Associates, Inc.
11250 Roger Bacon Road, Suite 8
Reston, VA 20190–5202
703–234–4149
www.therapeutic-touch.org

Spiritual Emergence Network
California Institute of Integral Studies
1453 Mission Street
San Francisco, CA 94103
415–648–2610
sen@cruzio.com

Educational Centers

Esalen Institute
Big Sur, CA 93920
408–667–3000

Institute of Noetic Sciences
475 Gate 5 Road, Suite 300
Sausalito, CA 94965
415–331–5650

Institute of Transpersonal Psychology
744 San Antonio Road
Palo Alto, CA 94303
650–493–4430
www.itp.edu

International Society for the Study of Subtle Energies and Energy
    Medicine (ISSSEEM)
11005 Ralston Road
Arvada, Colorado 80004
303–425–4625

Intuition Network
369-B Third Street, Mailbox 161
San Rafael, CA 94901–3581
www.intuition.org

Kripalu Center for Yoga and Health
P.O. Box 793
Lenox, MA 01240
413–448–3400
www.kripalu.org

Omega Institute for Holistic Studies
260 Lake Drive
Rhinebeck, New York 12572–3212
800–944–1001
www.omega-inst.org

Prayer Lines

Association for Research and Enlightenment
215 Sixty-seventh Street
Virginia Beach, VA 23451
757–428–3588

Guideposts Magazine
39 Seminary Hill Road
Carmel, New York 10512
800–204–3772

Science of Mind World Ministry of Prayer
3251 West Sixth Street
Los Angeles, CA 90020–5096
800–421–9600
213–385–0209

Silent Unity
Unity Village, MO 64065–0001
800–669–7729
816–969–2026 (Spanish speaking)

Alternative Medicine Programs

(For an extended list, contact the National Institutes of Health, Office of Alternative Medicine.)

Columbia-Presbyterian Medical Center
Department of Alternative Medicine
622 West 168th Street
New York, NY 10032
212–305–9628
www.complementarycare.org

Harvard Medical Center
Beth Israel–Deaconess Hospital
330 Brookline Avenue
Boston, MA 02215
617–632–7770
www.compmed.caregroup.harvard.edu

Stanford University Medical School
Complementary and Alternative Medicine Program
730 Welch Road, Suite B
Palo Alto, CA 94304
650–723–8628
http://scrdp.stanford.edu/camps.html

University of Minnesota
Academic Health Center
Center for Spirituality and Healing
Box 505
420 Delaware Street, SE
Minneapolis, MN 55455
612–624–9459
www.csh.umn.edu

INDEX

"Abnormal" behavior, 178
Abuse: in relationships, 213, 216; and sexual histories, 283, 285, 292–93, 294–95, 300; substance, 179–80, 192, 198, 201
Adversity: toughing out, 25
Aging, 138, 247, 269
AIDS, 95–96, 125
Aikido, 53
Akhmatova, Anna, 241
Alcoholism, 192, 198, 201
Alliance for Women, 213
Alternative medicine, 49, 55, 67
American Medical Association, 49
Ancestors, 122, 223–24, 247, 284–85
Anima, 151
Archetypes, 69, 151, 285, 302, 321–22
Asclepius, 92–93, 94, 321
Asking for inner guidance: and acting on guidance, 256–57; and centering, 168–72; and darkness, 192–96; and death, 116–19; and doctor-patient relationship, 61–64; and emotions, 143–47; and finding and enhancing intuition, 10–11; and guides, 169–70; and health, 35–37; and how to ask, 36–37; and illness, 88–92; and

intimacy, 275–77; and relationships, 220–24; and selecting health care practitioners, 61–64; and sexual energy, 317–19; and sexual histories, 295–99; and sexuality, 254–57; and silence, 143–44. *See also* Meditation; Remote viewing
Attractions, 212–13, 255, 259, 267–70, 273
Aura, 29, 59
Auschwitz prison camp (Poland), 176–77
Authors: death of, 109

Barasch, Marc, 93–94
Beagle, Peter, 211
Bearing Witness Retreats, 176–77
Beattie, Melody, 167
Beauty, 17, 74, 133–34, 247, 250–51, 266, 268, 270
Being in body: and centering and protection, 160–63; and darkness, 181–87, 195; and death, 110–13; and doctor-patient relationship, 56–59; and emotions, 136–38; and erotic zones, 309–13; and finding and enhancing intuition, 10; and

Being in body (*cont'd*)
health, 24–29; and illness, 79–84; and intimacy, 266–70; and puberty, 286–89; and relationships, 211–15; and sexual attraction, 212–13; and sexual histories, 286–89; and sexuality, 248–51; and suicide, 195

Beliefs: and darkness, 190; and dreams, 260; empowering, 132–35; functions of, 9; and health, 21–24, 42–43; of health care practitioner, 51; and illness, 77; impact of, 77; negative, 72–74; for new sexuality, 246–47; of parents, 23–24; positive, 22, 23, 72–73, 74–77; power of, 22, 190; that drain power, 157–60. *See also* Noticing beliefs

Benson, Herbert, 187

Berlin, Germany, 13–14

Bertolucci, Bernardo, 306

Beth Israel Medical School (New York), 55

Birth: and death, 16, 237

Biziou, Barbara, 287

Body: acting out life's traumas in, 76–78; attitudes about, 27, 57–58, 74; awareness of, 26–28, 181; beliefs about, 74; change in, 138; chemistry of, 73, 181–84, 194, 268–69; and compatibility of bodies, 289; and death, 105–6, 110–13; and doctor-patient relationship, 58–59; doctor's attitudes about, 58–59; as energy, 313; and environment, 137; and general guide to body-based intuitions, 211–12; imbalances in, 31–34, 181–84, 194; internal pictures of, 83–84; messages/ signals from, 25, 26, 31–32, 34–35, 79, 136, 137, 162, 211, 212, 213, 215; and mind connection, 84, 106, 184, 307, 317–19; organs of, 27–28; seeing, 250; self-care of, 26–27; and self-love, 29; sensitivity to, 186; sensuousness of, 10; and

soul, 214; and spirit, 184; as temporal, 106; trusting, 59; visualizing of, 30. *See also* Being in body; Body language; Sensing body's subtle energy

Body language, 31, 54, 139

Body scanning, 32

Bradley, Marion Zimmer, 251

Brown, Denise, 213

Brown University, 42

Buddhism, 29, 80–81, 88, 103, 104, 170, 176, 188, 255, 270. *See also* Zen Buddhism

Bukowski, Charles, 180

Byrd, Randolph, 92

Cameron, Julia, 22

Canada: workshop meditation in, 201–2

Castaneda, Carlos, 109

Casual sex, 247, 307

"Cellular memories," 99–100, 213–14

Cemeteries, 108

Censorship, 64, 258

Centering: and asking for inner guidance, 168–72; and being in body, 160–63; and danger, 160–61, 173–74, 175; and darkness, 190, 195; and fear, 167–68, 173, 174; and giving, 162, 167, 168; and gunman story, 155; importance of, 155–56; and listening to dreams, 172–75; meaning of, 156; and noticing beliefs, 156–60; questions for reflection about, 160; and relationships, 212; and sensing body's subtle energy, 163–68; and sexuality, 254, 255; techniques for, 161–63, 190; and war and peace, 174–75; when attracted to someone, 255

Chakras: and darkness, 188; definition/meaning of, 29, 85; feeling of, 30; functions of, 30; and health, 29–30; and heart, 85–88, 188; imbalances in, 85; and intimacy, 270–75; location of, 271;

overview about, 29–30, 270–71; and reading energy, 139; and relationships, 236; and sensing body's subtle energy, 10, 251–52, 253; and sexual histories, 290, 292; and sexuality, 251–52, 253; symbols of, 85

Chi (energy), 29, 82, 247

Childbirth, 137–38, 171, 302

China: centering and protection in lore of, 175; and feng shui, 320–21; gods and goddesses in, 170

Chinese medicine, 29, 55, 82, 87, 181

Chumash medicine woman: story of, 174

Codependency, 167

Comas, 191–92

Commitment, 204, 206, 208, 258

Communication, 201, 264–65. See also Nonverbal interactions

Compartmentalization, 244

Compassion: for body, 81; and centering, 159–60, 168; and darkness, 179, 182, 193, 197, 201; and death, 106, 121, 125; development of, 130; and doctor-patient relationship, 57; and dreams, 150; and emotions, 130, 132, 138, 144, 150; and illness, 71, 75, 80–81, 82, 88, 91; and relationships, 222–23, 225, 229, 231, 234; self-, 15, 82, 102, 135, 150; and sexual histories, 283–84, 302; and total healing, 324

Conception, 248–49

Connectedness, 7, 70, 214, 244

Contagion, 88, 105

Core essence, 156–60

Credentials: medical, 67

Cyclops, 69, 151, 285, 302

Danbury (Connecticut) Federal Prison: Orloff presentation at, 3–7

Danger, 160–61, 173–74, 175, 227

Dark matter, 177–78

Darkness: and asking for inner guidance, 192–96; and being in body, 181–87; and beliefs, 177–81, 190; and centering, 190, 195; and chemical imbalances, 181–84; and energy, 181; examples of, 177; finding light in, 176–202; and listening to dreams, 196–202; and medications, 181–87, 194; and protection, 193; questions for reflection about, 180–81; and sensing body's subtle energy, 187–92; and spirit/spirituality, 179–80, 182, 184, 188, 194, 196. See also Illness

Dartmouth-Hitchcock Medical Center, 76

Death: and asking for inner guidance, 116–19; and assisting dying, 119–20, 122–23; of authors, 109; and beauty, 17; and birth, 16, 237; and body, 105–6, 110–13; and bonding with ancestors, 122; as contagious, 105; cultural views of, 103–4; denial of, 103; doctors' dread of, 102–3; dreams about, 108, 120–23; as end, 106–7; and expectations, 115; as failure, 102–3; fear of, 101, 102, 103, 107, 110, 112, 118, 119, 173, 237; feel of, 114; and freedom, 101; head-on encounter with, 102; as healer and teacher, 101–25; and health care practitioners, 102–3, 112; and illness, 104–5; and intellect, 104, 124; legal definition of physical, 110; and letting go, 114–15, 232–39; and love, 112, 114, 119, 120, 124, 125; and messages from loved ones, 119, 121–22; as mirror of life, 123; multidimensional nature of, 116–18; myths about, 104–7; and near-death experience, 118–19; and noticing beliefs, 103–10; as part of life, 108–9; premonitions of, 119, 120–21; preparation for, 17; questions for reflection about,

Death (*cont'd*)
110; and relationships with loved
ones, 223–24; and remote viewing,
116–18, 223–24; and sensing
body's subtle energy, 113–16; and
sleep, 173; and spirit/spirituality,
106, 111, 112, 125; themes of,
119–23; and a year to live, 123–24.
See also Grief

Déjà vu, 213–14

Dementia, 235

Denial: of body's warning signals, 26,
79; of death, 103

Dependency: chemical, 179–80; co-,
167. *See also* Abuse

Depression, 137, 140–41, 181,
182–83, 186–87, 195, 196, 199,
201, 293

Detachment, 213, 255

Devils: story about, 129

*Diagnostic and Statistical Manual of
Mental Disorders (DSM-IV)*, 178,
179, 194

Diet: and centering, 161–62

Dionysius myth, 245

Divine being, 265

Doctor-patient relationship: and
asking for inner guidance, 61–64;
and being in body, 56–59; and
beliefs of practitioner, 51; and
doctor's attitudes about body,
58–59; feedback in, 57; and
listening to dreams, 64–68; and
love, 54; and medications, 185–87;
and noticing beliefs, 50–56; as
partnership, 46–47; and questions
for reflection, 56; and respect for
patient, 68; role models for, 44–45;
and sensing body's subtle energy,
59–61; and spirituality, 55–56

Domestic violence, 213

Dossey, Larry, 51, 67

Dreams: accuracy of, 94; asking
questions of, 64, 94, 198–99, 227,
277–78; "bad," 148; belief in, 153,
260; choosing healers by, 64–65;
clues about intuitive information

in, 39–40; context and quality of,
259; and darkness, 197; and
death, 108, 120–23; and emotions,
147–54; and fear, 150; as form of
intuition, 11; and freedom, 258,
260; healing nature of, 199–200;
and illness, 77, 93–94; and
insecurities, 148; and intellect, 11;
interpretation of, 39, 95, 279;
language of, 198; and letting go of
relationships, 234; messages in,
197, 198, 228, 258; not listening
to, 259; and perceptions, 150;
predictive nature of, 148, 197–98,
258; as premonitions, 95, 96–97,
151–52, 197, 214, 227, 301; and
protection, 173–74; with
psychological themes, 147–48;
recording of, 40, 41, 94, 95, 121,
199, 227, 258, 259, 277;
recurring/repetitive, 150, 198;
relationship with, 40, 64, 94–95,
200; and relationships, 203, 214,
224–29, 234; remembering, 40–41,
94; rules for, 40; separating
content from reactions to, 40; and
sexual attraction, 259; and
sexuality, 248; symbols in, 94–95,
197–98; telling others about,
97–98; themes in, 198; therapeutic
impact of, 99; and transitional
stage between waking and sleep,
227–28. *See also* Listening to
dreams; Nightmares

Egyptian culture/mythology, 74, 106,
278

Einstein, Albert, 42, 61

Emotions: and asking for inner
guidance, 143–47; and being in
body, 136–38; in conflict, 130,
131; and dreams, 147–54; and
emotional wholeness, 200–201;
expressing, 75; facing, 131; fear
of, 133–34; fluctuations in,
142–43; going with/surrendering
to, 134–35; and noticing beliefs,

131–35; out of control, 181–87; periodic housecleaning of, 136; questions for reflection about, 135; and reading energy, 138–40; role in healing of, 129–30; and sensing body's subtle energy, 138–43; sharing of, 131; and spirituality, 130, 138, 153–54; strata of, 140–41; and timetable for healing, 134. *See also* Darkness; Relationships; *specific emotion*

Empathy, 139, 159–60, 163–68, 201, 276, 305

Energy: avoiding other people's, 165–67; balancing of, 31–34, 87; body as, 313; and centering, 163–68; continuity of, 116; and darkness, 181; effects of, 142–43; in everyday life, 31; functions of, 141; as gift, 85; and health, 29–35; identification of, 10; of "inanimate" objects, 276–77; and intimacy, 276–77, 278; language of, 115; manifestations of, 10, 273; medical science's lack of understanding of, 32; of medications, 184; of organs of body, 27; of other people, 31, 53–54, 59–60, 156, 163–68; projection of, 190; protection from people who drain, 156; reading, 138–40; and relationships, 236; sensing emotional, 140; and sexual histories, 292, 295; and sexuality, 244, 247, 260, 306; sharing of, 86–87; and symptoms of illness, 87–88; tactics for deflecting negative, 53–54; as transcending language, 60; and warning signals from body, 31–32. *See also* Sensing body's subtle energy; Sexual energy; *type of energy, e.g.* Chi

Energy medicine, 29, 30–31

Energy vampires, 165

Energy work, 77, 98, 188–89, 292

Environment: and body, 137; for sleep, 172–73

Erotic zones, 309–13

Eroticism. *See* Intimacy; Organism

Etcoff, Nancy, 267

Evolution, 69, 177, 267, 280–81, 288, 319–20

Expectations, 15–17, 57, 115

Faith: and centering, 171; and darkness, 184; and death, 106, 112, 125; of doctor, 50; and doctor-patient relationship, 62; and emotions, 143, 147, 153; and fear, 73; and illness, 76; and relationships, 207, 217; in therapy, 187

Faith and Medicine (medical school course), 42

Family ritual: joy of, 287

Fantasies, 298–99, 318–19

Fear: and centering, 167–68, 173, 174; of death, 101, 102, 103, 107, 110, 112, 118, 119, 173, 237; and dreams, 150; of emotions, 133–34; and empathy, 167–68; and faith, 73; intuition as antidote to, 13; of male anatomy, 289; naming of, 107; noticing, 24; and relationships, 208, 212, 213, 227; releasing, 24; and sexual energy, 321–22

Feelings: learning to express, 16–17

Feminine, 207–8, 249, 280–81, 285, 320, 321, 322. *See also* Yin and yang

Feng shui, 320–21

Final good-byes, 232–39

First sexual encounter, 282–83

First time making love, 289–91

Five steps: overview of, 3–9. *See also specific step*

Flag story, 230–31

Forest Lawn cemetery (Los Angeles), 108, 109

Forgiveness, 229–31

Freedom, 6–7, 101, 177, 258, 260, 303, 313

Freud, Sigmund, 95, 145, 247, 279, 284, 287, 288, 309, 321

Freudians, 121, 181
Funerals, 238

G-spot, 309–11
Garfield, Patricia, 39
Gender preference, 67
Generational patterns: and sexual
    histories, 284–85
Genius, 8
Germany: Orloff's tour of, 143
Giving, 162, 167, 168, 201, 305
Glassman, Roshi Bernard, 177
God, 229, 244, 265
Goddess quilt, 285
Goddesses (spiritual women's circle),
    275
Grafenberg, Ernst, 309
Great Healer story, 71
Greece/Greek, 92, 93, 283
Grief, 107–8, 115, 201, 238
Grof, Stanislav, 194
Guardian angels, 169
Guides: contacting, 169–70
Gunman story, 155
Gut feelings: as form of intuition, 11

Hadi (healer), 59–60
Happiness, 129–30, 318
Happy family story, 175
Harvard Medical School, 55
Hawking, Stephen, 229
Healers: dreams for choosing, 64–65.
    See also Health care practitioners
Healing: attitudes toward, 200; core
    elements of, 99; formula for, 130;
    as from inside out, 14; and health,
    15; and love, 130, 307; origins of,
    69–70; and sexuality, 306; and
    spirituality, 306; timetable for, 134;
    total, 324–25; unsuspected ways
    of, 15–17
Health: and asking for inner
    guidance, 35–37; attitudes as
    shapers of, 23; and being in body,
    24–29; and beliefs, 21–24, 42–43;
    and healing, 15; inventory of, 26;
    and listening to dreams, 37–41;

questions for reflection about, 26;
    and self-care, 26–27; and sensing
    body's subtle energy, 29–35; and
    sensing and heeding warning
    signs, 7–8; and spirituality, 42–43;
    and what is intuitive healing, 7–8
Health care practitioners: alternative,
    49; beliefs of, 51; confronting
    difficult, 52–54; credentials of, 67;
    and death, 102–3, 112; faith of, 50;
    interviewing of, 49; qualities to
    avoid in, 48; qualities to look for
    in, 47–48; referrals for, 49; as role
    models, 59, 66, 68, 304; selecting,
    46, 47–68, 189; and sexual issues,
    304–5; style of, 56–57; tactics for
    dealing with, 53–54; touch of, 57,
    59–60; training of, 67, 178–79, 180.
    See also Doctor-patient relationship
Health maintenance organizations
    (HMOs), 45–46, 48, 49, 54–55, 66
Heart: broken, 217; and centering,
    175; as chakra, 85–88, 188; and
    darkness, 177; and death, 106,
    110; and emotions, 135; as energy
    center, 85–88; and finding and
    enhancing intuition, 12–13; illness
    as call for, 72; medicine as calling
    of, 46; meditation as opening,
    85–86; and relationships, 217; and
    sexual energy, 305; and sexuality,
    253–54; as stabilizer, 12–13
Heaven: picturing, 171–72
Heinlein, Robert, 247
Heroes: need for new medical, 66–67
Hexing, medical, 51
Hillman, James, 137–38
Hinduism, 29, 260–61, 270–75, 310,
    321
Hippocrates, 25, 59, 70
Hoffmann, Yoel, 115
Humor, sense of, 8, 121
Hypnagogic state, 41

I Ching, 153–54, 174, 207
Icarus myth, 134
Idealization, 260

Iglulic Eskimos, 27
Illness: acute, 71; and asking for inner guidance, 88–92; and being in body, 79–84; and beliefs, 23–24, 71–79; as call for heart, 72; chronic, 71, 80–81; and death, 104–5; deciding on best way to treat, 89; detecting and reversing, 20–21; and dreams, 77, 93–94; explanations of, 31, 77–78, 87–88; expressing emotions about, 75; factors contributing to, 77; as failure, 15; as form of healing, 100; harmonizing with, 81–82; as initiation by fire, 70–71; and integration, 70; and listening to dreams, 92–100; mystery of, 78; and natural world, 71–72, 77–78; as not failure, 100; personas of, 69; questions for reflection about, 72; and reliability of intuitions, 89–90; and sensing body's subtle energy, 84–88; and sexual energy, 305, 318; and spirit/spirituality, 76, 77, 184; as teacher, 21. *See also* Darkness
Illusion, 14
Immune system, 50, 88, 100, 306
India. *See* Hinduism
Infants: character in, 138
Innocence, 154
Insomnia, 173
Intellect, 8, 10, 11, 71, 104, 124
Intelligence gathering, 61
Intimacy: and asking for guidance, 275–77; and balancing masculine and feminine aspects, 280–81; and being in body, 266–270; and building blocks for conscious sexuality, 264; and common values, 264; and communication, 264–65; and energy, 276–77, 278; and eroticism, 307–8; and listening to dreams, 277–81; and noticing beliefs, 263–66; and passion, 263, 264–65, 273, 279, 296, 297; potential versus reality

in, 297–98; questions for reflection about, 266; and sensing body's subtle energy, 270–75; and sexual attractiveness, 267–70, 273; and sexual energy, 270–75, 307, 316; and shame, 265–66; and soul, 298; and spirit/spirituality, 263, 264, 265, 270, 272, 273–74, 281; and synchronicities, 276–77; ways for improving, 296–99
Intuition: as blessing, 13; forms of, 11–12, 193; honoring of, 207; integrity of, 214; and intuitive styles, 12; and life-changes, 9; questions for reflection about, 12; reliability of, 89–90; spirit for approaching, 12; steps for finding or enhancing, 9–11; that doesn't make apparent sense, 91–92; trusting of, 20, 102, 132
Intuitive healing: what is, 3–17

Japan: burial in, 108; commuter in, 107; returning flag to, 230–31
Johns Hopkins University, 42
Johnson, Virginia, 309
Journal of Alternative Therapies, 67
Journal of the American Medical Association (JAMA), 55, 189–90
Journals: importance of, 12; looking back at, 259; recording dreams in, 40, 41, 94, 95, 121, 258, 259, 277
Joy, Brugh, 287
Jung, Carl, 39, 94, 151, 219, 323

Kauai, Hawaii: spirituality workshop on, 273–74
"Knowings," 63
Kuan Yin (Chinese goddess), 170, 285
Kundalini (sexuality), 260–61, 290, 321

Laênnec, Renè, 83
The Last Unicorn (Beagle), 211
Le Guin, Ursula, 150
Leary, Timothy, 109

Letting go: and death, 114–15, 232–39; and fantasies, 298–99; of relationships, 232–39, 298–99; of shame, 265–66

Levine, Stephen, 123

Life: cherishing events in, 154; death as mirror of, 123; feel of, 114; as not as appears, 177

Lifestyle: and centering, 163

Lingum, 310

Listening: art of, 192–93; and sexuality, 256, 257. *See also* Listening to dreams

Listening to dreams: and centering, 172–75; and darkness, 196–202; and death, 119–25; and doctor-patient relationship, 64–68; and emotions, 147–54; and finding and enhancing intuition, 11; and health, 37–41; and illness, 92–100; and intimacy, 277–81; and protection, 172–75; and relationships, 224–29; and sexual energy, 319–23; and sexual histories, 299–302; and sexuality, 257–60

Love: and asking for inner guidance, 37; and beliefs, 23, 74; and centering, 168, 172; circularity of, 238; and darkness, 177, 188, 189; and death, 112, 114, 119, 120, 124, 125; and doctor-patient relationship, 54; and emotions, 132, 150; and energy, 188, 189; and freedom, 6–7; and healing, 130, 307; and health, 35; and illness, 72, 74, 75, 79, 86–87; and intimacy, 296–97; letting go of, 298–99; and letting others love you, 130; power of, 6; presence as radiating, 13; and relationships, 216, 223, 296–97; self-, 29, 130, 132–33; and sexual energy, 317, 318; and total healing, 324; as underpinning of intuitive healing, 7; unrequited, 298

Loyola University, 42

LSD, 106

Lucille: dream about, 121

Lust, 296–97

McClintock, Martha, 287

Maharaji (Indian sage), 229–30

Maharishi, Ramana, 130

Mandela, Nelson, 6–7

Mapplethorpe, Robert, 288

Marcelle (prison caseworker), 3, 4, 6

Marriage, 323

Masculine: energy, 278, 314–17; feminine blending with, 249, 280–81. *See also* Yin and yang

Masters, William, 309

Medical practice: recent changes in, 45–46; specialization in, 45

Medical schools: and need for new medical heroes, 67

Medical science: lack of understanding of energy by, 32

Medications, 181–87, 194

Medicine: brief history of, 200; as calling of heart, 46; future of, 324–25; need for new heroes in, 66–67

Meditation: and asking for inner guidance, 10, 36–37; and centering, 162, 166–67; characteristics and functions of, 10; at Danbury prison, 6; and darkness, 176, 180, 184, 190, 191, 201–2; and death, 108, 117–18; and doctor-patient relationship, 55; and emotions, 136; and finding intuitive voice, 5, 6; and illness, 74, 77, 81; and intimacy, 269, 272, 276, 296–97; and love, 6; as opening heart, 85–86; for pain, 81; and positive beliefs, 74; and relationships, 207, 212, 213, 221, 236, 237, 238, 296–97; and sexual energy, 306, 319, 322; and sexual histories, 292; and sexuality, 244, 247, 256

Meerha, Mother, 143

Memories, 99–100, 213–14, 294–95

Menstruation, 287–88
Mental illness: labels for, 179–80. *See also* Darkness
Mexico: Castaneda's ashes in, 109; Day of the Dead in, 103–4
Mind: and body connection, 84, 106, 184, 307, 317–19; capacity for healing of, 78; power of, 78–79
The Miracle of Life (TV-film), 248–49
Mojave Indians, 287
Moss, Thelma, 8
Muir, Caroline and Charles, 310–11, 314–15

Names: sacredness of, 62; tuning in to, 62–63, 146, 147, 221–22, 223–24
Naming: of fear, 107
National Federation of Spiritual Healers (Great Britain), 67
National Institute on Aging, 76
National Institutes of Health (NIH), 55
Native Americans, 103, 106, 122, 161, 162, 170, 184
Natural world, 13, 77–78, 162, 218, 273–74, 322, 325
Near-death experience, 118–19
Negativity, 23, 158, 171, 193, 212
New York City: spiritual circle of women in, 275
Nightmares, 149–53, 301
Nonhuman relationships, 218
Nonverbal interactions, 191, 205
Noticing beliefs: and centering, 156–60; and core essence, 156–60; and darkness, 177–81; and death, 103–10; and deciphering healing code, 21–24; and doctor-patient relationship, 50–56; and emotions, 131–35; and finding or enhancing intuition, 9; and health, 21–24; and illness, 71–79; and intimacy, 263–66; and protection, 156–60; and relationships, 205–10; and sexual energy, 305–8; and sexual histories, 284–86; and sexuality, 245–48

Nurse Healers Professional Associates, 60
Nursing homes, 91

Office of Alternative Medicine (NIH), 55
Orgasm: female, 309–13; male, 314–17; without external ejaculation, 315–16
Orloff, Judith: AIDS dreams of, 95–96; ankle injury of, 52; attempted suicide of, 282–83; childhood/youth of, 8–9, 44–45, 131–32, 134–35, 163, 196–97, 211, 218, 223, 262, 282–83, 284, 286, 287, 290–91, 310; dream of being psychiatrist of, 8; and father's illness/death, 15–17, 37–38, 75, 90–91, 92, 115, 225–26, 232–39; first sexual encounter of, 282–83; first workshop of, 154; and grandmother's death, 104, 105, 121; healing of, 8–9; medical training of, 3, 110, 114, 131, 154, 194, 252; and mother's illness/death, 23–24, 84–85, 102–3, 108, 111–12, 121–22, 197, 232, 234, 235, 237, 264; and Pipe's death, 114–15; role models for, 44–45; *Second Sight* by, 3, 86, 123, 152, 306; sexual energy of, 311–12, 322; sexual history of, 282–83, 284, 286, 287, 290–91, 295–96, 300–301
Other people: comparing self with, 14, 132–33; energy of, 31, 53–54, 59–60, 156, 163–68; and negative thoughts of others as harmful, 158; sensing body's subtle energy in, 138–43; supporting, 159–60; taking on pain of, 159–60

Pain: and asking pain for help, 80; embracing, 81; harmonizing with, 81–82; as healing, 131; ignoring, 25; managing of, 80–81; in relationships, 217, 229–30, 231;

Pain (*cont'd*)
and sexual energy, 318; and sexual
histories, 282, 293; and sharing
energy, 86–87; as speaking to you,
80; suffering distinguished from,
82; taking on other's, 159–60;
tuning in to, 79; and visualizing
organs of body, 28
Pandora's box: and sexual histories,
283
Parapsychology, 78–79
Parent-child relationships, 223, 226,
232–39, 285–86
Parents: beliefs of, 23–24; role in
sexual histories of, 284–86. *See also*
Ancestors
Parvarandeh, Osted "Hadi," 59–60
Passion: of body, 246; and
communication, 264–65; and
dreams, 319; and intimacy, 263,
264–65, 273, 279, 296, 297; and
relationships, 204, 205, 206, 208,
213, 217, 220, 296; and sexual
energy, 305, 317, 323; and
sexuality, 241–61
Patient care, 18–20
Peace, 174–75, 176, 177, 270
Penis size, 288–89
Peptic ulcers, 33, 77
Perceptions, 37, 119, 129, 150,
190–91, 233, 294
Personal space, 31
Physicians' Desk Reference (PDR), 186,
187
Physicians. *See* Health care
practitioners
Picturing. *See* Visualizing
Power: of beliefs, 22, 190; beliefs that
drain, 157–60; feel of, 133–34; of
feminine, 207–8; in relationships,
209–10
Prayer: and asking for inner
guidance, 68, 91, 92; and centering, 171; and dreams, 98; healing
power of, 55, 92; and illness, 74,
77; not granting, 229; and positive
beliefs, 74; and relationships, 224,

229; as revolutionary, 325; and
sexuality, 247, 256; and total
healing, 325
Prayer lines, 92
Predictions, 145, 148, 197–98, 258.
See also Premonitions
Preferred provider organizations
(PPOs), 45
Premonitions: of death, 119, 120–21;
dreams as, 95, 96–97, 151–52, 197,
214, 227, 301; and forms of
intuition, 90
Prescience, 96–97
Presence, 13, 14, 28–29
Prevention. *See* Health
Priests, 153
Principles of Internal Medicine
(Harrison), 102, 104
Prisons, 3–7
Program for Integrative Medicine
(University of Arizona, Tucson),
67
Projection, 209
Protection: and being in body,
160–63; and danger, 160–61,
173–74, 175; and darkness, 193;
and dreams, 172–75; from people
who drain energy, 156; importance
of, 155–56; meaning of, 156; and
noticing beliefs, 156–60; and
picturing heaven, 171–72; and
relationships, 211, 214; sacred
objects as, 170; and sensing body's
subtle energy, 166; and sexual
histories, 300; shields as, 166;
spiritual figures as, 169–70; and
war and peace, 174–75. *See also*
Centering
Psychiatric labels, 179–80
Psychiatrists, 153, 178–79, 180. *See
also* Health care practitioners
Psychic: intuition as differentiated
from, 19; as sign of psychosis,
19
Psychometry, 276–77
Psychoneuroimmunology, 88
Psychosis, 178, 182, 184, 194

Psychotherapy, 77, 118, 131, 168, 184, 189
Psychotic voice, 193
Puberty, 286–89, 300

Quackwatch Inc., 189–90
Questionable Nurse Practices Task Force, 189–90
Questions for reflection: and finding and enhancing intuition, 12. *See also specific topic*

Radin, Dean, 161
Reading energy, 138–40, 216, 251–54
Reading people, 205, 221–24
Relationships: abuse in, 213, 216, 283, 285, 292–93, 294–95, 300; acceptance in, 260; with ancestors, 223–24; and asking for inner guidance, 220–24; and being in body, 211–15; betrayal in, 230, 282–83; as boring, 206–7; and broken heart, 217; and centering, 212; and commitment, 204, 206, 208; communication in, 210; continuation of, 224; and déjà vu, 213–14; and dreams, 203, 214, 224–29, 234; and energy, 236; and faith, 207, 217; and fear, 208, 212, 213, 227; feminine in, 207–8; forgiveness in, 229–31; foundations of intuitive, 206–9; honoring, 203–31; and idealization, 260; lessons as part of, 204; letting go of, 232–39, 298–99; love as means for transforming, 216, 223, 296–97; and mirrors for each other, 208–9; negative intuitions about, 212; nonhuman, 218; and noticing beliefs, 205–10; pain in, 217, 229–30, 231; parent-child, 223, 226, 232–39, 285–86; positive intuitions about, 212; power struggles in, 209–10; problems and conflicts in, 208, 211, 227; and protection, 211, 214; questions for reflection about, 210; and reading people, 205; salvaging of, 216, 279–80; and sensing body's subtle energy, 215–20; and sexual attraction, 212–13; and sexual energy, 319; and sexuality, 246–47; and spirit/spirituality, 206–7, 208, 215, 222, 223, 230, 233, 236, 238; and synchronicities, 218–20, 234–35, 236; traditional model of, 204, 205–6; and trust, 204, 207, 229, 233; tuning in to, 221–22; ways intuition can improve, 296–99. *See also* Emotions; Intimacy; Sexual histories; Sexuality
REM sleep stage, 11
Remote viewing: and asking for inner guidance, 10–11; characteristics and functions of, 10–11; and darkness, 193; and death, 116–18, 223–24; and doctor-patient relationship, 61–64; in an emotional pinch, 193; and emotions, 146–47; and experiencing death, 117–18; functions of, 64; and illness, 89; for intelligence gathering, 61; as method for reading people, 221; and names, 62–63, 146; and relationships, 221–24
Rinpoche, Sogyal, 80
Roddenberry, Gene, 109
Role models, 22–23, 44–45, 59, 66, 68, 304
Romantic life: ways intuition can improve, 296–99
Royale, Candida, 307–8
Rumi, 20, 262

Sacred objects, 170
Sacred prostitutes, 304
Sacred space, 272, 310
Sacred spots, 227, 309–13
Sage plants: burning, 170–71
San Francisco General Hospital, 55, 92

Scientific method, 70, 190

Second Sight (Orloff), 3, 86, 123, 152, 306

Seinfeld (TV program): death episode on, 101

Self: awareness of, 168; comparing others with, 14, 132–33; compassion for, 15, 82, 102, 135, 150; confronting, 195–96; knowledge of, 177; love of, 29, 130, 132–33; as male and female, 308; as tabula rasa, 42; trust of, 193; uniqueness of, 14, 132, 134

Self-care, 26–27

Self-discovery, 130

Self-fulfilling prophecies, 22, 50, 98, 105

Self-perception, 129, 190–91

Sensing body's subtle energy: and centering, 163–68; in daily life, 140–41; and darkness, 187–92; and death, 113–16; and doctor-patient relationship, 59–61; and emotions, 138–43; and finding and enhancing intuition, 10; and health, 29–35; and illness, 84–88; and intimacy, 270–75; and orgasm, 314–17; in others, 138–43; and re-lationships, 215–20; and sexual histories, 289–95; and sexuality, 251–54

Sensitivity, 158–59, 160, 186, 228, 249, 254, 265

Sex: addiction to, 307; casual, 247, 307. *See also* Abuse; Intimacy; Orgasm; Sexual energy; Sexual histories; Sexuality

Sexual attractions. *See* Attractions

Sexual energy: and asking for inner guidance, 317–19; and fantasies, 318–19; and fear, 321–22; and freedom, 313; healing gift of, 304–23; and illness, 305, 318; and intimacy, 270–75, 307, 316; and listening to dreams, 319–23; and love, 317, 318; and noticing beliefs, 305–8; questions for

reflection about, 308; and relationships, 319; and sacred spots, 309–13; and sexuality, 250, 251–54, 259; and soul, 304, 323; and spirit/spirituality, 307, 322, 323; tips for reading, 253. *See also* Intimacy; Orgasm; Sexuality

Sexual histories: and abuse, 283, 285, 292–93, 294–95, 300; and asking for inner guidance, 295–99; and being in body, 286–89; and energy, 292, 295; and first sexual encounter, 282–83; and first time making love, 289–91; and freedom, 303; and generational patterns, 284–85; and identification of sexual traumas, 293–94; and intergenerational dialogues, 287; and listening to dreams, 299–302; and memories, 294–95; and noticing beliefs, 284–86; and pain, 282; parents' role in, 284–86; and puberty, 286–89, 300; questions for reflection about, 286; and sensing body's subtle energy, 289–95; and spirituality, 283, 290, 302; and synchronicities, 302

Sexual power: awakening, 262–81. *See also* Intimacy

Sexuality: and aging, 247; and asking for inner guidance, 254–57; attitudes about, 251; and being in body, 248–51; beliefs about, 245–48; building blocks for conscious, 264–66; and casual sex, 247; and centering, 254, 255; and commitment, 258; and compartmentalization, 244; and dreams, 248, 257–60; and energy, 244, 247, 260, 306; evolution of human, 267; healing attributes of, 304, 306; and listening, 256, 257–60; masculine and feminine aspects of, 249; new way of viewing, 241–42; questions for reflection about, 248; and reading sexual energy, 250, 251–54; and relationships, 246–47; and sensing body's subtle energy, 251–54; and sexual attraction, 255; and sleep, 257–58; and soul, 254, 257, 261; and spirit/spirituality, 241–61, 270, 280–81, 304, 306. *See also* Intimacy; Sexual energy

Shakti. *See* Chi; Energy; Sensing body's subtle energy

Shame, 250, 265–66, 286, 292, 300, 301

Shielding, 166, 278

Silence, 143–44, 188

Simonton, Carl, 184

Singer, Don, 111, 153, 176–77

Sleep, 172–73, 227–28, 257–58. *See also* Dreams; Nightmares

Smith, Mary, 250

Snakes: as archetypes, 321–22

Soul, 214, 254, 257, 261, 298, 304, 323

South Carolina: Orloff workshop in, 223–24

Spirit/spirituality: and body, 184; and darkness, 179–80, 182, 184, 188, 194, 196; and death, 106, 111, 112, 125; and doctor-patient relationship, 55–56; and emotions, 130, 138, 153–54; and healing, 306; and health, 42–43; and illness, 76, 77, 184; and intimacy, 263, 264, 265, 270, 272, 273–74, 281; of medications, 185; merger of intuition and technology and, 67–68; and need for new medical heroes, 67; and relationships, 206–7, 208, 215, 222, 223, 230, 233, 236, 238; and sexual energy, 307, 322, 323; and sexual histories, 283, 290, 302; and sexuality, 241–61, 270, 280–81, 304, 306; and spiritual housecleaning, 247–48; and total healing, 324; and traditional medicine, 55–56; and training of health care

practitioners, 179; types of, 180; witnessing absence of, 111. *See also* Meditation

Stanford Medical School, 55

Stanford Research Institute, 61

Starobinski, Jean, 69

Step 1. *See* Noticing beliefs

Step 2. *See* Being in body

Step 3. *See* Sensing body's subtle energy

Step 4. *See* Asking for inner guidance

Step 5. *See* Listening to dreams

Stereotypes, 179, 241, 267, 268, 281, 308

Stevens, Wallace, 324

Styron, William, 195

Substance abuse, 179–80, 198

Suffering, 82, 131, 159–60, 189

Suicide, 144–45, 195–96, 282–83

Support: for other people, 159–60

Support groups, 275

Survival mechanisms, 160–61

Sylvia, Claire, 99, 100

Synchronicities, 218–20, 234–35, 236, 276–77, 287, 302

Tabula rasa: imagining self as, 42

Tantra, 270–75, 279–80, 290, 310–13, 314–17

Technology, 66–67, 83–84

Temescal Canyon Park: Orloff workshop in, 154

Therapeutic touch, 55, 189–90

Therapy: as collaboration, 184; faith in, 187. *See also* Psychotherapy

The Tibetan Book of Living and Dying, 80–81

Tibetans, 101, 162, 170

Tigers: story about, 266–67

Tomes, Nancy, 88

Tonglen, 80–81, 82

Total healing, 324–25

Touch, 55, 59–60, 189–90, 306

Transplant patients, 99–100

Traumas: acting out, 76–78; acute, 119; identification of sexual, 293–94

Trust: of body, 59; and darkness, 196; and doctor-patient relationship, 56; of intuition, 20, 102, 132; and letting go of relationships, 233; and relationships, 204, 207, 229; of self, 193; and sexuality, 257

Tuning in: to medications, 184–87; to names, 62–63, 146, 147, 221–22, 223–24; to relationships, 221–24; and sexuality, 256–57

Twelve Steps (Alcoholics Anonymous), 179

UCLA: alternative care program at, 55; and Orloff's inner censor, 64; Orloff's work at, 3, 8, 78–79, 114; psychiatric training programs at, 180

University of Arizona at Tucson, 67

University of Chicago, 42

University of Nevada at Las Vegas, 161

University of Nevada Medical School: Orloff's grand rounds presentation at, 18–20

University of Southern California (USC), 194

Unrequited love, 298

Unresponsive people, 191–92

Urology, 67–68

Ventura, Michael, 245

Vibrations, 32–33, 62, 305

Visualizing: and centering, 174; and darkness, 184, 199; heaven, 171–72; and intimacy, 277; and letting go of relationships, 299; organs of body, 28; and sensing body's subtle energy, 166; and sexual energy, 318–19, 322; wellness, 184

Vulnerability, 166, 228–29

Wadsworth VA Hospital (Los Angeles), 110

War, 174–75, 230–31

Watts, Alan, 265

Weddings: in cemeteries, 108, 109

Weil, Andrew, 67

Wesselman, Hank, 174

Whitman, Walt, 101

Williamson, Marianne, 129, 133, 134

Wishing, 201–2, 324

Wordsworth, William, 162

Yin and yang, 207–8, 210, 291, 308

Yoni, 310

Zen Buddhism, 82, 104, 105, 111, 153, 318